The Book of Customs

BOOK of CUSTOMS

A Complete Handbook for the Jewish Year

BY

Scott-Martin Kosofsky

inspired by the Yiddish *Minhogimbukh*, Venice, 1593

with a foreword by

RABBI LAWRENCE KUSHNER

HarperSanFrancisco

Designed and composed by Scott-Martin Kosofsky at The Philidor Company, Cambridge. The text typefaces are Philidor Schmidt and Philidor Vilna (Hebrew), designed by Mr. Kosofsky. The titles are set in Galliard, designed by Matthew Carter.

Consultant for Yiddish translation: Szonja Ráhel Komoróczy
Consultant for Jewish law and custom: Dr. Ruth Langer

FIRST EDITION

The Library of Congress Cataloging-in-Publication data is available upon request.
ISBN: 0-06-052437-5

04 05 06 07 08 RRD(C) 10 9 8 7 6 5 4 3 2

Contents

Foreword

YOU ARE HOLDING A HOLY BOOK. It is also an example of graphic art at its finest. The author, who is also the designer, has, with meticulous and loving care, revived a lost Jewish literary format as well as a tradition. But even more noteworthy, he and his publisher have inadvertently placed a new volume on Judaism's shelf of sacred books. But how dare we call even such a beautiful book holy? That is where theology comes in.

Like all revealed religions, Judaism is classically taught by expounding sacred text. But the weekly Torah portion is more than merely the next chapter in an unfolding saga or the touchstone for homiletics; its literary, legal, theological, and mythic rhythms serve as menu and master outline for every conceivable moral and religious topic. (Indeed, the present volume offers synopses of each Torah lection.) There is, however, another, less well known, yet equally potent didactic tradition.

In addition to scripture, Jews over the centuries have also come to "read" the customs surrounding the fasts and festivals of their religious calendar as a kind of second sacred text. Rabbinic study bibles, collections of Hasidic teachings, and contemporary sermonica all routinely intersperse holiday teachings *within* the cycle of the weekly lectionary. In this way the *minhagim*, or "customs," are effectively transformed into what we could reasonably call another mode of revelation. Indeed, as Scott-Martin Kosofsky once suggested to me, these inseparable, twin strands of scripture and custom create a double-helix of Jewish life-learning. The "other" Torah of the holiday cycle is also to be plumbed, expounded, and comprehended. But this second sacred text of liturgy and custom differs from its scriptural twin in one deliciously interactive way: it is not fixed. And it is just these two interwoven strands of Torah and custom that this present *Book of Customs*, responding to the needs of our less than fully literate generation, presents together.

There are myriad legends about arguments among the sages over the correct interpretation of the scriptural law. One genre is especially instructive here. According to one legend, the dispute was about the actual appearance of the first sliver of the new moon of the month of Tishrei (and therefore the onset of Rosh Hashanah and, with it, the commencement of the entire year-long sacred calendar). Since it was daytime, however, the moon was barely visible. In desperation the scholars sought divine guidance but, to their astonishment, the heavenly voice only replied, "Why do you ask Me? Go outside and see [in Aramaic: *pok ḥazi*] what the Jews are doing!" And, sure enough, when they looked outside they saw the Jews carrying flowers for their celebration of the New Year. And from this the sages concluded that the New Year indeed must have begun. In the words of the rabbinic maxim: *Minhag avoteinu Torah hi,* "The custom of our parents is [also] the way."

This legend and others like it transmit a primary principle of Judaism: what the Jews wind up doing as they attempt to negotiate, comprehend, and live by God's laws attains independent and authentic religious status. Somehow, the Jewish people, through trying to lead sacred lives and make ends meet, are mysteriously, despite themselves, inescapably drawn to what God wants them to do. This is certainly not a matter of privilege or superiority but an expression of vocation and obligation. And just this is the reason that the Jews regard their customs and ceremonies as subjects to be studied, expounded, and taught. For not only do they teach us about who we are, they are a window into the sacred! You might say, in this way, that scripture is from the top down (from God to the Jews) while the customs that flower around God's laws are from the bottom up (from the Jews to God). The Torah tells the Jews about God, the minhagim tell God about the Jews.

Consider two examples. For a rabbi to expound upon the meaning of the custom of breaking a glass at the conclusion of a wedding is as appropriate as expounding a passage from Song of Songs. For a rabbi to draw religious lessons from the fact that Jews customarily have two *hallot* (braided loaves of egg bread) at the Sabbath table is as acceptable as interpreting the laws of Sabbath observance themselves. Such an attitude toward minhagim may also effectively serve to balance any overly rigid reading of Jewish legal tradition. (God says do it this way but this is how *we* do it.)

Dr. Lawrence Hoffman, of the Hebrew Union College-Jewish Institute of Religion, noting the fixity of scripture and the fluidity of liturgy, once suggested that Torah is our head but the prayerbook, and by extension, the festival calendar and the life-cycle ceremonies marking the passages of life of each Jew, is our heart. Torah's vitality comes from its lability. Responding to the unanticipatable exigencies of each new generation, the holiday observances and life-cycle customs sway and dance to the melodies of each new generation.

Most Jews know about Joseph Karo's monumental legal code, the *Shulḥan arukh* ("The Set Table") and that it is the apogee of Jewish law. Far fewer know that, based on Sephardic (Spanish-Portuguese) practice, the *Shulḥan arukh* remained unacceptable to Ashkenazic (German) Jews—half of world Jewry—until Moses Isserles published his extensive commentary, the *Mapah* ("The Tablecloth"), which incorporated *their* customs into the legal system. In this way, we are reminded that customs are the mechanism through which the divine will can be comprehended and practiced in lived lives. And that mechanism is unequivocally populist.

As many observers have observed, Judaism is less a religion than it is a people, a folk. And because Judaism is a people, then what the Jewish people does acquires a theological dimension. Ordinary Jews—as far as Judaism is concerned anyway—possess an almost ontic status. They enjoy a mode of being beyond their individual, personal identities; they are *am Yisrael,* the people of Israel; they are an *am kadosh,* a holy people. Somehow, when it comes to intuitively knowing what Judaism truly requires, they seem to have an inside track. And, while it routinely drives Jewish teachers and compilers of minhagim to annoyance and distraction, this includes even uninspired, boorish, and illiterate Jews as well. And this sets up another double-helix: On one hand we have rabbinic authorities expounding divine law and, on the other, we have ordinary people leading ordinary lives. Neither could survive alone!

In addition to the six hundred thirteen commandments that symbolically represent the definitive catalogue of what God wants, there are seven more that are found nowhere in the Torah: lighting Sabbath candles; observing *Ḥanukkah*; reciting blessings of enjoyment; washing the hands; reading the Megillah; singing the Psalms of *Hallel*; and setting Sabbath boundaries.

These customs, nevertheless, have been elevated to the status of scriptural commandment. In this way, some observers have suggested that minhagim that have been in force for five hundred years are raised to the status of law, even as laws in force for five hundred years are themselves raised to the status of (divine!) commandments. The theologian Eugene Borowitz, noting a widespread social custom in the liberal Jewish community, observes that it now seems to have become a religious law that, with the sweet feeling that fills the room upon the conclusion of a Sabbath eve service, you *must* kiss the person sitting next to you.

In this way, customs become laws and laws become commandments. And thus, while the author of this and probably every *Minhogimbukh* would be the first to renounce any such implication, since it might, God forbid, imply that they considered themselves as arbiters of the divine word, you might say nevertheless that the minhagim described on the following pages are proto-*mitzvot*, commandments *in utero*.

LAWRENCE KUSHNER
San Francisco, California
4 July 2004 / 15 Tamuz 5764

CUSTOMS

MUCH NICER THAN THE PREVIOUS VERSIONS

Everyone will enjoy reading it!

CONTAINS ALL THE CUSTOMS in Ashkenaz for the entire year
and includes customs for Italy, Poland, Bohemia, Moravia,
and several more.

LAWS EXPLAINED WELL, so you will know
how to live like a good person.

And it was not forgotten to include a CALENDAR for seventy
years, counted precisely, containing the zodiac and the times
for Rosh Ḥodesh, which were not included previously.

FOREVER AND EVER, HE

"THIS IS GOD, OUR GOD

WILL BE OUR GUIDE"

גונצבורג

שמעון
לוי

— PSALMS 48:14 —

Printed for the second time in the Big City of
VENICE
in the year 5353 /1593
at the house of Zuan di Gara

*This is a word-for-word translation of the title page of the first illustrated Yiddish edition of the
Book of Customs, Venice, 1593. It's a classic of mass marketing, utterly familiar in its style—and
with all the usual hype: "new and improved version," "will work everywhere," "helps you live like
a good person," and "made by smart people in the Big City." Who could ask for anything more?*

A Discovery

FIFTEEN YEARS AGO, while looking for illustrations to use in my first Judaica project, *The Harvard Hillel Sabbath Songbook*, I came across reproductions of several Renaissance woodcuts in an old Jewish encyclopedia. Their source was given as "*Sefer minhagim, Amsterdam, 1645.*" At the time I had reclaimed only enough of my Hebrew school education to know that *sefer* means "book"; the other word was familiar, but I couldn't quite remember its meaning. To learn more, I would have to see the book. The Harvard libraries had several books with that name or similar names, and still more on microfilm, including one that matched the particulars given in the encyclopedia. When I saw how *minhagim* was spelled in Hebrew, I looked it up and found that it means "customs." What I had stumbled upon was the *Book of Customs.*

I was charmed at first sight. I had in my hands something I had never seen before: a compact guide to the Jewish year, complete with over forty delightful illustrations of the main holidays and rituals. I knew this because, despite the Hebrew title by which it was cataloged, the book was in Yiddish with prayers in Hebrew. So rather than a lofty *Sefer minhagim* or *Sefer haminhagim*, it was in reality a humble Yiddish customs book, the *Minhogimbukh*. I grew up in a household in which

Yiddish was a principal language, and that I still had some ability in the language gave me an entrée. That it was a fine example of book design brought it into my professional realm. I noticed interesting differences in the six editions I saw at Harvard, which inspired me to ask about the books at other institutions and before long I saw some thirty more at the libraries of the Jewish Theological Seminary, Hebrew Union College, and Brandeis University and still others from the Bodleian Library at Oxford. Their dates were spread across the range of the book's history, 1566 to 1874.

I was surprised to discover that while a few of the illustrations were known, having been reproduced here and there, the book itself had no reputation. It was just one of the myriads of old Jewish books. I learned from a few Judaica librarians that it was especially well neglected because scholars of Judaism have paid little attention to books in Yiddish, written as they were for the unwashed and unlettered; Yiddish scholars, as a rule, are interested in literature, not in religion. That the early editions are in *Old* Yiddish, before the Slavic influences had become so much a part of the language, placed it even further from mainstream interests. Curiously, this book, which had been so useful for so long, had no successor. I was quite pleased to hear this; the book's outsider status made it available to become *my* book, my point of departure for a journey into the realm of Jewish learning.

From the many editions of the *Minhogimbukh* I had photocopied, ten of the woodcuts made their way into *The Harvard Hillel Sabbath Songbook*. The others were pasted into a scrapbook, arranged by theme: Sabbath cuts on one page, Passover cuts on another, whole sets bundled at the back. The thought of preparing a new edition occurred to me early on, but it was years before I felt capable of doing so. Fortunately, the *Songbook* was a success (it's still in print after all these years), and many more Judaica projects came my way, each an opportunity to become more engaged with Judaism. This wasn't to be a

Homeric journey home through rough seas and great perils. Instead, it was an near-accidental discovery that became an ever-increasing influence on my work and life. Perhaps it was *bashert*—"meant to be," as one says in Yiddish. My grandmothers would have thought so.

A History of the Minhogimbukh

For over four hundred years, the *Minhogimbukh* was among the most popular Jewish books in the European Diaspora, just after the Bible, the siddur (prayer book), and the Passover haggadah. It was published as the people's guide to the Jewish year in dozens of editions from Amsterdam to Venice to Warsaw and Kiev. In addition to its rich presentation of the rituals and prayers, the book's illustrated editions featured the zodiac and the seasons of farm life, giving it an additional role as a kind of Jewish *Old Farmers' Almanac*. Its roots were in the Hebrew *Sefer minhagim* written in the late fourteenth or early fifteenth century by the Hungarian rabbi Eyzik

The woodcut for the month of Av (Leo). It bears a quotation from Joel (2:24): "And the threshing floors will be full of grain."

(Isaac) Tyrnau, one of a number of such works from the late Middle Ages. The Tyrnau text circulated in manuscript for about one hundred fifty years before its first printed edition, still in Hebrew, was published in 1566 in Venice.

Eyzik Tyrnau's time was one of tragedy and loss. His book was written in the aftermath of the Black Death (1348–1350) in the belief that there was a kind of symbolic equivalence between a people and its customs. By preserving its customs, even if only in writing, the community would survive the pestilence, expulsions, harsh laws, and persecution that characterized Jewish life of the period. Tyrnau's work was thorough and well organized, setting the pattern for the later books of customs. The simplicity of his language suggests that he wrote for laypeople rather than for other rabbis. His book's basic outline was this: the Jewish week from the end of Sabbath through evening prayers on Thursday; preparations for Sabbath and the Sabbath day itself; the twelve months including all the holidays; and last, the life cycle events of marriage, birth, and death.

In 1590, again in Venice, which was one of the centers of Jewish life in Italy, the *Sefer minhagim* was published for the first time in Yiddish, which would be the language of most of its editions for the next three hundred years. Leaning heavily on Tyrnau's model, the author-editor-translator of this edition was Simon Levi ben Yehuda Gunzburg, who had come to Italy from Swabia; the printer was Giovanni ("Zuan" in Venetian dialect) di Gara, a Christian who specialized in Jewish works. The book was a tremendous success, as stated in the preface to the second edition of 1593:

> This useful little chapbook containing the traditional customs was first brought to the printing house by the honorable Rabbi Shimon Ashkenazi [Simon Levi Gunzburg] three years ago. The book has been praised and admired by all for its great usefulness and as a comprehensible guide to the customs and traditions of all Israel and Judah, especially to those of Ashkenaz [German Jewry and its sphere], which are explained by the author in great detail and with precision, following the sages and the rabbis. . . .
>
> Gunzburg soon saw the need for a second edition since all the copies of the first left his hands in great haste because everyone knew they were worth their weight in gold. But he did not see that as the reason to leave well enough alone; he now extended his view to include all the customs from other places he researched and collected, sparing no time and effort. . . . Also, there is more splendor and glory added [a reference to the forty woodcut illustrations and improved typography], in quality as well as quantity. Everyone will notice, nobles and small children alike, that this volume is thicker than the previous one.

It is this second edition, published in "the big city of Venice" in 1593, that I believe is the standard upon which almost all of the subsequent editions were based. I have used it as both the framework and as a regularly recurring point of reference for this book. Seeing that Gunzburg treated the book so flexibly, I realized that the *Minhogimbukh* was more of a *form* than it was a specific *text*, and a very adaptable form at that.

No records have been uncovered about the circulation of the customs books, but contemporary reports on other Jewish books of the time suggest that a success like the one decribed in the 1593 preface would translate to sales of between 1,500 and 3,000 copies. Clearly the sales were broad, since there were only about 1,500 Jews living in Venice at the time. Including customs from throughout Ashkenaz was clearly part of the publisher's marketing strategy.

JEWISH BOOKS OF THE PERIOD. The *Minhogimbukh* was one of about thirty-five Yiddish books published in Europe, many in northern Italy, between 1545 and 1609. The audience was mainly women and "men who are like women," meaning men who were not literate in Hebrew. Among the more popular Yiddish titles were racy verse romances and fables based on popular European literature, a book of religious commandments for women, and an enduring volume of Torah paraphrases called *Tsenerene* ("Go Forth and Behold"), so long-lived that my maternal grandmother, who came to America from Bessarabia as a young woman in 1914, used to refer to it disparagingly as a synonym for "old hat." My uncle Yankel would ask her, "So, Gittel, how was the sermon?" "Same old *Tsenerene*" was her slightly bored reply.

By the time the first Yiddish *Minhogimbukh* appeared in 1590, an extraordinary body of learned works was already in print in Hebrew, including major rabbinical works about Jewish law that remain among the cornerstones of Jewish legal discourse. Between the 1520s and the 1550s, the Iberian-born Joseph Caro produced a prodigious codification of Jewish law (halakhah) and its sources called *Bet Yosef,* "The

House of Joseph," best known through its digest form, the *Shulḥan arukh* ("A Set Table"). Written by a Sephardic Jew, it made little account of Ashkenazic customs. To address the deficit, Rabbi Moses Isserles of Cracow published in 1564/65 an extensive series of glosses on Caro's work that he entitled *Mapah* (literally, "tablecloth"). Isserles drew heavily upon various Ashkenazic customs books and Eyzik Tyrnau was one of his frequently quoted informants. The sheer physical enormity of these Hebrew works, intended as they were for only the most learned of rabbis and scholars, makes obvious the need for a digestible pocket guide like the people's *Minhogimbukh*.

AN EXCELLENT AND USEFUL DESIGN. The grace of the design of the *Minhogimbukh* enabled its readers to navigate easily through the Jewish year. Its refined, well-crafted typography—retained in most of the later editions—enabled one to differentiate Hebrew from Yiddish and liturgy from commentary and to easily find the major passages and commandments. It was in the best tradition of the Renaissance book—and of the great Jewish books of the Renaissance—in which beauty was achieved through clarity and balance, regardless of the complexity of the material and the number of layers of information presented. The typefaces of the early editions were especially interesting to me and learning about them led me in some unexpected directions. The text typeface, which I first believed was of the kind known as Rashi, or rabbinic, turned out to be another old semicursive form called *vaybertaytsh*, literally, "ladies' German." The older scholarly literature that I first consulted suggested that the use of this typeface meant that the book was intended for women. As intriguing as that theory appeared, the book's contents indicated that it was not true, at least not completely. Since the book is replete with certain rituals and liturgy that in its period would have been performed only by men, it was clear that it was not published primarily as a women's book.

פורים

צו אנחה ליימט און רחל אוב׳ גאנט עניו אוב׳ אונט קיין תחנה אוב׳ וורט אערב מוא בו־ מוד׳ מוד׳ אוב׳ מין
שמונה עשרה׃ אלטט און מין (על הניס׳ם) (על הניס׳ם) ו׳ם וומו׳ רם און דימ(מגילה) נאך ניט גליימט התט׃

תענית אחר׳) מ׳ו ניט מו מ המרב מו מגדר׳ (תענית) ׳ דרומ אעלן טרמ מגגדר׳ פרומו מרד דער
ניט וומו׳ מוך׳ ל׳ו וומו׳ ל׳ו און דעמ(תענית כתי׳) ׳ ׳ין דען דער (תנית) סטיט ניט ג׳ו ובט מיס
פסוק רע׳ן רט מ׳ו ניט רע דער (תע׳ ׳ דעמ אכחר) ג׳מ מסט המט ׳ מ המט מין פסח ג׳מ מסט מוב׳ מך הט
׳ימ דר׳ימ טמ מג ג׳מ מסט ׳ מכר ד׳מ וו׳ל מ׳דרמן מ׳ו קומן מס ערב פורים ד׳מ מ׳ל מ לו העדן רמ המבן
חכמים ג מ מכט און מ׳ ג מ מסטן זכר לתע׳ית אסר ׳

עש וומל מ׳ו ולכר ג׳ובן לו מ׳חה וואן מין
מול ׳ גים מה׳ת מה קל רם ו׳ובן ג הומרט מין ׳רוסלים מורד ג׳ובן ל׳ו סט׳מור רעלן ו׳ו בן ו׳ מין מ ין ׳ ׳ן ׳סר׳ל
וו׳לן ל׳ה׳ון מ׳ו מ׳ ג׳ובט מך מ׳צת פורים רם ט׳׳לט מ׳ רעלן עניים מ׳ו מ ר׳ים פר׳ים רו מ׳ ׳מל קען קו׳פן
ורים ג׳ל׳׳ג ׳ ׳מו׳ן ׳ פר׳ים מן ו׳מ ר׳מ ל׳גט מ׳ (תע׳ית אסתר) מ׳ך׳ ד׳ג ר׳ט מג ׳ רעל מ׳ך׳ פר׳׳טג
׳ס׳ מ׳ון עט ניט ל׳ג ר׳מ ו׳ל׳ מ׳ מ׳ מ׳ פר׳ ו׳בן ד׳ עט׳ן לום סכ ׳ מול׳רמ ל׳גט מ׳ן עט ג׳ל׳׳ך מ׳ך פר׳׳טג
רמ ׳ ׳ל מ׳ון רמ מ׳ין רמ׳ מ׳ן תחנה ו מ׳גט מ׳ מ׳ונסט ׳ מוב׳ מ׳גט ניט צרקחך ׃

פורים

פורים ווען עם ולכט מ׳ו מ׳ל׳גט מ׳ן רו עט עם ו׳מחה ומ׳ ו׳׳ן מ׳וב׳רער חדן ספר׳׳ט ד׳מ מג׳לה
מום ג׳ל׳ך ו׳מ מ׳ין בר׳ל ל׳מ׳ ו׳מ ניט מ׳בר מ גגר ג׳ו׳ק ׳ט מוב׳ ו׳מגט ר׳ימ כרבות ׃

נָרוּךְ אַתָּה יְיָ אֱלֹהֵינוּ כֶּלֶךְ הָעוֹלָם אֲשֶׁר קַרְשָׁנוּ וְצִוְּנוּ עַל מִקְרָא מְגִילָה
בָּרוּךְ אַתָּה יְיָ אֱלֹהֵינוּ כֶּלֶךְ הָעוֹלָם שֶׁעָשָׂה נִסִּים לַאֲבוֹתֵינוּ בַיָּמִים הָהֵם זְמַן הֶזָּה ׃
בָּרוּךְ אַתָּה יְיָ אֱלֹהֵינוּ כֶּלֶךְ הָעוֹלָם שֶׁהֶחֱיָנוּ וְקִיְּמָנוּ וְהִגִיעָנוּ לַזְמַן הֶזָּה ׃

אוב׳ היכט ד׳ימ מג׳לה מ׳ן לו ל׳׳מן מוב׳ ווען ער קומט
מן רע׳ן פסוק מ׳ש ׳הור׳ מוב׳ רע׳ן פסוק ׳ מורדכ׳
מוב׳ ל׳הור׳ים מ׳תחמ׳ המורח ׳ מוב׳ וכל מ׳עשה תקפו ו׳בורתו ׃
ו׳מ ו׳מגט רם קה׳ל ד׳ימ מוב׳ינ׳ ג׳ס׳קים הוך ׳ מוב׳ דער חדן
ו׳מ גט ו׳מ ו׳רדר ׳ רם ט׳ט מ׳ן דרומ פ׳ן ו׳מחה ו׳עגן מורד
רס ר׳ימ ׳ונגן ומ׳ן דר׳ך׳ וו׳רטן ׳ וו׳ען מ׳ן ד׳ימ פס׳קים הוך
ו׳מ גט ו׳מ ו׳ררן ו׳מ ד׳מ מ׳ט מ׳ ל׳ העדן ד׳ימ מג׳לה מוב׳
רע׳מ ה׳נטרסטן ׳ פסוק מך ׳ ׳ רט ו׳מ ו׳מל ד׳ימ כרלות
העדן נך דער גר׳ מג׳לה ׃

מן ׳מל מ׳ש מוב׳ עשרת כני המן מ׳ן נם מ׳ו נם מ׳וטט ומ׳גן
רע׳ן ד׳מ נ׳מחה מ׳ו מ׳ן מ׳ן מ׳וך׳ מ׳ין מ׳מו׳ מ׳ ׳גמן ׃
המט רע׳ן מ׳ה ד רם ר׳ימ ׳ונגן מ׳ון מ׳ הו׳ן (ל׳מ׳ף) ר׳ום
קומ׳ העדר פ׳ן רע׳ם מ׳ה ד רט ו׳מ המבן ל׳ר ׳מרן
ג׳ט המבכן מ׳ן מ׳ין סט׳ין ג׳סר׳בן הבן מוב׳ הבן רע׳ן ו׳ו׳ובן
סט׳ין מ׳ך׳ מ׳ין מ׳נדרן סט׳ין ג׳ומ׳גן ׳ ו׳ען מ׳ן ג׳נ׳נ׳
המט ה׳מן מ׳ן דער מ׳ג׳׳לה ׳ רט ו׳ך׳ רע׳ב שם ה׳מט מוב׳ מ׳ו׳

ג׳מ׳קט (כליפר ׳חמ ׳שמו ׳ מורד שם רשע׳ם ׳רקב ׃

ד׳ומ נ׳ים ו׳׳ן מ׳ך׳ ח׳ב ד׳ ר׳ מג׳לה ל׳ העדן וו׳מ וומו׳ ע׳ מ׳ו מ׳ן מ׳צ׳ תחנה ד׳ עשה ד׳ רם קומ כמ׳ס׳׳מ׳ ׳מר
לום מ׳נדרן מ׳ו מ׳ן ג׳סר׳בן הב ב׳ימ ק׳טה מם פר׳׳טג ל׳ו ובט רע׳ן ד׳ וו׳בר ׳ין מ׳ך׳ מ׳׳לובן נ׳ס
ג׳ו׳ון ׃

A typical page from an edition of Minhogimbukh, *this one published in Amsterdam in 1645, reduced here from its actual size, 6¾" x 10¼", the size typical of the earlier editions. This page shows part of the section on Purim.*

THE LATER EDITIONS. The third Venetian edition in Yiddish, published in 1601, gives the impression that there was a need to restimulate interest in the book. Its sophisticated woodcuts show a family that appears to have moved from the modest surroundings of the Ghetto to

sumptuous digs on the Grand Canal. The men are in stately Venetian dress while the women wear low-cut gowns—even while baking matzoh! Yiddish editions closer in style to the 1593 Venice edition were published in Basel in 1610 and 1611, and a Prague edition also appeared in 1611, one of the few to mention the name of Eyzik Tyrnau. The first

The third Yiddish edition, published in Venice in 1601, stands apart from all the others in the sophistication of its woodcuts. The illustration above shows the Havdalah ceremony (see p. 85).

in a long list of Amsterdam editions appeared in 1645. Also published in Amsterdam were four illustrated editions in Hebrew (1685 to 1774), and one in Ladino, the Spanish-based vernacular tongue of the Sephardic Jews, in 1768, also illustrated. New Yiddish editions appeared regularly in Germany from the 1690s well into the nineteenth century. From the late eighteenth century through the time of the last editions, in the late 1800s, the places of publication moved steadily eastward, from small towns in Germany to Poland and the Ukraine. Warsaw editions were published in 1871 and 1884 and a Kiev edition in 1874. An edition published in Piotrkow Trybunalski, Poland, in 1891, is the last that I've found that follows the printed format established in Venice three hundred years earlier and the mansucript text of Eyzik Tyrnau.

Interestingly, the first and only surviving Yiddish manuscript is an illustrated customs book from northern Italy that was made by or before 1503 (a back page records a death in that year). The manuscript is at the Bibliothèque Nationale in Paris. The calligraphy and the illustrations appear to be the work of the same hand. One imagines that it was made for teaching purposes or perhaps as a mock-up for a more elaborate illumination, though none resembling it exists.

The variations in the editions are found mainly in minor customs and additional liturgies, especially in the choice of liturgical hymns (piyutim), which often follows local tradition and the taste of the clergy. The seasonal references made in the captions to the zodiac woodcuts are missing entirely from the later, unillustrated editions.

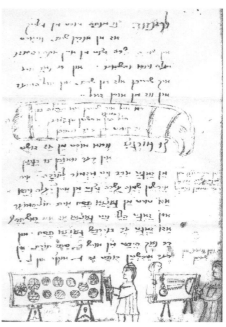

A page from an early sixteenth-century Italian manuscript on Jewish customs (Paris: Bibliothèque Nationale MS Hebr. 586). Shown here is matzoh baking.

THE ILLUSTRATIONS. Woodcut illustrations appeared in many, but not all, of the editions from 1593 (Venice) to 1774 (Amsterdam), and they show remarkable continuity of style. With the exception of the 1601 Venice edition, they differ only in small details. The full complement of illustrations numbers forty, five of which are repeated: twenty-eight squarish woodcuts of holiday and weekly customs; and twelve smaller, horizontal ones showing the month's zodiac and farming activity. By the time of Gunzburg's first illustrated edition, this style of woodcut was well established in illustrated Passover haggadot, such as the famous ones printed in Prague in 1526 and Mantua in 1560. (In 1609 a famous illustrated haggadah was printed in Venice by Giovanni di Gara, the printer of the Venice editions of the *Minhogimbukh*). The

Elijah in the Prague   *Noah's Ark, from* Tsenerene, *Frankfurt, 1741*
Haggadah, 1526

pictures migrate not only among haggadot and customs books, but also between Christian and Jewish books. A bearded man riding an ass may appear as Elijah in a haggadah and Jesus in a book of Gospels. A number of the illustrations of biblical scenes in the *Sefer Yosifon* and *Tsenerene* are adapted from the famous ones by Hans Holbein. The *Sefer Yosifon* is a Yiddish adaptation of a Hebrew translation of *The War of the Jews* by the Roman-era Jewish historian Flavius Josephus—a book of disasters. The woodcut genre survived in haggadot into the late nineteenth century, long after its last appearance in the customs books.

Among scholars of Old Yiddish, there has been some discussion as to whether the *Minhogimbukh* woodcuts were made by Jews or Gentiles, but little can be proven conclusively. There is a possibility that the woodcuts in the 1593 Venice edition were made by Jakob Bak of Prague, who spent the 1590s working in Venice at the publishing house of Giovanni di Gara and whose sons published editions of the *Minhogimbukh* in Prague between 1620 and 1660. The woodcuts in the 1611 and later Prague editions are virtually identical to those that appeared in the first illustrated edition in 1593.

Havdalah, the "separation" ceremony that ends the Sabbath, is depicted here in the first illustrated edition, Venice, 1593.

A slightly different version of the Havdalah ceremony in the Amsterdam edition of 1723. Note the white-and-black Dutch floor tiles and windows.

That these charming, simple pictures were retained for so long may be without parallel in the history of publishing. For the Jews of central and western Europe, they formed a ubiquitous iconography and it's hard to imagine why they fell from favor or why they didn't survive in updated versions or, in the least, as educational art for children. Similar scenes of Sabbath candlelighting ceremonies and Passover customs can be found in manuscripts and printed in pamphlets and broadsides, but the images as a group—as a visual vocabulary—vanished. It may well have been because of the increased strictness that characterized orthodoxy and Hasidism from the eighteenth century onward and, with it, a rigid interpretation of the biblical injunction against graven images.

WHY DID THE *MINHOGIMBUKH* FALL FROM FAVOR? The slow demise of the illustrations leads one to wonder why the *Minhogimbukh* itself lost its popularity. One can only speculate. After the Emancipation that began with Napoleon, Jews became increasingly splintered in the nineteenth century. There were two new directions in Jewish life of western and central Europe: the Reform movement with its radical reconsideration of traditional customs and a modernized learned culture called *Die Wissenschaft des Judentums* (the Science of Judaism) with its emphasis on historical and archaeological studies. European national languages gradually replaced Yiddish as the vernacular in many Jewish households, especially those of higher economic status. Books of personal prayers, a kind called *Tekhines*, often associated with women and long published in Yiddish, were now being written and published in German and other mainstream languages. One can imagine that some of the old woodcuts made nineteenth-century "enlightened" Jews more than a bit squeamish.

The Middle Ages had been recast in a Romantic context—everyone read Sir Walter Scott. The primitive was far from fashion and no one recoils from the primitive past more than the newly—and tentatively—assimilated. Where the book held its audience, albeit in unillustrated editions, was in eastern Europe, where lives were still conducted in Yiddish and opportunities for education fewer.

A Strategy for Revival

The spare, telegraphic prose of the *Minhogimbukh* was well suited to the readers of its times. Though the book was intended for those with a limited knowledge of Hebrew, it nonetheless assumed a familiarity with the Bible, the basic commandments, the principal prayers, and the cycle of synagogue services. Memorizing such material was a fundamental part of the education of Jewish boys and, to a lesser extent, girls, at every level. Thus the *Minhogimbukh* offered more than just basic rote facts; it also dished up bits of talmudic lore and references to the legal works of the great rabbis of the Middle Ages. Some key blessings were printed in their entirety, just in case the memorization didn't stick. On the whole, it did a superb job of helping its readers feel comfortable and competent in the Jewish world.

Comfortable and competent—that's what I was looking for: to know the home rituals and to be able to walk into a synagogue and understand what's going on. It wasn't quite enough for me to just "do Judaism," to know that on this day we recite this prayer or those Torah verses. I wanted to know what the words meant in the context in which they were written. If these explanations were added to the structural frame of the *Minhogimbukh*, I thought, then it might become an excellent vehicle for the chattering twenty-first century. I imagined that the readers for a newly reconstituted book of customs would be those who, like me, wanted to know the customs for a given day and to have a clear yet concise idea of the words that are spoken and heard on that day: the blessings, prayers, and Bible readings. There is a need, especially among those who do not know Hebrew and Aramaic, for something that is beween a book of Jewish holiday lore, on the one hand, and a prayer book and Bible, on the other—a concise, vernacular guide to how a Jewish life is lived from day to day and throughout the year. For three hundred years this was the role of the *Minhogimbukh*.

Using the 1593 Venice *Minhogimbukh* as a skeleton, I added to this edition a number of discursive elements: introductions to the book's major divisions and concepts, descriptions of all of the prayers and many of the Bible readings, a chart of the Amidah benedictions and the various names for its components, a general chapter on Jewish law and custom, and one on Jewish prayer to explain how the daily prayer rituals are performed—something the author of the *Minhogimbukh* took for granted. Also added are chapters on customs and holidays that weren't mentioned or didn't exist in 1593, such as bar and bat mitzvah and Holocaust Remembrance Day. The annotations in the margins point to some variant customs of different Jewish groups, references to the Bible and other key texts, historical notes and sources, and suggestions for further exploration.

The 1593 edition included a seventy-year calendar and a detailed accounting of the minutiae of the calendrical cycle in each monthly

xxviii   THE BOOK OF CUSTOMS

chapter, giving the reader a set of conditional propositions such as, "If the beginning of the month falls on a Thursday, then the Torah reading is *X*; if it falls on the Sabbath, then the Torah reading is *Y*," and so on. Because we live at a time when Jewish calendar information is available on many Web sites or at any synagogue, I have dispensed with it entirely. Instead, to give the reader a sense of the substance of the synagogue experience, I give synopses of all the Bible readings according to a hypothetical model year but always with a notice to the reader that the schedule of these readings varies somewhat from year to year.

Within the traditional sphere, Jewish practice has not changed greatly since 1593, but it has changed. To have followed the old book exclusively would have resulted in some strange affectations. For example, the well-known prayer *Modeh ani*, which Jews recite upon awakening, is not in the 1593 *Minhogimbukh*; though it was published for the first time in 1569, it was not widely recited until some time in the seventeenth century. To publish a modern book without it would be very odd, indeed. So to reconcile the old practices with those of today, I used as a general—though not exclusive—guide Ashkenazic Orthodox prayer books such as ArtScroll's siddur (the prayer book for weekdays) and maḥzor (the prayer book for Sabbath and festivals). These are the most commonly used prayer books in traditional circles.

Of What Denomination Is This Book?

The customs in this book are based in the Ashkenazic orthodox tradition, with many noted exceptions. I chose this path for two reasons: because it is similar to the 1593 model and because it is the basis for all other forms of Jewish worship. What we call traditional or orthodox Judaism today was, generally speaking, the only kind of Judaism practiced in the sixteenth century, though there were, of course, differences among rites—Ashkenazic, Sephardic, Eastern, and so on—which were the byproducts of the geography of the Diaspora. Though these rites continue to exist, the big differences among today's Jews are more philosophical and political—what Americans call denominational.

I offer this revival of the old *Minhogimbukh* as an attempt to describe a traditional baseline of Jewish custom without denominational particularity, though with a consciousness of the many varieties of Jewish religious experience of both the past and the present. If it is "cafeteria religion," then it's one that serves the traditional main courses. Some might find my approach singularly *un*orthodox and wonder why I, as a liberal, didn't opt instead for a more modernized basis, such as Conservative or Reform or Reconstructionist Judaism. In fact, there are parts of the book in which the views of those groups have been quite influential. Nowhere is that more evident than in matters of gender. Inspired by the congregations of every stripe in which women and men play equal roles in the liturgy, I have purged most gender differences with regard to commandments and customs, though the old way is mentioned, too. I was amazed at how easily this could be accomplished, without compromise to language or sense. I should say, though, that I have kept the masculine pronouns for God; to do otherwise is to jettison nearly three thousand years of mental images, continuity of sound, and literary sensibility.

I did not go back to the traditional customs and liturgies expecting to find lost meaning, but there it was. Even more surprisingly, I found deep meaning in texts that had been dropped or modified by the liberal denominations: the prayers of supplication and confession, the tragic liturgies of Tishah b'Av, and the even the *Avodah*, the daily call for the restoration of the Temple and a return to the sacrifices of old. What can a post-Freudian person like me find in such things? I found these: a broad and intimate confrontation with myself and with God, a sense of community for better or for worse, an appreciation of God's greatness, miracles, and ambiguities—all together, a clearer view of the moral and the immoral. We do not have to agree or find goodness in all of these liturgies, but if we choose to revile some of them, we must do so consciously, and, as in psychotherapy, which for many has taken the place of such confrontations, the regularity of the sessions is part of the treatment.

In the years after the Holocaust, fire-and-brimstone liturgies were pretty hard to take, and the more liberal denominations emphasized messages of consolation. Rightly so. What was set aside, though, was the human balance, the depth of confrontation with God and one's self—the sense, if I dare say it, of sin and of our bad tendencies. If we lack a relationship with these difficult parts, the inspiring and redemptive moments are deprived of their power. We don't need a Tishah b'Av with a triumphal, happy ending; the real one will do just fine, thanks. The traditional Jewish liturgies and customs are worth one's time and attention because they help us to ask ourselves—on a regular basis—who we were, who we are now, and who we aspire to be.

SCOTT-MARTIN KOSOFSKY
Cambridge, Massachusetts
Shushan Purim 2004 / 5764

A Welcome from 1593

THE LONGTIME CUSTOM of the prefatory poem has mostly died out, except in books that are entirely poetic. Since ancient times, such poems were the means by which the reader was enticed to buy the work. The poem might be an encomium or elegy for the writer— Ben Jonson's in the *First Folio* of Shakespeare was both—or a clever synopsis in rhyme. Today we have more books than we have Ben Jonsons, though we do have celebrity endorsements and an unspoken hierarchy of quotable reviewers. What has taken the place of the prefatory poem is not the preface or foreword but the dust jacket with its well-understood expectations of flap copy, back ad, and blurbs.

The "improved, expanded, and illustrated" *Minhogimbukh* of 1593, the old Book of Customs, which inspired this book, included a delightful prefatory poem that describes, commends, and celebrates the book's contents; one can't imagine a more concise rendering. The poem comprises thirty-five long lines (seventy lines written in the standard English form), each a rhymed couplet. Poetic forms were prominent in Old Yiddish literature, especially in secular works, though they are by no means unusual in paraphrases of religious stories; in fact, among the earliest surviving Yiddish texts is a racy narrative poem about the enslaved Joseph and Potiphar's wife. A Yiddish verse translation of the Italian version of the medieval romance *Bovo d'Antona* (*Bevis of Hampton* in English) was first published in 1541, and a book of Yiddish animal fables, *The Book of Cows*, set in rhyming couplets, was published in Verona in 1595. Through these, Yiddish literature entered the European mainstream.

The following translation of the original *Minhogimbukh* poem was rendered into rhyming English especially for this book by the British poet Arthur Boyars, the son of a noted cantor. It is faithful to both the substance and spirit of the Yiddish original.

> All praise be to the Lord our God
> > Who brought us to this present road
> With laws and customs fit for printing
> > And lovely pictures fit for minting.
> Near and distant are their sources,
> > From starters to those who've done their courses.
> Even those who cannot lift or read it
> > Will soon find out they really need it.
> All will be pros alike and know the ruling
> > For every possible occasion, and no fooling!
> Just like Rabbi Ḥutzpis, on one leg standing
> > Learned the whole Torah—a thing demanding!
> As if he'd spent a lifetime learning
> > And got the answers right, simply by yearning!
> Shofar, *lulav*, sukkah, *eruv tavshilin*,
> > And chores like kashering, and ḥametz-searching
> > > —all time filling!
> The women must not be bare-jointed, this causes wrath,
> > Also how they should cover challah with a cloth;
> Hands in front of Sabbath lights to hold—
> > Doesn't matter if you're young or old.
> For *Oseh shalom* we step back,
> > For *Kadosh, kadosh* our very heels we clack;
> Elijah the Prophet we sing on Sabbath eve,
> > Mondays and Thursdays a *Vehu raḥum* we'll weave.

For *Raḥum veḥanun* faces should be covered
    And facing where will also be discovered.
On Sabbath seven are called to Torah, on Rosh Ḥodesh four,
    Five for festivals, for Yom Kippur six, not more!
When making kiddush, keep the bread covered,
    Another rule you surely have discovered!
Spices should be smelled on Saturday night,
    Nails should be scanned by Havdalah's light!
Why eating fruit on Sabbath is prescribed
    And how the sukkah's measure is described.
This and much more for every season,
    And things which have no rhyme or reason!
And those not practicing the laws aright
    Will find themselves in a dreadful plight,
And those who wrong ideas are shaping
    Will soon find out that Hell is gaping—!
So read the *Customs* or listen for the knell
    That takes you by the fastest route to hell!
And so I'll start, trusting to God's might,
    with customs we're ordained for Saturday night,
For that's the proper start of every week,
    When light the darkness is obliged to seek!
Then follows on the seven-day week, don't fear
    With Sabbath days arranged for all the year.
First there's Rosh Ḥodesh and its laws
    Then the whole month follows without pause.
With Rosh Ḥodesh Nisan I'll get going,
    The good sections will set my juices flowing.
How the twelve months fall, and when,
    And why they're thirteen now and then,
To which add hymns, haftarot, blessings,
    Circumcision services, weddings with the seven blessings,
And lots of other things, a real anthology
    All served up here with no apology!
On how to run a business without delay
    Or, without a full minyan, how to pray!

Why no Taḥanun is said on certain days
  Why on Hoshana Rabbah seek the new moon's rays.
Therefore buy our *Book of Customs* and don't delay,
  And then make sure you use it night and day.
On Tishah b'Av as well as Purim.
  On Rosh Hashanahs and Yom Kippurim;
Whatever joy or pain's your measure
  This book will prove your greatest treasure.
Our God of blessed name guard us from all that's vile,
  Return Your people Israel from long Exile!

Amen.

Custom and Law

C USTOMS ARE THE POINT OF DEPARTURE for a Jewish
life. There is a well-known expression, "Judaism is a religion of
deed, Christianity is a religion of creed." It's a gross oversimplification,
for sure, but not without some truth. Judaism stresses that if you begin
with the right actions, you'll come upon the right beliefs; Christianity
works the other way around. In the Talmud, there is a passage that's
considered fundamental in Jewish education, "Let a man busy himself
with observing the commandments and customs even if his heart is
not in them, for eventually the hand will teach the heart."

The Hebrew word for custom is minhag, which comes from the word
nahag, "to lead," and it is the leading edge of tradition in the sense of
its being the most visible part. Minhagim (plural) are popular practices
that were either the basis of Jewish law or were performed to fulfill
God's commandments or practices that come and go over time. The
word minhag is also used collectively to refer to a community and its
customs, including its prayer rites (*nushaot*, singular *nusah*). Thus, to
speak of a community's minhag is to speak of its identity. Jewish customs have five objectives that remain pretty much the same regardless
of time or place or, in contemporary Judaism, of denomination:

1. To make a "fence around the law," for those who know it and for

those who may violate it inadvertently

2. To keep one involved in the faith through its rituals and to keep one from falling into bad habits or indifference

3. To instill a sense of community and inhibit assimilation, which is warned against in several passages of the Torah

4. To glorify the commandments in ways that go beyond the basic requirements, such as the making of certain foods or lavish ceremonial objects for the home or synagogue

5. To provide a mechanism by which Jewish law may be applied and updated

But Judaism is much more than custom. Jews must also observe the commandments (mitzvot; singular, mitzvah, from the word *tzivah*, "he commanded") and the laws (halakhot; singular, halakhah, "the way to go," from the word *halakh*, "to go"). There are many more than ten commandments: God gave 613 of them to Moses and through him to all Israel. They subsume the "Noahide Laws," the "natural" laws of morality of our common ancestor Noah, which include the injunctions against murder, theft, the eating of live flesh, and the bearing of false witness. They also include the *hukim*: commandments for which there are no explanations, such as the sacrifice of a red heifer for the purpose of ritual cleansing, the act of which renders the sacrificer unclean; not even King Solomon could understand that one (see Shabbat Parah, p. 359). Also in Jewish law there are *takanot* and *gezerot*, ordinances or regulations instituted by the sages of the Talmud or by community leaders.

It is a fundamental principle of traditional Jewish belief that Moses received from God on Mount Sinai not only the tablets of the Ten Commandments but the entire "written law" (the Torah) and the "oral law" (codified as the Mishnah, which is the basis of the Talmud). The concept appears first in the literature of the later Second Temple period in the

Pharisees' teaching of the interdependency and simultaneous existence of the written and oral law. This Pharisaic interpretation of Exodus 24:12, later identified with rabbinic Judaism, expresses the principle clearly (interpretation in italic):

BIBLE TEXT, EXODUS 24:12	PHARISAIC INTERPRETATION
[God said] And I will give to you the tablets of stone,	*the Ten Commandments*
the law,	*the word torah, interpreted here as the written Pentateuch*
and the commandments,	*the word mitzvah, interpreted here as oral law, later called the Mishnah*
that I have written to teach them.	*them — the Children of Israel*

This is the belief, despite the obvious historical disorder that it creates. Over the centuries it has not been embraced without dissent. A change of punctuation—ancient languages had no punctuation—is enough to change its meaning. Here it is again, with a change of commas: "And I will give to you the tablets of stone, the law and the commandments, that I have written to teach them." Nevertheless, the first became the accepted interpretation.

The Mishnah was completed around 210 C.E.; the Talmud comprises the Mishnah's text as well as commentaries and disputes concerning the text called *gemara*. It is a vast oceanic work and is considered the main collection of oral law, lore, legends, rabbinical commandments, and commentaries. It was collected in two versions: the first, called the Jerusalem Talmud, was completed around 420 C.E., and the larger Babylonian Talmud around 500 C.E.

The sages of the Mishnah presided over a period of great transition in the practice of Judaism that was brought about by a calamity: the destruction of the Second Temple in 70 C.E. This marked the end of sacrifices and offerings. Intercession with God had been the work of Temple priests; now it became an individual's responsibility. What took the place of the sacrifices was prayer, and it was during this time that a good bit of the liturgy practiced today was formally established. This was also the time when the synagogue became the central institution of Jewish life and with it the rise of the rabbi as community leader and local legal authority.

The end of Temple-based Judaism eventually brought the end of the supreme judicial court, the Sanhedrin, and with it the end of central authority in Jewish law. While legal interpretation and codification continued unabated, individual cases could be adjudicated only by local courts run by panels of rabbis and *posekim* (rabbinic scholar-judges). Their decisions are confined to the interpretation of existing statutes, but creative solutions are found nevertheless, and a good bit of the creative power in Jewish law is derived from the minhagim, the customs that the people make and the judges recognize. The treatment of customs is somewhat akin to the Anglo-American legal tradition of common law, in which custom is endowed with a subsistent authority, playing a comparably important part in the development of law and reflecting the same kind of political genius.

CUSTOM INTO LAW. Three times we are told in the Torah, "Do not boil a kid in its mother's milk." This is a commandment—a mitzvah. The direction seems straightforward enough, but by the time of the Tannaim, the arbiters of oral law in the period before the Talmud, it was interpreted as restricting the consumption of all permissible meat with milk of any kind, and so it became rabbinic law. In talmudic times, rabbis disagreed as to whether the eating of fowl with milk was also forbidden. In some communities the two foods were mixed freely; in others they were not mixed as a matter of custom—of minhag. Yet even in those places where the two foods were eaten together, some individuals chose not to do so as a *ḥumra*—a restriction one takes upon oneself as an expression of piety. By the Middle Ages, the ban on mixing fowl with milk was observed universally—as a matter of decided rabbinic law—but the length of time one had to wait after eating meat before consuming milk varied from one to six hours—again as a matter of local minhag.

But there is also the example of bar mitzvah, which for much of the twentieth century was celebrated lavishly in Conservative communities in the United States but was embraced only slowly in the same way by the Orthodox. Reform Judaism had instituted a confirmation ceremony in the nineteenth century that, in effect, replaced bar mitzvah, but by the late twentieth century the denomination also celebrated bar mitzvah. Though the idea of bar mitzvah is based in oral law, it is not mentioned at all in the *Minhogimbukh*. The earliest reference to a ceremony and feast similar to the kind we know today is from the sixteenth-century Polish rabbi Solomon Luria, who described it as a German custom. It wasn't until the late nineteenth century that it was endowed with the importance it has today. A more contentious example is that of bat mitzvah, the equivalent ceremony for girls, which was practiced first in Germany in the mid-nineteenth century, though not on a regular basis. It was introduced in America in 1922 by Mordecai Kaplan, the founder of the Reconstructionist movement. At first it was widely rejected—and even ridiculed—in Orthodox circles, but by the late twentieth century it became commonplace, albeit under certain halakhic regulations. Bar and bat mitzvah may not have stature in Torah, but they surely have stature in customs.

CENTURIES OF CHANGE. The advent in the eighteenth century of the populist revival movement known as Ḥasidism brought with it new customs, many of them particular to specific communities. This created a great rift with the traditionalists, who saw it as a breakdown of traditional authority. However dramatic their movement seemed at the time, the Ḥasidim did not, generally, abandon the established customs and liturgies; they tended more to add than subtract. In contrast, the nineteenth-century formulators of Reform Judaism saw customs as agents for change, as superseding the practice of many of the mitzvot. This flexibility was enough to accommodate the lives of western European Jews who had become integrated into the fabric of the larger society in the wake of the Jewish Emancipation. The reformers argued that since some laws and commandments were created to govern circumstances that no longer existed, such as those related to the Temple and its sacrifices, references to them should be expunged from the liturgy. The traditional view, on the other hand, was that study of the commandments that couldn't be performed for one reason or another was still necessary—and sufficient for their fulfillment. To the orthodox, changing a custom was one thing, but changing a commandment was heresy.

The cleft is deeply embedded in issues of social class and community, assimilation and identity—powerful (yet mobile) dividers in free, desegregated societies. As a result, the great differences in Jewish custom today are defined not by family heritage but by choice. Nowhere is this more true than in America, where the number of Jewish groups has continued to increase: Ḥasidim, Ḥaredim (fundamentalist Orthodox), Modern Orthodox, Conservative, Reform, Reconstructionist, New Age Kabbalist, and even groups that call to mind Pentecostal Christianity. Within each, one finds a range of custom. To some this pluralism is anathema, sinful straying from the path; to others it is a healthy sign of Jewish vitality and survival. Yet despite this panoply—perhaps because of it—there has been a shift back toward tradition in recent years. Customs and liturgies long ago abandoned in the process of reform are being revived by popular demand. People seem to want more, not less, of traditional custom and ritual.

Fundamentals of Prayer

O F ALL THE LAWS and customs, none is more central than prayer. Its purpose is to create a space, both communal and personal, in which people may come to understand their lives in regard to God's morals, laws, and teachings. Both its objective and its meaning can be found in the Hebrew word for prayer, *tefilah*, which comes from the root *palal*, meaning to intercede, to judge, to mediate. The sages who initiated the formulation of the service referred to it as *avodah shebalev*, "the service of the heart." The poetry of Jewish prayer comes from placing oneself in God's realm, the words acting as reminders of what that realm encompasses and all the things most valued within it. The constancy of prayer's framework enables our contemplation and accommodates our changing perspectives, experiences, and needs.

It was not always so. Though the Bible includes many examples of prayer—about eighty of them—few of them were recited formally in the biblical period. Moses's prayer for Miriam, who had become afflicted by leprosy (Numbers 12:13), or Hannah's silent prayer for fertility (1 Samuel 1:11)—these were spontaneous outpourings that set a precedent for later prayers. In biblical times, intercession with God was expressed mostly in the sacrifices and offerings of animals and grain brought to the Tabernacle, later to the Temple. It has been conjectured that during the Babylonian Exile, 586–538 B.C.E., which followed the Temple's destruction, prayer rituals were developed to take the place of the sacrifices, though there is no evidence for it. Sacrifices resumed during the Second Temple period, but after the Temple's demise in 70 C.E., prayer became their substitute. With the end of Temple-based Judaism came the rise of the synagogue as the main institution of Jewish life, and it was then that many of the prayers—and the structure of the prayer service—we know today were established. That's not to say that all Jewish prayers are two thousand years old, but some of them are, though others are more recent and yet others much older.

Jewish prayer comprises several categories and includes two large, daily prayer sets: the Shema—three paragraphs from Deuteronomy and Numbers that are the cornerstone of the faith; and the Amidah, a group of benedictions that is the central feature of every prayer service. A third major set surrounds the reading of the Torah, "the Law," which is apportioned through the year and is read on Sabbaths, Mondays, and Thursdays, thus combining study and prayer. There are blessings, *berakhot*, which bless God's connection to all things and His ultimate kingship; they are often based on the familiar formulation, "Blessed are You, O Lord our God, king of the universe...." Many prayers of petition, thanksgiving, and sanctification also appear throughout Jewish life, as well as prayers of supplication, of confession, and of penitence and prayers in the form of hymns and dirges.

Still, the symbols of the old Temple sacrifices remain: the morning (shaharit) and afternoon (minhah) services correspond to the two daily offerings. The additional service called "musaf," recited after the morning service on Sabbath and special days, is also analogous to a sacrifice ritual. Only the evening (maariv) service is not related to a sacrifice and thus it began as nonobligatory. Today, long after the demise of the Temple, the specific formulas for the sacrifices are recited in festival musaf services, directly from the Torah, and every day in the traditional morning service, quoted from passages in the Mishnah.

In this book, the communal prayer services are described mainly in the chapters "Days of the Week," "Sabbath," "The Conclusion of the Sabbath," and "Rosh Ḥodesh." Prayers that are particular to specific festivals (holidays) and other observances are described in the chapters about the months in which they occur. The number of prayers is large and what is especially daunting for the novice is the variety of names used to describe some of the same ones. For example, the central part of all services is a group of benedictions called the Amidah, also known as the Shemoneh esrei, sometimes simply called *Tefilah* ("prayer"). Amidah is the word for "standing," and, indeed, one stands while saying it; Shemoneh esrei means "eighteen," a reference to the original eighteen benedictions. One was added later, bringing the total to nineteen; on Sabbaths and special days, one recites fewer. The individual components of the Amidah are called by different names in different communities. And so on. But as one begins to understand the context of the prayers and learn the customs of a home community, figuring out the variant names becomes easier.

Congregational and Private Prayer

In Judaism, prayer provides a means of contact with the divine, a way to appeal for justice or mercy or knowledge. But the prayers for such requests—even those said silently—emphasize community rather than individual need: "Grant *us* relief from affliction." Judaism stresses community, and so most Jewish liturgy is intended to be recited congregationally. Distinctions are made between the standardized statutory prayers and those that are personal expressions of prayerfulness. Some prayers in the obligatory class have certain requirements, such as a mandatory prayer quorum of ten adults, called a "minyan," that must be present to conduct certain parts of synagogue services. For example, the Torah may not be read without a minyan, nor may the mourner's Kaddish be recited. Some synagogues employ *batlanim*, synagogue-goers whose presence guarantees the minimum number.

There are also many personal prayers and prayers said in the home, such as the those recited upon awakening and going to bed, the Grace after Meals (one of the most elaborate prayer sets), and the blessings and rituals at the beginning and end of the Sabbath. An important category of personal prayer is called Teḥinot, or in Yiddish, *Tekhines*. These are personal supplications, sometimes based on formulas that begin, "May it be Your will, O God," or "Master of the Universe," but are often completely free in form, especially those in the vernacular.

Kavanah

"Hear O Israel, the Lord our God, the Lord is One!" begins the Shema (Deuteronomy 6:4). It is the next verse, "You shall love the Lord with all your heart and all your soul and all your might," that is the basis of *kavanah*, the devoted concentration that is considered an essential component of prayer. To many, *kavanah* (literally "to aim") is synonymous with the repeated knee-bending and bowing that one associates with Ḥasidic prayer, but *kavanah* is really about intention, about the individual state of mind one brings to prayer. There is a well-known saying that appears as the motto a 1709 Yiddish prayerbook, "*Tfile on kavone iẓ vi a guf on neshome*," which is to say, "Prayer without *kavanah* is like a body without a soul." The repetition of conscious prayer, day after day and through the yearly cycle, is intended to create a framework for our thoughts and self-examination, not as mindless utterances.

The Language of Prayer

Hebrew is the language in which most prayers and blessings were composed, though there are some notable exceptions, such as Kaddish, which is in Aramaic, a Semitic language closely related to Hebrew that became a vernacular tongue in the Holy Land during the Second Temple period. (Since that time, Hebrew has been written in the Aramaic alphabet, not the other way around, as is commonly assumed.) Aramaic is the language of Jewish legal documents, still used in wedding contracts and divorce decrees, and also in legal formulas that are part of the liturgy such as the famous *Kol nidrei* of Yom Kippur. It is the primary language of the Talmud and language of the *Zohar*, a key work in the writings of Kabbalah, the well-known school of Jewish mysticism.

The ratio of Hebrew to vernacular prayer remains a division between denominations and individual synagogues. There are many issues at stake: group identity, national identity, philosophy of education, priestly control, and of course custom. Wherever one stands in this debate, it must be recognized that Hebrew words often possess meaning and context that are not always apparent in a given translation. This contention, which is by no means unique to Judaism, is not so much about translation as it is about belief in language's mystical powers. As with all literature, it's best to read the original, but a fine translation, especially one with perceptive annotations, may shed light on a text in ways that wouldn't be apparent to any but the most learned readers.

The Tallit, the Tzitzit, and the Tefillin

The origin of the tallit, the familiar Jewish prayer shawl, and more particularly the tzitzit, the tassels at its ends (often translated as "fringes"), may be found in the book of Numbers with God's instruction to Moses:

> Speak to the Israelites and instruct them to make for themselves tassels [tzitzit] on the corners of their garments throughout the generations; let them attach a cord of blue to the tassel at each corner. That shall be your tassel; look at it and recall all the commandments of the Lord and observe them, so that you do not follow your heart and eyes in your

lustful urge. Thus you shall be reminded to observe all My commandments and to be holy to your God. (Numbers 15:38-40)

And so the tallit began as a tasseled garment to be worn all the time, not just for prayer. Ḥasidim and some traditional Orthodox Jews wear a tasseled tunic, as described in the verses above, as an undergarment. It is the custom of some to let the tassels hang outside the trousers. Over time, regulations were developed as to the details of the twists and knots of the tassels, so that the knots and the numerical value of the word *tzitzit* (600) add up to 613, the number of the commandments in the Torah. Why tassels? Scholars have shown that at the time of the Exodus, tassels worn on the clothing were a sign of dignity and importance in other Middle Eastern cultures.

Tefillin, called "phylacteries" in English, from the Greek word for "protector," are two amulets worn for prayer—one on the head, the

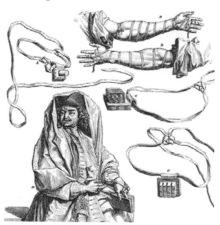

Tefillin and the manner in which they are tied.
Engraving by Bernard Picart, Amsterdam, 1725.

other on the left arm and hand (right arm for lefties). They are first mentioned in Exodus 13:9 (and again in 13:16) but are described in more detail in Deuteronomy 6:8 (repeated in 11:18), which is part of the Shema: "You are to tie them as a sign upon your hand, and they are to be for browbands between your eyes." What this means exactly is not altogether clear, but, as in the case of the tzitzit, there is no indication that these tied-on words are to be worn only for prayer. The interpretation of these amulets eventually became this: two small, black, leather-covered boxes to which are attached a black leather strap, one on each. The boxes contain four sections of the Torah: Exodus 13:1-10 and 13:11-16 and Deuteronomy 6:4-9 and 11:13-21, texts that one might call the cornerstones of Judaism: the commandments to remember how God brought us out from Egypt and to say the Shema. On the outside of the one worn on the head is the letter *shin*, which stands for *Shaddai*, "Almighty God." The custom that developed for the donning of tefillin is that they are worn on weekdays, with some exceptions, for the morning service. There are some Hasidic groups in which it is the custom to wear tefillin all day.

Though not an object related to prayer per se the mezuzah, which is affixed to the doorposts of Jewish homes (the word itself means "doorpost"), originates in the same Bible passages that describe tefillin. It is, in a sense, an amulet for the home, affixed to the doorposts. There is an old custom to kiss the mezuzah when entering one's home.

Headcovering, most familiar as the yarmulke, or *kipah*, is mentioned only in the later rabbinic literature as a symbol of piety. There is no blessing specific to it and its standing is based entirely in custom, not law. Some Hasidic communities have their own style of headdress worn in addition to a yarmulke; sometimes this is just a hat of the fedora type or more elaborate hats based on the styles of non-Jewish headwear popular in the groups' late-eighteenth-century eastern European places of origin. It was long the custom for married women to keep their heads covered, too. Orthodox women wear a scarf or hat in public and the once-ubiquitous customary wig (*sheytl* in Yiddish) is still worn in some devout circles. In non-Orthodox synagogues, women's headwear has become the same as for men, which is to say a yarmulke or not, depending on generation and congregation.

Music and Prayer

The weekly readings from the Bible are traditionally sung—or rather chanted—not read. Also sung are the liturgical hymns (piyutim) as well as a number of blessings and prayers. Music is frequently mentioned in the Bible, as early as the fourth chapter of Genesis. Altogether, about seven or eight types of musical instruments are mentioned: lyre, harp, flute, cymbal, trumpet—all typical of the ancient world. In 1 Samuel, David sings to Saul; the psalms are musical works, plentiful in musical references and allusions. At the Temple, a choir of Levites sang psalms. But after the Second Temple's destruction, this practice fell away.

As to the sound of any of this music making, we can only speculate. The notation of Jewish chant, codified in the ninth and tenth centuries C.E., is a system of twenty-nine diacritical marks called *teamim*, or "tropes," which indicate not pitch, meter, or tempo but rather musical phrase patterns. How these are interpreted is a matter of time, culture, and place. Recent scholars have codified eight basic Jewish musical styles defined along geopolitical lines, but that hardly describes the variety. Since so much of music making depends on the talent and skill of its practitioners, considerable variations can be found even within neighborhoods. For many Jews, their only education in formal chant comes with training for bar or bat mitzvah, when a Bible portion with its musical tropes is traditionally learned.

Beside the high art of interpreting the *teamim*, there is also the congregational and personal style of chant known as *nusah*, a word that also means "rite," as in the Ashkenazic rite or Sephardic rite. *Nusah* is far less formal than the cantorial style, but it is important nonetheless that it be appropriate to the occasion. And so a more festive musical mood and style are adopted for the Sabbath than would be considered appropriate to a weekday. Likewise, different *nushaot* (plural of *nusah*) are deemed suitable to the mood of various festivals.

The musical styles found among different congregations and denominations vary greatly. Vernacular music and musical forms have been adapted to Jewish liturgy to one degree or another in all rites. Jewish music is at least as much a reflection of the outside world as it is something consciously apart from it. Since Jews were travelers, their musical influences were diverse.

Since the early nineteenth century a steady stream of new Jewish liturgical music has been created by professional composers, mostly Jewish and largely associated with Reform Judaism. While some of the music of the early Reform composers remains influential, most of it was short-lived. The mixing of Western art music and Jewish liturgy predates Jewish Emancipation in the early 1800s by at least two centuries. Contemporaneous with the early editions of the *Minhogimbukh*, in the late sixteenth and early seventeenth centuries a number of Jewish musicians were involved with the revolution in the greater musical culture going on at the time. In 1622 the composer Salamone Rossi of Mantua, a colleague of Claudio Monteverdi's, published cantatas and madrigals for synagogue use that differed from the latest Christian and secular music only in their Hebrew texts. Rossi's style was widely imitated, from Italy to France and the Low Countries. The dramatic possibilities of the forms were well suited to Jewish liturgy, emphasizing as they did the meaning of the words over the beauty of the melody. Not everyone was so pleased: some rabbis discouraged the performance of such music as *ḥukat hagoy*, the practices of the gentiles forbidden in Leviticus 20:23, a charge that has long marked the relationship of Western art music and Orthodox synagogue practice. Rossi's works have enjoyed a revival in recent years.

The music that has had a more lasting influence on Jewish liturgy has tended to be that which does not require highly trained musical forces. The songs of the pioneers of the modern state of Israel have been enormously influential, as has been the work of modern Hebrew songwriters. An example is the work of the late Rabbi Shlomo Carlebach, whose musical influences included Woody Guthrie. Carlebach, a charismatic figure with a loyal following, led musical services throughout the world, from Indian ashrams to Manhattan jazz clubs. His influence continues unabated.

Jewish Time

When approaching Jewish customs, it is important to understand how Jewish time is counted. The Jewish day begins and ends in the evening, at sunset, reflecting the description of the days of Creation in the first chapter of Genesis: "The evening and the morning were the first day." Sabbaths and festivals always begin at sunset, and it is considered important to proper observance of the rituals that the exact time of sunset be known by everyone. Neither in the Torah nor in modern Hebrew do the six weekdays have names; they are, rather, referred to by number. Only the seventh day has a name: *Shabbat*. This regularly occurring day of devotion and rest was an innovation of Judaism.

The Jewish calendar, though often described as lunar, is actually a "lunisolar" calendar, since it is adjusted to ensure that the major festivals occur in the appropriate seasons. There are twelve months of twenty-nine or thirty days. In order to keep seasonal synchronization, a thirteenth month (a second month of Adar) is added seven times during a nineteen-year cycle, in years 3, 6, 8, 11, 14, 17, and 19. An ordinary year has between 353 and 355 days, or 50 weeks; a leap year between 383 and 385 days, or 54 weeks. The flexibility in the number of days in a year, whether a standard year or a leap year, allows for the proper placement of the dates of certain observances in regard to the Sabbath. Though the Torah refers to seasons and to some specific months as well as to the observance of the new moon, the names of the Jewish months were introduced only after the Babylonian Exile, 586–538 B.C.E., and their names are, in fact, adaptations from the Babylonian language, Akkadian.

Major festivals that in the Torah and in the state of Israel are observed for one day, are traditionally observed for two days in the Diaspora. These include the three pilgrimage festivals (when the Israelites brought personal sacrifices to the Temple) of Passover (the last two days of which are also observed as holidays), Shavuot, and Sukkot. Rosh Hashanah is celebrated for two days everywhere. Yom Kippur is observed for only a single day because one cannot fast for two consecutive days. This practice of a second day in the Diaspora stems from Temple times, when the occurrence of the new moon was determined by the reports of field observers to Temple officials, who in turn sent messengers to all the communities. If the messengers arrived on the thirtieth day of the month, in the morning, then that day was considered the beginning of the next month, and it was counted as the first day of the month, retroactively making the previous month twenty-nine days long. However, if the observers did not come on the thirtieth day of the month, the next month was counted from the thirty-first day, making the previous month thirty days long. In the case of Passover, for example, if the messengers came on the thirtieth of Adar, then Nisan would be counted from that day and Passover would be observed fifteen days later. But if the messengers did not arrive on the thirtieth of Adar, Adar would be thirty days long and Nisan would be counted from the thirty-first day only, and then the sixteenth day after the thirtieth would be Passover. The issue was, in essence, how soon distant communities could learn of the date and how far the messengers could travel within two weeks' time. Therefore, Passover is celebrated for two days, on the fifteenth and the sixteenth, to be sure the actual day is covered. Although we now (since the fourth or fifth centuries C.E.) can predict time with near-perfect accuracy, two-day observance in the Diaspora continued. Reform leaders in the nineteenth century had widely moved to single-day observance—the issue being the centrality of the Land of Israel—but in recent years they have tended toward the traditional observance.

Hebrew years are calculated from the date of Creation, which corresponds to the Gregorian date of October 7, 3760 B.C.E. It is Jewish practice in the English-speaking world to use the nonsectarian C.E. and B.C.E., "Common Era" and "Before the Common Era," in place of A.D. and B.C. We continue that usage here.

How Prayer Is Presented in This Book

The early editions of the *Minhogimbukh* gave prayer instructions for all the days of the year. They did not give the texts of the prayers, only their names, assuming that the reader either knew them by heart or had at hand a siddur (the daily prayer book) and maḥzor (the prayer book for Sabbath and festivals). This edition, though not a prayer book, gives more flesh to the prayers than did the old *Minhogimbikher*. This book is based mostly in modern Orthodox practice, not for the sake of espousing the observance of a specific community, but because it comprises the broadest and oldest material. Annotations mark some places where differences exist in other rites and denominations: Sephardic, Conservative, Reform, and so on. Are the prayers presented here relevant to people from non-Orthodox denominations? They are, because all Jewish prayer books are, at their core, based in the same liturgical tradition, regardless of prayers that have been dropped or altered or whether they're said in Hebrew or the vernacular.

The history and nature of Jewish prayer are well covered in a number of popular books: Reuven Hammer's excellent *Entering Jewish Prayer*, Adin Steinsaltz's learned *A Guide to Jewish Prayer*, Hayim Halevy Donin's methodical *To Pray as a Jew*, and Lawrence Hoffman's multivolume *My People's Prayerbook*. Macy Nulman's *The Encyclopedia of Jewish Prayer* is a very useful, concise reference. Perhaps the greatest work available in English is Ismar Elbogen's *Jewish Liturgy*; today it is regarded mainly for its commentaries, its historical aspects having been replaced by more recent scholarship. Sadly, relatively few books about prayer from the Reform and Reconstructionist perspectives are currently available; comparative studies of Jewish prayer among the denominations are virtually nonexistent. However, Jewish liturgy in general is an active area of interest, and new books appear regularly. The volumes mentioned above and prayer books of every stripe, shape, and size can be found in Jewish bookstores and on the Internet.

Cartouche from the Amsterdam edition of 1722

The Days of the Week

IN THE WEEKDAY CUSTOMS of Jewish life, we have inherited a collective consciousness to help us conduct and measure our lives. While the world of the Sabbath is a world apart, a day of immersion in our relationship with God, the weekday rituals give us the principal criteria that we use to relate to others and confront ourselves. Where these ideas and words are found is mainly in the three daily synagogue services, called in Hebrew shaḥarit, minḥah, and maariv.

The observances described in the 1593 *Minhogimbukh* are more or less the same as in today's traditional Ashkenazic orthodoxy. While the book might give the impression that Jews of the sixteenth century did little but pray, that was no truer then than it is today. As in any good instructional work, complete observance is the standard. Where it differs most from today's style of Jewish instruction is in its homiletics—the little stories used as examples. They retain what one might describe as Old World earthiness:

> One should wear tzitzit the whole day, because its fringes are like the knots that one ties in order not to forget things, reminders of all the commandments we must observe. Everyone knows the story of the wise scholar who went to

This well-known story is from Talmud Menaḥot *43a, but the moral has its origin in the Torah, specifically Numbers 15:39, in which it is said of the tzitzit, "You will see it and you will remember [God's commandments]."*

see a whore. He traveled a long way and gave her lots of money. She got undressed and lay down on a fancy bed. When he went to caress her, his tzitzit slapped his face, making him step back and suppress his desire. The whore wanted to know if he found fault in her; he answered that he had never seen a lovelier woman in his life but that Jews were commanded to wear fringes, which act like four witnesses when one transgressed a commandment. Hearing this, the whore gave one-third of her wealth to the king and one-third to charity, moved to the study house of the scholar, and became a pious Jew. The wise scholar married her and she became his pious wife. And so the bed that was first forbidden by a commandment became one prescribed by a commandment, and together they had pious children.

One imagines from this that wives were greatly encouraging of their husbands' wearing of tzitzit.

While the washing of hands before a meal is a ritual act rather than a cleansing one (one begins with clean hands), one could hardly fault this standard of personal hygiene:

> Before eating a meal, one should wash one's hands using a vessel full of clear water that has not been used previously. The water should not be mixed with wine or anything else, nor should it stink so much that a dog wouldn't drink it.

On occasion, though, the microbiology gets a bit weird:

This has various talmudic sources, including the Babylonian Talmud Bava metsia *107b, which says eighty-three portions (!).*

> One should get into the habit of eating at least a small portion of bread for breakfast, because according to our sages— may their memory be blessed—there are sixty-three portions of scum in one's bladders, and a small portion of bread with some water washes it all out. However, according to Rashi— may his memory be blessed—water is only for those who do not have wine.

Suffice it to say that Rashi, the renowned eleventh-century commentator on the Bible and Talmud whose interpretations are often among the most *peshat*, "plain-meaning," was both a Frenchman and a professional vintner.

The Jewish passion for prayer sometimes comes through in curious ways:

> After finishing the meal, one should put away the knives from the table. The reason for this custom is that there was once a man who recited the Grace after Meals with great devotion, and when saying the section *Uvenei Yerushalayim*, he remembered the destruction of the Temple in Jerusalem, grabbed the knife on the table, and stabbed himself in the heart.

Such stories aside, the book is pious, thorough, and methodical. What follows is not a strict translation but an expansion on the original framework for today's readers who might not be familiar with the texts of all the prayers.

Prayers upon Waking

It is the custom to wake up early, in order to begin the Shema no later than when the sun is shining brightly. Upon waking, one says a brief prayer of thanksgiving, *Modeh ani*, which is based upon the belief that in sleep, as in death, the soul leaves the body; every time one awakens, the body and soul are reunited. The prayer is simple and brief: "I give thanks to You, living and eternal king, for having mercifully restored my soul within me. Great is Your faithfulness."

To wash away the "impurities of the night," one follows with the ritual of *Netilat yadayim*: Wash hands using a pitcher and a receiving basin (usually a sink, today). Pour the water three times over one hand and then three times over the other. Then recite the blessing:

> Blessed are You, Lord our God, king of the universe, who has sanctified us through His commandments and commanded us to wash our hands.

The prayer Modeh ani *first appeared in print as early as 1569 but seems not to have been widely recited until the seventeenth century. It was not mentioned in the earliest Yiddish editions of the* Minhogimbukh. *Since* Modeh ani *does not mention the name of God, it may be said before the ritual handwashing.*

As there is a blessing for nearly everything, the third blessing of the day is the one said in the morning as well as after performing one's bodily functions, *Asher yatzar*:

> Blessed are You, Lord our God, king of the universe, who fashioned the human body in wisdom, creating openings, arteries, glands, and organs, marvelous in structure and intricate in design. Should but one of them fail by being blocked or opened, it would be impossible to exist. Praised are You, God, healer of all flesh, sustaining our bodies in wondrous ways.

Sephardim and some Ashkenazim now recite the prayer *Elohai devarim*, "These are the precepts that have no measure." The prayer is from the Talmud, which mentions it as a prayer said upon awakening, though it is now most familiar as a prayer said in fulfillment of the blessings for Torah study. Since one may study the Torah at various times of day, at home or in the synagogue, blessings for Torah study are said in the morning and need not be repeated. But since a blessing must be followed immediately by a commandment, the blessings include passages from both the written law (the Torah) and the oral law (the Talmud). The latter emphasizes those personal virtues that are considered highest and explains the stature of Torah study among them. One may say them at home, but they are also part of the morning synagogue service.

Talmud Berakhot 6ob

See pp. 2–3 for more on the concepts of written law and oral law.

Shaḥarit: The Morning Synagogue Service

Mah tovu is the series of verses said upon entering the synagogue by Ashkenazim. Its formulation has varied over the

ENTERING THE SYNAGOGUE. The prayers said upon entering the synagogue in the morning vary in different traditions. Those in the *Minhogimbukh* are what one might call classical Ashkenazic liturgy. The first prayer said upon entering the synagogue is *Mah tovu*, which in the 1593 edition is described as being said while bowing toward the Torah ark:

> How lovely are your tents, O Jacob, and your dwelling places, O Israel. As for me, through Your abundant kindness I will enter Your house and filled with awe for You I will bow down toward Your holy Temple. O Lord, I love the house of Your abode, the dwelling place of Your glory.

It is followed by two hymns. The first, *Yigdal* ("May the living God be magnified and praised"), written around the year 1300 by Daniel ben Judah, of Rome, is a verse version of Maimonides' Thirteen Articles of Faith, a credo in which the body of Jewish beliefs is expressed in thirteen statements. (See page 80 for further explanation.) *Adon olam* ("The Lord of the universe reigned before anything was created"), one of the most popular of Jewish hymns, is second. It was often attributed to Solomon ibn Gabirol, one of the great masters of Hebrew poetry of medieval Spain (eleventh century), but earlier sources have also been suggested.

TALLIT AND TEFILLIN. The congregant puts on the tallit and tefillin upon entering the synagogue. In traditional Orthodox circles, these ritual objects are worn only by men, but that is no longer the case in many congregations. One examines the tallit before putting it on, making sure that all its fringes have the required eight threads and five knots and are long enough to wind around one's finger. It is the custom to grasp the corners, two in each hand, and kiss them as part of the ritual. The blessing *Lehitatef batzitzit* is recited over it:

> Blessed are You, Lord our God, king of the universe, who commanded us to wrap ourselves in tzitzit.

As the tallit is wrapped around the head and over body, another prayer, *Mah yakar*, is said. It begins, "How great is Your kindness, O God. Mankind takes shelter in Your wings."

years. The form most familiar today is this. The initial words are a quotation from Numbers 24:5, the remainder taken from various Psalms. Sephardic Jews recite Psalm 5:8 upon entering the synagogue and Psalm 5:9 upon leaving it.

Adon olam has enjoyed remarkable versatility, used in various traditions in morning and evening prayers, on Sabbath, as a wedding song in Morocco, and even as a deathbed prayer. There are many musical settings, including one for double choir by Salamone Rossi, Venice, in 1623.

The wearing of tallit and tefillin by women is not a new custom; it was recorded at least as far back as the daughter of the eleventh-century sage Rashi. More recently, the writer Isaac Bashevis Singer wrote of his grandmother's wearing of them.

After the tallit, the tefillin are put on, beginning and ending with the one for the hand. The strap of the hand tefillin is
wound around the arm while tightening the box and reciting
the blessing *Lehaniaḥ tefilin*:

> Blessed are You, Lord our God, king of the universe, who
> has sanctified us with His commandments and has com-
> manded us to put on tefillin.

Then the one for the head is put on, placed on the forehead
with the box at the hairline, centered above the eyes. It
should be visible as a sign of one's acceptance of the covenant. (The arm tefillin does not have to be seen.) When the
head tefillin is placed, one says the blessing *Al mitzvat tefilin*:

> Blessed are You, Lord our God, king of the universe, who
> has sanctified us with His commandments and has com-
> manded regarding the commandment of tefillin.

It is then that one continues to wrap the strap of the arm
tefillin around the wrist and the fingers so that it forms the letter *shin*, which stands for the word *Shaddai*, one of the divine
names. The box should be above the elbow, facing the heart.

MORNING BLESSINGS. The service proper begins with *Birkhot hashaḥar*, morning blessings, which also have a place in
the home liturgy. The morning blessings are a series of fifteen benedictions, each beginning with the customary formulation, "Blessed are You, Lord our God, king of the universe."

*The phrase, "who
has made me a
Jew" is an adapta-
tion of the tradi-
tionally recited*

who endows the cock with the ability to distinguish
    between day and night.
who has made me a Jew.
who has made me free.
who has made me in His image.
who enlightens the blind.

who clothes the naked.
who releases the bound.
who raises they who are bowed down.
who stretches out the earth upon the waters.
who has provided me with all my necessities.
who has strengthened the steps of humanity.
who girds Israel with might.
who crowns Israel with glory.
who gives strength to the weary.
who causes sleep to pass from my eyes.

"who has not made me a gentile." Similarly, "who has made me free" is an adaptation of the original "who has not made me a slave," and "made me according in His image" is a modern, egalitarian version of the original "who has not made me a woman."

THE AKEDAH AND THE SACRIFICES. Absent from the 1593 *Minhogimbukh*, but part of most Orthodox services, is the daily recitation of the *Akedah*, "the binding [of Isaac]," the story of God's most difficult test of Abraham's faith and of the covenant that God swore to Abraham that day at Mount Moriah (Genesis 22:1–19). The *Zohar*, the thirteenth-century "Book of Splendor," which is the key work of the Kabbalah and the cornerstone of Jewish mysticism, states that daily recitation of the *Akedah* is itself a source of God's mercy. The liturgy comprises the reading of the passage from Genesis and a series of related prayers that emphasize the theme of covenant and everlasting loyalty. In synagogues where the reading of the *Akedah* is observed, it is usually followed by the *korbanot*, the reading of the passages relating to the daily burnt offerings in the Temple. After these, the prayer *Barukh sheamar*, "Blessed is He who willed it and the world came into being," is recited, followed by the rabbis' Kaddish.

Regarding the korbanot, see p. 8.

PESUKEI DEZIMRA—VERSES OF SONG. The next part of the service is the *Pesukei dezimra*, the "verses of song," which is introduced by Psalm 30, "A psalm for the inauguration of the Temple." The choice of texts for these verses is not set in the Talmud, but it is customary that they include Psalms 145-

The rabbis' Kaddish is explained on the next page.

For more on
Ashrei, *see pp. 41*
and 81.

150, which are all praises for God's work in the world. Psalm 145, known as *Ashrei*, is said three times in the daily prayers, including this time, and is considered essential among the group. The Song of the Sea (Exodus 14:30–15:19), which Moses and the Israelites sang in thanks to God upon their miraculous deliverance, is also considered an important element here. The closing blessing of *Pesukei dezimra* is *Yishtabah*, "Praised may Your name be forever." The cantor repeats *Yishtabah* aloud, and if there is a minyan in the synagogue, he says Kaddish and then Barkhu.

KADDISH. "Sanctification" is the English meaning of the name of this basic Jewish prayer. Its text is in Aramaic, the language of many Jews of the Second Temple and talmudic periods. There are four main forms, each requiring a minyan (prayer quorum of ten) for its recitation. The "full Kaddish" is said by the prayer leader after the Amidah.

> Magnified and sanctified be His great name in the world He created according to His will. And may He establish His kingdom during your life and during your days, and during the life of all the house of Israel, speedily and in the near future, and say: Amen.
>
> *Response:* Blessed be His great name forever and ever.
>
> Blessed, praised and glorified, exalted, extolled and honored, adored and lauded be the name of the Holy One, blessed be He, beyond all blessings and hymns, praises and songs that are uttered in the world, and say: Amen.
>
> May the prayers and supplications of the entire family of Israel be accepted before their Father who is in heaven, and say: Amen.
>
> May there be abundant peace from heaven and life for us and for all Israel, and say: Amen. May He who makes peace in the heavens make peace for us and for all Israel, and say: Amen.

The "half Kaddish," comprising the first two major paragraphs, is used to conclude major sections of the service. The "rabbis' Kaddish" is the full Kaddish with an added paragraph in which we pray for those who study the scriptures; the word "rabbi" in this case means a learned person, which is to say someone learned in Judaism. In the "mourner's Kaddish," the third paragraph is not recited.

THE CALL TO PRAYER. Barkhu is the official summons to congregational prayer, said only when a minyan is present. The cantor, who begins in a straight, upright position, bows saying the word *barkhu*, then straightens upon invoking God's name:

ברכו את יהוה המברך.

Blessed be the Lord, the blessed One.

The congregation bows and straightens in the same way:

ברוך יהוה המברך לעולם ועד.

Blessed is the Lord, the blessed One, forever and ever.

THE SHEMA AND ITS BLESSINGS. It cannot be overstressed that the Shema is the heart of Jewish prayers, the one to know if you know no others. It has held this status since ancient times. It is said at every morning and evening service and at bedtime; it is the martyr's cry and an essential part of a deathbed confession. As Moses instructed the Israelites, it is to be taught to one's children and worn on one's person, placed on one's gates and on one's doorposts.

The recitation of the Shema in the morning service begins with two preceding blessings. The first one, which has several parts, is called *Yotzer*, "He who makes light and creates darkness." It is punctuated by the Kedushah, the Sanctification of the Angels, which is said by the entire congregation: "Holy,

The medieval sage
Moses Maimonides
noted eleven levels
of angels in his
Mishneh Torah
(Hilkhot yesodei
hatorah 2:7).

holy, holy is the Lord of hosts; the whole world is filled by His glory" (from Isaiah 6:3). This is a quotation of the words of the Ofanim, one of the orders of angels in heaven, who are mentioned in the second line, recited by the cantor: "And the Ofanim and the holy Ḥayot with great noise raise themselves toward the Seraphim and, facing them, offer praise and proclaim. . . ." The congregation completes the sentence: "Blessed is the glory of the Lord from His place" (from Ezekiel 3:12). The blessing concludes with the section *Leel barukh neimot*, "To the God who is blessed, sweet melodies do they offer." Both *Yotzer* and *Ofan* are points in the service that were traditionally elaborated with liturgical poems (hymns) called piyutim, different ones for various occasions, their choice subject to local custom.

Ahavah rabah ("With an abundant love You have loved us"), the second blessing before the Shema, speaks of God's compassion and mercy, his love of our ancestors, to whom he taught the precepts. At the verse that begins *Vehavienu leshalom* ("Bring us in peace from the four corners of the earth"), one places the four corners of the tallit between the fourth and fifth fingers of the left hand and holds them there throughout the Shema. If one is praying alone, or if there is no minyan at the synagogue, three words are spoken before the Shema, *El melekh neeman* ("God, king, who is trustworthy"). And then the Shema is recited—slowly, clearly, and with *kavanah*—concentration and intent.

The full Shema comprises three paragraphs: Deuteronomy 6:4-9, 11:13-21, and Numbers 15:37-41. These are the words that God told to the Israelites through Moses, before they crossed the Jordan into the Promised Land (Deuteronomy) and in the Wilderness (Numbers). The first verse, Deuteronomy 6:4, proclaims God's singularity:

Shema, first verse

שמע ישראל, יהוה אלהינו, יהוה אחד:
Hear, O Israel, the Lord our God, the Lord is One!

If one knows but a single sentence of Jewish prayer, it should be this one. The *Minhogimbukh* teaches, as does every other work on Jewish law and life, that every syllable should be pronounced clearly and emphatically.

Then follows an interjection proclaiming God's kingship. It is recited softly, except on Yom Kippur, when it is said loudly and in unison by the entire congregation:

ברוך שם כבוד מלכותו לעולם ועד.
Blessed is the name of His glorious kingdom forever and ever.

The remainder of the first paragraph concerns the acceptance of God's rule:

*Deuteronomy
6:5–9*

> You shall love the Lord your God with all your heart
>   and with all your soul and with all your might!
> Take to heart these instructions with which I charge
>   you this day.
> Impress them upon your children.
> Recite them when you stay at home and when you are
>   away, when you lie down and when you get up.
> Bind them as a sign on your hand and let them serve
>   as a symbol on your forehead;
> inscribe them on the doorposts of your house and
>   on your gates.

The second paragraph urges the acceptance of God's commandments—the rewards of so doing and the punishment for disobeying:

*Shema,
second paragraph,
Deuteronomy
11:13–17*

> If, then, you obey the commandments that I enjoin upon
>   you this day,
> loving the Lord your God and serving Him with all your
>   heart and soul,

> I will grant the rain for your land in season, the early rain
> and the late. You shall gather in your new grain and
> wine and oil.
> I will also provide grass in the fields for your cattle—and
> thus you shall eat your fill.
> Take care not to be lured away to serve other gods and
> bow to them. For the Lord's anger will flare up against
> you, and He will shut up the skies so that there will be
> no rain and the ground will not yield its produce; and
> you will soon perish from the good land that the Lord is
> giving to you.

The remainder is a paraphrase of the instructions that begin
"You are to repeat them with your children."

The third paragraph, from the book of Numbers, begins
with the tzitzit and their role as a mnemonic for the commandments and ends with the Exodus from Egypt.

Shema,
third paragraph,
Numbers 15:37–41

> The Lord said to Moses, saying:
> Speak to the Israelite people and instruct them to make
> for themselves tassels on the corners of their garments
> throughout the generations; tell them to attach a cord
> of blue-violet to the tassel at each corner.
> That shall be your tassel; look at it and recall all the
> commandments of the Lord and observe them, so
> that you do not follow your heart and eyes in your
> lustful urge.
> Thus you shall be reminded to observe all My command-
> ments and to be holy to your God.
> I the Lord am your God, who brought you out of the land
> of Egypt to be your God: I, the Lord your God.

Thus ends the Shema. The last phrase is repeated by the
cantor in order that the number of words comes to 248, the
same as the number of bones in the human body. It continues immediately with the first word of the blessing of

redemption, the *Geulah*: "*emet.*" The *Geulah*, the only blessing after the Shema, ends with two excerpts from the Song of
the Sea (Exodus 15:11, 18), the song led by Moses as the
Israelites crossed the Red Sea. The congregants join in their
redemption by reciting the verses:

> Who is like You, O Lord, among the gods! *Exodus 15:11*
> Who is like You, magnificent in holiness, awesome in
> praises, doer of wonders!
> The Lord shall reign forever and ever. *Exodus 15:18*

THE AMIDAH. If the Shema, the affirmation of faith, lies at the
center of all Jewish belief, then the Amidah, the series of petitions that invoke future hope, is a main feature of the synagogue experience as well as private prayer. The word *amidah*
means "standing," and indeed, one stands with feet together
when saying this series of benedictions. The Amidah is
known also as *Hatefilah*, "The Prayer," and as Shemoneh esrei,
or "eighteen benedictions," because the series had originally
eighteen parts (later, nineteen). Tradition ascribes it to the
Men of the Great Assembly, of the early Second Temple
period, but it was reordered after the Temple was destroyed
in 70 C.E. Modern scholarship suggests that the prayer originated then but took several more centuries to develop and
become widespread.

The nineteen benedictions, which are sometimes referred
to by their opening words, are listed and described briefly on
the next page, along with some of their related customs.

The Amidah is said at all three of the daily services. When
a minyan is present in the morning and afternoon services, it
is said twice: once silently by the congregants and once by
the cantor or prayer leader, in order to say it for those who
cannot pray on their own. Of particular significance in the
repetition of the Amidah is the recitation, once again, of the

The Weekday Amidah

Benedictions in Praise of God

1. *Avot*	*Magen Avraham*	Patriarchs' covenant with God
See note 3, below.		
2. *Gevurot*	*Atah gibor*	God's powers of life and healing
3. *Kedushat Hashem*	*Atah kadosh*	Proclaiming God's holiness

Petitions for Personal and Community Needs

4. *Binah*	*Atah honen*	Give us knowledge and insight
5. *Teshuvah*	*Hashivenu*	Bring us back to You in repentance
6. *Selihah*	*Selah lanu*	Forgive us for our sins
7. *Geulah*	*Reeh veonyenu*	Redeem us from our struggles
8. *Refuah*	*Refaenu*	Save us from illnesses
9. *Birkat hashanim*	*Barekh alenu*	Bless the year for prosperity
10. *Kibutz galuyot*	*Teka beshofar*	Bring our people from exile
11. *Birkat hamishpat*	*Hashivah shoftenu*	Bring us righteousness and justice
12. *Birkat haminim*	*Velamalshinim*	Stamp out wickedness and malice
13. *Birkat hatzadikim*	*Al hatzadikim*	Grant favor to the righteous
14. *Birkat Yerushalayim*	*Velirushalayim*	Rebuild Jerusalem
15. *Birkat David*	*Et tzemah David*	Bring a messiah from David's house
16. *Kabalat tefilah*	*Shema kolenu*	Hear our prayers with favor

Benedictions of Thanksgiving

17. *Avodah*	*Retzei*	Accept our prayers in lieu of sacrifice
18. *Birkat hodaah*	*Modim*	Prayer of thanksgiving
Bend the knees and bow at the beginning and the end.		
19. *Birkat shalom*	*Sim shalom/Shalom rav*	Grant us peace

At the end of the silent recitation of the Amidah, one says a prayer of supplication, *Elohai netzor*, "God, guard my tongue from evil." At the end, take steps, bend knees, and bow, as described in note 3, below.

SOME NOTES ON THE AMIDAH

1. It is to be said while facing Jerusalem, whether or not there is a minyan.

2. It is recited silently, standing with feet together and every word articulated. It is then repeated by the cantor or prayer leader, with the congregation seated, except during the third blessing. In the repetition, the congregation recites an alternative version of the eighteenth benediction.

3. One begins by taking three steps forward and ends by taking three steps back and bowing.

4. No conversation is permitted during the Amidah.

Kedushah ("Holy, holy, holy is the Lord of hosts"), which is added to the third benediction. The congregation recites aloud this invocation of holiness—not only standing, but rising on their toes three times, at each *kadosh* ("holy"). The basis for this amazing evocation of holy awe is Isaiah's call to prophecy, whence the blessing comes.

> In the year that king Uzziah died I saw also the Lord sitting upon a throne, high and lifted up, and his robe filled the temple. About him were attendant seraphim; each one had six wings: with two he covered his face, with two he covered his feet, and two were spread in flight. They called ceaselessly to one another,
> Holy, holy, holy is the Lord of hosts:
> the whole earth is full of His glory.
> And, as each one called, the threshold shook to its foundations, while the house was filled with smoke. Then said I, Woe is me! for I am lost, for I am a man of unclean lips and I dwell in the midst of a people of unclean lips: yet with these eyes I have seen the king, the Lord of hosts.

Isaiah 6:1–5

The *Minhogimbukh* puts it this way: "If wood and stone shook from the holy voice, then obviously humans have to tremble as well when reciting the Kedushah."

The benediction continues with the angelic praise of God from Ezekiel, "Blessed is the glory of the Lord from His abode" (Ezekiel 3:12), and concludes with Psalm 146:10, "The Lord shall reign forever, thy God, O Zion, for all generations; praise the Lord." Both are said by the congregation. The cantor recites the rest of the Amidah until he reaches the eighteenth benediction, *Birkat hodaah*, the blessing of thanksgiving. While the cantor recites the one version, the congregation recites a shorter one. Then the cantor recalls—but does not actually give—the Priestly Blessing and then finishes the

For the full details of the Priestly Blessing, see p. 133.

repetition of the Amidah with the last benediction, *Birkat shalom*. The Priestly Blessing is one of the high ceremonies of Judaism, and it is given every day in Jerusalem at this point of the morning service, once a week (on the Sabbath) elsewhere in Israel, and on the High Holidays and pilgrimage festivals (Passover, Shavuot, Sukkot) in the Diaspora.

CONFESSION AND SUPPLICATION. The traditional service of most weekday mornings follows the Amidah with a series of personal prayers: Viduy, or confession; Taḥanun, or supplication; and *nefilat apayim*, or prostration. While the supplication prayers are widely said, the confession of sins is not always part of the morning service and in many places has been relegated to Yom Kippur, whose liturgy is related to Viduy. But there has been something of a revival of it recently among those who study Kabbalah, since its cornerstone work, the *Zohar*, is a source of its recitation before Taḥanun. The confession has three parts, each to be recited while standing with head and body somewhat bent. First, a collective prayer, in which we confess that "we and our forefathers have sinned"; then the listing of the sins as we strike the left side of our chest with our right fist; and the singing of the Thirteen Attributes of Mercy, the passage in Exodus (34:6–7) that tells of God's nature, the words with which Moses could always seek God's mercy. The thirteen are reckoned in the Talmud this way:

The verses in Exodus read: "The Lord, the Lord, God, showing mercy, showing favor, long-suffering in anger, abundant in loyalty and faith-

1. Lord
2. Lord
3. God
4. compassionate
5. gracious
6. patient
7. abounding in loving-kindness

8. and truth
9. keeping kindnesses to the thousandth generation
10. bearing with sin
11. and transgression
12. and error
13. and forgiving.

fulness, keeping loyalty to the thousandth generation, bearing iniquity, rebellion, and sin, yet not clearing the guilty, calling to account the iniquity of the fathers upon the sons and upon son's sons, to the third and fourth generation."

The Taḥanun prayers begin. In the morning, one leans to the right, to show respect for the tefillin, which is on the left arm (right arm for lefties). And in the afternoon, one leans to the left. On Monday and Thursday, a longer version of Taḥanun, also known as the "long *Vehu raḥum*," is said, with additional supplications before and after the core prayer. On those days, one recites the following prayers:

Vehu raḥum, "The merciful one, He is forgiving of iniquity and does not destroy," which quotes from Daniel, 9:15-17.
Hateh Adonai oznekha, "Incline, my God, Your ear and listen," is drawn from Daniel 9:18-19, Isaiah 64:7, and Joel 2:17.
Habet na, "Look, we beg You, have mercy on Your people," invokes the unbreakability of the covenant with Abraham.
Ana, "Please, O king . . . remember the binding of Isaac."
El raḥum, "O God who is compassionate," includes a verse from Jeremiah 14:9.
En kamokha, "There is none like You," is drawn from various parts of the Scripture.
Hapoteaḥ yad, "You, who open a hand for repentance," speaks of God's willingness to hear the plea of those who have committed terrible sins.

All are seated. If there is a Torah scroll in the room, one should cover one's face, placing it in the bend of one's left arm. This is the *nefilat apayim*, the "falling on one's face," symbolizing how Moses, Aaron, and Joshua had cast themselves down before God in times of trouble. It is also said that we cover our faces because in ancient times people used to stand at least four *amot* (cubits) apart in order not to hear the others' confessions. Then begins the main supplication, the one that is said every day that supplications are said. *Vayomer David*, 2 Samuel 24:14, is said as an introduction.

> And David said to the prophet Gad, I am deeply troubled; let me fall into the hand of the Lord, for His mercies are many, but let me not fall into the hand of man.

And then Psalm 6:2–11, the core of the supplication liturgy:

> O Lord, do not rebuke me in Your anger, or chastise me
>   in indignation.
> Be gracious to me, O Lord, for I am wretched.
> Heal me, O Lord, for my bones are trembling.
> My soul is terrified; how long, my Lord?
> Return, O Lord, extricate me from my plight, if only for
>   the sake of Your loving-kindness.
> For in death there is no remembering You; who in the
>   grave will thank You?
> I am tired from my groaning; every night I swim in tears;
> With my tears I melt my couch.
> My eye is dimmed from vexation; it grows old from
>   adversity.
> Let me be, all of you who do me wrong,
> For the Lord heard the voice of my weeping.
> The Lord heard my supplication; the Lord will
>   receive my prayer.
> Let all my enemies be ashamed and frightened;
> They shall turn back, ashamed.

On Monday and Thursday, the extended Taḥanun is continued:

> *Adonai elohei Yisrael*, "Lord, God of Israel, withdraw from
>   Your flaring anger."
> *Habet mishamayim ureeh*, "Look from heaven and see that
>   we have become an object of scorn," from Isaiah 53:7.

Zarim omerim, "Foreigners say there is no expectation or
hope," a passage from Lamentations 5:5.

Husah Adonai, "Lord, have pity on us in Your mercy."

Kolenu tishma vetahon, "Hear and accept our voices with
grace."

Ozrenu elohei yishenu, "Assist us, Lord, in our salvation," a
passage from Psalm 79:9.

Then on all days the congregation recites a pained plea for
protection, *Shomer Yisrael*, a medieval piyut whose author is
not known, that in a few words speaks volumes of a people's
tragedies:

> Guardian of Israel, guard the remnant of Israel.
> Let not those perish who say, "Hear, O Israel."
> Guardian of one nation, guard the remnant of one nation.
> Let not one nation perish who unify Your name,
> "The Lord our God, the Lord is One."
> Guardian of a holy nation,
>   guard of the remnant of a holy nation.
> Let not a holy nation perish
>   who three times a day say, "Holy, holy, holy."

All stand for the final prayer of this section of the service,
Veanahnu lo neda, "We know not what we should do, so our
eyes are upon You. Remember Your mercies, O Lord, and
Your kindnesses."

Tahanun is not said in a house of mourning during a
shivah period or in the presence of newlyweds or in the synagogue when a circumcision will take place later that day.
Neither is it said on Sabbath Rosh Hodesh or during festivals.

For mourning customs, see the chapter beginning on p. 391.

THE TORAH READING. On Mondays and Thursdays (as well
as on Rosh Hodesh and festivals), the Torah is brought out
from the ark. The portion of it that is read on these days is an
abbreviated one: the first verses of the full portion that will be

read the following Sabbath morning. Before the ark is opened, a short prayer of supplication is said: *El erekh apayim*, "O God, slow to anger." And as the ark is opened, two verses are recited by the congregation. The first, *Vayehi binsoa*, recalls the Ark in the Wilderness and how the Children of Israel carried it to the front when they met their enemies in battle:

Numbers 10:35   When the Ark was brought forth on the march,
              Moses would say:
         Advance, O Lord,
              that Your enemies may scatter,
              that those who hate You may flee before You!

The second verse comes from near the beginning of Isaiah's vision (2:3):

         The Torah shall come from Zion,
              and out of Jerusalem comes the word of the Lord.

And in response is said:

         Blessed is He who in His holiness
              gave the Torah to His people Israel.

In some synagogues, this is followed by an Aramaic prayer *Berikh shemeh*, "Blessed is the name of the Master of the Universe," which at other synagogues is said only on Sabbath morning. Then, taking the Torah out, the cantor or prayer leader turns toward the ark, holding the Torah, and says *Gadlu*, "Declare the greatness of the Lord with me, and let us exalt His name in unison." As the prayer leader turns, carrying the Torah to the *bimah* (the rostrum), the congregation responds with *Lekha Adonai*, "Yours, Lord, is the greatness, the strength, the glory, the triumph, and the majesty," then *Romemu*, "Exalt the Lord our God and bow down at His footstool." As the cantor carries the Torah, the congregation recites *Av harahamim*, "Father of compassion, may He have mercy on the people who are borne by Him."

Three people are called up to the Torah for the weekday readings. The ritual begins like this: The gabbai, the elected "moderator" of the synagogue, recites the formalized invitation to the *aliyah*, the coming up to the Torah. The congregation responds with a verse from Deuteronomy (4:4), "And you who cling to the Lord your God, all of you are alive today." The *oleh* (a woman is an *olah*), as the invitee is called, is mentioned by name, though not by his or her secular name but rather as *Hebrew Name son of/daughter of Hebrew Name*. Approaching the Torah, the *oleh* takes the corner of his or her tallit, touches it to the place where the reading begins, and kisses the corner of the tallit. Then, holding on to the staves of the Torah (each an *etz hayim*, a "tree of life"), the *oleh* begins the Barkhu, the same responsory call to prayer said before the Shema, and follows it with the blessing before the reading:

ברוך אתה יהוה אלהינו מלך העולם, אשר בחר בנו מכל
העמים, ונתן לנו את תורתו. ברוך אתה יהוה, נותן התורה.

Blessed are You, Lord our God, king of the universe, who
selected us from all peoples and gave us His Torah.
Blessed are You, Lord, giver of the Torah.

Then the first part of the portion is read, either by the person called up—which is rare—or, as is usually the case, by a designated reader. After the verses are read, the *oleh* recites another blessing:

ברוך אתה יהוה אלהינו מלך העולם, אשר נתן לנו תורת אמת,
וחיי עולם נטע בתוכנו. ברוך אתה יהוה, נותן התורה.

Blessed are You, Lord our God, king of the universe, who
has given us the Torah of truth and planted within us
everlasting life. Blessed are You, Lord, giver of the Torah.

Following each blessing is a congregational "amen." After the Torah reading there is a series of prayers, each of which is called a *Mi sheberakh* and begins, "He who blessed our fathers Abraham, Isaac, and Jacob, may He bless [person's name]...." They follow a number of different formulations: blessing the *oleh* who just read from the Torah; blessing a sick or needy person whose name has been brought forth by a congregant; and in honor of a bar or bat mitzvah, a bride or bridegroom, or someone who has made a major charitable gift to the community. These are all recited by the gabbai.

Another formulation of the Mi sheberakh prayers is said on Sabbaths and holidays; see p. 77.

Several other customs surround the honor of *aliyah*, such as the traditional order in which people are called: by bloodline (that is, kohen, levite, or Israelite) and in regard to special occasions such as marriage, a birth, or the commemoration of a death. (By custom, one does not call members of the same family consecutively.) Two additional honors are given to those who participate in the ritual of *hagbahah*, the holding up of the unfurled scroll for all the congregation to see, and *gelilah*, the replacement of the Torah's binder, covering, and ornamental fittings. As the Torah is returned to the ark, the prayer said includes a continuation of the passage from Numbers recited when the Torah was taken from the ark:

The designations kohen, levite, and Israelite refer to ancient lineage passed on through a father's family. The levites, leviyim, are those descended from the tribe of Levi, third son of Jacob. The priests, the kohanim, are a subgroup of levites descended from Aaron. (The priesthood of the Temple was an inherited position.) The term Israelite—yisrael—used in this connection refers to all others among the Children of Israel.

> And when the Ark halted, he would say: "Return, O Lord, to the ten thousands of the families of Israel." (Numbers 10:36)

It is followed by a number of intervening verses, from Proverbs and Lamentations, on these themes:

Proverbs 4:2, 3:18, 3:17

> For I give you good instruction;
> Do not forsake My Torah.

> It is a tree of life to those who grasp it,
> And whoever holds onto it is happy.

> Its ways are pleasant ways,
> All its paths peaceful.

Take us back, O Lord, to Yourself,
And let us come back;
Renew our days as of old!

Lamentations 5:21

Sephardim return the Torah after Uva letziyon; see below.

Half Kaddish completes this section of the service.

THE CLOSING PRAYERS: The last major protion of the service begins with two psalms recited by the congregation: Psalm 145, always referred to by its first word, *Ashrei* ("Happy are they"), a psalm of praise that is an important part of this liturgy, and Psalm 20, known as *Lamenatzeah*, which begins "May God answer you on the day of distress; may you be made invulnerable by the name of the God of Israel."

A key passage, however, is in the third prayer, *Uva letziyon*, "a redeemer shall come to Zion," a message of hope and consolation taken from Isaiah 59:20–21.

A redeemer shall come to Zion,
To those in Israel who turn away from willful sin
—thus says the Lord.
And this shall be My covenant with them, said the Lord:
My spirit which is upon you, and the words which I have
put in your mouth, shall not be absent from your mouth,
not from the mouth of your children, nor from the mouth
of your children's children—henceforth and for all time.

And then the return of the angelic sanctification: *Kadosh kadosh kadosh Adonai tzevaot* ("Holy, holy, holy is the Lord of hosts"), to which are added Aramaic explications of the aspects of God's holiness:

It is the custom to recite the three verses of the Kedushah in Hebrew, then silently in Aramaic, which was the vernacular language in the Second Temple period.

Holy in the lofty heavens on high, the dwelling place of
His shekhinah (presence).
Holy on earth, the product of His might.
Holy forever and for all eternity.

A full Kaddish follows, recited by the cantor.

The end of the formal liturgy—though not of the entire service—is *Alenu*, "It is our duty to praise the Master of all." The prayer has been ascribed to the school of Rav, the great Babylonian sage, in the third century C.E. Another legend ascribes it to Joshua, who is said to have recited it after the Battle of Jericho. Be that as it may, it was intended as a special prayer for Rosh Hashanah, but by the thirteenth century it became the closing of all daily services. *Alenu* has two paragraphs. The first is a statement of creed, the unwavering belief in a one-and-only God and an acknowledgment of a special relationship with him. Both paragraphs originated in the Rosh Hashanah liturgy for the blowing of the shofar and to glorify God's kingship and triumph over idolatry.

Alenu is said by the congregation while standing and it is a well-known custom to bend one's knees and bow at the waist upon reciting the line, "for we bend the knee and bow in worship."

In the presence of a minyan, the mourners in the congregation recite the mourner's Kaddish. The full congregation responds to the prayer according to the custom.

Ashkenazic Jews close the service with the Psalm of the Day, psalms sung by the levites during the time of the Temple, selected for their appropriateness to the six days of Creation. These are recited by Sephardic Jews as well, though they do so before *Alenu*.

> Sunday: Psalm 24, a psalm of David. All belongs to God, because it was He who created it all from the void.
> Monday: Psalm 48, a psalm of the sons of Korach, who instigated a rebellion against the authority of Moses. Because on the second day God created the heaven and the earth, this psalm was chosen to symbolize the struggle between the heavenly and the earthly.

Tuesday: Psalm 82, a psalm of Asaph. The theme of this
psalm is equity and justice, the key to coexistence on
earth. On the third day, God separated land from sea,
creating the physical prerequisite to human existence.

Wednesday: Psalms 94:1–95:3. These are psalms of God's
vengeance and intolerance for the worship of things. On
the fourth day, God created the sun, the moon, and the
stars, things that had become, to many, gods in themselves.

Thursday: Psalm 81, a psalm of Asaph. On the fifth day, God
made the creatures of the sea and the air, bringing a joyful noise. Psalm 81 is a joyous song, filled with the sound
of music.

Friday: Psalm 93. God completed the Creation on the sixth
day and this brief psalm decribes God's grandeur.

After the psalm is recited, the worshipers remove their
tefillin, in reverse order from the way they were put on. The
tallit is also removed and put away with care.

Sephardim and Ḥasidim complete the morning service
with the famous hymn *En kelohenu*. Ashkenazim sing it only
on the Sabbath. The *Minhogimbukh* recommends that after
the synagogue service one should spend some time studying.
"Those who cannot understand the holy tongue should at
least read some holy books in Yiddish (or in the language
with which they are most comfortable), because after death
our first judgment in the heavens depends on whether we
have studied every day, either much or just a little."

For En kelohenu,
see p. 79.

Blessings of Food and Drink

BLESSINGS BEFORE EATING. Whatever one partakes of with
pleasure, be it food, beverage, or a fragrance, it is the law to
make a blessing over it in order to thank and praise God. The
rituals concerning food are the most elaborate, since Jews

bless God, the source of their food, both before and after it is eaten. The blessings said before eating follow the formulaic pattern, *Barukh atah Adonai, elohenu melekh haolam . . .* , "Blessed are You, Lord our God, king of the universe . . . ," followed by one of six phrases, each representing a category of food, although wine is a category of its own. When bread is part of a meal and its blessing, *Hamotzi*, is said, one is exempted from saying the other food blessings. It is a commandment to precede the *Hamotzi* with the ritual hand washing and its blessing, *Al netilat yadayim.*

See p. 21 for the handwashing ritual.

Hamotzi leḥem min haaretz
"Who brings forth bread from the earth"
　　Bread made from the five grains listed below.

Borei minei mezonot
"Who creates various kinds of nourishment"
　　Food made from—but not if baked as bread—the five grains mentioned in the Bible: wheat, barley, oats, rye, and spelt. Rice is also included. The category includes most cereals, cakes, cookies, pasta, and dough-covered foods.

Borei peri hagafen
Deuteronomy 8:10
"Who creates the fruit of the vine"
　　This applies only to grape wine or juice.

Borei peri haetz
"Who creates the fruit of the tree"
　　All tree fruits and nuts, including olives and coconuts.

Borei peri haadamah
"Who creates the food of the earth"
　　Nearly all vegetables, legumes, tubers (such as potatoes), roots, and fruits not from trees.

Shehakol nihyeh bidvaro
"through whose word all things were called into being"

All foods that do not grow from the earth: water, milk and dairy foods, meat, eggs, fish, fowl, all beverages except wine (but including other alcoholic beverages), soups, sugar, sauces, candy, as well as all foods that one is unable to categorize.

GRACE AFTER MEALS. Of all the blessings that have become indelible parts of Jewish custom, *Birkat hamazon* is one of the small number that have direct mandate in the Torah. As the Children of Israel were about to cross the Jordan into the Promised Land, Moses included in his instructions: "When you have eaten and are satisfied, you shall bless the Lord your God for the good land that He has given you." Though it means "blessing of food," *Birkat hamazon* is referred to in English as the Grace after Meals. While blessing food before it is eaten is considered important, the Grace after Meals is considered more important still. What the Amidah is to synagogue liturgy, the Grace after Meals is to prayer in the home. It is a liturgy that comprises a call to prayer, four major blessings, concluding petitions, and additional material added on special days. Some include a special blessing said by a guest. In fact, a guest is often asked to lead the prayers.

Deuteronomy 8:10

Before the first blessing is said, all the knives are removed from the table—as first described on page 21. The generally accepted explanation for the custom is this: After the destruction of the Second Temple, the dining table has symbolically taken the place of the altar. God's instruction for the building of the altar specifically precluded the use of metal cutting tools. "You shall not build it of hewn stones for if you lift up your sword on it, you will have profaned it" (Exodus 20:25)." Another widespread custom is that of leaving a piece of bread on the table while the Grace after Meals is said, to signify satisfaction.

There are other explanations for the custom of the removal of knives, including the association of knives with Esau, who accepted his father Jacob's blessing, "By the sword shall you live."

When three or more people are present at the table, the Grace after Meals is preceded by a *zimun*, or Call to Grace. The ritual, more often performed in public settings than in private homes—most often during festivals—is this: the prayer leader (a guest, if one is present) holds up a glass of wine and proclaims, "Come, let us recite the benediction." The others respond, "May the name of the Lord be blessed, now and forever."

The wine is not a requirement of a zimun, but rather a hidur mitzvah, an "enhancement of a mitzvah" associated with special occasions.

The four blessings are each a full-length paragraph. The first is the *Birkat hazan*, the blessing for the food:

> Blessed are You, O Lord our God . . . who nourishes the whole world . . . He gives food to all flesh . . . in His great goodness we have never lacked for food. . . . ;

The second, *Birkat haaretz*, is the Blessing of the Land.

> We thank You . . . for the good and spacious land You gave our forefathers as our heritage . . . for having brought us out of Egypt . . . for Your covenant . . . for Your Torah and teachings . . . for Your loving-kindness. . . .

Birkat Yerushalayim, the Blessing for Jerusalem, is the third blessing. It is said that it had once been a prayer of thanksgiving for God's gifts of Jerusalem, the Temple, and the Land of Israel. After the destruction of the Second Temple, it was modified to become a prayer for their rebuilding. Of special significance is the plea for sovereignty, "And please, Lord, let us not need other people's gifts or loans." A call for the reestablishment of the royal house of David is a further expression of this—and for the coming of the Messiah.

The fourth blessing is called *Hatov vehametiv*, which concludes thus:

> He [God] has done good to us, does good to us, and will do good to us. He who has bestowed, does bestow, and will

always bestow on us grace, loving-kindness, mercy, and relief; rescue, success, blessing, salvation; consolation, sustenance, and maintenance; mercy, life, peace, and all good; and of everything good, may we never lack.

The fourth blessing was a later addition to the Grace after Meals. Exactly when it was added is a matter of contention that may bear on one's understanding of it. Moses Maimonides, the great twelfth-century sage, said that it was composed after the destruction of the Second Temple, in 70 C.E.; Naḥmanides, the thirteenth-century sage, who frequently disagrees with Maimonides, says it was written in the aftermath of the Romans' defeat of Bar Kokhba and the fall of the fortress of Betar in 135 C.E., the final blow to any form of Jewish sovereignty in the ancient Land of Israel. Some recent scholars have suggested a time between the two events. Be that as it may, this blessing, which stresses the bounteous, unalloyed goodness of God, comes from a time of great loss.

In the writings of Maimonides and Naḥmanides, there is a curious debate over whether or not one should say the Grace after Meals following the eating of forbidden foods. Maimonides was completely against it, saying it would make a mockery of God's word; Naḥmanides said yes—so long as one was satisfied by what was eaten.

Thus ends the obligatory part of the liturgy. But it is the custom to continue the Grace with brief petitions that each begins with the word *haraḥaman*, "May the Merciful One . . ." Other petitions are added for special occasions, for example, in honor of a host or in honor of one's parents when eating in their home. Like the Amidah, these petitions conclude with the prayer *Oseh shalom bimromav*, "May He who makes peace in heaven, may He make peace for us and all of Israel, and say Amen."

In talmudic times, abbreviated versions of the Grace after Meals were devised for farm laborers, and these became the precedent for the short Grace after Meals that is recited today after meals that don't include bread. This version still includes the themes of the four blessings, but they are now summarized in a single blessing.

There has always been some difference of opinion over when the Grace after Meals must be said, especially with regard to snacks. Some authorities are of the opinion that the presence of bread is the criterion and that as little as an olive-sized piece of it is enough to constitute bread's presence; others say the key is recognizing God's role in all that we have and consume.

Minḥah: The Afternoon Synagogue Service

The afternoon service is the second of the three required daily services. It is the descendant of the daily afternoon offering at the Temple. The service may be held anytime between one half hour after the sun's zenith and one hour before sundown. It is the common custom that the afternoon service is scheduled at a time when the evening service can follow it immediately. However, where there is a community to support them, there are midday afternoon services.

The main liturgical components of the afternoon service are *Ashrei* (Psalm 145), followed by half Kaddish; the Amidah, its repetition by the cantor, and full Kaddish; Taḥanun (the prayers of supplication); and *Alenu*. The Priestly Blessing in the last blessing of the Amidah is said only on fast days; Taḥanun is not recited on those days when it is omitted from the morning prayers.

The *Minhogimbukh* explains two of the details of the afternoon service thus:

> Everyone should recite *Ashrei* at the beginning of the service, because those who recite *Ashrei* three times a day will definitely win a place in the world to come. . . . The reason for omitting the Priestly Blessing is that the kohanim were not allowed to drink wine in the times of the Temple before they blessed the people of Israel, and by the time of the

afternoon and the evening prayers they may well have had some wine.

Maariv: The Evening Synagogue Service

Maariv means "to make it evening" and the name of the service is derived from the first evening blessing before the Shema, "[God] who by His word makes the evenings." The evening service began as a voluntary one, gaining obligatory status only during talmudic times. It may take place anytime from one hour before nightfall through the evening hours, though as mentioned above, it most often follows on the heels of the afternoon service.

The liturgy for the weekday evening service has three main components: the Shema, the Amidah, and *Alenu.* The service is introduced by one of the prayers of supplication, *Vehu rahum*, "The merciful one, He is forgiving of iniquity," and is followed by the Barkhu, the call to prayer.

As in the morning prayers, two blessings precede the Shema, but they are different ones, appropriate to the time of day. The first, the *Birkat maariv*, the evening blessing, is an especially poetic liturgy, in part from Isaiah, that recalls the Creation itself:

> Blessed are You, Lord our God, king of the universe, who
> with His word brings on the evening,
> With wisdom opens the gates,
> With understanding alters the phases, varies the seasons,
> And arranges the stars in their heavenly orbit according to
> His will.
> He creates day and night.
> He rolls away the light from before the darkness and the
> darkness from before the light,
> He makes the day pass and the night to come, and divides
> between day and night;

Lord of Hosts is His name.
A living and everlasting God, who shall reign over us forever
and ever.
Blessed are You, Lord, who brings on the evenings.

The second blessing before the Shema, *Ahavat olam*, recognizes God's everlasting love for His people and their gratitude for His precious gift of Torah, which will be acknowledged both day and night, not as obligation, but in meditation and rejoicing.

It is followed by the three paragraphs of the Shema. Whereas the morning recitation of the Shema is followed by one blessing, the evening recitation is followed by two. *Birkat geulah*, the Blessing of Redemption, is the first. It is not the same as the blessing of the same name said in the morning service.

The second blessing is *Hashkivenu*, "Lay us down to sleep." Its words are rather like a lullaby, and it seems to have originated as a bedtime prayer:

> Lay us down to sleep in peace, O Lord our God, and raise us up again unto life, O our king. Spread over us the canopy of Your peace. . . . Shelter us in the shadow of Your wings. . . . Safeguard our going forth and coming in, for life and peace, for now and forever.

At this place in the evening liturgy, some Ashkenazic Jews in the Diaspora recite *Barukh Adonai leolam*, known also as the Blessing of Verses, a set of prayers drawn from a number of biblical passages, mostly the Psalms. It was created as an abbreviated substitute for the Amidah and contains, as a symbol of it, nineteen occurrences of the phrase "Blessed is the Lord." It is followed by half Kaddish, the Amidah—not repeated by the cantor in the evening, then full Kaddish,

Alenu, and for those in mourning, the mourner's Kaddish. Thus ends the day's synagogue prayers.

The Bedtime Shema

The Shema, the prayer of all prayers, is the focus of the bed-time prayer ritual, in which it is considered a talisman against the "dangers of the night." It is the usual custom to precede the Shema with the prayer *Hamapil*, a prayer for safe and restful sleep in the vein of *Hashkivenu* but this time as a personal plea rather than a communal one.

> Blessed are You, Lord our God, king of the universe, who casts the bonds of sleep upon my eyes and slumber upon my eyelids. May it be Your will, Lord my God, God of my ancestors, that You lay me down to sleep in peace and raise me up in peace. May I not be troubled by bad dreams and thoughts. May my offspring be perfect before You. And may You illuminate my eyes lest I sleep the sleep of death, for it is You who illuminates the pupil of the eye. Blessed are You, Lord, who illuminates the entire world with His glory.

The three paragraphs of the Shema are to be recited aloud, with *kavanah*. And so concludes the day.

Sabbath

WHEN THE SABBATH is formally introduced to us in the fourth of the Ten Commandments, it is with the immediate declaration that it is to be kept holy.

Woodcut from the Minhogimbukh, Amsterdam, 1721.

> Remember the Sabbath day and keep it holy. Six days you shall labor and do all your work, but the seventh day is a Sabbath of the Lord your God: you shall not do any work—not you, your sons, your daughters, your servants and your maids, your cattle, or the stranger who is within your gates. For in six days the Eternal made heaven and earth and sea and all that is in them, and rested on the seventh day; therefore the Lord blessed the seventh day and hallowed it.

Exodus 20:8–11

Sabbath (shabbat) has its root in the Hebrew verb shavat, which means "to cease."

The word "holy" is connected so closely to the Sabbath that to understand this divinely commanded day of rest, we would do well to begin with an idea of what holiness is all about. *Kedushah*, the Hebrew word for holiness, has at its root the meaning "to be set apart," and indeed, Sabbath is set apart from the rest of the week. In the Hebrew language, it is set apart as the only day of the week that has a name. God, who exemplifies all that is holy, is both immanent—part of the palpable universe—and set apart, "exalted" above and beyond his creations. In Jewish parlance, God is often referred to as "the

Holy One, blessed be He." Set apart, too, are holy objects like the Torah, holy places like the Temple, the holy name of God that we say only euphemistically, holy rituals like the kiddush said over wine, and holy days like Yom Kippur. So, then, holiness is a thing set apart *by* God and *for* God.

"You shall be holy, for I, the Lord your God, am holy" is the instruction given by God to the Children of Israel in Leviticus 19:2, a verse from the Torah portion called *Kedoshim*, or "holy ones." How, exactly, do we follow it? The instructions can be found in the surrounding chapters of Leviticus, 17–26, which modern Bible scholars refer to as the Holiness Code. There the franchise of holiness is extended to almost every aspect of life: sexual, social, legal (both civil and criminal), business, personal, and of course religious. In other words, we are enjoined to imitate God, not as creators of all things, but as God's moral and ethical creations. If the Bible comprised only these chapters, it would still stand as one of the world's most powerful documents.

What stands out in this realm of holiness is the centrality of the Sabbath. In the Ten Commandments (Exodus 20:2–14), keeping the Sabbath is the first positive commandment—the first "do" rather than "do not." But in Leviticus, Sabbath appears in the first sentence following the injunction to be holy like God, coupled with respect for father and mother: "You are to hold in awe your father and mother, and keep My Sabbaths." There it is, right up there with honoring one's parents and with the injunctions against murder and false witness, idolatry, adultery, stealing, and covetousness. It is the one commandment that is directed to the inner person, toward a cessation of life as usual and a day of personal intimacy with God. God's rest and blessing dictate our rest and blessing—of ourselves, our employees, our animals, and all.

The term "Holiness Code" as applied to Leviticus 17–26 is a modern construct, first coined by a German theologian, A. Klostermann, in 1877.

The major biblical passages mentioning Sabbath are: Genesis 2:2–3; Exodus 16:23, 20:8–11, 23:12, 31:12–17, 34:21, 35:2–3; Leviticus 19:3, 23:3; Numbers 15:32–36; Isaiah 58:13; Jeremiah 17:21–24; Amos 8:5; and Nehemiah 10:32, 13:15–22.

Later in Exodus, just as Moses is about to receive the stone
tablets, God speaks of the Sabbath as a symbol, a sign of the
holiness of the Children of Israel.

> The Lord said to Moses: Speak to the Children of Israel and
> tell them: Above all, you must keep My Sabbaths since they
> are a sign between Me and you, throughout your genera-
> tions so that you know that I, the Lord, have consecrated
> you. You shall keep the Sabbath for it is holiness for you. . . .
> Whoever profanes it and whoever does work on the Sabbath
> shall be put to death—yes, death! . . . The Children of Israel
> are to keep the Sabbath, observing it throughout their gen-
> erations as a covenant for all time.

*Exodus 31:12–13,
15, 16*

Sabbath's holiness: *above all—a covenant for all time.* Its
stature is unique; the only days of comparable importance
being Yom Kippur—the Day of Atonement, the Sabbath of
Sabbaths—whose importance "overrides" Sabbath, and the
three pilgrimage festivals of Passover, Shavuot, and Sukkot.
These are the days that God commanded us to remember—
zakhor—the events that define our relationship with him.
Sabbath, too, is a day of remembrance, recalling both Exodus
and the Creation, of which it is the crowning conclusion.

As a "covenant for the ages," Sabbath is a promise not to
be broken or taken lightly—on penalty of death. When the
Israelites were in the Wilderness, a man was found collecting
wood on Sabbath and brought to Moses and Aaron who
placed him under guard while they sought clarification from
God on what should be done with him. God ordered Moses
to have the man stoned to death before the entire community.
An example was set.

*The incident is in
Numbers 15:32–36.*

Cultural values have changed over three thousand years
and hardly any would consider nonobservance of Sabbath to
be in the realm of the death penalty. But awareness of where

we came from has great value, to remind us just how central this day is and how Judaism carries within it the power to change. The *Minhogimbukh* makes very clear that the observance of the Sabbath makes for a remarkably full day, the virtues of which speak for themselves. For those who want more, there are some very good books on this subject: Abraham Joshua Heschel's *The Sabbath: Its Meaning for Modern Man* (1951), a post-Freudian, post-Holocaust look at the human relationship with God, in print since it was first published; and Francine Klagsbrun's *The Fourth Commandment: Remember the Sabbath Day* (2002), which explains the Sabbath through a well-chosen sampling of its rich traditions and lore. A look at a prayer book, one that contains the full, traditional synagogue and home liturgies, will also yield many riches.

Preparations for the Sabbath

The first mention in the Torah of the Sabbath as a day of rest for the Children of Israel appears in Exodus 16:23—before Moses's encounter with God on Mount Sinai in chapter 20. The passage speaks of the special advance preparations of food that will be eaten on Sabbath, a day on which one may not cook.

Some modern scholars have conjectured that the sources may have been out of sequence.

Exodus 16:23

> This is what the Lord meant: Tomorrow is a day of rest, a Sabbath of holiness of the Lord. Whatever you wish to bake, bake, and whatever you wish to boil, boil. And all that is left over, put aside for yourselves in safekeeping until morning.

The food that was being baked and boiled was, of course, manna, that divinely delivered, all-purpose edible that was described as being "like coriander seed, whitish, and its taste like that of a wafer with honey" (Exodus 16:31). It was the staff of life in the Wilderness—all the way through Numbers and Deuteronomy and into the book of Joshua. When it first appeared in the Torah, the word *hallah* meant "cake," but in Number 15:18-21 it is used specifically for the cake or loaf of manna that was mandated to be set aside for the priests. It is the set-aside that is commemorated today, though how it became the familiar braided bread is a matter of speculation. Challah is always made from a larger batch of dough; the 1593 *Minhogimbukh* describes it thus:

The dividing of the priestly portion is described in Numbers 15:18-21.

> On Fridays it is the custom that women make a large amount of dough from which the challah is taken. The dough should be at least the volume of a little more than 43 eggs [the egg, *betzah*, was used as a unit of measure and refers to volume, not weight]. If the dough is less, one should not take challah from it. If there are two portions of dough, each one less than the appropriate amount, they may be counted together. In that case, the two portions of dough should be covered with the same cloth, because the cloth that covers them makes them then belong together and challah should be taken from underneath the cloth. But if there is a portion of dough that is the appropriate amount by itself, it does not have to be covered.

The precepts of challah are the subject of a special tractate of the Mishnah, in the order Zeraim, as well as in commentaries in the Jerusalem Talmud. Maimonides discusses it in his Mishneh Torah, Bikkurim 5-8; as does the Shulhan arukh, in Yoreh deah 322-330.

Beside the challah, other foods are prepared in advance as well since no work may be done on the Sabbath. Because energy sources may not be directly engaged on this day, it is the custom for hot meals to be placed in a preheated warming oven so that they may be enjoyed throughout the day.

FRIDAY AFTERNOON. On the cusp of Sabbath, no later than eighteen minutes before sunset, the Sabbath candles are lit at home in the room where the Sabbath meal will be eaten and the festive table has been prepared. Though the Mishnah specifies only one light, it is the custom that at least two lights be lit, to symbolize the commandments to "remember" and "observe." Some people have adopted the custom of lighting one candle for each household member. Festive star-shaped lamps, as shown in the various *Minhogimbukh* woodcuts, came into general use during the later Middle Ages, when the hanging lamp became a characteristically Jewish ornament.

Candlelighting is an act of both physical and spiritual illumination, performed with a sense of miracle and reverence for the day of peace and serenity that follows. The order of the ritual is unusual in that the blessing follows the act rather than the other way around. First, the candles are placed and lit—keeping in mind that it is not yet Sabbath—then, as the day turns, one covers the lights with the hands, reciting the blessing:

ברוך אתה יהוה אלהינו מלך העולם, אשר קדשנו
במצותיו וצונו להדליק נר של שבת.

Blessed are You, Lord our God, king of the universe, who has made us holy through His commandments and commanded us to light the Sabbath lights.

The blessing is modified when a holiday falls on Sabbath:

ברוך אתה יהוה אלהינו מלך העולם, אשר קדשנו
במצותיו וצונו להדליק נר של שבת ושל יום טוב.

Blessed are You, Lord our God, king of the universe, who has made us holy through His commandments and commanded us to light the Sabbath and holiday lights.

On all festivals *except* the last two days of Passover, one also adds the following:

ברוך אתה יהוה אלהינו מלך העולם, שהחינו וקימנו
והגיענו לזמן הזה.

Blessed are You, Lord our God, king of the universe, who has kept us alive and sustained us and brought us to this time.

After the candlelighting, it was a
common Ashkenazic custom for
women to add personal prayers in
Yiddish—*Tekhines.* The ArtScroll
siddur, the most popular in American Orthodox congregations, mentions in this connection the Hebrew prayer *Yehi ratzon,* "May it be

Your will," a prayer for God's consideration to the members
of the family and all Israel, invoking the memory of God's
goodness to the ancestors.

*Woodcut from the
Minhogimbukh,
Venice, 1601.*

Friday Evening: Kabbalat Shabbat

It has been conjectured that in the aftermath of the disas-
trous destruction of the Second Temple and the crushing of
Bar Kokhba's revolt, the sages of the Talmud invoked the
alternating images of the Sabbath Queen and the Sabbath
Bride so that a crushed people, without a Messiah, could find
comfort and joy. In the special service that precedes the
evening prayers known as Kabbalat Shabbat, "Welcoming the
Sabbath," the Queen has a very special place, indeed, for it
was she who inspired the service. This relatively recent addition to the Sabbath observance developed from the custom of
the mystic rabbis of Safed in the sixteenth century, the great
interpreters of Kabbalah, including Isaac Luria and Moses
Cordovero, who would go into the fields to "greet the Sabbath
Queen." As with all Jewish customs, actions are very soon
followed by words, and it appears that early on, the walks in
the fields were accompanied by the recitation of texts that
later became a formal liturgy. Kabbalat Shabbat is not mentioned in the early editions of the *Minhogimbukh,* having

*The Sabbath
Queen and Sab-
bath Bride are
mentioned in
Talmud Shabbat
119a and Bava
kama 32b.*

*Safed, called Tsefat
in Hebrew, is in the
north of modern-
day Israel. It
became a great
center of Jewish
learning, following
the expulsion of the
Jews from Spain in
1492.*

been adopted gradually during the seventeenth and eighteenth centuries.

In many communities it is customary to begin the service with the poem *Yedid nefesh*, written by another of the great Kabbalists of the sixteenth century, Eliezer Azikri, whose famous work, *Sefer haredim*, emphasizes that all religious practice must begin with an intense love of God. *Yedid nefesh* expresses this intensity in a way worthy of the Psalms. The last of its four verses evokes the feeling of the coming of Sabbath:

> Reveal and tenderly spread over me
> The shelter of Your peace;
> The earth will be illuminated with Your glory.
> We will rejoice and celebrate in You.
> Hurry, my beloved, because the appointed time approaches,
> And have mercy on me forever.

The formal service begins with Psalms 95 through 98, which announce the splendor of God's reign with voices and instruments, trumpeting glory, victory, salvation, and, in Psalm 99, trembling before the Lord enthroned atop the Cherubim who attend the Ark. This is followed by Psalm 29, a psalm of David, which describes God's might in harrowing earthly terms, but ends on a note of peace. This sets a calmer tone for the famous piyut (hymn or liturgical poem) that follows, *Lekha dodi*, a poem written by another sixteenth-century Safed poet, Shlomo Halevi Alkabetz. For a people long downtrodden, this is one of the great liturgical pep talks, filled with inspiration, hope, encouragement, and rejuvenation. Nothing better characterizes the Sabbath.

Like many piyutim, Lekha dodi is an acrostic in which the first letters of each verse together spell the author's name.

> Come, my beloved, to welcome the bride!
> Let us receive the Sabbath's presence! (*after each verse*)
> Come, let us go to welcome the Sabbath, for it is the

source of blessing. From the beginning, in olden times, she may have been last in Creation, but she was first in God's thoughts.

Shake off the dust! Arise and don your splendid garments, my people. Through the son of Jesse of Bethlehem, draw near to my soul—redeem Jerusalem!

Wake up! Wake up, for your light has come! Rise up and shine! Awake and sing! The glory of the Lord is revealed!

Do not be ashamed; do not feel humiliated. Why so downcast? Why so agitated? In you the afflicted of my people will find shelter, in the city rebuilt upon the hill.

Those who have trampled you will be trampled themselves, and all who have devoured you will be heaved away. Your God will rejoice over you as a bridegroom rejoices over his bride.

To the right and the left you shall spread out, and the Lord you shall extol through the man who is a descendant of Peretz, over him we shall rejoice and be happy!

[Rise and face the rear of the synagogue to greet the Sabbath bride when saying, "Enter, O bride!"]
Enter in peace, O crown of her husband, in jubilation and gladness among the faithful and treasured people. Enter, O bride! Enter, O bride!

Many parts of this lyric are references to the Messiah: David's descent from Jesse and Peretz, the rebuilding of Jerusalem. The messianic idea presented here is that of redemption, God's glory as already revealed, which one must simply wake up and see.

Psalms 92 and 93, which are recited next, were associated with the beginning of the Sabbath service long before the advent of Kabbalat Shabbat. Psalm 92 is titled "A Psalm for the Sabbath Day," though Sabbath itself is never mentioned;

Peretz was the son of Judah (son of Jacob) born to Tamar. Jesse was the father of King David.

its theme is the pleasure of praising God's deeds in full
knowledge of long-term rewards that will come:

> ... though the wicked grow like grass
> and every evildoer prospers,
>   they will be destroyed forever.
> While You, Lord, reign on high eternally,
>   Thy foes will surely perish,
>   all evildoers will be scattered.

There is an amazing story about the custom of reciting
Psalm 92 twice in the Altneushul, the beloved "old-new" synagogue in Prague. It stems from Rabbi Judah Loew (1525–
1609), known as "the Maharal," one of the greatest Jewish
thinkers of the postmedieval period and a person to whom
more than a few amazing stories have been attributed. Loew
is most famous today as purported creator of a giant living

The story of the
Golem was
the inspiration
for Mary
Wollstonecraft
Shelley's novel
Frankenstein.

being, the Golem, to be the protector of the Jews of Prague.
As the story tells it, one Friday afternoon, as the Sabbath
evening service had just begun, the Golem went wild, destroying property and menacing the people. The rabbi was
summoned to disarm it. Turning off a Golem is not covered
specifically by any halakhic dispensation and doing so would
be a breach of the Sabbath. Rabbi Loew managed to quell the

The idea for the
headplate was
inspired by the
headdress of the
Temple priests,
which bore the
words "Holiness for
the Lord." (See
p. 352 for reference
to Exodus
28:36–38.)

Golem by wiping from its headplate the tetragrammaton,
Yhwh, the letters of God's name. He worked around his violation of the Sabbath thus: As the congregation had just
begun the service, having recited only Psalm 92, they said a
Kaddish while the rabbi was gone and recited the same psalm
again upon his return. And so, according to the story, it
became the synagogue's custom.

The story suggests the breadth of prohibited activity on
Sabbath, albeit facetiously, since the saving of lives always
takes precedence over rules of observance. Just what is it that

one may not do on the Sabbath? The old editions of the *Min-hogimbukh* do not address the question directly, probably because of its complexity. The Mishnah lists thirty-nine categories of *melakhah*, the word for "purposeful action" used in reference to the prohibitions. Here is a list of them, though one should keep in mind they refer to broad *categories* of action that have been elaborated upon over the centuries in various rabbinical writings. As technology develops, new interpretations are issued by influential rabbis.

Talmud Shabbat 73a

1. Carrying	14. Plowing	27. Chain-stitching
2. Burning	15. Planting	28. Warping
3. Extinguishing	16. Reaping	29. Weaving
4. Finishing	17. Harvesting	30. Unraveling
5. Writing	18. Threshing	31. Building
6. Erasing	19. Winnowing	32. Demolishing
7. Cooking	20. Selecting	33. Trapping
8. Washing	21. Sifting	34. Shearing
9. Sewing	22. Grinding	35. Slaughtering
10. Tearing	23. Kneading	36. Skinning
11. Knotting	24. Combing	37. Tanning
12. Untying	25. Spinning	38. Smoothing
13. Shaping	26. Dyeing	39. Marking

Kabbalat Shabbat concludes with the mourner's Kaddish, a recitation of the *Bameh madlikin*, and the rabbis' Kaddish. *Bameh madlikin* are the rules for candlelighting that constitute the second chapter of Mishnah *Shabbat*, one of the tractates of the Mishnah, the oldest part of the Talmud. It states all that may or may not be used as candle or lamp material and fuel, separating the holy from the tainted, and such.

For mourner's Kaddish and the rabbis' Kaddish, see p. 26.

Friday Evening Service

The Kabbalat Shabbat having concluded, the Friday evening service continues along the lines of the weekday evening service — Barkhu, Shema, Amidah, *Alenu*, and mourner's Kaddish — but with some notable differences and a rather different set of expectations. As the week becomes the Sabbath, the theme of redemption is introduced into the liturgy.

Barkhu is recited with a special tune; the Shema is the same as on weekdays, up until the blessing *Hashkivenu*, "Lay us down to sleep," to which is added a repetition of the sentence that describes the Sabbath mood, "And spread over us the shelter of Your peace." The congregation rises and remains standing through the Amidah, but before it begins, the cantor chants *Veshamru*, the verses from Exodus (31:16-17), in which God proclaims the Sabbath a covenant. Half Kaddish follows.

See weekday evening service on p. 49.

As is the case throughout Sabbath, the evening Amidah has seven benedictions. The first three and last three are the same as in the weekday version, but the fourth, called *Kedushat hayom*, "Sanctification of the Day," is particular to the Sabbath. It is preceded by the hymn *Atah kidashta*, which speaks of God's sanctification of the Sabbath after the work of Creation was complete: "Thus were finished the heaven and the earth and all their legion" (Genesis 2:1-3), about

Talmud Shabbat 119b

which the Talmud says that everyone who recognizes God's Creation also participates in it. The Amidah is followed by *Magen avot* (Shield of Our Fathers), called the "Seven-Faceted Blessing" because it epitomizes the seven benedictions of the Amidah, thus forming an abbreviated repetition of the Amidah — and used as such in the Palestinian rite. After it full Kaddish is said.

See p. 66 for the Sabbath kiddush ceremony.

The remainder of the service varies in different synagogues. In most, the kiddush over the wine is said by the cantor, a custom that is believed to have begun in Babylonia, where wine was scarce. *Alenu* and the mourner's Kaddish are recited invariably. To conclude, congregations recite either *Adon olam* or *Yigdal.*

For Adon olam *and* Yigdal, *see p. 23.*

Friday Evening at Home

The home observance of Sabbath eve is redolent with song, food, ritual, and good company—a festive occasion, albeit under certain restrictions. After the evening prayers one is supposed to get home quickly. According to the 1593 *Minhogimbukh*, the walk home is never made alone:

> There are two angels who accompany every Jew on his walk home from synagogue on Friday night. One is a good angel, the other one is a bad angel. If the house is well prepared—the Sabbath candles are burning and the table is set nicely—the good angel says, "May it be God's will that it should be like this next week as well." The bad angel then has to reply, "Amen." But if the situation is, God forbid, the opposite, then the bad angel will say·that it should be like that the following week, to which the good angel must also reply, "Amen." Therefore, one should always honor the Sabbath—especially since this happens everywhere.

The story comes from Talmud Shabbat *119b.*

The customs prior to the festive meal vary a bit in different households and in different locales. Many begin with the angels still in mind, with the song *Shalom aleikhem,* "Peace to you, ministering angels, messengers from above." It is a popular custom to add here the song *Eshet ḥayil,* from the last chapter of the book of Proverbs, in which the lady of the house is praised for all her abilities, goodness, and virtues. Then, with parents placing their hands upon the heads of their children, each is blessed thus: to girls, it is recited, "May God make you like Sarah, Rebecca, Rachel, and Leah"; to boys, "May God make you like Ephraim and Manasseh."

BLESSINGS: Three things follow: kiddush, the sanctification with wine; *Netilat yadayim*, the ceremonial washing of hands; and *Hamotzi*, the blessing of the bread. After these, the meal may begin. The kiddush is not simply a blessing, like that said over the bread, but an extended sanctification to help fulfill the commandment to make the Sabbath holy. It begins with these defining verses from Genesis:

Genesis 1:31–2:3

There was evening, there was morning on the sixth day. The heavens and the earth, and everything they contained, were finished. On the seventh day, God finished the work that He had been doing. God rested on the seventh day from all the work He had done. God blessed the seventh day, and called it holy, because on it God rested from all the work of Creation that He had done.

The Minhogim-bukh *says that one should look into the light of the candles while reciting the blessing over wine. The reason given is this: "According to our sages—may their memory be blessed—if one takes a big step, that takes away ¹⁄₅₀₀th of one's vision, and the remedy for it, the way to gain back one's vision, is to look into the Sabbath candles while reciting kiddush, because the numerical value of the two candles is two times 250, which equals exactly 500."*

Then two blessings: on the wine and the Sabbath itself.

Blessed are You, Lord our God, king of the universe, who created the fruit of the vine. Blessed are You, Lord our God, king of the universe, who made us holy with Your commandments, and showed favor to us by lovingly giving us His holy Sabbath as an inheritance and a memorial to the Creation. It is the first among the holy days, a remembrabce of the Exodus from Egypt. For You have chosen us and made us holy from among the nations, and have lovingly given us Your holy Sabbath as an inheritance. Blessed are You, God, who makes the Sabbath holy.

When one says kiddush on behalf of others present, it is prefaced by the phrase, "Attention, distinguished people, rabbis, and gentlemen." In some circles, everyone joins in at the words "For you have chosen us." After the blessing, everyone should say "amen" and partake of the wine.

Everyone present washes their hands in the ritual manner:

using a pitcher and a receiving basin. Pour the water three times over one hand and then three times over the other. Then recite the blessing:

ברוך אתה יהוה אלהינו מלך העולם, אשר קדשנו
במצותיו וצונו על נטילת ידים.

Blessed are You, Lord our God, king of the universe, who has sanctified us through His commandments and commanded us to wash our hands.

And then the familar *Hamotzi*, the blessing over bread. There are two loaves of bread—challah—on the table, in remembrance of the double portion of manna that was given to the Israelites in the Wilderness. During kiddush, they sit covered by a special Sabbath cloth. In many Jewish households the cloth is a revered item, often highly decorated with embroidery. Before the blessing of the bread, the cloth is removed.

ברוך אתה יהוה אלהינו מלך העולם, המוציא לחם
מן הארץ.

Blessed are You, Lord our God, king of the universe, who brings forth bread from the earth.

After the blessing everyone is given a generous slice of bread. Each person is obligated to bless the bread, so when one blesses on behalf of others, it is acknowledged in a manner such as the kiddush. In regard to the cloth and its purpose, the 1593 *Minhogimbukh* relates two well-known anecdotes:

> Before saying kiddush one should cover the challah with a cloth. This is done in order to prevent the bread from seeing its own shame, stemming from the fact that the blessing over wine comes before the blessing over bread, despite the fact that bread is mentioned before wine in the verse, "a land of wheat and barley, of vines and fig

trees and pomegranates, a land of olive trees and honey"
(Deuteronomy 8:8). According to another opinion, the
challah is covered for a different reason: In the desert, the
manna did not fall directly on the ground, because then
it would have become dirty. Dew fell from the heavens
first, then the manna fell on the dew, and then again dew
fell to cover the manna (Exodus 16:11–27). So the manna
lay between two layers of dew. Therefore, there should be
a cloth on the table, and another cloth above the bread,
and thus the bread should be between the two layers of
cloth, in a commemoration of the manna. Pious women
have the custom of preparing pie (*pashtida*) on the
Sabbath for the same reason: the filling is between two
layers of dough.

A bit of rabbinic law was mentioned at this point in the
1593 book; it gives some insights into the realm of Jewish
legal reasoning:

> If one has only one glass or two of wine, then the one
> glass should be saved for havdalah [the closing ceremony
> of Sabbath], because it is more important to have wine
> for havdalah than for kiddush. If there is enough wine for
> havdalah but only a bit left for kiddush, then wine for the
> evening kiddush has priority over the morning kiddush.
> If one has made a vow not to drink wine, one may say
> kiddush and give the wine that was blessed to the some-
> one else to drink. But if one is alone, then one should say
> kiddush over the bread.

THE SABBATH EVE MEAL: The spirit of the meal is governed
by two commandments: that we are "to rejoice during the festival" (Deuteronomy 16:14) and that we "call the Sabbath a
delight and the holy day of the Lord honorable" (Isaiah
58:13). The Hebrew word for delight is *oneg* and the term
oneg shabbat, "Sabbath delight," is used to describe many

Sabbath customs, perhaps the best known being the wine and sweets reception held after Sabbath services in many synagogues. To eat and drink well on the Sabbath is far more than custom—it is a commandment. Fasting is prohibited. There are no foods that are mandated "in" or "out" on the Sabbath, though meat has a great traditional presence and it is customary to eat fruits. There is a passage in the Talmud that recommends eating fruit because it requires a special blessing and since we are supposed to say a hundred blessings in the course of the day and the Amidah is shortened for the Sabbath, the eating of fruit is a way to pick up another one. Many customs have evolved around the Sabbath meal, and special dishes are to be found everywhere, from gefilte fish, an Ashkenazic favorite for Friday nights, to *cholnt*, a kind of cassoulet beloved to the Jews of eastern Europe, served on Saturdays because it is long cooking, to *kubaneh*, a steamed sweet bread favored by the Jews of Yemen. Every region and family has its favorites. The key, though, is that they are dishes that may be prepared in advance because the meal must be cooked by the time the candles are lit and the Sabbath begins.

One source for this story is Shibolei haleket, *a compendium of Jewish law written by Zedekiah ben Abraham Anav, Italy, thirteenth century.*

Punctuating the meal are the Zemirot, the "table songs," a sizable repertory based mostly on medieval poems. While the texts are well established, the tunes vary with region and tradition rather like the food, much in the way that music and food are always linked to local culture. The themes are those of the Sabbath itself: rest and joy, God's kindness, the holiness of the day. The *zemer* (singular) *Mah yedidut*, on a text by an anonymous "Menashe" (his name appears as an acrostic), written in the early Middle Ages, is a typical example of the genre, complete with biblical references. Here are three representative verses:

Isaiah 58:14
mentions the fine
clothing worn
on the Sabbath.

How beloved is the rest you bring, Sabbath Queen!
And so we run to greet you: Come, regal bride!
Wearing our fine clothes and lighting the candles
    with a blessing—
All our labors have ceased, "Thou shalt not work."
Celebrating with delightful things: geese, quail, and fish.

Be leisurely and at ease, for the Sabbath has been called
    a delight,
Sleep is to be praised, for it revives the soul,
And so my soul longs for You, to rest in Your affection,
As roses protected by a fence, boy and girl will rest
    on Sabbath.
Celebrating with delightful things: geese, quail, and fish.

A taste of the world to come is the rest of Sabbath,
Everyone who celebrates it will be rewarded
    with much happiness.
They will be rescued and relieved from the
    tribulations that precede the Messiah,
Cause our redemption to blossom, and banish
    misery and anguish.
Celebrating with delightful things: geese, quail, and fish.

On Sabbath and festivals, the Grace after Meals is preceded by *Shir hamaalot*, one of the fifteen Psalms (120–134)
called "Songs of Ascents," corresponding to the fifteen steps
to the inner courtyard of the Temple. This particular song
takes its text from from Psalm 126, though at its end several
lines are sometimes added from other psalms.

The Grace after Meals for Sabbath is the same as that for
weekdays, but with a few additions. Into the third blessing,
the Blessing for Jerusalem, one should insert the prayer *Retzei
vehahalitzenu*, "May it be pleasing, Lord our God, to give us
rest . . . through the commandment of the seventh day." Later,
in the series of *Harahaman* petitions (each beginning, "May
the merciful One . . ."), one must insert, "May the merciful

One cause us to inherit the day that will be completely a Sabbath and a rest day for life that is eternal."

MISCELLANEOUS SABBATH CUSTOMS: In the Sabbath chapter of the *Minhogimbukh*, there is at this point in the text a miscellany of Sabbath eve customs:

> On Friday in the evening it is even more appropriate to "take care" of one's wife than it is on other days of the week, especially so for a scholar. One should caress her and should concentrate on having pious children who follow the ways of God.
>
> It is forbidden to kill fleas on the Sabbath; one should whisk them away instead. But if they are biting us, it is permissable to kill them.
>
> It is forbidden to instruct a gentile on the Sabbath to do any work that is not permitted to be done by a Jew.

Such is the power of concentration. Note, however, the choice of words regarding the work of the *shabbes goy*, the non-Jew hired to perform forbidden tasks on the Sabbath: "It is forbidden to *instruct* a gentile *on* the Sabbath. . . ." Indeed, according to Jewish law, one may not instruct anyone to do anything forbidden, but some have "interpreted" the law in such a way as to arrange for things to be done in advance or by *inferring* that certain things need doing: "Wouldn't it be nice if there was light in the parlor?" The exception is for sick people's needs; these may be requested directly. One may be surprised to learn that according to a recent book, employment of *shabbes goyim* for personal needs rarely occurred before the nineteenth century.

Saturday Morning

Sabbath morning is marked by a number of differences from the weekday routine. One may sleep later—another example of *oneg shabbat*—since the synagogue service usually begins later, a reference to the burnt offerings at the Temple, which on Sabbath were not required to begin at sunrise. Also, tefillin are not worn on Sabbath since the Sabbath itself is considered a sufficient sign of covenant. The passage in Exodus (13:10) that commands us to wear tefillin specifies they be worn "all the days," and Sabbath is not just another day.

See the chapter beginning on p.19 for the weekday rituals and prayers for home and synagogue.

The Sabbath morning prayers upon awakening are the same as on weekdays: *Modeh ani*, the washing of the hands, *Birkhot hashaḥar* (the morning blessings, which many say in the synagogue), and the donning of the tzitzit. Likewise, the synagogue service begins in the usual way: *Mah tovu, Adon olam, Yigdal*, and the bessings of the Torah are said. In those synagogues that recite the *korbanot*, the sections of the Torah regarding the Temple offerings, a section on the Sabbath sacrifice is added, though the prayers that begin *Yehi ratzon* ("May it be Thy will") are not said after it.

The *Pesukei dezimra*, the Verses of Song, is longer on Sabbath than on weekdays. There are many psalms that refer to Sabbath in one way or another and additional ones are chosen in various rites and by individual synagogues. Regardless of the choices, the *Pesukei dezimra* concludes on the Sabbath with a beautiful, long prose poem woven from verses from Psalms and Isaiah. It is known as *Nishmat* and begins *nishmat kol ḥai*, "The soul of every living thing." It was held in very high esteem by the talmudic sages. A number of great rabbinical poets of the Middle Ages wrote introductions to it, some of which are now known as Zemirot. It offers praise and thanks to the Lord at a height beyond the highest, stretching the power of language to mingle in the realm of the superlative. This is the poetry one sets to music with high trumpets and drums. Here are some excerpts:

The soul of every living thing shall bless Your name,
O Lord our God.
The spirit of all flesh shall continually adore and exalt
the mention of You, O our king.
You are God from everlasting to everlasting.
Other than You we have no king, redeemer, savior,
liberator, and deliverer. . . .

He awakens the sleepers and arouses the slumberers.
He makes the dumb speak,
Frees those who are imprisoned,
Sustains those who fall,
Straightens those who are bowed down. . . .

Were our mouths filled with song as the sea,
Our tongues with melody as the multitude of its waves,
Our lips with praise as the expanse of the heavens,
Our eyes bright as the sun and the moon,
Our hands spread out as the eagles of heaven,
Our feet swift as the deer,
We would still be unable to adequately acknowledge
You and bless Your name, O Lord our God and God
of our fathers,
For even one thousand-thousand-myriad-myriad part
of the favors You have bestowed upon our fathers
and upon us. . . .

God—in the greatness of Your might
Great—in the glory of Your name
Mighty—for all time
Awesome—in Your awesome deeds. . . .
By the myriad choirs of Your people, the house of Israel.
Your name will be glorified, O our king, in every generation.
For it is the duty of all creatures to thank and acknowl-
edge, praise, laud, glorify, exalt, adore, bless, uplift,
and acclaim You, O Lord our God. . . .

Translation by Reuven Hammer from Entering Jewish Prayer *(Schocken Books, 1994).*

Nishmat concludes with *Yishtabaḥ*, the "fifteen expressions of praise," which brings to an end the *Pesukei dezimra*, as it does every day. Afterward, the cantor says half Kaddish.

THE SHEMA THROUGH THE AMIDAH: One might say that all up to this point has been an introduction, with the "real" prayer beginning only now with the Barkhu, the call to prayer, same as on weekdays, followed, as then, by the Shema. As it is on weekdays, the Shema is preceded by two blessings and followed by one. It had long been the custom to insert piyutim (hymns) at each of the Shema blessings, though this is seldom done today except on the High Holidays. These hymns are often referred to collectively as *yotzerot*, in reference to the first blessing before the Shema, *Yotzer or*, "He who makes light and creates darkness." These are the points of the service where the old editions of the *Minhogimbukh* describe the greatest diversity of material: in Poland they add this hymn, but in Bohemia they add that one. However, three such hymns that are widely known are *Hakol yodukha* and *El adon al kol hamaasim*, both of which speak of God as the "director" of all things, and *Lael asher shavat*, "To the God who rested," which refers to the origin of the Sabbath.

For Yotzer, *see p. 27.*

The Sabbath morning Amidah comprises seven blessings, same as the other Sabbath services, though there is an addition before the fourth benediction: *Yismaḥ Moshe*, "Moses rejoiced [that God considered him] His faithful servant," its text referring to passages in Numbers (12:7) and Exodus (32:15; 31:16–17). Moses is mentioned on Sabbath because it was through him that God delivered the gift of the Sabbath. In the cantor's repetition of the Amidah, the Kedushah is expanded and includes material from Isaiah, Ezekiel, and Psalms. It begins, "We shall sanctify Your name in this world

For an explanation of the full weekday Amidah, see p. 31.

as they sanctify it in heaven," then quoting the angels, "Holy, holy, holy is the Lord of hosts." As the silent Amidah is followed by *Elohai netzor*, "My God guard my tongue from evil," the cantor's repetition is followed by the prayer *Yehi ratzon* ("May it be the will") and the recitation of the full Kaddish. Thus concludes the Amidah section of the service.

THE SABBATH TORAH READING: The week's full Torah portion is read in the Sabbath morning service, the readings on the preceding Monday and Thursday mornings having been just a taste of what is to come. The reading ritual is similar to that described in the chapter about the days of the week but expanded as one might expect given the time made available to prayer on the Sabbath. But since it is a joyous day, the prayer of supplication *El erekh apayim* is not said.

The Torah portion of the service begins with a recitation of *En kamokha*, "There is none like You among the gods, O Lord," a prayer comprising a number of Psalm passages. Then, a call for God's compassion: *Av harahamim*, "Father of compassion." The ark is opened and before the Torah is removed, the congregation recites the verse from Numbers, *Vayehi binsoa*, "It would be that when the Ark was brought forth," and the Aramaic prayer *Berikh shemeh*, "Blessed is the name of the master of the universe.... May it be with mercy." A single Torah is removed from the ark and placed in the right arm of the cantor, who raises it high and with the congregation recites the first line of the Shema. This is followed by *Ehad elohenu gadol adonenu*, "One is our God, great is our master, holy is His name." Turning toward the ark, the cantor bows while raising the Torah and says *Gadlu*, "Declare the greatness of the Lord." The congregation responds with *Lekha Adonai*, "Yours, Lord, is the greatness, the strength, the glory, the triumph, and the majesty," then *Romemu*, "Exalt the Lord our God and bow down at His footstool." The cantor carries the Torah scroll through the standing congregation, which recites *Al hakol*, "For everything may it be exalted," and everyone reaches out to kiss the Torah with a corner of the tallit or a prayer book that will in turn be kissed. The cantor returns the Torah to the *bimah* (the pulpit) and places it upon the reading desk, where the scroll's decorative metal fittings, mantle, and binder are removed and set aside.

In some places it is the custom to just bow as the Torah passes.

The Sabbath Torah reading is divided into seven parts, each with at least three verses (usually many more), representing the seven days of the week. One person (called an *oleh* [m] or *olah* [f]) is called up for each part; the coming up is known as an *aliyah*. After the seventh person reads, the maftir is called up. *Maftir* means "one who closes," and the person so designated is called to read the last three verses from the weekly portion or, on holidays, to read from a separate scroll a portion designated specifically for that day. To be called up to the Torah as maftir is considered a special honor, often given to a bar or bat mitzvah. After each *oleh* has come up, the gabbai calls the next *oleh* and recites a *Mi sheberakh* prayer for the previous one. When the reading is complete, the Torah scroll is lifted in its opened-for-reading position for all the congregation to see—the ritual of *hagbahah*—and the congregations sings, "This is the Torah that Moses placed before the Children of Israel, according to the word of the Lord, and through the hand of Moses." This is followed by the *gelilah* ritual, the dressing of the Torah with its binder, mantle, and metal fittings, an honor performed by two persons from the congregation. And to conclude, the cantor says a half Kaddish.

See also the section on the weekday readings that begins on p. 39.

There may be more than seven; Sabbath is the only day when there may be extra aliyot.

Mi sheberakh means "the One who blessed" and may be said for the oleh, *for a bar or bat mitzvah, for a mother and newborn child, for a sick person, etc.*

THE HAFTARAH READING: The next part of the Sabbath morning service has no weekday counterpart: the reading by the maftir of the haftarah, the apportioned readings taken from the books of prophets that are read throughout the year in parallel with the Torah readings. Like the Torah portions, the haftarah readings often make for interesting counterpoint to the Torah portions, offering a different perspective on the themes. Festival haftarot are related to the festival. While the Torah is read in its entirety—and in order—over the course of a year, the haftarah readings are neither systematic nor complete. The maftir may be a bar or bat mitzvah.

The reading of the haftarah is both preceded and followed by blessings. After the concluding blessings, two Aramaic prayers composed in Babylonia are recited, both beginning *Yekum purkan*, "May there arise salvation." The first one is for the leaders of the community, specifically those who study and lead the study of the Torah; the other for the welfare of the members of the community. Then a *Mi sheberakh* prayer is said for the congregation and all congregations, for their spouses and children, for those who study, and for those who provide for all the ritual and charitable needs of the community. In some synagogues there are prayers for the government and its leaders and for the state of Israel. When the new moon, which marks the new month (Rosh Ḥodesh), will appear before the next Sabbath, the exact time of its appearance is announced at this point in the service.

See the chapter "Rosh Ḥodesh," p. 91

PRAYERS FOR THE DEAD: In some congregations after the *Mi sheberakh* or the announcement of Rosh Ḥodesh, prayers are said for those who died during the past year and for those whose anniversary of death (*yortsait* in Yiddish) will be observed in the coming week. In the prayer *El malei raḥamim*,

For Yizkor, see
p. 265.

"O God, full of mercy," the *gabbai* of the congregation reads out the names of the deceased as part of the text. A special memorial service called Yizkor, "May God remember," includes *El malei rahamim* on Yom Kippur, the last day of Passover, Shavuot, and Shemini Atzeret.

THE CONCLUSION OF THE SERVICE: The final major parts of the liturgy are the recitation of *Ashrei* (Psalm 145) and the standing recitation of *Yehalelu* as the Torah is again carried through the congregation and returned to the ark. In most congregations, there is a recitation of Psalm 29, "Render unto the Lord, you sons of the powerful, glory and might," and, as always, a half Kaddish.

Musaf (Additional) Service

Numbers 28:9–29:39 mandates additional offerings that were to be brought to the Temple on Sabbaths and festivals. Since they were in addition to the usual morning offerings, they were termed *musaf*, "additional." When prayer services took the place of the additional Temple offerings, musaf services were instituted to take their place, and so they are held on the Sabbath, Rosh Ḥodesh, the High Holidays (Rosh Hashanah and Yom Kippur), and the pilgrimage festivals (Passover, Shavuot, and Sukkot). It is the general custom for the musaf service to take place immediately following the morning service, though there is no legal reason for doing so.

The mood of the service is one of elevated holiness. The half Kaddish that is recited by the cantor at the end of the Sabbath morning service serves as a segue. The service itself begins with the Amidah, again comprising only seven benedictions and again with a specially formulated middle one. The middle benediction concerns the holiness of the day and the special offering and begins with an acrostic of twenty-two words, each starting with a letter of the alphabet in retrograde order, א to ת: "*Tikanta shabat ratzita korbenoteha...*," "You established the Sabbath; you found favor in its offerings." It is followed by the reading of the musaf sacrifices:

> On the sabbath day: two yearling lambs without blemish, together with two-tenths of a measure of flour with oil mixed in ... and on Rosh Ḥodesh you shall present a burnt offering to the Lord: two young bulls, one ram, and seven yearling lambs, without blemish. As meal offering for each bull: three-tenths of a measure of flour with oil mixed in....

Numbers 28:9–10.
For more on the Temple sacrifices, see p. 8.

The cantor's repetition of the Amidah includes an extended Kedushah that has within it a congregational recitation of the Shema.

The service continues with full Kaddish and the hymn *En kelohenu*, "There is none like our God," best known to Ashkenazic Jews with the tune published in 1841 by the German Reform cantor Hirsch Goldberg and composer Julius Freudenthal. In the traditional service, the congregants recite *Pitom haketoret*, which is composed of passages from the Talmud and Torah (Exodus 30:34–37:7–8) that pertain to the particulars of the incense offering that God commanded Moses to instruct:

> Drop gum, onycha, galbanum, and frankincense weighing each seventy *maneh*; myrrh, cassia, spikenard, saffron weighing each sixteen *maneh*; costus, twelve [*maneh*]; aromatic bark, three; and cinnamon, nine; lye of Carshina, nine *kab*; wine of Cyprus, three *seah* and three *kab*; salt of Sodom, a quarter of a *kab*....

The conclusion of the service varies somewhat in different rites and denominations. In Ashkenazic orthodoxy, the common order is the rabbis' Kaddish, *Alenu*, mourner's Kaddish, *Shir hakavod* ("Song of Glory," a medieval German hymn), and the Psalm of the Day (Psalm 92 on Sabbath). The hymn of praise *Adon olam*, "The Lord of the Universe," closes most Ashkenazic services; *Yigdal*, the Thirteen Principles of Faith by Maimonides, holds pride of place in the Sephardic rites. In the *Minhogimbukh*, *Adon olam* is mentioned only in connection with the beginning of the morning service, not with musaf. Yet it has been popular as a closer at least since the nineteenth century and is among the most popular texts with composers of Jewish liturgical music.

Maimonides' Thirteen Principles may be summarized as follows: Belief in God's existence, perfection, and presence as Creator of all things; God's unity; his noncorporeality; his eternity; his exclusivity; his communication with us through prophecy; Moses's primacy among prophets; divine origin of Torah; immutability of Torah; divine omniscience and providence; divine reward and retribution; coming of the Messiah; resurrection of the dead.

The Sabbath Day Meal

Even when kiddush is said after the synagogue service, it is the custom to perform the ritual at home before the Sabbath day meal. This particular kiddush is referred to in Aramaic as *Kidusha raba*, the "great kiddush." While it was prescribed in the time of the sages, it has been added to many times over the centuries. The 1593 *Minhogimbukh* mentions one addition that is still commonly said: *Veshamru venei yisrael*, "The Children of Israel shall observe" (Exodus 31:16–17), said before the blessing over wine. The blessing over bread, with two loaves covered by the cloth, and the Grace after Meals are the same as on Friday night.

As on Friday night, there is a great encouragement of singing during and after the Sabbath day meal. One of the very best examples of Sabbath-day Zemirot repertory is *Yom shabbaton*, by the great medieval poet, philosopher, and physician Yehudah Halevi (1075–1141), who lived in Toledo, Spain. Its text is rich in biblical allusions: to Noah's dove who could find no place to rest, and to the Song of Songs, in which the beloved is spoken of as a dove. Here are three of its verses:

None can forget Shabbat,
Its memory is like a pleasant scent.
    refrain: Noah's dove found a resting place on this day,
        And on it all the weary will rest.
At Sinai all the people joined in the covenant,
Saying with one voice: "Let us do and obey."
"For God is One," they proclaimed,
"Blessed is He who gives strength to the tired."
The people who wandered like lost sheep
Will remember God's covenant and pledge,
So that no evil should befall them,
In accordance with the promise made to Noah
    after the Flood.

It is the custom to spend at least some time studying Torah after the Sabbath meal.

Sabbath Afternoon Service

The Sabbath afternoon service, coming as it does during a day of spiritual refreshment, is considered one of heightened spirituality, said to be the time of the week when one is most open to revelation. In the literature of Kabbalah, it is described as the time when God is most likely to hear our prayers favorably as it is the time when he himself yearns for redemption.

This is a service in which the Torah is read, so its order is somewhat different from its weekday counterpart and it contains some prayers that are specific to this service. As on weekdays, it begins with *Ashrei* (Psalm 45), with its special emphasis on the verse that begins, "You open Your hand and satisfy the needs of every living thing." An oft-quoted passage of the Talmud says that the sages assured their followers a place in the world to come if they repeated *Ashrei* three times a day. It is followed by *Uva letziyon*, "A redeemer shall

For Ashrei *and*
Uva letziyon,
see p. 41.

Psalm 69:14

See p. 40 for more
on the bloodline
"castes."

come to Zion," derived from Isaiah and familiar from the Monday and Thursday morning services. Then half Kaddish and the Psalm verse *Vaani tefilati* ("May my prayer . . . be at a time that is favorable").

The service then continues with the Torah reading and its attendant blessings. One scroll is taken from the ark and three persons are called: a kohen, a levite, and an Israelite, representing the three castes of ancient Israelite society. It is required that no fewer than ten verses be read from the beginning of the following week's portion (usually the entire first *aliyah*). The Amidah is similar in structure to that of the preceding Sabbath services: seven benedictions, each with its variant in the middle, which in this case emphasizes the oneness of God, the redemption that will come from its recognition, and the redemptive tranquility of the Sabbath.

A return to the tone of supplication and of the concerns that will be upon us once again in the week to come is found in the prayer *Tzidkatkha*, "Your righteousness is a righteousness everlasting," which follows the Amidah. In connection with this brief prayer, the *Zohar*, the chief work of the Kabbalah, points out that Moses, Joseph, and David all died at the time of afternoon prayers on Sabbath. In the *Minhogimbukh*, the prayer is explained as related to the furlough from hell (*gehinom*) that is granted on Sabbath:

The "hell" referred
to here is, in
Hebrew, gehenna,
closer to the Chris-
tian concept of
purgatory than to
hell. That is to say,
it is not an eternal
destination.

> *Tzidkatkha* is recited on Sabbath in the afternoon be-
> cause the souls of the sinners will have to return to hell
> soon, after the end of Sabbath, and we should accept the
> reason for their verdict. On Friday evening one lets out a
> cry that the souls of the sinners be allowed to leave hell
> in order to rest on the Sabbath like all the other people of
> Israel. And on Sabbath, in the evening, one lets out a cry
> once again so that they go back when the people of Israel
> finish their prayers.

The prayer is followed by full Kaddish, *Alenu*, and the mourner's Kaddish. In pious communities on winter Sabbath afternoons, it is the custom to recite alone the *Shir hamaalot*, the Songs of Ascent, which are Psalms 120–134. In some communities, *Pirkei avot*, "The Ethics of the Fathers," one of the great collections of Jewish wisdom, is read at this time between Passover and Shavuot; in others it is read through the summer months, up to Rosh Hashanah.

See p. 154 for more about The Ethics of the Fathers.

The Third Sabbath Meal

It is considered an especially great mitzvah to eat three meals on the Sabbath, since the meals are not meals in the ordinary sense but are in themselves forms of prayer. The Hebrew term for this meal is *Seudah shelishit*, but it is known to most Jews as "*shaloshudos*." Exactly when to eat the third meal varies according to community custom and sometimes according to season. The *Minhogimbukh* recommends that the most appropriate time is in the afternoon, following the afternoon prayers, which allows the three meals to be evenly distributed throughout the day, though it recognizes that others eat the meal before the afternoon service. The custom is fulfilled if one eats bread alone for the third meal; however, some authorities say that it may not be fulfilled by eating fruits only. Whether or not two full loaves of bread are required for the blessing of the third meal is also a matter of varying opinion. However, one should always leave a small bit of bread on the table for the Grace after Meals. There is a custom that one should not consume or use water between the afternoon and evening prayers. This is how it was explained in 1593:

> Between the afternoon and evening prayers it is forbidden to drink water or to draw water, because at this time the souls of the sinners cool themselves in the waters of

the world in order to cool down before returning to the fires of hell. Thus, if one drank water or drew water, he would be doing harm to the souls. According to another opinion, the souls cool down in the waters Friday in the evening, after coming out from the fires of hell.

The Conclusion of Sabbath

THE CONCLUSION OF SABBATH marks a separation of holy time from the rest of the week, of sacred
from profane. The demarcation of Sabbath's end is a ceremony called *havdalah*, which itself means "separation" or
"distinction." It is one of Judaism's most beautiful rituals and
surely one of its most edifying, a ritual in which the Sabbath
day that was ushered in as bride is escorted out as a queen.
This takes place on Saturday evening, already into the next
day—a belated ceremony since one is reluctant to see the Sabbath pass. There is a Havdalah at the conclusion of all festival
days, though not of this ceremonial splendor.

Havdalah developed as a ritual for the home, which it is
still, though like kiddush, a version is also practiced in the
synagogue. The 1593 *Minhogimbukh* says that it is the custom
"to make Havdalah in the synagogue in certain communities" in the Saturday evening service. The synagogue service
follows the general weekday pattern for the evening service,
though with various obligatory and customary additions and
insertions. A mandatory insertion into the Amidah is the
benediction that officially concludes the Sabbath: *Atah
ḥonantanu*, "You have graciously endowed us with the intelli-

*A depiction of
Havdalah from
Venice, 1601. The
woodcut's caption
reads, "The master
of the house makes
Havdalah with
great devotion and
ceremony and thus
draws his children
to commandments
and good deeds."
Note the presence
of both boys and
girls in this educa-
tional context. It is
the tradition that
women bring in the
Sabbath and men
escort her out.*

*For the weekday
evening service, see
p. 49.*

gence to study your Torah." According to local custom, other prayers are added after the Amidah, such as *Viyhi noam* (Psalm 90:17), "May the pleasantness of the Lord be upon us," and Psalm 91, "The Soldiers' Psalm," which describes the many dangers from which God will protect us. The synagogue Havdalah ceremony may take place either before the *Alenu* or after it.

THE PRAYERS that are specific to the Havdalah ceremony are considered to be in a special class and are known collectively as *havdalot*, prayers of separation. These are prayers that separate the sacred from the profane, holiday from ordinary day, or light from dark. But first, the Havdalah ritual begins with a group of short biblical verses, begun by the prayer leader (in the synagogue it is usually the cantor):

> Behold, God is my savior, I will trust Him and not be afraid, for my strong faith and song of praise for God will be my salvation. (Isaiah 12:2)

> You will draw water joyously from the wellsprings of salvation. (Isaiah 12:3)

> Salvation is God's; may Your blessing rest upon Your people, Selah. (Psalms 3:9)

> The Lord of hosts is with us, the God of Israel is our heavenly tower. Selah. (Psalms 46:12)

> O the Lord of hosts, happy is the man that trust in You. (Psalms 84:13)

> God, redeem us! The king will answer us on the day we call Him. (Psalms 20:10)

Those present respond:
> The Jews had light, happiness, joy, and honor. (Esther 8:16)
> May we have the same [liturgical addition].

The leader repeats and then continues:
I will raise the cup of salvation and call out in the name of
God. (Psalms 116:13)

The last verse leads directly to the blessing for wine, *borei
peri hagafen,* "Blessed are you . . . who creates the fruit of the
vine." As in the Sabbath eve kiddush, it is the custom to
overfill the wine goblet slightly, allowing some to spill; the
overflowing cup is a symbol of good fortune. It is the general
rule that things are held in the right hand when being
blessed, and so it is with the wine goblet.

Two other objects are part of the Havdalah ceremony: a
spice box, often an elaborately made silver object; and a candle with at least two wicks. It says in the Talmud, "The Holy
One, blessed be He, gives a person an extra soul on Sabbath   *Talmud* Betzah
eve and takes it back at Sabbath's end." The purpose of that   *16a*
soul is to fully absorb the contentment and pleasures of the
Sabbath day. The spices, which represent joy and pleasure,
are said to be a compensation for the loss of the second soul.
The candle with multiple wicks represents a torch rather than
a mere candle, and it is to commemorate the gift of fire and a
return to the free use of it after the Sabbath that a blessing is
said. As one transfers the goblet to the left hand and picks up
the spice box with the right, the following blessing is said:

ברוך אתה יהוה אלהינו מלך העולם, בורא מיני בשמים.
Blessed are You, Lord our God, king of the universe, who
creates various kinds of fragrant spices.

We inhale the aroma, the spice box is put down, and the goblet is transfered back to the right hand. A blessing is said over
the fire:

ברוך אתה יהוה אלהינו מלך העולם, בורא מאורי האש.
Blessed are You, Lord our God, king of the universe, who
creates the lights of fire.

As this is said one holds the hands in such a way that one's fingernails and palms can be seen at the same time, again transferring the goblet from right hand to left so that both hands can be examined. A number of reasons are given for this odd custom, but the halakhic one is simply to make use of the torch's light.

Then the wine glass is transferred to the right hand again, and the Havdalah blessing itself is recited:

ברוך אתה יהוה אלהינו מלך העולם, המבדיל בין קדש לחול,
בין אור לחשך, בין ישראל לעמים, בין יום השביעי לששת
ימי המעשה. ברוך אתה יהוה, המבדיל בין קדש לחול.

The "distinctions" in this blassing are derived from Leviticus 10:10, Genesis 1:4., and Leviticus 20:26.

Blessed are You, Lord our God, king of the universe, who separates between the holy and the everyday, between the light and the darkness, between Israel and the other nations, between the seventh day and the six days of creation. Blessed are You, Lord, who separates the holy from the everyday.

Again, some wine is spilled during the blessing. The candle is then put out, and the prayer leader drinks the wine.

At Havdalah's end, it is the custom to sing *Eliyahu hanavi* for the coming of the immortal prophet Elijah, that he may bring news of the Messiah.

> Elijah the Prophet, Elijah the Tishbite,
> Elijah the Gileadite.
> Speedily in our days may he come to us,
> with the Messiah, the son of David.

The *Minhogimbukh* describes the popular legend behind the custom of calling Elijah thus:

> After the synagogue service one should go home and sing songs, especially *Eliyahu hanavi*, because we know that Elijah the Prophet will not come on the day before the

Sabbath or a holiday, but now that Sabbath has ended, he may indeed come. So we call him—some say it is good for our memory to call Elijah several times at the end of Sabbath. Also, it is taught that at the conclusion of Sabbath, Elijah sits underneath the Tree of Wisdom in the Garden of Eden and writes down the good deeds that the people of Israel did on that Sabbath.

In recent times, it has become a custom in liberal circles to add to the call to Elijah a parallel call to Miriam the Prophetess, the sister of Moses and Aaron, and to set aside a cup of water in her honor, just as a cup of wine is set aside for Elijah on Passover. The custom refers to the story of Miriam's Well, which is told in chapters 20 and 21 of the book of Numbers. In the desert, the Israelites were supplied with plentiful water from a rock that Moses struck with his staff. The rock seemed to follow them in their journey, but coinciding with the death of Miriam, the water supply became perilously short. This led to numerous interpretations that the two events were somehow related, and the source became known as Miriam's Well. It is believed that the well still exists, though its location has been obscured. In medieval Ashkenaz, there was a precedent for the custom of the cup of water in Miriam's honor, and the *Minhogimbukh* describes it:

Havdalah from the Minhogimbukh, Amsterdam, 1722. Note the three ceremonial objects: the wine goblet held in the father's right hand, the double-wicked candle, and the spice box.

Rabbinic sources for the drawing of water and Miriam's Well say that the well was created during the twilight on the eve of the first Sabbath (Avot 5:6) and that it traveled with the Children of Israel in the Wilderness (Talmud Taanit 9a, Numbers Rabbah 1:2).

> It is customary for women to go to the well to draw water right after the call to prayer, because Miriam's Well reappears on Saturday nights. Miriam's Well is now part of the Sea of Tiberias, and its waters mix with the waters of other wells and there is a chance of tapping into it. Whoever drinks from the water of Miriam's Well will be cured of all illnesses. Once there was a woman who went to draw water

on Saturday night and it happened that she tapped into the waters of Miriam's Well. She stayed out for a long time and her ailing husband was very angry with her when she returned. So afraid of her husband's anger was she that as soon as he spoke to her she dropped the jug. Nevertheless, her husband healed wherever the water touched him. Our sages say that anger causes only further anger and frustration. Had he been more moderate, her husband would have drunk the water and healed fully.

The Melaveh malkah *is mentioned as early as the third century* C.E. *by Rabbi Ḥanina, who said that a table should be set and refreshments should be served on Saturday nights. It is also mentioned in the* Shulḥan arukh.

It is the custom in some devout circles to eat a small meal after the conclusion of Sabbath. The meal is known as *Maleveh malkah*, "escorting the queen." As the Sabbath bride is welcomed with a festive meal, she is similarly ushered out. There are varying customs regarding the preparation of this meal and differences of opinion as to whether it is to be prepared in advance like other Sabbath meals, or made fresh as the first meal of the new week. The custom of the meal is mentioned as early as the third century C.E., but it was the Kabbalists of sixteenth-century Safed who established its popular observance. Isaac Luria, prominent member of that circle, said that the *neshamah yeterah*, the "second soul" that we are granted on Sabbath, lingers on until the end of this meal, so the longer we celebrate, the longer it stays with us. There are many Zemirot (table songs) that are specific to this meal and quite a number of them mention King David, because it was said that King David knew that he would die on a Sabbath, so he celebrated life every Saturday evening.

The remainder of the day is the same as other weekdays, concluding with the bedtime Shema.

Rosh Ḥodesh

ROSH HODESH means "beginning of the month," and it is recognized at the new moon. The moon is the main regulator of Jewish time, and before a fixed calendar was established in the fourth century C.E., by Hillel II, the occurrence of the new moon was determined by direct observation and announced throughout the land. From its first mention in the Torah, Rosh Ḥodesh was considered a festive day:

Kidush levanah, "blessing the new moon," from the Minhogimbukh, Venice, 1593.

> Also in the day of your gladness, and in your appointed seasons, and in your new moons, you shall blow the trumpets over your burnt offerings and over your peace offerings; and they shall be to you for a memorial before your God: for I am the Lord your God.

Numbers 10:10

The indication, then, was for a musaf offering on Rosh Ḥodesh, same as on Sabbath; today it is observed as an additional prayer service. The sages of the Mishnah regarded Rosh Ḥodesh as an observance of the rank of Ḥanukkah and Purim, but later it came to hold the status of a minor holiday, similar to the intermediate days (*hol hamoed*) of Passover and Sukkot. Nonetheless, it is an important observance and there is a ritual to announce its coming during the morning service

For Sabbath musaf service, see p. 78. The specific offering for Rosh Ḥodesh is described in Numbers 28:11–15.

on the preceding Sabbath, immediately after the haftarah

This addition to Yehi ratzon appeared first in the late eighteenth century. For more on this prayer, see pp. 59 and 74.

reading. A special version of the prayer *Yehi ratzon* is recited at the conclusion of the Amidah: "May it be Your will . . . that You inaugurate for us the month," followed by the announcement of the exact time of the occurrence of the new moon. This is referred to as the *molad*, or "birth," and is followed by a prayer of redemption and renewal:

> [*Congregation, repeated by the prayer leader*] The One who performed miracles for our forefathers and redeemed them from slavery to freedom, may He redeem us soon and gather in our dispersed from the four corners of the earth; then comrades shall all Israel be. Now let us say: Amen. [*Prayer leader then congregation*] The beginning of [name of month] will be on [day of week] at [hour and minute]; it is a good thing coming to us and to all Israel.

In announcing the *molad*, there is an old custom to announce not only the hour and minute, but the second as well—calculated by the *ḥelek*, an old division of the minute into eighteen three-and-one-third-second segments. While

For more on Jewish time, see p. 16.

the *molad* marks the astronomical new moon, the observance of Rosh Ḥodesh might be as much as several days later, to accommodate adjustments in the calendar made in order to prevent the High Holidays and Passover from falling on forbidden days.

Despite the "downgrading" of Rosh Ḥodesh from medium to minor holiday status, medieval talmudic commentators argued whether or not work was permitted on that day, since a musaf service was added to the morning prayers, requiring more time. It was resolved that men would be permitted to

Pirkei deRabbi Eliezer, 45

work but that women would be exempt (though not prohibited). Rashi (Rabbi Shlomo ben Yitzḥak, 1040–1105) explains it thus: When Aaron told the Israelites to bring him the gold earrings from their wives and children for the making of the Golden Calf, the women refused; when the Tabernacle was constructed, they gladly surrendered their jewels. The work was completed on Rosh Ḥodesh (of the month of Nisan), and for their steadfastness the women were rewarded with a work-free day on Rosh Ḥodesh.

The Kabbalists of sixteenth-century Safed, notably Moses Cordovero, saw in the observance of Rosh Ḥodesh an opportunity for the forgiveness of sin, since the burnt offerings for the day included a "sin offering." As they explained it, the moon's inequality to the sun, its waxing and waning, were imperfections brought about by Adam's sin. To atone, they instituted the custom of *Yom Kippur katan,* "little Yom Kippur," in which one fasted part of the day prior to Rosh Ḥodesh. Those who follow this practice add penitential prayers and a haftarah reading designated for fast days. On Rosh Ḥodesh itself it is not permitted to fast, nor is it permitted to deliver eulogies, since these might spoil the spirit of this festival day, albeit one of minor stature.

The Prayers for Rosh Ḥodesh

Rosh Ḥodesh services follow the general pattern of the day's services with special inserted prayers for the occasion and a Torah reading specific to the day. A musaf service follows after the morning prayers. In this chapter, only the prayers specific to Rosh Ḥodesh will be described.

THE AFTERNOON SERVICE BEFORE AND THE EVENING SERVICE OF ROSH ḤODESH: The only variation in the afternoon service before Rosh Ḥodesh is that Taḥanun, the group of supplication prayers, is omitted. The only addition to the evening service of Rosh Ḥodesh is in the Amidah, where the prayer

On days that are considered joyous, Taḥanun is always omitted, as are funeral lamentations and eulogies.

On days when Yaaleh veyavo is inserted into the Amidah, it is also inserted into the Grace after Meals.

Yaaleh veyavo, "May there rise, approach, and reach You," is inserted into the *Avodah,* the benediction for the restoration of the Temple. *Yaaleh veyavo* is a prayer of curious syntax and direction, more suggesting than asking or telling. Through gentle suggestion, it reminds God to think of us, expressing hope that we be heard, considered, remembered for kindness, goodness, grace, compassion, salvation, and pity. There is also a mention of David and the Messiah who will come of David's line. The prayer is also said, with minor variations, on *hol hamoed,* the intermediate days of Passover and Sukkot.

MORNING SERVICE: In the Orthodox synagogues where the *korbanot* (the order of the weekday burnt offerings) are read, the instruction for the Rosh Hodesh offering is inserted. In the Amidah, *Yaaleh veyavo* is added again, as it is on all festivals, both here and in the Grace after Meals. After the repetition of the Amidah, a half Hallel is recited standing. Hallel is the name given to a group of Psalms, numbers 113-118, that are said after the Amidah on certain holidays. The word *hallel* means praise, as in "hallelujah" (praise the Lord). These psalms have been an important part of the liturgy since ancient times. Half Hallel is a somewhat abbreviated version—far more than a half; in fact, only the first eleven verses of Psalms 115 and 116 are eliminated. It is a custom that is said to have begun in Babylonia in the third century C.E. One might say that the distinction between the half and full versions is made to differentiate the special days from the *very* special days. The half Hallel is followed by a full Kaddish.

The Hallel psalms are treated at length on p. 129, in the discussion of the Passover liturgy.

Generally, half Hallel is said on days when work is permitted; the full Hallel is said on days when one may not work.

When Rosh Hodesh falls on a weekday (except on Hanukkah), one Torah scroll is taken out from the ark, and the portion for the new moon is read: Numbers 28:1-15, which recounts the order of burnt offerings, including those for the new moon (Numbers 28:11-14). Four readers are called up, one more than for an ordinary Monday or Thursday Torah reading. The 1593 *Minhogimbukh* offers a mnemonic for remembering how many people are called up to the Torah:

> Four people are called up to the Torah to show that Rosh Ḥodesh is more of a holiday than an ordinary weekday. Major holidays are holier, so five people are called up. Yom Kippur is holier than the other holidays, so six people are called up. And since Sabbath is the holiest day, seven people are called up. I will now teach you a trick how to remember this: you just have to remember the verse *Shema Yisrael Adonai elohenu Adonai eḥad* (Deuteronomy 6:4). There are three letters in the word *Shema* (שמע), so three people are called up on the Sabbath in the afternoon, on Monday and Thursday, and on Ḥanukkah and Purim. In the word *Yisrael* (ישראל) there are five letters, and accordingly, five people are called up on holidays. There are four letters in God's name (יהוה), and accordingly, four people are called up on Rosh Ḥodesh and on the intermediate days of holidays (*ḥol hamoed*). In *elohenu* (אלהינו) there are six letters, so six people are called up on Yom Kippur, and finally the two words *Adonai eḥad* (יהוה אחד) have between them seven letters, so seven people are called up on the Sabbath.

After the Torah reading, half Kaddish is recited. The tefillin are removed prior to the beginning of the musaf service.

MUSAF SERVICE: The first and last three benedictions of the Amidah are as on weekdays, but the fourth is *Rashei ḥodashim*, a benediction specifically for the day. It begins, "New moons You have given to Your people, a time of atonement for all their offspring. . . ." The atonement is explained in the Talmud (*Shevuot* 2b) as that connected to the sin

offering, which concerns the inadvertent contamination of
the Sanctuary. The cantor repeats the Amidah aloud. The
service ends with *Alenu* and mourner's Kaddish.

AFTERNOON SERVICE AND OTHER ASPECTS OF THE DAY: In the
afternoon service, *Yaaleh veyavo* is again inserted in the Amidah, with an added phrase, as it is when reciting the Grace
after Meals. Taḥanun is again omitted. If the beginning of the
month is celebrated for two days, the second day is celebrated
the same as on the first day.

*Taḥanun is omitted
on all days that are
considered joyous.*

When Rosh Ḥodesh Falls on Sabbath

When Rosh Ḥodesh falls on Sabbath, the synagogue services
follow their basic Sabbath patterns, with the addition of the
verses and readings that mark the new month. The prayer
Yaaleh veyavo is inserted in the Amidah in all four services
(the usual three plus musaf, which is a requirement of both
Sabbath and Rosh Ḥodesh). Two Torah scrolls are taken from
the ark. The weekly portion is read from the first scroll, for
which seven people are called up. Then the second scroll is
put on the table and half Kaddish is recited over both scrolls.
The first scroll is lifted (the ritual of *hagbahah*) and then
rolled, dressed in its binder, mantle, and silver fittings (the ritual of *gelilah*), and the maftir is called up to the second scroll.
The maftir's reading is from the portion of the new moon,
Numbers 28:9–15, from the sentence that begins "And on the
Sabbath."

The haftarah reading for Rosh Ḥodesh is Isaiah 66:1–24,
the entire last chapter of that prophet. The last verses make
specific mention of the the new month:

> For as the new heavens and the new earth, which I will
> make, shall remain before Me, saith the Lord, so shall

your seed and your name remain.

And it shall come to pass, that from one new moon to
another, and from one Sabbath to another, shall all flesh
come to worship before Me, saith the Lord.

And they shall go forth, and look upon the carcasses of the
men that have rebelled against Me; for their worm shall
not die, neither shall their fire be quenched; and they
shall be an abhorring unto all flesh.

*The penultimate
verse is repeated so
as not to end on a
troublesome note.*

In the Amidah of the musaf service, the prayer *Atah
yatzarta* is inserted after the third blessing. This addition for
Sabbath Rosh Ḥodesh is the only Amidah prayer that refers
to God as creator. After the repetition of the Amidah, the cantor says full Kaddish, and the service ends as usual.

The afternoon service is as usual on a Sabbath, except that
Yaaleh veyavo is inserted in the Amidah, again with the a special phrase referring to Rosh Ḥodesh. *Tzidkatkha*, the prayer
that strikes a somewhat somber note on the otherwise joyful
Sabbath, is omitted from this service, as on most festive days.

Shabbat Maḥar Ḥodesh

When Rosh Ḥodesh falls on a Sunday, a special haftarah is
read on the preceding day, which is the Sabbath. The portion,
1 Samuel 20:18-42, begins, "Jonathan said to him, tomorrow
is the new moon," a part of the story of David's escape from
the clutches of Saul and of Jonathan's loyalty to David. Many
haftarot are designated for special days, but this is the only
one designated in advance of a special day.

*Maḥar is the
Hebrew word for
"tomorrow."*

Blessing the New Moon

Every month, the new moon is blessed in the ritual called
Kidush levanah. The custom is said to date from talmudic
times. The sage Rabbi Yoḥanan, who lived around the time

Rabbi Yohanan in
Sanhedrin *42a*

Exodus Rabbah *15*

the Second Temple was destroyed, said that one who blesses the new moon is like one who greets the shekhinah (the Divine Presence). In the midrash, the waxing and waning of the moon are seen as symbolic of Israel's rising and falling in God's favor, with the new moon as a favorable sign.

These are some of the customs of *Kidush levanah*: The blessing is to be said standing—as one must be when approaching the Divine Presence—under an open sky, in clear view of the moon, and with a minyan. (If any of these conditions are not feasible, the whole may be waived.) If the night is cloudy, one should wait for another night, within these limits: The blessing over the new moon should be recited no earlier than three days after the *molad*, the "birth" of the new moon, and before the fifteenth day, after which the moon will be full and is no longer considered new. However, it is considered best to recite it between the eighth and the eighteenth hour of the fourteenth day of the month. It is customary to wait until the conclusion of the Sabbath to recite the blessing, in order to approach the Divine Presence in nice clothes and in a festive mood. If the conclusion of the Sabbath falls on the tenth day of the month, then one should wait for that day, but if it falls later than that, one should not wait, since the sky might get cloudy.

The blessing is as follows:

> Blessed are You, Lord our God, king of the universe, who with His utterance created the heavens and with the breath of His mouth all their legion. A rule and a schedule He gave them, that they not alter their assigned task. They are joyous and happy to perform the will of their maker, the one who does truth, whose deed is truth. He told the moon that it should renew itself as a crown of splendor for those who are destined to renew themselves in the same way and to glorify

their maker for the sake of His glorious kingdom, Blessed
are You, Lord our God, who renews the months.

At this point one jumps or rises on one's toes, as if dancing,
and says three times, "As I dance toward thee, but cannot
touch thee, so shall none of my evil-inclined enemies be able
to touch me." Then, standing in place, one says three times,
"Let there fall upon them terror and dread and fear at the
greatness of Your arm, they should become still as a stone"
(Exodus 15:16), and afterward the same sentence backward,
"As a stone let them be still at Your arm's greatness, fear and
terror upon them let there fall." The reversal is explained as a
reflection of how God works in the world: sometimes in natural order, other times through miracles.

After this, it has become the custom to recite the song
David melekh Yisrael ḥai vekayam, "Long live David, king of
Israel," and then to greet one another with *Shalom aleikhem*,
"May peace be with you," to which one answers, *Aleikhem
shalom, shalom aleikhem, shalom al Yisrael*, "May with you be
peace, may peace be with you, may peace be with Israel."

Kidush levanah
from the
Minhogimbukh,
Venice, 1601.

"The time of singing has come"
(Song of Songs 2:12)

The Month of Nisan

NISAN, THE MONTH OF PASSOVER, is imbued with the status of holiness. It is described in the Torah as the first of all months: "Let this new moon be the first of all new moons, the new moon of the year," God says to Moses and Aaron. The statement suggests something far greater than the counting of time: a new beginning, a rebirth. In the story of the patriarchs, which occupies most of the book of Genesis, God created a tribe, a seed he then placed into the hothouse of slavery in Egypt. It was only with the Exodus that the Children of Israel were established as a nation, a people with a full system of belief and a body of practical and ritual law.

Exodus 12:2

Jewish New Year is celebrated on the first two days of Tishrei.

The narrative of Passover and Exodus is one of salvation on a massive scale: over 600,000 souls are brought out of Egypt in the aftermath of ten devastating blows to the Egyptian empire delivered directly by God. The story has a prophet, Moses, who is God's instrument and interlocutor, as well as the people's advocate, but it is God himself who is the main actor in this story, the one who determines and directs the course of human events, responds directly to human needs, and writes a code of civil, criminal, moral, and ritual law—

which is to be followed to the letter as a requirement for his interest and continuance.

In the Torah, Nisan is referred to as *Aviv*, "spring"; the name Nisan is Akkadian-Persian and comes from the period of the Babylonian Exile. True to its time of spring and rebirth, Passover is the first of the three pilgrimage festivals, in which the Israelites presented themselves at the Temple, bringing with them personal sacrifices appropriate to the growing season. Fifty days from the second day of Passover is the second pilgrimage festival, Shavuot; the third is Sukkot, which takes place in fall. Rosh Ḥodesh Nisan is observed for one day only.

In a sense, the entire month of Nisan is deemed holy and reflects a joyous and elevated spirit; in keeping with this, Taḥanun, the weekday prayers of supplication, *Tzidkatkha*, the prayer of supplication in the Sabbath afternoon service, and the memorial prayers for the dead are not said during Nisan. The *Minhogimbukh* says that one should not fast during Nisan but then goes on to mention various fasting customs: on the first day of Nisan in remembrance of the children of Aaron who died then; on the sixth, commemorating the death of Joshua; and on the tenth in memory of Miriam, who died that day. In many communities, the firstborn sons fast on the fourteenth, to commemorate the tenth plague, in which God took the lives of the firstborn of Egypt while the Jewish ones were spared.

When Rosh Ḥodesh Nisan falls on the Sabbath, it is a special Sabbath: Shabbat Haḥodesh, the last of the "Four Portions." As described in the chapter "Fundamentals of Prayer," the Jewish calendar shifts somewhat over a nineteen-year cycle. To give something of the flavor of the Bible readings that are apportioned throughout the year, we have based this book on a model year in which Shabbat Haḥodesh falls in the

See p. 34 for Taḥanun; p. 82 for Tzidkatkha.

See p. 177 for the story of the death of Miriam.

See p. 16 for a description of the Jewish calendar.

preceding month of Adar, making it the last Sabbath described in this book.

For Shabbat
Hahodesh, see
p. 364

Shabbat Hagadol, the Great Sabbath

The Sabbath preceding Passover is called Shabbat Hagadol,
the "Great Sabbath." The Talmud speaks of "great miracles"
that happened in Egypt on that day, the Sabbath before the
Passover, and offers two stories in connection with it, each of
them involving the sacrifice of the paschal lamb and how the
Israelites answered the Egyptians, frightening them with the
story of what was to come, eventually inciting a riot. To someone in a free society, the story seems less than "great," but to
a people who had been enslaved for over four hundred years
and to their descendants who also knew the yoke of oppression, it was a great symbol—a declaration of independence.

Talmud Shabbat
87b

Sacrifice of the
lambs: Exodus
12:3–11.

THE CUSTOMS OF SHABBAT HAGADOL: The *Minhogimbukh*
mentions a number of hymns particular to Shabbat Hagadol
that are inserted into the prayers of the Shema and in the repetition of the Amidah. These vary in different rites but are all
based on themes of redemption, appropriate to the occasion.

One Torah scroll is taken out from which the weekly portion is read. In our model year, that portion is *Aharei mot*,
Leviticus 16:1–18:30. Verses in chapters 16 and 17 pertain to
ritual purification and atonement for bodily pollution; chapter 18 describes forbidden sexual unions (addressed to men):
any incestuous relationship with mother, father, father's wife,
sister or stepsister, grandchildren, aunts and uncles (including those by marriage), daughters-in-law; and, generally, a
mother and daughter together, a woman and her sister together, a menstruating woman, a woman married to someone
else, a man and a man "in the manner of a man lying with a

The Minhogim-
bukh *mentions
many such hymns
that are no longer
recited.*

*Leviticus chapters
17 through 26 are
known as the
Holiness Code.
See p. 54.*

Shabbat Hagadol,
Venice, 1593.
Depicted is the
special sermon
given by the con-
gregation's leading
Torah scholar.

woman," and animals. The regular haftarah is Ezekiel 22:1–19, which tells how Jerusalem had polluted itself through such behaviors and how God's punishment shall be exile (pointing to the period of the Babylonian Exile).

Specific to Shabbat Hagadol is the haftarah Malachi 3:4–24. The text is a counterpoint to the reading from Ezekiel and speaks of redemption through offerings and good behavior in the aftermath of the Babylonian Exile. It is a well-established custom on Shabbat Hagadol that the sermon is to be given by the congregation's leading Torah scholar, who instructs the people about the special preparations for Passover as well as their meaning. The musaf service is as usual, though in some congregations special hymns are added to the repetition of the Amidah.

The *Minhogimbukh* mentions that in the Sabbath afternoon service, a portion of the Passover haggadah is read, beginning *Avadim hayinu,* "We were slaves to Pharaoh in Egypt." This takes the place of the series of psalms beginning with *Borkhi nafshi* (Psalm 104), which have been said every Sabbath afternoon since Sukkot, six months earlier.

The Preparations for Passover

The preparations for Passover follow a specific order, somewhat different from that described in Exodus 12. The slaughter of the sacrificial lamb on the fourteenth day of Nisan was particular to the original Passover meal, whereas the removal of all leaven (ḥametz) from the home by the time of the

Passover and the eating of matzoh for seven days is a commandment for "all your generations," to be observed every
year from the fourteenth through the twenty-first days of
Nisan. Anyone who eats that which is leavened during this
time is to be "cut off from Israel." The most elaborate preparations described in the *Minhogimbukh* are the steps in the
making of matzoh. Nowadays, most matzoh is purchased,
made in factories under rabbinic supervision. Yet the description of its manufacture in the *Minhogimbukh* provides a
glimpse into the home lives of Jews not long ago.

*In the Diaspora,
matzoh is eaten for
eight days; seven
among Reform
Jews.*

Preparing the Flour for Matzoh

Regarding the grinding and care of the matzoh flour, these
are the instructions from the *Minhogimbukh*:

> The flour for the matzoh should be ground at least three
> days before the matzoh is baked to make sure that it cools
> down before kneading, since the flour gets warm from
> grinding. It is for this reason that one should not place bags
> of flour on top of one another.
>
> The ground wheat should be carefully watched, covered
> with white linen to make sure that
> the crop does not touch the regu-
> lar leavened packs. In the mill, the
> entire area around the millstone
> should be cleansed thoroughly,
> though it is considered best to use
> a new millstone, since an old mill-
> stone tends to be damp, causing
> flour to stick to it, which risks
> mixing. Even if one uses special
> containers for the Passover flour,
> they should be lined with linen in
> case the flour sticks to a container

*Bringing the
matzoh wheat to
the mill,
Amsterdam, 1722.*

that has become damp. One should take good care of the flour and make sure that it does not get damp. Even salt and spices should be examined to be certain there are no grains mixed into it, because then it all is considered ḥametz, forbidden for Passover.

Though it is not mandated by Jewish law (nor is it mentioned in the *Minhogimbukh*), there is a custom in certain devout circles to use only *matzoh shemurah*, matzot made from wheat that was protected from leaven from the time of its harvesting.

THE KASHERING OF VESSELS AND UTENSILS

The word *kasher* or "kosher" means fit for use or consumption by the standards of *kashrut*, the Jewish dietary and use laws that are based in the Torah and were developed further by rabbinic authorities over centuries. The word comes from the Talmud and is commonly used in English both as an adjective and as a verb, with either spelling. In the Torah, the word commonly used is *tahor* ("clean"), as opposed to the words *tamei* ("unclean") or *sheketz* ("an abomination").

Kashering the vessels and utensils, Venice, 1593.

There are special requirements for becoming kosher for Passover, and the words used to describe the process of meeting those requirements are *kasher* and *kashering*, terms used not only for Passover. As food must be kosher for Passover, so too must all vessels and utensils. There are four methods, each considered appropriate to specific objects: incinerating (*libun*), purging (*hagalah*), purging through pouring hot water (*eruy rothim*), and soaking (*miluy veeruy*). The following are the methods for kashering as described in the 1593 *Minhogimbukh*:

One should start kashering utensils [here meaning all cooking and eating vessels and implements] at least two days before Passover or even earlier, and should make sure that it does not take longer, since it is forbidden to kasher utensils after midday on the day before Passover. . . .

For kashering, one should take a Passover vessel, fill it with water, and bring the water to the boil. When it is boiling, one should put in it the utensils made out of metal—spoons, goblets, and the like—then take them out and quickly put them under cold water. It is forbidden to kasher any other utensil except those intended for Passover use. If there is rust or other irregularities on the utensil, or if it is badly worn or chipped, it may not be kashered. Goblets painted or enameled on the inside may not be kashered, but those that are painted on the outside may.

Wooden utensils that are not used inside a pot may be kashered. To do so, one should take with tongs a piece of red-hot iron or a glowing hot stone, pour boiling water over the iron or the stone and onto the wooden utensil. . . . A ladle or a turner that is used only partially in the pot is kashered in the same way. All utensils that are used for hot food, such as bowls and plates, are kashered in the vessel as described above. But utensils used with fire and water, such as a roaster or a skewer or pans used for baking or frying, and similar utensils must be heated red-hot, not with boiling water. The general rule is that a utensil can become kosher and fit for Passover the same way as it became hametz. . . .

Earthenware cannot be kashered.

If one wants to kasher a big pot used for boiling water, first the pot has to be cleaned thoroughly, making sure that it has not been scraped. It should be filled to its rim with water, and the water should be brought to a boil. When the

"Passover vessel" means one that has been properly kashered and used exclusively for Passover.

water is boiling, three glowing hot bricks have to be thrown inside, making sure that the water overflows its sides. The hot water has to be poured out right away and the pot should be rinsed with cold water. Now the pot is kosher.

When kashering metal utensils or anything else that requires tongs, one should have two pairs of tongs, letting go with both tongs, one at a time under the water, because where the tong touches the utensil, it will not become kosher.

Once cleaned, tables or cutting boards can be kashered with boiling water and a red-hot iron or a glowing stone.... The cupboards that are used throughout the year have to be cleaned thoroughly, too. . . . The utensils not kashered for Passover should be cleaned thoroughly and put away in a separate room, away from view. . . .

The Web site kashrut.com makes available specific kashering instructions and offers resources for further information.

Modern ovens and stovetops require special cleaning (as do drawers, countertops, and tables), the methods for which vary according to the specifics of the models. Glass vessels that may not be heated are required to be submerged in water for three twenty-four-hour periods, each time in fresh water. Many people keep a separate set of dishes and glasses for exclusive use on Passover.

WATER FOR THE MATZOH

The drawing and preparation of water for the making of matzoh also has its rules. A pot already kashered for Passover on or before the thirteenth of Nisan should be used as a container. No sun or source of heat should reach the water for twenty-four hours prior to its use. When water was drawn from a well, the rule was to fetch the water after sunset but before the stars appeared in the sky. Since the water had been untouched by the sun when it was in the well, it only needed to be covered for twelve hours after it had been drawn.

The drawing of the water was traditionally the job of the master of the house, for whom, it was said, the task should not feel demeaning, since even the king of Israel used to carry the offerings of the firstfruits on his own shoulders.

The water for matzoh, Venice, 1601

SEARCHING FOR ḤAMETZ

A little while after water is taken for the matzoh, the search for leaven (*bedikat ḥametz*) begins. Rabbinical law instructs that one must do this at night, by candlelight, so that hidden spaces can be most clearly illuminated. A wax candle is specified and it is the custom to use a feather—a flight feather, specifically—to brush out the tight corners. One may not do any other work or study while the search is going on, nor may one eat nor hold any conversation other than that related to the demands of the search. The search begins with a blessing:

> Blessed are You, Lord our God, king of the universe, who sanctified us with His commandments and has commanded us concerning the removal of ḥametz.

If more than one person is involved, the others are to respond, "Amen."

One is to search all the rooms of the house, but not those places that are unreachable. If there is a hole in one's yard, that, too, should be searched. It is customary to put out some leaven to make sure that the blessing was not recited in vain. This leaven should be hard, not fresh, bread, to avoid crumbs. After the search is complete, one is to make the following statement in Aramaic:

> Any ḥametz that is in my possession and that I have not seen, that I have not observed, that I have not removed, and

that I do not know about, shall hereby be annulled and shall become ownerless like the dust of the earth.

This is a declaration, not a prayer, and as such, those who do not understand Aramaic are encouraged to say it in their own language. This applies also to the sentence said after the ḥametz is burned. Large amounts of ḥametz may also be sold—legally transferred, one might say—to a non-Jew and transferred back after the conclusion of Passover.

According to rabbinic law, if any of the gathered ḥametz is lost, or if any part of it is missing (mice again), the search has to be repeated.

Searching for ḥametz, Venice, 1593.

For those who find *bedikat ḥametz* odd or obsessive in the context of modern life, the Kabbalah explains it and its attendant silence and concentration as the symbolic brushing away of our evil inclinations—a kind of spiritual spring cleaning. Who among us does not need this?

THE DAY BEFORE PASSOVER

The day before Passover may fall either on a weekday or on a Sabbath, influencing the nature of the synagogue services. In either case, there are some alterations and special additions regardless of the day routine, as one might expect given the imminent approach of such a special occasion. In the case of the a weekday morning service, the psalm said in recognition of the thanksgiving offering, *Mizmor letodah* (Psalm 100), is dropped and replaced symbolically by the burning of the ḥametz.

One should finish eating ḥametz before the fifth hour of daylight; it is forbidden to even own any ḥametz after the sixth hour of daylight. The traditional method of disposal is burning, though any modern method of disposal, such as flushing down the sink or toilet, is acceptable. Following the disposal, one recites this sentence, originally in Aramaic:

> Any leavening or ḥametz that there is in my possession, whether I have seen it or whether I have not seen it, whether I have observed it or whether I have not observed it, whether I have removed it or whether I have not removed it, shall hereby be annulled and shall become ownerless like the dust of the earth.

If the day before Passover falls on a Sabbath, then the search for ḥametz must be made on Thursday. The disposal of the leaven then takes place on Friday morning. However, the proclamation should be recited on the Sabbath after the fifth hour of daylight. This is because the leaven in one's possession cannot be annulled on Friday, since Sabbath meals must be joyous and there are still two meals with bread to be eaten on the Sabbath. On Sabbath morning, though, one must finish eating ḥametz by the fourth hour of daylight.

FAST OF THE FIRSTBORN. It is a custom for all firstborn children to fast on the day before Passover (sunrise to sunset), because the Jewish firstborn sons were saved from the plague of the firstborn in Egypt. If the day before Passover falls on a Sabbath, the fast of the firstborn is observed on the preceding Thursday.

When there is a siyum, a public celebration of the completion of a major text, a ritual meal (seudat mitzvah) is made, which exempts those in attendance from the fast.

BAKING MATZOH

In the mid-1850s, in Austria-Hungary, matzoh-making machines were introduced for the first time, creating an uproar within the rabbinic establishment and forcing a careful examination of how the mechanisms of these devices might render the product unfit. Today few people make their own matzoh; matzoh made by machine according to the stringent requirements of Passover is readily available. Nevertheless, it is considered a good deed (a *mitsve* in the Yiddish sense) to bake matzoh at home after the ḥametz has been expunged, since what's missing from machine-made matzoh is *intent*, the opportunity to participate more completely in the fulfillment of a commandment. One assumes that the revival of interest in advanced home cookery will lead to a new interest in home matzoh making. What follows is an introduction to the process.

Three matzot (plural) are required for ceremonial use in the Seder, but those who cook matzoh at home usually prepare enough for the first two nights.

Men baking matzoh, Venice, 1593.

The process, which may not take more than eighteen minutes from mixing to oven, is as follows: working quickly and in a cool place in order to avoid any hint of fermentation, one prepares a batch of dough enough to make six pieces of matzoh. Flour and water are the only ingredients that may be used for the matzoh made for the Seder, which are called *leḥem oni*, "bread of poverty." Matzoh made with egg or milk, *matzah ashirah*, are not for ritual use but may be eaten the rest of the week. Before kneading the dough, one has to declare that all crumbs that fall from it are to be considered ownerless (*hefker*) so that if any fall on the floor and ferment, they will not be considered one's property. From the dough, one should take a portion as challah and recite the blessing, "Blessed are You, Lord our God, king

of the universe, who com-
mands us to separate challah." One then forms the
challah into a small ball and
throws it into the the oven
before the matzoh is baked,
making sure that the challah
burns so that we derive no
benefit from it. (Commer-

cially made Passover matzoh always carries the slogan on the
box "Challah is taken," meaning that they have done this for
you.) Working with a rolling pin that is free of ridges (to
inhibit dough from lodging and becoming ḥametz), one
takes an egg-sized piece of dough and rolls it out into a flat
round. A pricking wheel is used to make the familiar striated
pattern, used to inhibit rising. The dough is to be handled as
little as possible, to ensure that one's body heat does not
induce fermentation. If the dough is left unattended for more
than a quarter of an hour, it is considered ḥametz and must
be burnt. If the matzoh has been formed but cannot go into
the oven yet, it must be broken up, cooled down, and formed
again to make sure that it does not become leavened. After
the matzoh is baked it should be put into a special matzoh
container or on a wood surface.

Baking matzoh, Venice, 1601. Note the prominence of women and the production-line technique.

For challah, see p. 57.

There is a custom among pious Ashkenazic Jews to place
in the oven or use as fuel a bouquet (the *lulav*) of the Four
Species: the willow, myrtle, and palm branches, which are
part of the Sukkot observance.

See p. 276 for the Four Species. The etrog *(citron) is not burned.*

ERUV AND ERUV TAVSHILIN

The word *eruv* means "mixing" and it refers to a rabbinic legal
device to ease restrictions on the mixing of domains—private

Since this is the first monthly chapter, it covers the subject of eruvin for the entire book and follows the organization of the 1593 Minhogim-bukh.

and public spaces and time—that are prohibited by the Torah. It is forbidden on a festival such as Passover to prepare food for another day, even though one may prepare food for consumption the same day. This creates a problem when the day before the Sabbath is a festival day. To alleviate it, the sages instituted the *eruv tavshilin*, the "mixing of boundaries," which allows one to "mix" the cooking for the two days of the festival. This is accomplished by taking a piece of challah or matzoh and a cooked food, such as meat or egg or fish, and setting them aside for the Sabbath, followed by a blessing on the commandment of *eruv* and a declaration:

> Through this *eruv* we shall be permitted to bake, to cook, to insulate, to kindle a flame, to prepare, and to do anything necessary on the festival for the sake of the Sabbath, for ourselves, and for all Jews who live in this city.

It is also forbidden on the Sabbath to carry anything between a public and private domain or for four cubits (a cubit is about eighteen inches) in a public domain. Since there is no restriction on carrying between private domains, the *eruv ḥatzerot*, the "mixing of courtyards," was instituted to declare the space between private domains as commonly owned private space, such as among condominiums in a neighborhood. This is accomplished by collecting some bread or matzoh (or flour) from each of the families and placing it in the home of one of them to symbolize that all who have contributed are residents of that space. This enables strictly observant Jews to share meals on special days. More important, it enables observant families to use necessary items, such as baby strollers, wheelchairs, and walking sticks, within a carefully demarcated zone, thus enabling entire families to socialize and attend synagogue.

On Sabbaths and festivals, it is forbidden to go more than 2,000 cubits from the halakhically defined city limits. (Exodus 16:29: "Let no man go out of his place on the Sabbath.") To alleviate this somewhat, there is the *eruv tehumin*, the "mixing of boundaries," in which by placing enough food for two meals somewhere beyond one's home, but within the 2,000-cubit limit, one may extend that limit by another 2,000 cubits. It should be noted that these restrictions apply only to movement on the day itself, not before it.

PASSOVER

The First Night of Passover

On the day before Passover, the afternoon service is the same as usual, but the evening service that follows is a festival service with a specific liturgical order. Before the Amidah, the congregation recites the verse, "Thus Moses declared to the people of Israel the appointed festivals of the Lord." The fourth benediction of the Amidah includes the words, "this holiday of matzot, the time of our freedom."

See p. 48 for weekday afternoon and evening services.

"Thus Moses declared," Leviticus 23:44. This is also said on the other two pilgrimage festivals, Shavuot and Sukkot.

On years when it is also a Sabbath eve, the service follows the festival pattern, with additions recognizing the Sabbath. However, Kabbalat Shabbat, the series of prayers that welcomes in the Sabbath, is omitted until *Mizmor shir*, Psalms 92 and 93. *Magen avot*, "Shield of Our Fathers," is not said in most congregations, the rationale being that there are no evil spirits to be shielded from on Passover. *Bameh madlikin*, the instructions for candlelighting, is not read on festivals. It is customary that kiddush is not said in the synagogue since the Passover Seder includes four cups of wine that must be sanctified.

See p. 59 for Sabbath evening service.

The Hebrew word for festival is yom tov, *literally, "good day," which in Yiddish becomes* yontef.

On the eve of Passover one must light two candles, as on Sabbath, though without the ritual of covering the light. The blessing ends with *lehadlik ner shel yom tov*, "who commands us to light the festival candles." Unless it is Sabbath, the blessing precedes the lighting.

The Seder

The Seder is the ritual commemoration of the Passover and of God's deliverance of the Israelites from bondage—events of awe and miracle that are the core of Jewish identity and the nexus of the Hebrew Bible. Its narrative, taken from Exodus, tells the story of the origin of the people of Israel as a religious and political entity, linking inextricably the two aspects.

The Seder evolved over time, but its central components and the commandment for their commemoration were there from the beginning. In a sense, the first Seder occurred in real time, already commemorated while the events unfolded. The commandment to commemorate the Passover and the deliverance from Egypt appears extensively in chapters 12 and 13 of Exodus and later in Numbers and Deuteronomy. Here are some excerpts:

Exodus 12:14–15

This day shall be to you one of remembrance: you shall celebrate it as a pilgrimage festival to the Lord throughout your generations; you shall celebrate it as an institution for all time. For seven days you shall eat matzot; on the very first day you shall remove leaven from your houses, for whoever eats what is fermented from the first day to the seventh day shall be cut off from Israel.

Exodus 12:17–18

You shall observe the festival of matzot, for on this very day I brought your ranks out of the land of Egypt. . . . In the first month, from the fourteenth day of the month at evening, you shall eat matzoh until the twenty-first day of the month at evening.

And you shall observe this as law to you and your children forever. . . . And it shall come to pass, when your children shall say unto you: "What does this service mean to you?" that you shall say: "It is the Passover sacrifice of the Lord, for He passed over the houses of the Children of Israel in Egypt when He smote the Egyptians and delivered our houses."

Exodus 12:24–27

Note that the teaching of Passover to one's children is itself a commandment. The point has been well made: many Jews who observe nothing else of the Jewish year observe this. Such is the power of the story.

The Seder is specifically a home ceremony that takes place around a sumptuously set table; the participants are instructed to sit in a relaxed manner. The word *seder* means "order," and, indeed, every aspect of this most essential of commemorations is ordered. In Israel, the Seder is held on the first night of Passover; in the Diaspora, it is held on both the first and second nights. The ceremony is conducted by a leader (who by custom wears a white burial shroud), though with the participation of everyone present. It begins after dark, after the evening service has been completed. There is a particular affect to the event and to the posture of the participants, which is summed up nicely in the *Minhogim-bukh*:

The custom of the burial shroud has no single or simple explanation.

> The table has to be set nicely, all should indicate wealth. Whereas at most times one does not show off wealth and power, in remembrance of the destruction of the Temple, on the first two nights of Passover everyone should think he is an important lord or prince, as if he himself were a slave and weres let free. Therefore, we read the haggadah as if we were princes.

There are six ritual objects connected with the ceremony:

HAGGADAH: Serving as guide to the fourteen sections of the ritual is a special book, the haggadah, which means "the telling" or "narrative."

SEDER PLATE: A special Seder plate has on it the food items used in the ceremony. There are different customs for the arrangement of the plate, but the most common is:

> *Zeroa* (one o'clock position). This broiled shankbone represents the sacrificial lamb of the Passover sacrifice.
>
> *Ḥaroset* (four o'clock position). This mixture, made usually from fruits, nuts, and wine, symbolizes the clay and straw of the brickworks in which the enslaved Israelites worked.
>
> *Karpas* (eight o'clock position). A vegetable is the symbol of springtime and renewal, evoking the rebirth of the Jewish people at the Exodus. It is eaten dipped in saltwater or vinegar.
>
> At the six o'clock position is placed horseradish or another sharp herb, which has the same significance as the *maror* at the center.
>
> *Betzah* (eleven o'clock position). A roasted, hard-boiled egg is the symbol of the Passover sacrifice that was brought personally to the Temple. It is a reminder that Passover, along with Shavuot and Sukkot, is a pilgrimage festival.
>
> *Maror* (center). A bitter herb symbolizes the toil and bitter oppression suffered by the Israelites in Egypt.
>
> A bowl of saltwater representing the tears shed by the suffering Israelites is placed next to the Seder plate.

MATZOT: Three matzot are set upon each other on a plate, covered as for Sabbath. Two take the place of the loaves of challah used on Sabbaths and other festivals; the third is part of the Seder ritual. It is also said that the three matzot represent the three Jewish castes: kohen, levite, and Israelite.

For more about the castes, see p. 82.

WINE: Wineglasses are set in front of each adult. These are filled four times in the course of the Seder and represent the four terms of redemption described in Exodus 6:6–7: "I will bring you out. . . . I will rescue you. . . . I will redeem you. . . . I will take you."

ELIJAH'S CUP: There was a dispute among the sages as to whether there was a fifth term of redemption and since tradition holds that all disputes will one day be settled by Elijah, a fifth glass is filled in his honor. Elijah is the harbinger of all good things and will announce the coming of the Messiah. At a certain point in the Seder, the door is opened to let him in.

AFIKOMEN: The afikomen is part of the the third piece of matzoh referred to earlier. A piece of it is hidden at the beginning of the Seder, which at the end of the meal is distributed to all the participants. It symbolizes the Israelites' last meal before the Exodus—matzoh and the sacrificial lamb.

THE SEDER PROCEEDS AS FOLLOWS:

KADESH. The sanctification of the wine. Everyone picks up his or her glass of wine, and the Seder leader says the festival kiddush, starting with the blessing of the wine.

Blessed are You, Lord our God, king of the universe, who creates the fruit of the vine.

Blessed are You, Lord our God, king of the universe, who has chosen us from among all people, and raised us above all tongues, and made us holy through His commandments. And You, Lord our God, have given us in love festivals for happiness, feasts and festive seasons for rejoicing—the day of this festival of matzot and this festival of holy convocation, the season of our freedom, a holy convocation, commemorating the departure from Egypt. For You have chosen us and sanctified us from all the nations, and You have given us as a heritage Your holy festival, in happiness

Many stand to say the kiddush, but sit to drink the wine.

and joy. Blessed are You, Lord our God, who sanctifies Israel and the festive seasons.

This paragraph is the Sheheheyanu.

Blessed are You, Lord our God, king of the universe, who has granted us life, sustained us, and enabled us to reach this occasion.

Then everyone should recline toward the left and drink at least as much as would fit into the shell of an egg.

Hunting the Hare, from the Prague Haggadah, 1526.

See p. 85 for Havdalah.

If the first night of Passover falls on Saturday night, as it does in our model year, the order of blessings is: wine, kiddush (sanctification), candles, Havdalah, and the blessing of the time (that is, the day of this festival). The Hebrew acronym YaKNeHaZ was long used as a mnemonic. In Yiddish it sounds like the words for "hunting the hare" and is sometimes portrayed in old haggadot with a woodcut of a hare hunting scene. When it is also Sabbath, one starts the kiddush with the paragraph that begins, "And there was evening, there was morning, the sixth day."

URHATZ. Then the participants wash their hands but do not recite the blessing.

KARPAS. The word *karpas* is an anagram of *perekh samekh*, which means "600,000," the number of enslaved Israelites. The leader of the Seder picks up a piece of a vegetable, dips it in the saltwater, and recites the following blessing: "Blessed are You, Lord our God, king of the universe, who brings forth the fruits of the earth." The leader asks each participant to take a piece of the vegetable and dip it into the saltwater. The joy of rebirth tempered by tears is today the most familiar explanation. The *Minhogimbukh* gives two other explanations for the custom of dipping in vinegar: to arouse the

The Romans had a custom of dipping the first course of a meal. It is likely that this was the origin of the Passover custom.

curiosity of the children and to make us joyous by the time the matzoh is eaten, since vinegar has this effect.

YAHATZ. This "dividing" of the matzoh recalls, too, the dividing of the Red Sea. The middle piece of matzoh is taken and broken into two pieces. The smaller piece is put back between the other two pieces; the larger one is wrapped in a napkin and set aside as the afikomen, from a Greek word for "dessert." There is an old—and still popular—custom in which the afikomen is hidden somewhere in the house. After the meal, the children are sent to search for it, and the one who finds it gets a reward.

The sweet balsamic vinegar of Modena is said to have originated as a Jewish remedy in the fourteenth century.

MAGGID. The retelling of the story. First, the matzoh is lifted and *Ha lahma anyah* is recited from the haggadah.

> This is the bread of affliction, the poor bread our ancestors ate as slaves in the land of Egypt. Let all who are hungry come and eat. Let all who are needy share the hope of this Passover celebration. This year we are here; next year may we be in Jerusalem. This year we are still in bonds. Next year may we all be free.

The matzoh plate is put aside and the glasses are refilled with wine. Since one of the key Passover commandments is to teach children, the story of the Passover and the Exodus are not simply recited, but are rather posed in the answers to a series of "Four Questions" that are read by the children in attendance:

Where many children are in attendance, it is the usual custom to ask the youngest ones to read the questions. Where none are present, any adult may read them.

> Why is this night different from all other nights?
> On all nights we eat hametz or matzoh,
> but on this night we eat only matzoh.
> On all nights we eat whatever vegetables we wish,
> though on this night we must eat *maror*!
> On all nights we need not dip our food even once,
> yet on this night we do so twice.

On all nights we eat sitting upright or reclining,
but on this night we all recline!

The matzoh plate is placed on the table again and partly uncovered. The Seder leader begins the answer thus:

> We were slaves to Pharaoh in Egypt, and the Lord our God, took us out from there with a strong hand and with an outstretched arm. If the Holy One, blessed be He, had not taken our fathers out of Egypt, then we, our children, and our children's children would have remained enslaved to Pharaoh in Egypt. Even if all of us were wise, all of us understanding, all of us knowing the Torah, we would still be obligated to discuss the Exodus from Egypt; and everyone who discusses the Exodus from Egypt at length is praiseworthy. . . . Such an instance is that of the sages who in Roman times discussed the going out from Egypt all through the night.

The instruction to teach the story to children occurs four times in the Torah. From this comes the haggadah parable of the Four Children: one wise, one scornful, one simple, and one who does not know how to ask. The children represent four aspects of humankind; the responses change the narrative from chronicle to first-person experience: "It is because of that which the Lord did for *me* when *I* left Egypt."

> What does the wise child say? "What are the precepts, the statutes, and the laws that the Lord our God, has commanded you?" In response, we should explain thoroughly all the laws and customs of Passover, all the way through, "after the Passover lamb, there is no dessert."
>
> What does the scornful one say? "What is this service to you?!" Notice how the question is directed away from himself. By so doing he excludes himself from the community, denying that which is fundamental. To this child we respond sharply: "It is because of that which the Lord did

for me when I left Egypt; had you been there, you would not
have been redeemed!"

What does the simple child say? "What is this?" You
answer simply, "With a mighty arm the Lord took us out of
Egypt, from the house of slavery."

For the one who does not know how to ask, one must ini-
tiate the story: "You shall tell your child on that day, 'It is
because of that which the Lord did for me when I left
Egypt.' . . ."

The narration continues with a history of the Jewish people
from Abraham and his forebears to their slavery in Egypt.
This is told by means of connecting Torah passages with rabbinical narrative phrases and elaborations. In this way the
story of the Exodus is linked with the patriarchs Abraham
and Jacob:

> In the beginning our ancestors were idolators; but now have
> brought us close to God's service. "Joshua said to all the   *Joshua 24:2–4*
> people: Thus said the Lord, the God of Israel, 'Your fathers
> once lived on the other side of the Euphrates . . . and there
> served other gods.'
>
> "'And I took your father Abraham from beyond the river,
> and I led him throughout the whole land of Canaan. I
> increased his seed and gave him Isaac, and to Isaac I gave
> Jacob and Esau. To Esau I gave Mount Seir, while Jacob and
> his sons went down to Egypt.'"

And it was preordained:

> "And He said to Abraham, 'You shall know that your seed   *Genesis 15:13–14.*
> will be sojourners in a land that is not theirs, where they will
> be enslaved and made to suffer for four hundred years. But
> I shall also judge the nation whom they shall serve, and after
> that they will come out with great property.'"

The wine cup is now raised and the matzoh is covered. The
Seder leader continues:

> This is what has stood by our fathers and us! For not just
> one alone has risen up to destroy us, but in every generation
> they rise against us to destroy us; and the Holy One, blessed
> be He, saves us from their hand!

The wine cup is put down—without a drink taken—and the matzoh is uncovered. The story and its explication continue with Laban's plot against Jacob, the flight into Egypt, how Joseph gained favor with Pharaoh, and how the group so few in number (about seventy people) became a great nation within Egypt; how the tide turned after the death of Joseph and Pharaoh; how the Egyptians under a new Pharaoh made them suffer; and how God took notice of their plight and remembered his covenant.

The next paragraphs describe God's punishments of the Egyptians, and at two points in the reading, the Seder leader spills wine into a vessel, traditionally a broken or chipped bowl. Three spills of wine are made at the words "blood, fire, and pillars of smoke," a quotation from the prophet Joel (2:30). Ten spills are made during the recitation of the Ten Plagues, once after each plague: blood, frogs, lice, wild beasts, pestilence, boils, hail, locusts, darkness, and the slaying of the firstborn. This ritual has its roots in the Kabbalah: the cup symbolizes *malkhut* ("kingdom"), an aspect of anger and indignation; the broken bowl is the symbol of *kelipah*, a shell of evil that surrounds the sparks of divine light. It could be explained as the expiation of anger, of leaving the urge for revenge in God's hands while at the same time bearing the knowledge that with remembrance comes redemption.

Here follows *Dayenu*, a well-known hymn of thanksgiving. It means "it would have sufficed," which is the refrain of each of its fourteen verses.

> How many gifts has God bestowed upon us!
> If He had brought us out from Egypt, and had not carried

out judgments against them, [*dayenu*] it would have
sufficed! . . .
If He had given us the Torah, and had not brought us into
the land of Israel, it would have sufficed!
If He had brought us into the land of Israel, and had not
built for us the Temple, it would have sufficed!

And then, this summary paragraph:

How many are the reasons for our gratitude to God for the
many favors He has bestowed upon us. He has brought us
out of Egypt and carried out judgments against them, and
against their idols, and smote their firstborn, and gave us
their wealth, and split the sea for us and took us through it
onto dry land, and drowned our oppressors, and supplied
our needs in the desert for forty years, and fed us the manna,
and gave us the Sabbath, and brought us before Mount
Sinai, and gave us the Torah, and brought us into the land of
Israel, and built for us the Temple to atone for all our sins.

The Seder leader reads and participants respond:

Rabban Gamliel used to say: "Whoever does not discuss the
meaning of the following three things on Passover has not
fulfilled his duty, namely: *pesah* (paschal lamb), matzoh,
and *maror* (the bitter herb)."

What is the meaning of the paschal lamb that our fathers
ate during the time of the Temple? Why did they do so?

They ate the *pesah* lamb as a remembrance of how God
passed over (*pasah*) our fathers' houses in Egypt, and how
He had commanded us to offer him the lamb: "Then say: It
is the sacrifice meal of Passover to the Lord, who passed
over the houses of the Children of Israel in Egypt, when He
dealt the blow to Egypt but rescued our houses."

What is the meaning of this matzoh? [*At this phrase, the
leader takes a piece of matzoh in hand or points to it.*]

The matzoh is meant to recall how our people had fled
quickly and "they baked the dough that they had brought

These verses of
Dayenu *are the
traditional ones
from the eleventh
century C.E. Vari-
ants have been
written over the
centuries, the most
extraordinary
being a catalog of
catastrophes writ-
ten by survivors of
the Holocaust for
their first Passover
after liberation in
1946. See* A Sur-
vivors' Haggadah,
*by Saul Touster
(Philadelphia:
Jewish Publication
Society, 2000).*

Mishnah Pesaḥim
*10:5. "Rabban" is
the word for "great
rabbi."*

Exodus 12:27

Exodus 12:39 out of Egypt in matzoh cakes, for it had not fermented, for they had been driven out of Egypt and were not able to linger, neither had they made provision for themselves." And today we fulfill the commandment: "For seven days shall you eat matzoh, that you may remember your departure from Egypt as long as you live."

What is the meaning of the *maror*? [*At this phrase, the leader takes a piece of the bitter herb in hand.*]

Because the Egyptians embittered our fathers' lives in *Exodus 1:13–14* Egypt, as it is said: "They embittered their lives with hard servitude in mortar and bricks and with all kinds of servitude in the field—all their service in which they made them subservient with crushing labor."

And then, the essence of the Passover experience:

In every generation each of us should feel as though we ourselves had gone forth from Egypt, as it is written: "And you are to tell your child on that day, saying: It is because of what the Lord did for me, when I went out of Egypt."

While this ends the magid, some people choose to continue the readings with Torah passages that emphasize the remembrance of the experience of slavery, how strangers, orphans, and widows may not be oppressed nor their rights curtailed.

See p. 21 for the blessing and ritual washing of hands.

The wine cups are raised for the hymn "Therefore, let us rejoice at the wonder of our deliverance" and set down at the final word: "hallelujah." Then Hallel begins with Psalms 113 and 114. The wineglasses are lifted again, and this time the blessing is said, after which everyone drinks from this second glass—the Cup of Redemption. This ends the telling of the Passover story.

ROHTZAH. Everyone must now participate in the ritual washing of hands and the blessing *Al netilat yadayim*.

MOTZI MATZOH. The Seder leader takes the two whole matzot in hand and recites the blessing over bread and the blessing for eating matzoh. Before all may eat, the broken middle matzoh is taken and put on top of the top matzoh and this is blessed. Then a piece of the broken matzoh and a piece of the top matzoh are eaten together while we recline to the left. This is done because on a holiday, the blessing has to be recited over two pieces of bread, just as on the Sabbath. But on Passover, there is another reason for taking a broken piece: because matzoh is called *lehem oni*, "the bread of afflic- *Deuteronomy 16:3* tion," and the poor have only broken pieces of bread.

MAROR. Everyone takes a piece of the *maror* at least as big as an olive and dips it into the *haroset* and recites a blessing over the *maror*. Thus food is dipped a second time. "Blessed are you Lord our God, king of the universe, who hallows our lives through commandments and commands us to eat *maror*."

KOREKH. In this "binding together," the bottom matzoh is *Customs vary on* taken, some of the bitter herb dipped in *haroset* is put on it, *reclining for the* and it is eaten like a sandwich, without reclining. This is done *eating of the* in memory of the sage Hillel and with this recitation: *korekh.*

> Thus did Hillel do at the time of the Temple: He would combine the paschal lamb with matzoh and *maror* and eat them together, because it is written: "They shall eat it with matzoh and bitter herbs." *Numbers 9:11*

The modern interpretation of *korekh* is that it is a symbol of continuity with past tradition.

SHULHAN OREKH. At this point comes the "set table," the Passover meal that one should eat and drink well. The cooking traditions vary greatly from region to region, as a glance at any one of the many available Passover and holiday cookbooks will confirm. As for the specific proscriptions, the *Minhogimbukh* mentions these:

> One should not eat anything broiled on the two Seder nights, so as not to seem as if we prepared a sacrifice in the

Cracow rabbi
Moses Isserles was
the principal
sixteenth-century
codifier of
Ashkenazic law.
See p. xviii.

Diaspora. However, in his *Book of Customs*, Rabbi Isaac Tyrnau writes that in Israel it is customary to eat broiled food. In his annotations, our teacher and rabbi, Rabbi Moses Isserles, may his memory be blessed, writes that we should eat a hard-boiled egg in memory of the destruction of the Temple and mourning that we cannot bring the Passover sacrifice. But our custom is to eat the hard-boiled egg dipped in the vinegar [saltwater in most places] at the end of the meal in order not to forget the afikomen, which is hidden under the pillow and still must be eaten.

TZAFUN. "The hidden." Toward the end of the meal, the children are sent to find the afikomen, the symbol of the Passover sacrifice, which had been hidden earlier. Neither the meal nor the Seder may be concluded until after the afikomen is found and consumed—whence the tradition of rewarding its finder. It must be eaten before midnight, also while reclining to the left. After the afikomen is eaten, it is forbidden to eat anything else, so its taste can linger in the mouth.

For Grace after
Meals, see p. 45.

BAREKH. Then wineglasses are filled for the third time and the Grace after Meals is recited. It is customary to ensure that there will be the required number of people (three or more) on both Seder nights to do *zimun*, the Call to Grace, before the Grace after Meals and for the recitation of the responsory Hallel that follows it. As on all festivals and Sabbath, a special paragraph is added to the Grace after Meals. At the conclusion of the grace, the third cup of wine—the Cup of Blessing—is blessed and drunk.

HALLEL. Before the psalms in praise of God are recited, a child is sent to open the door. Holding up their wineglasses, all recite *Shefokh ḥamatkha*: "Pour out Your wrath upon the nations that do not know You," a plea for divine justice against persecutors. It is explained to the children that the door has been opened for Elijah the Prophet, who will announce our redemption before a Messiah comes. A glass of wine is poured for the prophet, and the children gather around his cup to see if he drinks from it. In addition to the glass of wine, it is a common custom to leave an empty chair and place setting for him. The song *Eliyahu hanavi* ("Elijah the Prophet") is sung:

The song Eliyahu hanavi *is also part of the Havdalah ceremony; see p. 88.*

> May the Merciful One send us Elijah the Prophet, so that he may be remembered for good and that he may bring us good tidings, salvation, and consolation.

Then the fourth glass of wine is poured. Psalms 115–118 continue the Hallel begun earlier. Psalm 136, known as the "Great Hallel," is added to the set. Hallel is recited on festival days as part of the liturgy, and it is also an important part of the Seder. While many groups customarily recite only excerpts of these psalms in song settings, others recite the entirety, which is the traditional way. These are psalms not only of praise, but also of thanksgiving. Given the centrality of the Exodus in the Jews' relationship with God, it is not surprising to find mention of it among the verses. Here are a few excerpts:

> Hallelujah! Sing praises, you servants of the Lord, praise His name . . . from sunrise to sunset. He raises the poor from the dust, He lifts the wretched from the dirt. . . .
>
> How can I repay the Lord for all His gifts? I will lift up the cup of deliverance and glorify the Lord by name. I will offer the tribute of Thanksgiving. . . . In distress I called upon the Lord; in answer He set me free. . . .

Psalm 136 is itself a retelling of the Passover story—with verses of thanksgiving and a bouncy refrain:

Give thanks to the Lord, for He is good. . . .
His love endures forever.

The body of water widely known as the Red Sea was actually the "Reed Sea" or "Sea of Reeds."

To Him who divided the Red Sea asunder
His love endures forever.
And brought Israel through the midst of it
His love endures forever.
But swept Pharaoh and his army into the Red Sea.
His love endures forever.

See p. 72 for Nishmat kol ḥai.

The Hallel psalms are followed by *Nishmat kol ḥai,* which is the blessing concluding the *Pesukei dezimra* in the Sabbath morning service. It continues the praise of God as an act of thanksgiving.

NIRTZAH. The Seder is "accepted." The fourth glass of wine is taken up, and the blessing is recited over it. One should drink it reclining to the left. Then an "afterblessing" over wine is said, since it was not included in the Grace after Meals. After the four glasses it is forbidden to drink any more wine.

And finally, the Seder concludes with songs, many intended for children, both as entertainment and education. *Adir hu* ("Mighty is God") is a series of epithets of praise with a chorus urging the rebuilding of the Temple.

Supreme is God, Great is God, Outstanding is God,
Glorious is God, Faithful is God. . . .
May God rebuild the Temple soon,
Speedily in our time, soon.
Build, God! Build, God!
Build Your house soon!

One of the best known is the "cumulative" song *Ḥad gadya,* "An only kid." Its origin is in the twelfth or thirteenth century C.E. and it is often explained as an allegory for God's repeated salvation of the Jewish people from a long line of conquerors.

An only kid, an only kid, my father bought for two zuzim.
Then came the cat that ate the kid.
   An only kid, an only kid, my father bought for two zuzim.
Then came the dog that bit the cat that ate the kid.
   An only kid, an only kid, my father bought for two zuzim.
[last verse] Then came the Holy One, blessed be He, and
   destroyed the angel of death that slew the butcher
   that killed the ox that drank the water that quenched
   the fire that burned the stick that beat the dog that bit
   the cat that ate the kid.
   An only kid, an only kid, my father bought for two zuzim.

It is a common custom to end this "different night" with
the singing of "Next Year in Jerusalem."

The First Day of Passover

MORNING SERVICE. The service for the first day of Passover
generally follows the weekday pattern, with some additions

See the chapter "The Days of the Week."

and special Torah readings. However, there are only seven
benedictions in the Amidah. It is the custom of many synagogues to add, before the recitation of the Amidah on the
first and second days of Passover, one of the hymns called
Berah dodi, "Flee, my beloved," which contain paraphrases of
the last verse of the Song of Songs, an allegory of flight and
renewal. Also particular to this day, the full Hallel is recited
before the Torah reading.

Two Torah scrolls are taken out and five people are called
up. From the first scroll are read the verses Exodus 12:21–51
(from the portion called *Bo*), which begin with the marking

For Bo, see p. 334

of the doorposts with the blood of the paschal lamb (it's actually either a goat or a lamb); then the decisive tenth plague—
God's destruction of the firstborn of Egypt; Pharaoh's ordering out all the Israelites and their property; the beginning of
the Exodus exactly 430 years after the Israelites first came

into Egypt; and the commandment that all who participate
in the Passover meal must be circumcised.

The first scroll is held up and shown, rolled up, bound, and

See p. 40 for hag-
bahah and gelilah.
dressed—the *hagbahah* and *gelilah*. Then the second scroll is
put on the table, next to the first one, and half Kaddish is
recited. The maftir is called up to the second scroll to read

Numbers 28:19–25
is from the portion
called Pinḥas; *see*
p. 179.
Numbers 28:19–25, which declares Passover a pilgrimage festival and describes the particulars of the sacrifice. *Hagbahah*
and *gelilah* follow the reading of the second scroll. The haftarah is from the book of Joshua (5:2–6:1) and tells how after
the crossing of the Jordan, God commanded Joshua to circumcise all the men, since those who were born in the Wilderness had not been circumcised. When this was complete,
it would be time for the first observance of Passover in the
Promised Land. Matzoh would be made from grain for the
first time since the Exodus; manna would not be eaten again.

When the first day of Passover is a Sabbath, the appropri-
For Sabbath
Shema blessings,
see p. 74.
ate passages are inserted into the Shema blessing, with additional phrases in recognition of the holiday. Seven people are
called up to the first Torah scroll, and the portion—the same
for Passover whether it is a weekday or Sabbath—is divided
into seven parts. The haftarah is also the same.

For a general view
of the musaf ser-
vice, see p. 78.
MUSAF SERVICE. The musaf service on the first day of Passover is considerably more elaborate than its counterparts on
Sabbath or Rosh Ḥodesh, though they are based on the same
framework. On Passover, the offering brought to the Temple
was quite elaborate; its description in the Torah is inserted
into the middle of the Amidah, along with the commandment
for the eating of matzoh and recitation of special verses for
the *Kedushat hayom,* the "sanctification of the day." In a similar vein, the cantor's repetition of the Amidah includes a

longish and sweet hymn for dew, known by its Hebrew name, *Tal*. Its counterpart is the prayer for rain, *Geshem*, which is said on Shemini Atzeret, the festival that occurs at the end of Sukkot and brings closure to the period that began with Rosh Hashanah. Similarly, at this service one ceases to mention rain in the *Gevurot* of the Amidah. *Tal* is said to have originated in the story of Isaac and Esau (Genesis 27), though it also makes reference to both the freedom from Egyptian bondage and to the rebuilding of Jerusalem after the Babylonian captivity:

For Geshem, see p. 291.

In Israel and in most Sephardic rites, one makes the seasonal substitution of dew for rain in the Gevurot.

> Dew—decree for a year that is good and crowned
> With fruit of the earth becoming its pride and splendor.
> The city that is like a hut left standing alone,
> Place it in Your hand as a crown   with dew.

> Dew—let it sweeten the honey of the mountains;
> And may the chosen ones savor Your bounty.
> Release Your favored ones from bondage,
> And melodies will we sweetly sing with
>   raised voices and—with dew.

THE PRIESTLY BLESSING. The cantor's repetition of the Amidah also includes the *Birkat kohanim*, the Priestly Blessing. This ritualized blessing is said every day in Jerusalem and every Sabbath elsewhere in Israel, but in the Diaspora it is the usual custom to say it only during the musaf service of festivals, Rosh Hashanah, Yom Kippur, and in the afternoon service of fast days. Though the blessing itself is only fifteen words long, the ritual is one of the grand gestures of Jewish liturgy: The "priests" in the congregation (that is, all those born into the priestly caste—the kohanim) remove their shoes and gather at the back of the synagogue, where their hands are ritually washed by those of the levite caste. The kohanim then assemble on the raised platform in front of the ark (the

The Minhogim-bukh *says that in some congregations the Priestly Blessing is performed also when the festival coincides with Sabbath.*

Hands positioned for the Priestly Blessing are shown here in a woodcut from Prague rabbi Shabbetai Sheftel Horowitz's 1612 Kabbalistic book Shefa tal (Abundance of Dew). Any similarity shown by Mr. Spock was purely intentional.

dukhan), with their backs toward the congregation. They cover their heads with their tallitot (prayer shawls) and, after their summons by the cantor, chant the benediction, "Who has hallowed us with the holiness of Aaron and commanded us to bless His people Israel with love." The congregation responds, "Amen." On the last word, "with love," the kohanim turn to face the congregation and make the two-handed gesture, variously explained as a symbol of a heart pouring forth and as the letter shin, ‫ש‬, which stands for *Shaddai*, "Almighty God." They then recite the verses from Numbers (6:24–26) that constitute the blessing. The congregants avert their eyes, since it is said that the shekhinah, the divine presence, is upon the hands of the kohanim:

> May the Lord bless you and safeguard you.
> May the Lord illuminate His countenance upon you
>   and be gracious to you.
> May the Lord show kindness toward you
>   and grant you peace.

After the word "peace" (*shalom*) the congregation and cantor say, "Amen." This is followed by the cantor's recitation of *Yehi ratzon*, "May it be Your will." The Ashkenazic liturgical custom of the Priestly Blessing is highly elaborate: the verses are not recited straight through but rather one word at a time, and between each one the congregation chants elaborate riffs of biblical verses. This is an extraordinary style of liturgy, similar in both aesthetic and intent to J. S. Bach's chorale preludes or elaborate jazz renditions of famous tunes—each note or word the opportunity to explore the universe.

General Laws of Festivals

It is at this point in the *Minhogimbukh* that the general laws of festivals are explained. It's a logical placement, since the customs of Sabbath and Rosh Ḥodesh have been covered already and we are now up to the second day of Passover, which in the Diaspora shares equal status with the first. Some of the intricacies of the Jewish calendar and the reason that most major festivals are observed for two days may be found beginning on page 16 in the chapter "Fundamentals of Prayer."

WORK AND COOKING ON A FESTIVAL DAY. In general, there is no difference between the Sabbath and a festival in terms of what work may be done. Whatever is forbidden on a Sabbath is forbidden on a festival, too. An exception, however, is the preparation of food, which is permitted so long as the food is to be consumed on the same festival day. This includes all the chores related to cooking. Things that can be done before the festival should not be left for the festival, though if preparing a dish before a festival would render it inferior, then it is considered preferable to wait for the festival day to prepare it.

If one stuffs a chicken on a festival, it is permitted to stitch it closed, but one should thread the needle before the festival.

One may grind matzoh on a festival, but it is forbidden to put it through a colander to separate the big from the small.

One should not wash the lunch dishes after eating in order to use them in the evening. However, it is permitted to cook for the next day, so long as some will be eaten that day, too.

ENERGY USE. On a festival, a Jew is permitted to heat water to bathe a small child, but an adult Jew should not bathe in warm water unless it was warmed by a non-Jew—this is the halakhah as quoted in the *Minhogimbukh*. Today, warming water does not involve making a fire, and opinions differ about the use of electric, gas, and solar-powered hot water heaters, as they do about the use of continuous current electricity and dimmers.

INTERACTIONS WITH GENTILES. The customs described in the *Minhogimbukh* with regard to interactions with gentiles at the time of festivals reflect the complexity of intergroup relations both then and now, albeit with a different focus. The Torah teaches both universal justice and the potential dangers of intermingling. Talmudic and later law take up matters more specifically, differentiating between a *ger toshav*, a "resident alien," who believes in and lives by the seven Noahide Laws, and an *akum*, a pagan (an acronym for a "worshiper of stars and planets"). The Noahide Laws are those revealed to Noah, the common ancestor of Jews, Christians, and Muslims, and represent their shared belief. They are: belief in one God; no blasphemy (including false witness); no idolatry; no forbidden sexual practices; no murder; no theft; and no eating of flesh cut from a living animal.

For Noahide Laws, see also p. 2.

This sense of common ground is expressed in the *Minhogimbukh*, but not without a degree of caution and suspicion for potential misunderstanding and violation:

In many circles today, it has become a custom to welcome gentiles to the Seder. Multi-faith Seders are held in many cities, often in recognition of other groups who have suffered under slavery and oppression.

One should not invite a gentile for a festival, because there is the possibility that one might do more work for his sake than is permissible. However, if a gentile comes into the home of a Jew, he may be invited to join the table and eat. On a Sabbath, when it is forbidden to cook anyway, one is allowed to invite gentiles. . . .

If a gentile brings eggs on a festival day, though not for any Jew in particular, and he says that the eggs were laid the day before, he should be trusted because it would have been in his interest to claim the eggs were fresher. Thus the eggs may be accepted.

But the greatest caution expressed is to prevent Jews from using the work of gentiles to get around the rules:

> This prohibition [against food brought from outside the Sabbath boundary] was instituted by our sages, may their memory be blessed, because if a Jew were allowed to eat it right after the holiday, he could easily tell the gentile to bring him such things, looking forward to eating them right after the holiday. But if he knows that he cannot eat them even then . . . he will not tell the gentile to do this.

Forbidden and Permitted Foods on Passover

The prohibition against ḥametz is so strict that even when the leaven constitutes just a sixtieth of the weight of the food (a general standard in kashrut), it is still not annulled. Whereas all other food prohibitions are valid throughout the year, the prohibition against ḥametz is valid on Passover only, and therefore one is commanded to be extra cautious. In the world of the *Minhogimbukh*—in fact, at any time prior to the 1920s—the mere suspicion of the possibility of encountering leaven was enough to lead to a prohibition. For example:

The factor of the sixtieth in kashrut is known as batel beshishim *and is applicable to most other dietary prohibitions. For example, if a bit of cream finds its way into a pot of beef stew but constitutes less than one-sixtieth of it, then the cream is annulled and the stew is still considered kosher.*

> Saffron is usually not used during Passover because when it loses its color, shopkeepers often put it into fermented dough so that it gets its color back. In Germany it is customary not to eat sugar on Passover because the shopkeepers often mix flour into it. This rule applies to rock candy as well because if rock candy were allowed, then one would eat the other type of sugar, too. And figs are not eaten either because of their taste. (In Italy, they do eat sugar and they eat freshly picked figs.) One should not eat honey during Passover because there is often flour in it. Even if one takes

the honey from the bees himself and knows for sure that there is no flour in it, the honey is forbidden because of the other types of honey.

Nowadays, commercial food manufacturers gladly accommodate the requirements and supervision of rabbinical authorities. Selling food with a *hekhsher*, the official label of a rabbinical organization, along with the signature of a reputable rabbi, is good business, since it is as attractive to those interested in food purity as to Jews who wish to meet the ritual requirements.

PROHIBITED FOODS: Prohibited foods include leavened bread, cakes, biscuits, crackers, cereal, coffee made with cereal derivatives, and all liquids containing ingredients or flavors made from grain alcohol. Wheat, barley, oats, spelt, and rye are all prohibited unless made into matzoh. Most traditional Ashkenazic authorities have added *kitniyot* to the forbidden list: rice, corn, millet, legumes (beans and peas, though string beans are specifically permitted). However, Orthodox rabbis in the United States have ruled that peanuts and peanut oil are permissible since peanuts are not true legumes. Some, but not all, Ashkenazic authorities permit the use of legumes in a form other than their natural state, for example, corn sweeteners, corn oil, soy oil. Sephardic authorities make no restrictions on *kitniyot*.

PERMITTED FOODS: Currently, the following foods do not require a "Kosher for Passover" label if purchased prior to Passover: unopened packages or containers of natural coffee without cereal additives, sugar, pure tea, salt, pepper, natural spices, frozen fruit juices with no additives, frozen uncooked vegetables (see the previous paragraph regarding legumes), milk, butter, most cheeses, frozen uncooked fruit without additives, baking soda, canned permissible fish without additives.

The following foods do not require a Kosher for Passover label if purchased during Passover: fresh fruits, vegetables, and eggs. Fresh fish and meat depend on a number of variables of preparation.

The following foods *do* require a Kosher for Passover label, whether purchased before or during Passover: all baked products (cakes and any products containing matzoh in any form), canned or bottled fruit juices, fish preparations, wine, vinegar, liquor, oils, dried fruits, candy, chocolate-flavored milk, ice cream, yogurt, and soda.

The following processed foods (canned, bottled, or frozen) require a Kosher for Passover label if purchased during Passover: milk, butter, juices, vegetables, fruit, milk products, spices, coffee, tea, and fish.

Further information is available from various rabbinical Web sites.

The Second Night of Passover

In the Diaspora, a Seder is to be made on the second night of Passover. The synagogue service follows the pattern for a festival eve, like the previous night's service. It is the custom to hurry home after the service on the second night because the service was started later and one still must cook, lest the afikomen be eaten after midnight.

See p. 16 for an explanation of two-day festival observances in the Diaspora.

The second-night Seder is the same as the first except that at the end, after *Nishmat*, some add the hymn *Ometz gevuro-tekha*, which begins with the refrain "And you shall say: This is the Feast of Passover." And on this night one begins the counting of the Omer.

The Counting of the Omer

The book of Leviticus deals with matters of holiness in all aspects of life and time. Beginning in the twenty-third chapter, the holy calendars are set forth and the offerings and observances for the principal holy days are described. The number seven appears repeatedly: the day of the Sabbath, the number of days of Passover and Sukkot, and the number of weeks between the Omer offering on the second day of the Passover festival and the Festival of Weeks—Shavuot (Pentecost). *Omer* means "sheaf" (of barley), and it refers to the commandment in Leviticus 23:9–16:

> The Lord spoke to Moses, saying: Speak to the Children of Israel, say to them: When you enter the land I am giving you and you reap its harvest, you shall bring the first sheaf of your harvest to the priest. He shall elevate the sheaf before the the Lord, for acceptance in your behalf; . . . it is a law for all time, into your generations. . . . You are to count for yourselves, from the day after the Sabbath, from the day that you bring the elevated sheaf, seven weeks—they must be complete . . . forty-nine days, then you are to bring an offering of new crops to the Lord [the festival of Shavuot].

Tradition has it that the count has another meaning: it was seven weeks from the time of the Exodus to the receiving of the Law. It is also a commemoration of the killing of 24,000 students of Rabbi Akiva at the time of the Bar Kokhba's rebellion against Roman rule (132–135 C.E.) and various other tragedies during the period of the Crusades.

The commandment to count the forty-nine days of the Omer is observed in the post-Temple period with a brief service that may be said at home or in the synagogue, near the end of the evening service. It begins with the blessing *Al sefirat haomer*, ". . . who has commanded us in regard to the counting of the Omer," and is followed by the enumeration of the day, for example: "Today is forty days, which are five weeks and five days of the Omer." The counting of the Omer begins on the second night of Passover, and then it is continued every night until the day before Shavuot.

For other customs and restrictions related to the Omer, see p. 153.

In synagogues and in homes, one finds special Omer counters, devices with replaceable numbers so that all will know the appropriate number to insert into the blessing. Today there are also Internet reminders.

The Second Day of Passover

The morning service of the second day of Passover is quite similar to that of the previous day. Two Torah scrolls are taken out of the ark. Five people are called up to the first, from which is read Leviticus 22:26–23:44, part of the portion called *Emor*, from which the instruction for the counting of the Omer comes. The remainder of the reading consists of instructions for offerings and observances on other major festival days: Shavuot, Rosh Hashanah, Yom Kippur, and Sukkot. The second scroll is then put on the table next to the first and half Kaddish is recited. The maftir is called up to read Numbers 28: 19–25, same as the day before. The haftarah is 2 Kings 23:1–9, 21–25, a story of the reign of Josiah, the last righteous king of Judah, who had inherited from his father a nation so corrupt that the Temple was filled with idols and the Torah was forgotten. Josiah sets out on a campaign to destroy all vestiges of idolatry, and in an effort to restore the faith, he assembles all the people of Judah and Jerusalem and reads to them the entirety of the Torah, from beginning to end. He restores the Passover observance, "as prescribed in this scroll of the covenant," for the first time since the time of Samuel four hundred years earlier.

For the full portion of Emor, see p. 159.

The musaf service is the same as the previous day, including the Priestly Blessing, without *Tal*, the prayer for dew.

Since the second evening marks the end of the first statutory festival day of Passover, a Havdalah prayer is recited, thus separating holy time from ordinary days. (In Israel they perform the ritual on the first night.) If the end of the festival coincides with the end of Sabbath, then the spices and candle are deployed as usual. If it is a weekday night, then there is no blessing of the spices or the candle, simply the prayer "He who distinguishes."

For Sabbath Hav-dalah, see p. 85.

Ḥol Hamoed: The Intermediate Days of Passover

The intermediate days of Passover are called *ḥol hamoed* and are considered semiholidays. One may work, but within strict limitations. The governing principle is that one may not work for profit but only to prevent loss. In the home, one may water plants but may not do the laundry, unless one does not have enough clothing to otherwise get through the week. Weddings are not held because it is prohibted to mingle two joyous events. One does not sit shivah or give eulogies during the intermediate days.

For mourning and shivah, see p. 391.

On Sabbaths and festivals one never puts on tefillin for prayer, but during *ḥol hamoed* it is a matter of local custom. Some Ashkenazic Jews put on tefillin but do not say the blessings; in Israel, they are not worn at all. The laws of the intermediate days are contained in a tractate of the Talmud called *Moed katan*, "minor festivals."

The prayers during *ḥol hamoed* of Passover are similar to Rosh Ḥodesh services that fall on a weekday, with a Torah reading and a musaf service. Also like Rosh Ḥodesh, the prayer *Yaaleh veyavo* is inserted in the Amidah, and after the Amidah, half Hallel is said—a small differentiation between

For Yaaleh veyavo, see p. 94.

the first and last days of Passover when full Hallel is recited. *For half Hallel, see p. 94.*
The musaf service is like the first day but, like the second,
without *Tal*, the prayer for dew.

Each day of *hol hamoed* has a specified Torah portion to be
read from the first scroll by three readers; the last *aliyah*, read
from a second scroll, is the same as on the first days: Numbers
28:19–25. The first intermediate day's portion is Exodus 13:1–
16: God's instruction to Moses to make holy by sacrifice or
redemption (that is, monetary substitution) the firstborn of *The redemption of*
every man and beast. In the case of the firstborn sons, since *firstborn sons is*
child sacrifice was forbidden, the child is redeemed by *still practiced in a*
ceremony called
money. The portion twice says that the telling of the Passover *Pidyon haben (see*
story shall "be for you a sign on your hand and for a reminder *p. 384), in which*
the child is
between your eyes." This sentence, repeated twice in *redeemed by giving*
money to a priest.
Deuteronomy (6:4–9, 11:13–21), is the basis for tefillin.

On the second of the intermediate days, the reading is
Exodus 22:24–23:19. These verses come from the midst of the
giving of the law on Mount Sinai and conclude with the
commandments for the three pilgrimage festivals: "At three
points in the year all your males are to be seen before the
presence of the Lord, God." But the verses prior to these are
a mixture, mostly commandments in matters of social justice:
lending, the return of found property, the fair treatment of
animals and the land, against bribes and false witness, against
spreading rumors, and to protect the rights of sojourners.
Also, against blasphemy, idolatry, and the eating of carrion.

The reading of the third intermediate day is Exodus 34:1–
26, which tells part of the story of the replacement of the
stone tablets that Moses had smashed upon finding the
Israelites worshiping a Golden Calf they had made during his *For the text of the*
Thirteen Attri-
first absence on Mount Sinai. The verses include the Thirteen *butes, see pp. 34*
Attributes, God's revelation to Moses of his own character. *and 208.*

Numbers 9:1-14 is the reading of the fourth intermediate day and speaks of the first Passover commemoration, which followed the completion of the Tabernacle, one year after the Exodus. God tells Moses to instruct the Israelites to prepare for its observance. A practical question of observance arose: some men who had become ritually unclean as a result of handling dead bodies present themselves to Moses and Aaron and ask how they should proceed with the Passover sacrifice. A good question; Moses tells them to stand by while he asks God, now in residence at the Tabernacle, what should be done. God responds, saying that the men must make the sacrifice a month later and eat it with matzoh and *maror*, the bitter herbs, making sure it is entirely consumed by morning—without breaking any bones.

Take note: The preceding paragraphs describe the Torah readings during the intermediate days—if there is no Sabbath in between or if Sabbath is on the third of the intermediate days. But if Sabbath is on the first of the intermediate days, then its reading is an expanded version of that which is ordinarily read on the third intermediate day: Exodus 33:12–34:26. On the second day, the portion ordinarily designated for the first intermediate day is read: Exodus 13:1-16. On the third day, the portion for the second day is read (Exodus 22:24-23:19); the fourth day's portion remains the same.

Sabbath During the Intermediate Days of Passover

The Friday evening service that occurs during the intermediate days of Passover is as usual, though most omit the Kabbalat Shabbat until *Mizmor Shir,* Psalm 92, with the addition of special verses and phrases in recognition of the occasion: ". . . and on this festival of matzot." Customs vary with regard to the recitation of *Magen avot,* "Shield of Our Fathers," and

Bameh madlikin, the talmudic instructions related to Sabbath candles.

See p. 59 for the standard Sabbath observance and p. 93 with regard to Rosh Hodesh.

There is a major addition to the Sabbath morning service: the recitation of the Song of Songs. It is the Sephardic custom to sing it at the end of the Seder; Ashkenazic custom is to include it in this service. Among some Ashkenazim, it is a custom to recite it on Friday afternoons, before the afternoon service. The Song of Songs comprises 117 verses arranged into eight chapters and is traditionally attributed to the authorship of King Solomon. It is traditionally interpreted as an allegory of Israel's love of God, its exile, God's love of Israel, and Israel's redemption (whence its relation to Passover). This approach to the poem was emphasized in the *Zohar*, the central text of Kabbalah, in which the Song of Songs is described as the embodiment of the entire Torah. It is, in actuality, a profane, deeply erotic, and passionate poem, a dialogue of lovers that was composed in the late Persian or early Greek period. The sages of the Mishnah and Talmud created for it an entirely new meaning based on their allegorical interpretation. The modern reader may choose to embrace the Song of Songs either way, but in the context of a Seder or this synagogue service, it is intended as allegory.

Two Torah scrolls are taken out of the ark. Seven readers are called up to read from the first scroll Exodus 33:12–34:26. This extends the reading of the third intermediate day both backward and forward in order to make a full-length Sabbath portion. The verses that begin with 33:12 relate a key moment—*the* key moment—the establishment of a renewed covenant, which henceforth defines the intimate relationship between God and the Children of Israel. This takes place in the aftermath of the Golden Calf episode, as Moses realizes that things between God and the Israelites have become shaky. Earlier in the chapter, God told Moses, "You take this hard-necked bunch on the journey and I'll send some angels to clear the way, but I won't be going." This reading begins with Moses's responding plea: "If You're not going, don't bother sending us. How will they ever believe that we have a relationship?" God gives in: "All right, I'll go." Moses, realizing he had touched a nerve, takes the opportunity to ask God to reveal himself, which he does, on Mount Sinai. What God reveals there is not a physical manifestation but the words that describe his relationship with humankind, known as the Thirteen Attributes.

For the text of the Thirteen Attributes, see pp. 34 and 208. For a yet larger context, see p. 363.

As on all the days of Passover, the maftir reads Numbers 28:19–25 from the second scroll, then the haftarah: Ezekiel 36:37–37:14, the story of the Valley of Dry Bones. As Ezekiel comes upon a valley filled with dry bones, God commands him to prophesy to them, bringing them back to life. It is another allegory of renewal, part of the messianic overlay of the holiday that looks past the Passover redemption toward a future redemption:

Ezekiel 37:11–12

> Then He said unto me: "Son of man, these bones are the whole house of Israel; behold, they say: Our bones are dried up, and our hope is lost; we are clean cut off.
>
> Therefore prophesy, and say unto them: Thus saith the Lord God: Behold, I will open your graves, and cause you to come up out of your graves, O My people; and I will bring you into the land of Israel. . . ."

The afternoon and evening services are as usual.

The Last Days of Passover

The seventh and eighth days of Passover are, once again, full holidays in which work is forbidden. The services follow the festival pattern (as on the first two days) and include a musaf service after the morning prayers. The kiddush is the same as on the first two nights of Passover, except that *Sheheheyanu*, the general prayer of thanks for granting us life and bringing us to this day, is not said.

THE SEVENTH DAY: Two Torah scrolls are taken from the ark and five people are called up to read from the first one. The portion is Exodus 13:17-15:26, the climax of the Exodus story when the Israelites, carrying with them the mummified remains of Joseph, are led by God and Moses around the land of the Philistines and through the Red Sea. As the Egyptians are swallowed up in their wake, Moses and the Children of Israel, safe on the dry land of the eastern shore, break into the Song of the Sea, a poem of the highest exultation to God, who in it is called "king for the ages, eternity." The poem, which has been aptly described as "a veritable lexicon of military victory," has the quality of a spontaneous outburst, though it makes references to events that occurred some time after the parting of the sea. At the end, Miriam, the sister of Moses and Aaron, called here a prophetess, takes a timbrel in hand and leads the women in dance and in their own version of the song. It is customary to stand for the song.

The maftir reads from the second scroll, Numbers 28:19-25, as on the other days of Passover. The haftarah is 2 Samuel 22:1-51, a perfect complement to the Exodus reading, another great song of exultation that concludes an important chapter and story. After God rescues David "from the clutches of his enemies and from the clutches of Saul," he recites a poem of gratitude saying, in effect, "it was all God's greatness and His doing—He who led me, He who inspired me, He who saved me."

The text of David's song is nearly the same as Psalm 18.

The musaf service is the same as it was throughout the

intermediate days of the holiday, including the Priestly Blessing. The kiddush and the blessings for the food are the same as on the first day of Passover; so, too, the afternoon service.

THE EIGHTH DAY: Two Torah scrolls are taken out from the ark and five readers are called. The portion is another rendering of the laws for the pilgrimage festivals, Deuteronomy 15:19–16:17. In addition to the specifics of the offerings and observances, the verses also mention charitable acts and the obligation to share the pleasures of the celebration with all those "within your gates," including the sojourner and the orphan and the widow. The maftir is called up to read Numbers 28:19–25, as throughout Passover. The haftarah is Isaiah 10:32–12:6, which predicts the failure of the Assyrian invader Sennacherib and the coming of a Messiah, "a shoot shall grow out of the stump of Jesse."

For Yizkor, see p. 265.

Following the Reading of the Law, Yizkor, the memorial service for the dead, is begun. This distinctive feature of Ashkenazic Judaism, observed on Yom Kippur and on the three pilgrimage festivals (Passover, Shavuot, Sukkot/Shemini Atzeret), is described at length as part of the Yom Kippur liturgy, with which it was originally associated—and was, in the *Minhogimbukh*, described there alone. Associated with Yizkor is a custom for one of the dignitaries of the synagogue (*hashuv*) to take pledges for donations for the poor in the land of Israel.

If it is a Sabbath, the service changes accordingly; the portion from Deuteronomy is expanded to accommodate the increased number of readers from five to seven: 14:22–16:17.

The afternoon service is the same as it was the previous day. If it is a Sabbath, three sections of the next week's Torah portion are read. The evening service should begin after dark.

Havdalah is said, but unless it is Sabbath, without the spices and the double-wick candle.

One might expect that a festival as rich as Passover would have a commensurately grand conclusion, but it does not, at least not in most rites. The Talmud says Shavuot, the "Festival of Weeks" (Pentecost), which marks the fiftieth day after the beginning of the counting of the Omer, is the conclusion of Passover. The explanation given is that it wasn't until Moses received the Law on Shavuot that the promise of the Exodus was completed. But there is at least one group that marks the conclusion of the eighth day of Passover with something more than an unceremonious unpacking of the ḥametz: the Jews of Morocco, who celebrate with a festival called Mimouna, a lavish, all-night, outdoor party and barbecue with everyone dressed in their finest garb. As many Moroccan Jews have emigrated to Israel, the festival's popularity has spread.

For Sabbath Havdalah, see p. 85.

YOM HASHOAH
HOLOCAUST REMEMBRANCE DAY

Shoah means "disaster," the Hebrew word by which the Holocaust became known in Israel, having set aside the Yiddish *khurbn*, the word most familiar to the survivors of the horrific events of 1936 to 1945. In 1951 the Israeli parliament—the Knesset—declared that the twenty-seventh day of the month of Nisan would be Yom Hashoah, Holocaust Remembrance Day.

The Yiddish word khurbn *derives from the Hebrew* ḥurban *and is the word used in connection with the destruction of the Temple.*

It was not an easy path to its establishment. The chief rabbis of Israel were against it. They said that Jews already had a day on which they remember their worst catastrophes: Tishah b'Av, the ninth day of the month of Av. This was the day of

*For Tishah b'Av,
see p. 188. Most
Tishah b'Av litur-
gies now include
the Holocaust.*
the Temple's destruction, when the Second Temple burned, when Bar Kokhba's fortress fell to the Roman legions. Had it not been for these events, the chief rabbis reasoned, there would have been no Diaspora; and if there had been no Diaspora, they continued, the Shoah would not have happend. They also suggested the tenth of Tevet, the date on which the Babylonian siege of Jerusalem began. The catastrophes of Tishah b'Av continued to mount long after ancient times, with edicts of expulsion from England and France and later, in 1492, from Spain. Added to these were massacres and pogroms too numerous to recall, yet nonetheless deserving of our mourning. To add another, separate day of tragic memory, the chief rabbis argued, would risk creating a cult of victimhood.

So raw was the pain that many Jews reviled the rabbis' opinions. Most Jewish leaders argued that the magnitude and viciousness of the Holocaust placed it in a class of its own, and so the popular will was done, not by halakhah or persistence of custom, but by organized political will. The chief rabbis compromised and negotiations ensued over the date. Many survivors wanted it to be the fifteenth of Nisan, the day of the outbreak of the Warsaw Ghetto Uprising, but since that falls on the second night of Passover (observed as a major holiday in the Diaspora, though not in Israel), it was not acceptable to religious leaders. Other dates were proffered and finally the twenty-seventh of Nisan—after Passover yet still during the uprising—was agreed upon.

Recognition of Yom Hashoah quickly took hold throughout the Jewish world, and, of no small importance, it found a place on non-Jewish calendars. As yet, there is no established liturgy, though some creative attempts have been made. Some have suggested the reading of documentary material along with the traditional memorial prayers, others the literature of medieval lamentations and hymns written in the aftermath of the Crusades. It's probably too soon to know; there are still survivors among us—and other genocides being carried out with appalling regularity. What we do know, however, is that historical events and documents have rarely influenced Jewish liturgy immediately. Rather, it has been their retelling as legend and lore that has shaped the collective consciousness.

One thing is certain: whatever liturgy is adopted will draw upon the remarkable body of poetic works written by victims and witnesses. In 1949 the critic Theodor Adorno wrote, "After Auschwitz, it is barbaric to write poetry." No one was ever so far off the mark. Among the documentary works, historical studies, and even the photos and films, it is the poems that mark us so indelibly. Nelly Sachs, Primo Levi, Paul Celan, Miklós Radnóti, Dan Pagis, and even Yankev Glatshteyn, who never left New York: would that they had never suffered, yet we are grateful for what they had given us: a reaffirmation of the commandment *zakhor*—"remember!"—and verse worthy of eternal remembrance. Thus Primo Levi calls upon us in his "Shemà" to examine the most fundamental assumptions about the nature of humanity:

> Consider whether this is a man,
> Who labors in the mud
> Who knows no peace
> Who fights for a crust of bread
> Who dies at a yes or a no.
> Consider whether this is a woman,
> Without hair or name
> With no more strength to remember
> Eyes empty and womb cold
> As a frog in winter.

"A skillful hunter, a man of the field"
(Genesis 25:27)

The Month of Iyar

ETWEEN THE FESTIVALS of Passover and Shavuot
is the counting of the Omer, as discussed in the previous chapter. Since the entire month of Iyar falls within this
period, the laws and customs of the Omer prevail throughout
the month. One might imagine that a time between two pilgrimage festivals would be a joyous one, but events in Jewish
history have rendered it otherwise. A state of mourning is
observed up to the thirty-third day of the Omer; neither performances nor weddings may be held, neither shaving nor
haircutting is permitted. There are various accounts and legends as to what or whom we mourn, none of them definitive.
One story tells of the death from a mysterious plague of
24,000 disciples of Rabbi Akiva for "begrudging one
another." The plague ended on the thirty-third day of the
Omer. In another version of the story, the students had joined
Israel's second war against Rome in 132–135 C.E., known as
Bar Kokhba's Revolt, and they all were killed by Roman
legions. Simon Bar Kozeba (called Bar Kokhba, "son of a
star," by his followers) was held to be a messiah, the savior of
the Jews from the harsh rule of the Romans. But the revolt
was a disaster: about 600,000 Jewish combatants as well as an

For Omer, see p. 140.

Sephardic custom observes the state of mourning until the thirty-fourth day. Some Ashkenazic groups observe the period of mourning for forty-nine days.

"Begrudging one another," Talmud Yevamot 62b.

53

untold number of noncombatants were killed by Roman legions—one-third of a population already in ruins after an earlier revolt that led to the destruction of the Second Temple in 70 C.E. Rabbi Akiva was among the sages supporting Bar Kokhba. Israel was not to be a self-governing entity for more than eighteen hundred years.

Pious Jews today observe the traditional restrictions of the Omer period, but they are now mitigated through the festive recognition in the month of Iyar of Israel Independence Day and Yom Yerushalayim.

The special liturgy associated with the Omer is the reading from the Mishnah tractate *Pirkei avot*, "The Ethics of the Fathers," every Sabbath after Passover through Shavuot or, in some communities, through the seventeenth of the month of Tamuz. The Ethics of the Fathers is a book of wisdom, a compilation of the maxims of the great sages. Here are some excerpts, with their sources:

> The world is sustained by three things: by Torah, by worship, and by acts of loving-kindness.—*Simon the Just, 1.2*

> If I am not for myself, who will be for me? But if I am only for myself, what am I? And if not now, when?—*Hillel, 1.14*

> In a place where no one behaves like a human being, you must strive to be human.—*Hillel, 2.6*

> You are not required to complete the work, but neither are you at liberty to abstain from it.—*Rabbi Tarfon, 2.21*

> When our learning exceeds our deeds we are like trees whose branches are many but whose roots are few—easily uprooted by the wind. But when our deeds exceed our learning we are like trees whose branches are few but whose roots are many—unmovable by the wind.—*Rabbi Elazar ben Azaryah, 3.22*

> Do not try to placate your friends at the height of their

anger; do not attempt to comfort them in the first shock of bereavement; do not question their sincerity at the moment they make a solemn promise; do not be overeager to visit them in their hour of disgrace.—*Rabbi Shimon ben Elazar, 4.23*

There are four temperaments: easily angered and easily appeased—the loss is balanced by the gain; hard to anger and hard to appease—the gain is offset by the loss; hard to anger and easily appeased—a saint; and easily angered and hard to appease—wicked.—*no attribution, 5.14*

The Customs of Iyar

Rosh Ḥodesh Iyar is always celebrated for two days. There is an old custom to fast on the tenth of Iyar, the day when Eli the high priest and his two sons were killed by the Philistines, who captured the Ark of the Covenant (they returned it later). There is also the "Fast of Monday, Thursday, and Monday," observed not within a week but rather over several weeks following both Passover and Sukkot, to atone for possible misdeeds and overindulgences during the holidays. It is observed today only in the most devout communities, though one might imagine its successful revival as a religious post-holiday weight-loss program. The *Minhogimbukh* says it is a time to ask God's protection from the "evil winds" that blow between winter and summer.

On the fourteenth of Iyar falls *Pesaḥ Sheni*, "Second Passover," so called after a passage in Numbers 9:6–8, in which a group of people approach Moses and Aaron to ask how they should make up for the Passover sacrifice they missed as a result of becoming ritually unclean from the handling of dead bodies. They were assigned a makeup day and so the fourteenth of Iyar became known as a Second Passover. The *Minhogimbukh* says that some people observe the

The story is told in 1 Samuel 4:1–22.

The fast is known as Behav, *an acronym made from the Hebrew initials of the days.*

The story is told in the reading for the fourth day of Passover, see p. 144.

day by eating sandwiches of leftover matzoh and *maror*. Taḥanun, the prayers of supplication, are not said.

Yom Haẓikaron, Yom Haatẓmaut, Yom Yerushalayim

If either observance falls on a Friday or Saturday, then Yom Haẓikaron is moved to the preceding Wednesday and Yom Haatẓmaut to the preceding Thursday.

On the fourth and fifth of Iyar are two related observances, recently invented yet widely recognized by Jews throughout the world: Yom Hazikaron, Israel's memorial day for its fallen soldiers and, more recently, for those who have perished in acts of terrorism; and the joyous Yom Haatzmaut, Israel Independence Day. As with Holocaust Remembrance Day, there was considerable rabbinic debate over religious recognition of what are, in essence, civil holidays. The debate brought into relief two important strands in post-Holocaust Jewish life: the separation of the state and religion as a basic principle of successful democracy, a value held especially high by most American Jews, and the slow acceptance of Zionism among Jewish fundamentalists, the *haredim*. Added to these is the idea of *Klal Yisrael*, the notion of an "entire community of Israel" that must act with a sense of collective responsibility, both in joy and in mourning.

In 1948 Israeli Jews and Jews around the world celebrated Nation Day, which served both as independence celebration and as memorial for those who had fallen, in pursuit of a Jewish state. The next year it was renamed Israel Independence Day. This brought a cry from bereaved families for a more specific recognition of the fallen and a number of possible dates were placed under consideration as an Israel Memorial Day. The "twinning" of the two days had not been planned, but in 1950, after the coincidence of Sabbath had pushed the two days together, Israel's first prime minister, David Ben-

Gurion, became so adamant about continuing the juxtaposition that the debate over the date was effectively ended.

Both days are widely observed among Diasporan Jews, though not uniformly or with equal attention. For Yom Hazikaron, the memorial day, preexisting liturgies are fit into normal synagogue services: Yizkor, *El malei rahamim*, Kaddish—each readily adaptable to the needs and desires of each community. Some nonsynagogue groups use a rewritten, secularized Yizkor for public ceremonies. The Diaspora's observance of Israel Independence Day is commonly the province of major Jewish philanthropic organizations and Zionist groups—at least in big cities, where public ceremonies are planned, often including music and dance. In smaller towns, these functions are assumed by synagogue groups. In the synagogue per se the event has also been liturgized, with a recitation of Hallel, the psalms of praise, special Torah and haftarah readings, and the insertion into the Amidah of the prayer *Al hanisim*, "For the miracles." However, there is little uniformity of practice.

The twenty-eighth of Iyar is Yom Yerushalayim—Jerusalem Day—a holiday established after the reunification of Jerusalem in the aftermath of the 1967 war. Whether one regards this most recent of holidays a civil observance in the state of Israel or a universal Jewish holiday is a personal matter. There is no established liturgy for the day, but the possibilities are endless; this is the place where God chose to dwell, among the most conquered and lost real estate in the world, witness to strife for millennia, and source of literary inspiration for just as long. Whether or not Jerusalem remains entirely under Jewish governance is beside the point; the very idea of Jerusalem is a leading motif in Jewish life, one that we confront daily, whether it be in the recitation of the Amidah

The twenty-eighth of Iyar also marks the death of the prophet Samuel, and it is a custom in some places to observe a fast on that day.

The fourteenth benediction of the Amidah, Birkat Yerushalayim, calls for the rebuilding of the city; the seventeenth benediction, the Avodah, implores God to accept our prayers in lieu of the sacrifices and expresses hope that the true services— the Temple sacrifices—be restored. These benedictions are usually interpreted allegorically and, in some denominations, have been modified.

or on the front page of our newspapers. Whether it is for us a place that exists only in our souls or a city where the Temple should be rebuilt and the sacrifices renewed, it is where Jews define their faith, where they join and where they divide.

These observances, coming as they do between the redemption of Passover and giving of the Torah on Shavuot, may become the time when Jews contemplate the nature and meaning of nationhood and of Jewish nationhood, of the relations of religion and state, and the lessons and tensions of Torah and history. And so the Omer has been infused with new meaning.

Lag b'Omer

The letters גל, *lag*, means "thirty-three" and are used here to speak of the thirty-third day of the counting of the Omer, which falls always on the eighteenth of Iyar. The restrictions of the Omer period are suspended on that day in commemoration of the cessation of the dying of Rabbi Akiva's students. But there are other stories: a turnaround, albeit temporary, in the military fortunes of Bar Kokhba. The historian Flavius Josephus says the commemoration actually refers to events in

Haircutting on Lag b'Omer from the Minhogimbukh, Amsterdam, 1722.

66 C.E., in the first insurrection against Rome to which he was an eyewitness.

Lag b'Omer has no specifically prescribed customs, though it is the tradition to celebrate the cessation of the restrictions of mourning with weddings and performances—and haircuts. In Israel and elsewhere, it has become popular as a student holiday, a day of school festivals. The eighteenth of Iyar also marks the death of the second-century sage Shimon Bar Yoḥai, the legendary author of the *Zohar*, and on this day Sephardic and Ḥasidic Jews, as well as other connoisseurs of Kabbalah, make the pilgrimage to his burial place in Meron, near Safed.

The *Minhogimbukh* mentions here several community customs that are observed no more. For example: in the German city of Worms, the twenty-third of Iyar was observed with special penitential prayers and a memorial service in commemoration of the eight hundred Jews who were killed on that day in 1096, during the course of the First Crusade.

Torah Portions for Iyar

The portions read on the four Sabbaths of our model month of Iyar are the final chapters of Leviticus through the beginning of Numbers.

The first week's portion, *Emor* ("Speak!"), Leviticus 21:1–24:23, begins with rules of holiness that apply to the kohanim, the Temple priests, in regard to marriage and personal purity and also the physical blemishes and deformities that prohibit someone from serving in that capacity. Animals brought for sacrifice must also be free of blemish. Instructions are given for the observance of the Sabbath, Passover, the Omer, and Shavuot, as well as Rosh Hashanah (described not as New Year but as the first day of the seventh month, a "sacred assembly marked by shofar blasts"), Yom Kippur, and Sukkot. There follows, unrelated to the foregoing, the story of the blasphemer and God's instruction for his stoning, that all the community must participate in such action, not just those within earshot. And then some verses about the limiting factors of restitution: "If anyone takes the life of a human being, he must be put to death . . . an eye for an eye." These principles of justice are elaborated upon in later portions.

The reader is reminded that unlike the holiday readings, the weekly Torah and haftarah portions shift somewhat every year. A "model" year was established for this book to give a flavor of the whole synagogue experience.

The portion Emor, Leviticus 21:1–24:23; haftarah portion for Emor, Ezekiel 44:15–31.

The accompanying haftarah is Ezekiel 44:15–31, written in the aftermath of the Temple's destruction. It is concerned with some matters that parallel the first part of the Torah portion: rules for the priesthood to be observed upon the restoration of the Temple.

Torah portion Behar, Leviticus 25:1–26:2; haftarah portion for Behar, Jeremiah 32:6–27.

Behar ("On Mount [Sinai]"), Leviticus 25:1–26:2, is the portion of the second week. Beginning with the laws of Sabbatical and Jubilee Years, it continues the code of holiness that encompasses issues of land tenure and indentured servitude. "The land may not be sold permanently, because the land is mine," says God. Similarly, the Children of Israel may not be sold into slavery, "for they are my servants." The haftarah of Jeremiah 32:6–27 covers similar ground in writings about deeds to transfer land ownership, but with a twist: God tells Jeremiah to put the deeds in an earthenware vessel and hide them, for the land will soon be overtaken by the Babylonians, though the day will come when the Children of Israel will again trade upon that land. The harbingers of destruction that will culminate in Tishah b'Av have begun.

Torah portion Behukotai, Leviticus 26:3–27:34; haftarah portion for Behukotai, Jeremiah 16:19–17:14.

The next Torah portion, Leviticus 26:3–27:34, *Behukotai* ("My decrees"), also carries a stern warning from God. The Israelites are told that if they—as a people—obey God's laws, they shall benefit from his gifts beyond their imagining, but if they disobey, they will suffer an entire catalog of miseries. Nevertheless, God says, if the Children of Israel confess their iniquities, he will not forget his covenants with Abraham and Jacob and will reembrace them with mercy. Next order of business: raising shekels for the sanctuary. Republicans and Tories might do well to note that when God describes to Moses the tithes for support of the sanctuary, it is not as a head tax or a flat tax, but as a schedule according to age and sex, adjusted for the poor.

In the haftarah, Jeremiah 16:19–17:14, the warning of impending doom are dire, the chance for salvation slim:

> [*saith the Lord*] "Judah's sin is engraved with an iron tool, inscribed with a flint point on the tablets of their hearts and on the horns of their altars. . . .
> I will enslave you to your enemies in a land you do not know, for you have kindled my anger."

The fourth portion, *Bemidbar* ("In the Wilderness"), is the beginning of the book of Numbers (1:1–4:20). The first three chapters concern the taking of a detailed census of all males over age twenty, tribe by tribe, and all levites, aged thirty to fifty, who were assigned to attend to the "Dwelling," the movable sanctuary and the Ark. The firstborn are to be given over to the levites, but may be redeemed for five shekels each. This is the basis of the ceremony of Pidyon haben, described in the chapter on birth and circumcision.

Torah portion Bemidbar, Numbers 1:1–4:20; haftarah portion for Bemidbar, Hosea 2:1–22.

For Pidyon Haben, see p. 384.

Hosea 2:1–22 provides the haftarah, and in it we have another harbinger of the impending disaster, this time taking the form of a poetic allegory, the rebuke by a loyal husband of a faithless wife, the misery of separation and the goodness to come upon reconciliation.

"I would be asleep; then I would be at rest"
(Job 3:13)

The Month of Sivan

S IVAN IS THE MONTH OF SHAVUOT, the second
pilgrimage festival of late spring, observed on the fiftieth day of the counting of the Omer, which commenced on
the second day of Passover. Rosh Ḥodesh Sivan is observed
for one day only; Shavuot is observed on the sixth and seventh of the month.

The Sabbath before Shavuot was known as "Black Sabbath" in European communities, in reference to the murder
of thousands of Jews at this time in 1096, during the First
Crusade. In those places where Jews suffered most greatly—
Germany, Austria, Bohemia—it was the local custom to add a
special memorial service and to add special hymns.

✿

SHAVUOT

The word *shavuot* means "weeks." It is described first in Exodus 34:22: "The pilgrimage festival of Weeks you are to make
for yourselves, of the firstfruits of the grain cutting," and
again, with more detail, in Deuteronomy 16:9-10:

> You shall count for yourself seven weeks; start the count of
> the seven weeks when the sickle is first put to the standing
> grain. Then you shall observe the pilgrimage festival of

Weeks for the Lord your God, offering your freewill contribution according to how the Lord your God has blessed you.

And so on the fiftieth day (Greek "fiftieth"=*pentecost*), after the counting of seven weeks, a thanks offering of ripe grain or fruit was brought to the Temple. In Exodus 23:16 Shavuot is referred to as the "Harvest Festival"; in Numbers 28:26 it is *yom habikurim*, "the day of the ripe fruits." The Mishnah describes at length how during Temple times, the farmers made elaborate preparations and then a great procession to Jerusalem.

Mishnah Bikurim
3:2–3

Over time the meaning of Shavuot became obscure. The sages of the Talmud referred to it only by the name *Atzeret*, which indicates an abstention from work and is described further as a conclusion to Passover. The *Book of Jubilees*, an ancient text that survived in part in the Dead Sea Scrolls and in its entirety in the ancient Ethiopian language Ge'ez, gives an entirely different spin on Shavuot. The word *shavua*, "week," is a near-homonym to the word for "oath" (*shevuah*), and the anonymous author of Jubilees says that Shavuot was, in fact, the "Feast of Oaths," a holiday long before Moses, commemorating the oath sworn by Noah and his sons not to eat blood with flesh (Genesis 9:4). Abraham, says Jubilees, was alone in his keeping this oath. This interpretation was known to the talmudists and became part of their discourse.

*See also Shemini
Atzeret, p. 190.*

*For more on this
and the other
Noahide Laws, see
p. 2.*

But Shavuot gradually took on another meaning in post-Temple times—the one it has today—as *zeman matan toratenu*, the anniversary of the day when Moses received the Law on Mount Sinai. It is a fundamental principle of traditional Jewish belief that Moses received from God that day not only the tablets of the Ten Commandments, but the entire Torah (the written law) and the Mishnah (the oral law).

*For more on written and oral law,
see p. 2.*

Customs of Shavuot

Perhaps it is because of its different interpretations that Shavuot is less rich in custom than the other pilgrimage festivals, Passover and Sukkot. Nevertheless, it does have its characteristics and specific liturgies. Unlike the first two days of Passover, the customs are different on each day of Shavuot.

The custom of *Tikun lel shavuot*, "The Restoration of the Night of Shavuot," is to remain awake and study Torah the entire first night of Shavuot. There are several explanations for this, but the best one comes from the *Zohar*, which describes Shavuot as the wedding day on which the Children of Israel are the bride and the Torah the groom. To prepare her spiritual dowry, the bride remained awake all evening studying. For this purpose, the sixteenth-century Kabbalist Solomon Alkabets wrote a special anthology that comprises the first and last verses of each book of the Torah, the opening verses of every other book of the Bible, and the beginning of each of the sixty-three tractates of the Mishnah. Some communities add to these quotations from the *Zohar*. In Israel it has become a custom to gather at various places in Jerusalem for an all-night *tikun*, ending at the Western Wall; in the United States many synagogues hold study seminars. The connection between the Western Wall and Shavuot began with the Six Day War, which came just before Shavuot.

Tikun is more concept than word and as such is not easily translated. What it means is that through study one may achieve the mystic marriage in heaven, the tikun, *and in so doing repair on a cosmological level the duality of good and evil that separated at Creation. The concept is associated with the sixteenth-century Safed mystic Isaac Luria.*

The First Day of Shavuot

In the morning service, the splendid medieval Aramaic poem *Akdamut* ("Prelude") is recited before the Torah reading. Its author is Rabbi Meir of Worms, whose father, Rabbi Isaac, was murdered in the First Crusade. *Akdamut* was written as a prefatory ode to the Torah reading and comprises ninety-seven verses in double acrostic. Its verses include praise for

The Jews of Yemen read instead from Maimonides' Sefer hamitzvot, the "Book of Commandments."

the Creator and Creation, the angels' Kedushah, the persistence of the faithful despite efforts for their conversion, and
this summation of Jewish love of God and the written word:

> Could we with ink the ocean fill,
> Were every blade of grass a quill,
> Were the world of parchment made,
> And every man a scribe by trade,
> To write the love of God above
> Would drain the ocean dry;
> Nor would the scroll contain the whole,
> Though stretch from sky to sky.
> . . . [last] Then let us rejoice that He blessed us
>   and gave us the Law.

This is the familiar English verse rendering attributed to Frederick M. Lehman, who published it in 1917, having claimed to have found it written on the wall of an insane asylum.

The morning services follow the usual pattern for festival
mornings. It is held by tradition that King David was born
and died on Shavuot and so, in his honor, additional psalms
are read in many synagogues. Synagogues are decorated with
foliage on Shavuot, and several reasons are given for the custom: to represent the fringe of growth around the edge of
Mount Sinai, beyond which it was prohibited to go; to represent the harvest festival; to represent the reeds of the Nile
from which Moses was plucked by Pharaoh's daughter,
which, according to the sages, was also on Shavuot. Two
Torah scrolls are taken from the ark and five persons are
called up. (Some congregations read this way: the first aliyah
is read by a kohen, then *Akdamut* is recited, after which the
Torah reading resumes.) The portion is Exodus 19:1–20:23,
the story of God's revelation and the covenant at Mount
Sinai. The verses of the Ten Commandments are recited to a
special tune. The maftir reads Number 28:26–28:31, which
describes the details of the Shavuot offering. The haftarah is
Ezekiel 1:1–28 and 3:13, a parallel revelation. Where in Exo-

dus God's appearance is shrouded in a cloud of smoke, causing the mountain itself to tremble, Ezekiel's awesome vision is more lavish: four-headed angels with human hands and a single calf's hoof whose movements are followed by wheels of fire precede the appearance of God, who is manifest in human form, surrounded by radiance and the glow of amber and fire. In some

synagogues there is a custom of passing the Torah from person to person, a symbol of the acceptance of the covenant, rather than the usual carrying of it through the room.

Moses receiving the Law on Shavuot. Minhogimbukh, Amsterdam, 1722. Note the fence around Mount Sinai, through which no man or beast was to pass through and live.

If the two days of Shavuot fall on a Friday and a Saturday, then *eruv tavshilin* must be made to allow for advance preparation of food. This is the same as described for Passover. In the repetition of the Amidah of the musaf service, there is the ritual of the Priestly Blessing, as described for the first day of Passover. The repetition of the Amidah ends with *Sim shalom*, then Kaddish is recited and the service ends with *En kelohenu* and *Alenu*.

It is customary among Ashkenazim to eat dairy foods on Shavuot. There are a number of explanations; this one is from the *Minhogimbukh*: "We eat *milkhig* (dairy) foods because the Torah is as basic as milk, and the Torah was given to us on Shavuot." Mizrahi Jews observe the custom of going up on the roof of the synagogue and throwing apples off it. This has its basis in the verse "All that the Lord has spoken we shall do and we shall listen!" which the Children of Israel spoke when they were presented with the Law. It was later observed that in their proclamation of action before understanding, the

Exodus 24:7

Children of Israel were like a growing apple, in which the fruit begins to develop before the leaf.

The Second Day of Shavuot

The highlight of the second day's morning service is the reading of the book of Ruth. There are a number of explanations for its selection, which mostly follow along these lines: as with Shavuot, the story takes place at the barley harvest; like Ruth, the Children of Israel were also "converts" to Judaism at Mount Sinai.

This moving short story (eighty-five verses) is the epitome of compassion, loyalty, and loving-kindness. It has three main characters: Naomi, a Jewish woman of Bethlehem and the mother of two sons; Ruth, a Moabite woman who is married to one of Naomi's sons; and Boaz, a landowner near Bethlehem and the kinsman of Naomi's husband, Elimelech. Naomi, now a widow, and her two sons flee a famine in Judah and establish residence on Moab. The sons, who have taken Moabite wives, die after ten years, leaving the three women stranded and destitute. Naomi bids her daughters-in-law to return to their mothers' houses; one does, but the other, Ruth, pledges her loyalty to Naomi: "For wherever you go, I will go; wherever you lodge, I will lodge; your people will be my people and your God my God." The two women return to Bethlehem at the time of the barley harvest, and Naomi instructs Ruth to exercise her God-given right to glean the fallen grain from the harvest in the fields of Boaz, a kinsmen of her late husband's. Ruth's compassion and loyalty gain favor in the eyes of Boaz, who marries her after obtaining the right to do so. Naomi becomes the nurse to their son, Obed, the grandfather of King David.

After the conclusion of the book of Ruth, half Kaddish is

Ruth is one of the Bible's "Five Scrolls," along with Song of Songs, Lamentations, Ecclesiastes, and Esther.

Boaz obtains the right to marry Ruth. This refers to yibum and ḥalitzah, the laws of levirate marriage described in Deuteronomy 25:5–9, in which the brother of a deceased husband is obligated to marry his brother's widow, unless released from the obligation by the widow herself. The ceremony of release is called ḥalitzah, in which the widow removes the shoe from her brother-in-law's foot, spits in his face, and recites the verse, "Thus shall be done to the man who will not build up his brother's house."

recited, and two Torah scrolls are taken out from the ark and five readers are called. The portion is Deuteronomy 15:19-16:17, same as on the last day of Passover and Shemini Atzeret—days when charitable pledges are made. (If it is a Sabbath, seven people are called up and the reading begins with Deuteronomy 14:22.) In addition to the specifics of the list of holiday laws, the verses also mention charitable acts and the obligation to share the pleasures of the celebration with all those "within your gates," including the sojourner and the orphan and the widow. The maftir reads from the second scroll, Numbers 28:26-31, same as on the first day. In the *Mi sheberakh* prayers that follow the Torah verses, a special phrase is added: "for giving charity in honor of God, in honor of the Torah, and in honor of the pilgrimage festival." Following the haftarah, it is a custom for one of the dignitaries of the synagogue (*hashuv*) to collect donations for the poor in the land of Israel.

The haftarah is Habakkuk's Prayer (Habakkuk 3:1-19). After the great doubt brought by seeing the prevalence of oppression and injustice in the world, Habakkuk is reassured that God will come to save his people. Habakkuk's Prayer is the third and last chapter of this brief book and takes the form of a psalm, including a call for "string music." The last three verses are often quoted:

> For though the fig tree shall not blossom,   *Habakkuk 3:17-19*
>   neither shall fruit be on the vines,
>   the labor of the olive shall fail,
>   and the field shall yield no food,
>   the flock shall be cut off from the fold,
>   and there shall be no herd in the stalls;
>
> Yet I will rejoice in the Lord,
>   and I will exult in the God of my salvation.

God, the Lord is my strength,
and He maketh my feet like hinds' feet,
and He maketh me to walk upon my high places.

For Yizkor, see p. 265. Following the reading of the haftarah, Yizkor, the memorial service for the dead, is begun.

The Jewish concept of charity is not quite the same as that implied by the Latin *caritas*, with its emphasis on free will. The Hebrew word most often translated as charity is *tzedakah*, which derives from the root word for "justice" and applies to the commandment to care for the needs of the poor. It is part of a broader concept of *gemilut ḥasadim*, usually translated as "acts of loving-kindness." The Talmud points out the difference between the two concepts: while *tzedakah*, by its nature, applies to only the living and involves giving one's money, *gemilut ḥasadim* may apply more broadly to the needs of the community, living and dead, rich and poor, and may involve giving of one's physical self as well as of one's money.

Talmud Sukkot 49b and Ketubot 67b. The medieval sage Maimonides wrote a tract on the subject called Laws of Gifts to the Poor, which is quoted on p. 210.

The musaf service is the same as on the first day and again includes the Priestly Blessing. The afternoon and following evening service are as usual. Havdalah is made at the close of the day. If it is a Sabbath, then the blessings are said over the light and the spices; if it is the middle of the week, then these are not used.

Torah Portions for Sivan

The readings for our model month of Iyar continue in the book of Numbers, from 4:21 through 18:32. The portion *Naso* ("To Take") is read on the first Sabbath (Numbers 4:21–7:89). Various responsibilities for the Sanctuary are divided among the three clans of the Levites: Gershon, Kehat, and Merari. A series of laws and regulations are presented: keeping the camp pure and limiting its exposure to persons made impure by exposure to dead bodies or to various diseases that may be communicable (such persons must stay outside the camp for prescribed periods of time); procedures for an accused adulteress; and the prohibitions applied to Nazirites, ascetics who are consecrated by a vow of separateness. A *nazir* (who may be a woman or a man) may not cut his or her hair, may not drink anything fermented or derived from grapes, and may not come into contact with the dead. The Priestly Blessing is described. Further details are given in regard to the count of the firstborn. Finally, the gifts given by the princes of each tribe at the inauguration of the Altar in the Wilderness Tabernacle are listed in detail.

Torah portion Naso, Numbers 4:21–7:89; haftarah portion for Naso, Judges 13:2–25.

The first week's haftarah, Judges 13:2–25, tells the story of the birth of Samson, how he is born to a barren couple visted by an angel, who instructs the mother that he is to be raised as a *nazir*, for which he will be endowed with extraordinary strength. One should note that in Numbers, to become a *nazir* is an entirely elective state and not a permanent one.

The verses 6:24–26 constitute the Priestly Blessing. See p. 133.

The name of the second week's portion, *Behaalotekha* ("when you are to set up," Numbers 8:1–12:16), derives from the verses describing the making of the menorah, the seven-branched candelabrum in the sanctuary. The levites are purified—scrubbed up and shaved clean—for their sanctuary service. The matter of giving over the firstborn to the levites is made clearer and tied to God's killing of the firstborn of Egypt, the first anniversary of which is about to be observed. A remarkable series of verses describes God's manner of dwelling among the Israelites, how his cloud covered the Sanctuary when the Israelites came to rest, how it hovered over all night, and how when the cloud lifted the Israelites knew it was time to march on. As they prepared to move on,

Torah portion Behaalotekha, Numbers 8:1–12:16; haftarah portion for Behaalotekha, Zechariah 2:14–4:7.

Moses called out, "Arise, O Lord, that your enemies may scatter, that those who hate You may flee!" And as they rested, he would say, "Return, O Lord, You of the myriad thousands of Israel." These are the verses said when the Torah is removed from and returned to the ark in the synagogue. These passages are followed by grumblings: not long after commemoration of the Exodus, the Israelites, tired of manna, recall the delicious fruits of Egypt. Even Aaron and Miriam begin to grumble, and God strikes Moses's sister with lesions. Moses prays for her recovery, and she is banished from the camp for seven days as the Israelites await her recovery before moving on.

The haftarah from the late prophet Zechariah, 2:14–4:7, is an interesting one, filled with suggestive symbols: the high priest Joshua on trial before God is prosecuted by Satan; a stone with seven eyes; a messianic promise of a world united before God; a solid gold lampstand with a bowl at the top and seven lights on it—the Temple menorah. In the aftermath of the Babylonian Exile, Zechariah challenges the complacent Jews now living under Persian rule to rebuild the Temple: "Sing out and rejoice, O Daughter of Zion, for I am coming; And I will dwell within you, says the Lord."

Torah portion Shelaḥ, Numbers 13:1–15:41; haftarah portion for Shelaḥ, Joshua 2:1–24.

"Send!" is the meaning of *Shelaḥ*, the name of the portion for the third week (Numbers 13:1–15:41). Upon God's commandment, Moses sends spies to view the situation in the land of Canaan. One from each tribe is sent. Moses instructs them to look carefully at the land, character, and situation of the encountered inhabitants. They report back that, indeed, the land flows with milk and honey, and they bring with them a single bunch of grapes so large that it is carried on a pole by two men. But speaking before the whole community, the spies warn that the inhabitants are strong and their cities large and fortified. The people rebel, saying, "We should choose a leader and go back to Egypt." Moses and Aaron fall facedown before the assembly. Caleb and Joshua, who were among the spies but who have confidence in God's promise, tear their clothing, as in mourning. God says to Moses, "How long will they refuse to believe in me, despite all the miracles I have performed among them? I will strike them down with a plague and destroy them, but I will make you (Moses and the faithful ones) into a nation greater than they." Moses, ever faithful to God and his people, assuages God's anger, just as he did in the Golden Calf episode (Exodus 32:11): "Then the Egyptians will be able to say that You brought them out just to destroy them. . . . Where's the 'slow to anger, abounding in love, and forgiving of sin' God You told me about?" And so God changes his mind, but the price to the Israelites for his doing so is forty years in the Wilderness. It would be an entirely new generation who crossed the Jordan. In the remaining verses, the sin offerings are described, a Sabbath breaker is put to death, and the tasseled garments are prescribed.

"Slow to anger" is Moses's repetition of God's own self-description. See pp. 34 and 208 for the Thirteen Attributes of God as revealed to Moses on Mount Sinai.

The haftarah, Joshua 2:1–24, brings us to the fulfillment of the episode when, forty years later, Joshua, the heir to Moses, sends two men to go look over the land. Once in Jericho, they are hidden at the house of a prostitute, who offers to help and tells them of the widespread fear of their coming and the reputation of their deliverance from Egypt. The men agree and tell her to tie a scarlet cord to her window. All who will be within will be safe.

Korah, Numbers 16:1–18:32, is the fourth portion of the model month. Korach, Moses's cousin, along with Datan, Abiram, and two hundred fifty men from the tribe of Reuben, challenge Moses's and Aaron's leadership. Moses persuades

Torah portion
Koraḥ, *Numbers*
16:1–18:32;
haftarah portion
for Koraḥ,
1 Samuel 11:14–21.

Datan and Abiram to withdraw their challenge, but Korach cannot be persuaded. The next day God instructs Moses and the Israelites to separate themselves from the tents of Korach as well as from Datan and Abiram. Moses proclaims that his (and Aaron's) leadership will be divinely confirmed. The three rebels along with their families are swallowed up by the earth; the two hundred fifty men from the tribe of Reuben are consumed by heavenly fire. God sends a plague to consume the rest but advises Moses on stopping it, though not before 14,700 perish. Aaron's position as high priest is confirmed, as God causes his staff to miraculously sprout almonds.

The haftarah of 1 Samuel 11:14–21 describes the retirement of Samuel, last of the Judges, and establishment of Saul as the first king. The establishment of the kingship was evil, not in accordance with God's will, but Samuel instructs that if the Israelites hold to God's commandments, he will not abandon them for it. But if they do not, "both you and your king will be swept away."

"Harvest in mercy"
(Hosea 10:12)

The Month of Tamuz

TAMUZ MARKS THE BEGINNING of summer in Israel. Rosh Ḥodesh Tamuz is observed for two days. Like summer, Tamuz begins uneventfully, but on the seventeenth a fast is observed in recognition of several calamities that took place on that day, each with long-term implications. The day Shivah Asar b'Tamuz, the seventeenth of Tamuz, begins the "Three Weeks," a period of mourning that culminates in Tishah b'Av, the ninth of the month of Av, the day on which the destruction of the First and Second Temples took place—heading a list of other catastrophes.

It is a rabbinic tradition that Moses smashed the tablets on the seventeenth of Tamuz. But it was the breaching of the walls of Jerusalem by the armies of the Babylonian king Nebuchadnezzar that enshrined the day in infamy. This is how the event is reported in 2 Kings 25:2–7:

The Hebrew name for the Three Weeks is Ben hametzarim, "between the straits," derived from Lamentations 1:3, "all her (Jerusalem's) persecutors overtook her between the straits."

> In the fourth month of that year, on the ninth day, when famine was severe in the city and there was no food for the common people, the city was thrown open. When Zedekiah king of Judah saw this, he and all his armed escort fled the city by night. . . . But the Chaldean army pursued the king and overtook him in the lowlands of Jericho; and all his

army was dispersed. The king was seized and brought before the king of Babylon at Riblah, where he pleaded his case. Zedekiah's sons were slain before his eyes; then his eyes were put out and he was brought to Babylon in fetters of bronze.

The episode is recorded in Talmud Taanit 28b.

And it gets worse. There was also on this day, in Roman times, the burning of a Torah scroll by Apostomos, captain of the Roman guard.

The morning service includes penitential prayers (Selihot), which begin with *El erekh apayim*, a prayer for mercy that begins with a quotation from the Thirteen Attributes of God, which Moses quoted to quell God's anger in the Wilderness. That is followed by penitential prayers specific to the day, mentioning by name the infamous events.

The episode is in Numbers 14:18.

> We have come to you, O molder of spirits. Because of our many iniquities, our groans have been intensified. The decrees have become severe, and many are the outcries, for on the seventeenth day of Tamuz, the Tablets were smashed. We were exiled from the House You chose for us. . . .

There Torah reading for the seventeenth of Tamuz is the one designated for fast days: Exodus 32:11–14; 34:1–10. The portion recalls how Moses assuaged God's anger after the Golden Calf episode, how the covenant was renewed. After the reading, half Kaddish is recited, the Torah is returned to the ark, then *Ashrei, Lamenatzeah, Uva letziyon,* and concluding with Kaddish and *Alenu.* If the seventeenth of Tamuz falls on a Sabbath, the fast is postponed to the following day, to Sunday.

The period between the seventeenth of Tamuz and the ninth of Av is a time of great misfortune. The *Minhogimbukh* mentions in connection with it a number of old superstitions:

One should not walk alone between one o'clock and three o'clock in the afternoon because an evil spirit rules during those hours. And if a Jew goes to court with a gentile in this period, he should make sure that he can afford to lose because the luck of the Jews is—God forbid—not so good in these days.

Torah Portions for Tamuz

The portion *Ḥukat* ("Requirements of"), Numbers 19:1–22:1, contains a number of passages that are difficult to understand, most notably the one that begins the reading: the sacrifice of a red heifer, whose ashes purify the water that is used to purify sin. Yet both the priest who performs the sacrifice and the person who gathers the ashes are rendered unclean by their acts. In the fortieth year in the Wilderness, the prophetess Miriam dies and is buried. Miriam's traveling well, the Israelites' source of water, vanishes with her passing. Another rebellion: the people begin grumbling; God tells Moses to assemble the people, speak to the rock in front of them, that they may see the water flow. Moses, who does this, says, "Listen, you rebels, must we bring you water out of this rock?" He strikes the rock twice with his staff and it gushes water. But Moses and Aaron do not honor God in their act and God tells them they will not be given admittance to the Promised Land. Aaron dies and is mourned for thirty days; he is succeeded by his son Eleazar. The Edomites deny the Israelites passage, who instead skirt the land of the Moabites; the Canaanite king of Arad and his army are defeated and destroyed, as are King Sihon and the Amorites and King Og of Bashan. The Israelites continue to grumble, and God, angered by their complaints, sends serpents to bite them. Moses prays for them and on God's instruction makes a bronze serpent to protect the people.

The sacrifice of the red heifer is the theme of a special Sabbath, Shabbat Parah. See p. 359.

Torah portion Ḥukat, Numbers 19:1–22:1; haftarah portion for Ḥukat, Judges 11:1–33.

The beginning of the story of Jephthah is the subject of the haftarah, Judges 11:1–33, and it concerns a matter related to the Torah portion. Jephthah the Gileadite, the son of a concubine, had been hounded out of Israel by his brothers. Having become a noted warrior, part of a band of outlaws, he was sought out as a leader when the Israelites were under attack by the Ammonites, who were pressing a land claim dating back three hundred years. Jephthah attempts a diplomatic solution but to no avail.

Torah portion Balak, Numbers 22:2–25:9; haftarah portion for Balak, Micah 5:6–6:8.

The second week's portion tells the story of King Balak of Moab and the oracle Balaam, the first non-Israelite prophet to recognize the power of God. Balak, fearing the growing masses of Israelites, hires Balaam to place curses upon them. But each time Balaam tries, he is given words by God and every curse becomes a prophecy of doom for Balak and a blessing for the Israelites:

> How beautiful are your tents, O Jacob,
>   your dwelling places, O Israel.
> Like valleys they spread out,
>   like gardens beside a river. . . .
> God brought them out of Egypt;
>   they have the strength of a wild ox.
> They devour hostile nations
>   and break their bones in pieces.

The haftarah for Balak, Micah 5:6–6:8, begins with a prediction of the fall of the divided kingdoms of Israel and Judah into the hands of the Assyrians. Micah's touch is softer and more economical than that of the sharp-edged Jeremiah, but with sometimes shocking turns. In these verses he describes how in their moment of triumph, God would turn on Israel, smash their property, and destroy their cities for their idolatry and evildoing:

The remnant of Jacob will be in the midst of many peoples,
  like dew from the Lord, like showers on the grass. . . .
  like a lion among the beasts of the forest. . . .
Your hand will be lifted in triumph over your enemies,
  and all your foes will be destroyed.
In that day, declares the Lord, I will destroy your horses
  and demolish your chariots.
I will destroy the cities of your land. . . .
My people, what have I done to you?
How have I burdened you?
Answer me. . . .
My people, remember what Balak king of Moab counseled
  and what Balaam son of Beor answered.

The third week's portion, *Pinḥas* (Phineas), Numbers 25:10–30:1, includes the third of three stories of rebellion in the Wilderness. As the Israelites were encamped at the edge of Moab, the men began to indulge in sexual relations with the Moabite women, who invited them to participate in the sacrifices to their God, the idol Baal of Peor. God commands Moses to slay these men and display their corpses, facing the sun, so that his anger will be diverted from the other Israelites, whom he will spare from a plague. One who rises in rage to avenge the insult to God is Phineas, "zealous for God," a grandson of Aaron, who throws his spear through the private parts of an Israelite man and his Midianite mistress. God is greatly pleased and grants him *shalom* and "everlasting priesthood."

Torah portion Pinḥas, Numbers 25:10–30:1; haftarah portion for Pinḥas, 1 Kings 18:46–19:21. The regular haftarah may be preempted when this portion is read after the seventeenth of Tamuz.

In the following chapter God orders Moses and his nephew Eleazar to take a new census, by tribe, just as Moses and Aaron had done forty years earlier. This time the purpose is the fair parceling of the Promised Land among the tribes. What the census reveals is that it will be an entirely new generation that inherits the land; only two adults among those who came out of Egypt, Caleb and Joshua, will be with the Israelites when they cross the Jordan into Canaan.

A question of inheritance arises. The daughters of Zelophehad, of the tribe of Manasseh, present themselves to Moses asking if they may inherit their late father's land, since they have no brothers. Moses brings the question before God, who declares that any such inheritance may be transferred, whether to a daughter or any other rightful heir, following a specific line:

> When a man dies leaving no son, his patrimony shall pass to his daughter. If he has no daughter, you shall give it to his brothers. If he has no brothers, you shall give it to his father's brother. If his father had no brothers, then you shall give possession to the nearest survivor in the family. ... This shall be a legal precedent for the Israelites.

And for all the world—though by the end of the book of Numbers, the ruling is modified (see page 187). The last chapters of the portion concern the calendar of sacrifices and then, specifically, sacrifices for the festival of Rosh Ḥodesh, the new moon. These are more elaborate than those described in Leviticus.

The haftarah for *Pinḥas*, 1 Kings 18:46-19:21, describes God's revelation to the prophet Elijah and concludes the dramatic and magical story that begins when the idolatrous Ahab becomes king of Israel. After Elijah slays the four hundred fifty prophets of Baal in view of the king, he flees for his life, fearing the revenge of Queen Jezebel, and hides in a cave at Mount Sinai. He hears the voice of God, who commands him to do three things: anoint Hazael king of Aram (a friendly northern kingdom), anoint Jehu king of Israel, and anoint Elisha as his own successor. The connection between the Torah portion and the haftarah may seem obscure, but early Bible sources find many convergences in the stories of Phineas and Elijah. It was believed that God's grant of "everlasting priesthood" applied literally to Phineas, that he became immortal and that he and Elijah were one and the same. Indeed, Phineas's death is never reported, and in Judges 20:28 he is still alive, working as a priest long after the death of everyone associated with the Exodus. Like Phineas, Elijah is also described as "zealous for God"; his birth is never reported, and he, too, never dies but rather is taken to heaven in a chariot drawn by angels.

The book of Numbers jumps quickly from narrative passages of the Wilderness years to legal matters, and this last week's portion *Matot* ("tribes"), Numbers 30:2–32.42, is no exception. It begins by discussing vows and sworn oaths in general and vows taken by women in particular. Then, a sudden switch to a troubling episode: God instructs the Israelites to destroy the Midianites for having lured some of Israel into sinfulness. At first the large Israelite force destroys only all the adult males. Moses is furious and and commands them to go back and destroy all the male children and the women, except for those who are virgins. He also instructs them on the disposition of the Midianites' property, which of it is to be purified and which destroyed.

Torah portion Matot, Numbers 30:2–32:42; haftarah portion for Matot, Jeremiah 1:1–2:3.

Compare this with the story of Samuel, Saul, and the Amalekites in 1 Samuel 15:1–34.

The reading switches back to legal matters: the request of the tribes of Reuben, Gad, and half the tribe of Manasseh, who, because of their vast flocks, wish to remain on the east side of the Jordan River because of the superior grazing. They are permitted to do so as long as they help in the conquering of the land of Canaan.

The destruction of the Midianites is an especially discomfiting chapter. The threat posed by the Midianites was not military but cultural: they threatened the Israelites with temptation. To give this chapter a facile explanation and to suggest, as is often done, that it represents the behavior and values of an olden time during which monotheism was under attack is a dangerous simplification. Such slaughters are carried out in our time with numbing frequency, invariably by people with a belief that their actions are a form of purification or cleansing. And yet these actions do nothing to stave off "polluting" ideologies. During the Cold War, a number of influential political scientists, including Henry Kissinger, concluded that the Soviet Union would prevail because its cultural persistance was more robust than the permissive pluralism of the West. Nothing was ever more wrong.

The haftarah is the beginning of the book of the prophet Jeremiah, whose words loom large in the period between the seventeenth of Tamuz and Tishah b'Av. It is the first of three "Haftarot of Affliction," prophecies foretelling the disasters that will befall the the people on Tishah b'Av. The preamble to the reading identifies Jeremiah as son of the priest Hilkiah, of the tribe of Benjamin. He begins his prophecy in the thir-

Josiah was the last righteous king after years of decline. He attempted a revival of the Torah and of God's command- ments, but it proved to be for naught.

teenth year of the reign of Josiah, king of Judah, and he con- tinues his prophecy until the eleventh year of the reign of Zedekiah—a period of more than forty years. In the fifth month of that year, the people of Jerusalem were carried into exile by the Babylonians. The book of Lamentations was long thought to have been written by Jeremiah, too, since it is closely related in its subject matter and its period, but that is no longer believed to be true.

In these first verses, Jeremiah explains his call to prophecy and the words that God spoke to him. He has to bolster his own resolve to deliver God's exhortations. And then the

tirades against the evil ways of the people—the jeremiads—
begin. They come as a torrent.

The juxtaposition of the passages from Numbers and
Jeremiah makes for sad reading: the Children of Israel, who
had enjoyed such favor in God's eyes, are now about to be
punished, as they turn from God's offer of a last chance of
reconciliation. But reading Jeremiah, one wonders if a reconciliation between God and Israel was ever possible. There is
throughout the feeling of a marriage gone bad: the bitter-
sweet remembrances of better days that will never be relived,
the recitation of offenses, the talk of recriminations, the
(maybe) hollow offer of another chance, more anger, and,
finally, collapse. The metaphor of Jeremiah is the poetry of
divorce.

> I remember the unfailing devotion of your youth,
> > the love of your bridal days,
> > when you followed Me in the wilderness,
> > through a land unsown.
> Israel was then holy to the Lord,
> > the firstfruits of His harvest. . . .

Jeremiah 2:2–3

The sweet memories turn to accusations:

> How well you pick your way in search of lovers!
> Why! Even the worst of women can learn from you . . .
> If a man puts away his wife and she leaves him,
> > and if she becomes another's,
> > may he go back to her again? . . .
> You have played the harlot with many lovers;
> > can you come back to Me?

*Jeremiah 2:33–3:1.
This is beyond the
verses of the week's
portion.*

There are two wives here, the Kingdom of Israel and the
Kingdom of Judah, each with her own "issues." "Apostate
Israel is less to blame than that faithless woman Judah," God

Jeremiah 3:11

says to Jeremiah. With the first, there may be a chance for reconciliation.

Jeremiah 3:12   Come back to me, apostate Israel,
I will no longer frown on you.
My love is unfailing, I will not be angry forever.
Only you must acknowledge your wrongdoing.

But for second wife, Judah:

Jeremiah 4:11   A scorching wind from the high bare places in the wilderness
sweeps down upon my people,
no breeze for winnowing or for cleansing;
a wind too strong for these . . .

In the end, Israel and Judah were destroyed by Assyria and Babylon. It was a long, hard fall.

"And the threshing floors shall be full of wheat"
(Joel 2:24)

The Month of Av

THE WOODCUT SCENES of Leo basking in the summer sun and threshing floors full with wheat are hardly the images that come to mind as the month of Av begins. "When Av comes in, joy is diminished" is the talmudic dictum. Av begins in the midst of the Three Weeks, the period of mourning that recalls some of the greatest catastrophes of the Jewish people, which began the previous month, on the seventeenth of Tamuz. It was the Ashkenazic custom to restrict oneself from all joyous things during the entire period, in remembrance of the destruction of the Temple. Weddings and performances were banned, and it was forbidden from the seventeenth of Tamuz through the ninth of Av for adults to bathe, shave, or do laundry. Meat and wine, both joyous things, were also forbidden, the only exceptions being Sabbath and festive meals held on special occasions, such as a circumcision. Today, most observant Ashkenazim follow the Sephardic practice of obeying these restrictions from only the first through the ninth of Av—called the Nine Days.

Rosh Ḥodesh Av is observed for one day only. In our model year it falls on Sabbath, but given the grave nature of the Three Weeks, neither the special maftir's reading for Rosh

The 1593 Minhogimbukh states: "In Italy they drink wine until the last meal before the fast on Tishah b'Av, because they are incapable of drinking water alone for eight days."

Ḥodesh, Numbers 28:9–15, nor the special haftarah, Isaiah 66:1–24, is read. In many communities the festive dress associated with Sabbath is not worn during this time. *Kidush levanah*, the ritual blessing of the new moon, is held off until happier times after the ninth, since one is not supposed to confront the shekhinah, the Divine Presence, while in a sad frame of mind.

It is customary for the services during the Three Weeks to be humble, without much singing. The Torah reading for the first week of Av is Numbers 33:1–36:13, called *Masei* ("Journeys"): an end-of-book look back to the places where the Israelites stopped in the Wilderness on their way out of Egypt. The first was Sukkot, the same as the autumn festival. God describes the borders of Canaan as they are to appear after the conquest of the land by the Israelites. One legal innovation is the establishment of asylum towns, three in the land of Canaan and three outside it, for anyone who has allegedly killed someone by accident, so that they may escape the vengeance—the "blood redemption"—of the victim's family and await the judgment of the community. If the community decides in favor of the blood redeemer, then the person who has taken a life is to be put to death. If they decide in favor of the life taker, then he is to be returned to the town of asylum where he is to remain until the death of the high priest there, after which he may go back whence he came. The standard of innocence God establishes here is what became known in the Anglo-American law as the "absence of malice aforethought." If the life taker (still not adjudicated) leaves the town of asylum before the high priest's death, then he may be be killed by the blood redeemer without blood guilt. Also established here is the requirement of multiple witnesses in a capital cases; the

The death of the high priest is certainly an odd determinant of time. It would have to be considered as among the ḥukim —the inexplicable commandments.

word of one person alone is not suffiicient. The portion—
and the book—ends with an elaboration of the legal case of
the daughters of Zelophehad and the inheritance of their
father's property, first described in chapter 27, in the portion
Pinḥas. Here, the heads of the clans from the tribe of
Manasseh petition Moses, saying that if the daughters marry
outside the tribe, their property will be lost to the tribe's
aggregate inheritance. Moses, speaking on God's authority,
rules that the property would remain with the daughters only
if they married within their tribe. And so Zelophehad's
daughters—a practical group, for sure—married the sons of
their uncles.

For the beginning of the story of the daughters of Zelophehad, see p. 180.

This was reversed in later law, with the explanation that it applied to only the original generations in Israel.

The haftarah *Shimu*, Jeremiah 2:4-28, 3:4, 4:1-16, continues on the themes of the previous portion, which foretells the
punishments to come: the breakdown of the God-Israel marriage, faithlessness, treachery, and the other offenses. This is
the second Haftarah of Affliction.

See the previous haftarah on p. 182.

The second Sabbath in our model month is called Shabbat
Ḥazon, the "Sabbath of Foretelling," so named for the haftarah reading from the beginning of Isaiah, in which the
prophet foretells the destruction of Jerusalem. It is the third
and final Sabbath of the Three Weeks. The Torah portion is
the beginning of Deuteronomy, the fifth and last book of the
Torah. The Greek *deuteros* means "second"; *nomos* is the word
for "law." The name is apt, since in the book Moses repeats
and clarifies the commandments and laws he gave earlier. In
Hebrew the book is called *Devarim*—"words"—the same word
used by Moses in reference to the Ten Commandments. Thus
the book begins, "These are the words that Moses spoke to all
Israel." The book's tone is that of a great oration and all of it
is, in fact, Moses's farewell speech. His oratory is that of a
teacher, not a prince or a politician, and in no book of the

Shabbat Ḥazon always precedes Tishah b'Av.

Torah is instruction so central and urgent. With stern insistence, Moses instructs the Israelites to observe God's laws and warns them of the dire consequences if they do not.

The book begins with the Israelites camped along the Jordan River, before their entrance into the land of Canaan. After forty years in the Wilderness, Moses, who knows he will not make the journey into the Promised Land, speaks of the burden of age: "I am not able, I alone, to carry you." He speaks of the indigenous peoples of the land and God's instructions in their regard: whose land is not to be trespassed and whose is to be taken. Then he tells the tribes of Israel how the land will be divided among them, a matter that was discussed first in the last chapters of Numbers.

The haftarah, *Ḥazon Yeshayahu*, is the beginning (1:1–27) of Isaiah. It is the last of the three Haftarot of Affliction, and most of it is sung with a special tune of lament. Isaiah begins *The special tune is the* Eikha *trope, the same as used to sing the book of Lamentations.* his prediction of the fall of both Jerusalem and the Kingdom of Judah, citing the iniquity and sinfulness that has overtaken them, "like Sodom, another Gomorrah." He continues in God's voice, saying that all the observances and piety at the Temple, all the sacrifices and keeping of the calendar are but hollow, futile proclamations of false solemnity.

TISHAH B'AV

The ninth of Av (*tishah* = nine) is the traditional collective symbol of the Jewish people's greatest disasters: failures, oppressions, sufferings, and exiles. Its stature as a twenty-five-hour day of fasting is shared only with Yom Kippur. On this day in 586 B.C.E. the Temple and Jerusalem were destroyed by the Babylonian forces of King Nebuchadnezzar, and all the people of Judah and Jerusalem, its capital, were

taken captive. In 722 B.C.E. the Northern Kingdom had been destroyed by
the Assyrians. On or about the same
day six hundred years after the Babylonian siege, in 70 C.E., the Roman
legions of Titus destroyed the Second
Temple; again on the same day, in 135
C.E., Bar Kokhba's fortress at Betar fell
to Hadrian's army, marking the end of
the last vestige of Jewish self-gover-
nance until 1948. The iteration of
tragedies of the ninth of Av is only the beginning of Jewish
woes. It goes on to include the murder of Rhineland Jews
during the first Crusade in 1096, expulsion of the Jews from
England in 1290, from France in 1304 (and again over the
next century), and from Spain in 1492.

*Tishah b'Av,
Venice, 1593. A
mental image of
the Temple burns
in the background
as members of the
congregation sit on
the floor reading
the book of Lamen-
tations.*

For all of these tragedies to coincide on one day took some
"interpreting," but it has its own wisdom. The traditional
understanding is that they are all of a piece: all exiles that
stem from the first events in 586 B.C.E., which had been
brought about by God's will to punish his people who had
besmirched their capital, strayed from his teachings, and
sinned greatly. In both books of Kings, especially the second,
one reads of the slow decline of the two kingdoms. By the
time King Josiah discovers a long-lost book of laws—the
Torah!—and orders that it be read publicly from beginning to
end, it was too little, too late. It may be argued that the events
after the destruction of the Temple were political or military
failures or episodes in which the Jews in the Diaspora suffered at the hands of their non-Jewish neighbors. But there
the events of 586 B.C.E. were divine punishment for sin, especially the sin of idolatry. The five poems that comprise the

*The original refer-
ence is to a "scroll
of laws," which
may have been
Deuteronomy only.*

book of Lamentations, a central feature of the liturgy of Tishah b'Av, form a veritable catalog of the people's sins as well as of God's punishments.

To Jews who do not follow traditional observance, Tishah b'Av has become perhaps the least-known major festival. It calls for a rigorous confrontation with great tragedies and with our own malfeasances—and it does so in the middle of summer when many synagogues can barely raise a minyan and students (except for the most devout) are on vacation. Reform Judaism had largely written off Tishah b'Av as an anachronism, since it was tied to mourning for (and prayers for the restoration of) the Temple, an institution the movement had rejected as no longer relevant to Jewish belief. Today, the Union of American Hebrew Congregations, the organization of Reform synagogues, recognizes Tishah b'Av as a day on which various tragedies are remembered. What is lost in this generalized interpretation, however, is the deeper significance of Tishah b'Av, which lies well beyond one's feelings about the Temple: as a much-needed time to examine human failing and self-destructiveness.

See p. 149 for Yom Hashoah. Yet another reason for the decline of Tishah b'Av in the public imagination was the advent of Yom Hashoah, Holocaust Remembrance Day, the immediacy of which subsumed much Jewish energy for the commemoration of tragedy. Perhaps it is Yom Hashoah that should include other events in which Jews were victims and martyrs, leaving Tishah b'Av to its own realm, the one of God's punishments so devastatingly described by the prophets.

The Customs of Tishah b'Av

On the eve of Tishah b'Av, there is a ritual closing meal before the fast begins, a *seudah mafseket*. It is customary to eat round foods, such as lentils or eggs, which are symbols of mourning. The 1593 *Minhogimbukh* explains the eating of lentils—already associated with mourning in Genesis—in an especially poetic way:

> Lentils are round as mourning goes around; today it reaches one of us, tomorrow someone else. Peas are round, too, but some have a black line, like a mouth. Lentils don't have a mouth, the way a mourner does not speak.

If Tishah b'Av begins on a Saturday night, as it does in our model year, one is allowed to eat meat and drink wine; customs vary as to whether or not there is a ritual closing meal. However, in years when everyone does eat the ritual meal, one tries to do so alone, to avoid a *zimun*, a quorum for public blessing that arouses feelings of fellowship and requires special prayers in the Grace after Meals. The meal must be finished during daylight. It is customary to eat sitting on the floor or on a low stool, as one does in mourning. In fact, one follows this practice until afternoon prayers. Havdalah is abbreviated. The candlelighting is blessed, but there is no smelling of the spices, nor do we bless our children. At the conclusion of Tishah b'Av, Havdalah is made over a glass of wine but again without the spices.

See p.85 for Havdalah.

It is forbidden to wear leather shoes, to bathe, to wash anything, to eat or drink, or to have sexual relations. But it is allowed to wash the hands in a minimal way for the sake of ritual purity, to be able to recite the prayer *Netilat yadayim*. One does not greet friends or acquaintances. The Torah may not be studied except for those passages relevant to the day: Lamentations, Job, Jeremiah (but not the passages of consolation). Tefillin are not worn until afternoon prayers because they are considered *peer*, "glorification." The tzitzit are worn, but not blessed, but not the tallit until afternoon.

A special prayer book is used for Tishah b'Av. It is called Kinot, which means "elegies," the word also used for a series of dirges that are recited in the services.

In the evening prayers, the cantor starts softly, saying *Vehu raḥum*, "The merciful One, He is forgiving of iniquity," and is followed by the Barkhu, the call to prayer. The lights are kept low; only next to the cantor is a light; the *parokhet*, the curtain in front of the ark, is removed. The congregants take off their shoes (or wear nonleather ones) and pray by themselves, everyone sitting on the ground. Then the Amidah is recited, standing as always, followed by half Kaddish. Then everyone sits down on the ground again to begin the reading of the book of Lamentations, the principal text of Tishah b'Av. The cantor, also sitting on the floor, begins the reading.

The book of Lamentations is one of the five scrolls (megilot), the others being the Song of Songs, Ruth, Ecclesiastes, and Esther. If Lamentations is read from an actual scroll, which it usually is not, it requires a special blessing; see p. 355.

The scroll known in Hebrew by the word *Eikhah* ("how"), with which it begins, is known in English as the "Lamentations of Jeremiah," though the authorship of its five poems has been a matter of debate for some time. But whoever may have written them, the rawness of the pain and the immediacy of the suffering described suggests an author or authors who were contemporary with the destruction.

The first four poems are alphabetic acrostics, a device that symbolizes here the completeness—the A to Z—of the destruction and misery. The first poem begins in near silence, describing the state of Jerusalem:

Lamentations 1:1–2

How deserted she lies, the city, once so full of people.
Once great among nations, now like a widow;
She was the queen of provinces, but now is like a slave. . . .
Bitterly she weeps in the night, with no one to comfort her.

As to how this disaster came about, there is no doubt:

Lamentations 1:8

Jerusalem had sinned greatly,
   and so she was treated like a filthy rag. . . .

Lamentations 1:18

The Lord was in the right;
   it was I who rebelled against His commandments. . . .

Lamentations 2:17

The Lord has done what He had planned to do,
   He has fulfilled His threat.

So heavy is the hardship that in the third poem the poet becomes angry at God, suspecting his motives:

> Like a bear lying in wait, like a lion in hiding,   *Lamentations 3:10*
>   He dragged me from the path and mangled me
>   and left me without help. . . .
> He has broken my teeth with gravel   *Lamentations 3:16*
>   and He has trampled me in the dust. . . .
> My splendor is gone and all that I   *Lamentations 3:18*
>   had hoped from the Lord.

Then the poet remembers—where there is life, there is hope.

> Because of the Lord's great love we are not consumed,   *Lamentations 3:22*
>   for His compassion never fails. . . .
> For men are not cast off by the Lord forever.   *Lamentations 3:31*
> Though He brings grief, He will show compassion.

But suffer they did, the Children of Israel. None was spared and no one came to their rescue:

> The suckling infant's tongue cleaves to its palate in thirst;   *Lamentations 4:4*
>   young children beg for bread, but no one offers
>   them a crumb. . . .
>   and those nurtured in luxury now grovel   *Lamentations 4:5*
>   on dunghills. . . .

In the end, they beg to be remembered, but there is no sign of anyone's listening. It is a custom that the first three poems be chanted with increasing loudness but the fourth read quietly like the first. The penultimate verse *Hashivenu* (5:21), "Restore us, Lord!" is said loudly by the cantor, then repeated by the congregation; the cantor says the last verse and the congregation follows with *Hashivenu*, again, and the cantor repeats it, alone: "Restore us to Yourself, O Lord, that we may return; renew our days as of old."   *Lamentations 5:21*

The third poem has its own special tune.

Having finished Lamentations, the cantor begins the recitation of the Kinot, the latter-day poems of lamentation.

These are an accumulated literature, the most famous of which come from the Middle Ages. Some are paraphrases of the books of Lamentations and Jeremiah, others refer to later diasasters. The first *kinah* (sing.) is a paraphrase of the fifth poem of Lamentations. The tune is altered to accommodate the addition of the word *Oy* (O! in the sense of "woe!") in the middle of each verse and *Oy meh hayah lanu* (O! what has befallen us!) at the end of each verse, so that the verse that reads "Remember, O Lord, what has befallen us; look, and see our disgrace" now becomes "Remember, O Lord, what has befallen us—O!—look, and see our disgrace—O!—what has befallen us!" and so on through all the verses until verse nineteen, which is recited straight. The congregation says the *Hashivenu* verse, as before, and the cantor repeats it.

The number of Kinot recited in the evening service varies according to local custom but is usually five to seven. When they are concluded, the cantor stands up in front of the pulpit and recites the prayer *Atah kadosh*, "You are the Holy One," which includes the Kedushah, the angels' sanctification, which is said by the congregation. The surrounding interpretive translation in Aramaic is recited softly.

See p. 33 for Kedushah.

THE MORNING SERVICE starts early in the synagogue. Everyone prays by themselves. In some congregations the *Pesukei dezimra*, the songs that begin the morning prayer, are not recited aloud. Instead, the cantor starts with *Yishtabah* ("Praised may be Your name forever"), but quietly, as a mourner. As usual, it is followed by Kaddish and Barkhu, the call to prayer. Again, the tefillin are not put on; tzitzit are worn, but not the tallit. Everyone sits on the floor. The *Minhogimbukh* mentions here that after the repetition of the Amidah, the cantor sings a special hymn, *Aavikh beyom mevekh,* "On this day of confusion." This is a *kerovah,* one of a special class of hymns inserted into the prayers on special days but they are rarely included nowadays. As on all public fast days, the cantor inserts *Anenu* ("Answer us") after the seventh benediction (which asks for redemption) in the repetition of the Amidah. Taḥanun, the prayers of supplication, is not said.

For more about kerovot, see p. 280.

The Torah is taken out, and a section of the next week's Torah portion is read with a low voice: Deuteronomy 4:25–4:40. It is an appropriate choice for it provides a small measure of needed comfort. It says: even if you do ill in God's eyes and are punished because of it, you may still seek God's forgiveness, which will be generous. The third person who goes up to the Torah (three are called) also recites the haftarah, chanted in the dirge-like manner of Lamentations. It is Jeremiah 8:13–9:23, which is a vision of the destruction to come. Then the cantor sits down on the floor and starts reciting the Kinot. Though the tradition is to recite the Kinot for the rest of the morning, the number recited varies according to local custom and time available on certain days of the week—more on Sunday, fewer on weekdays. The repertory known to most American Jews is about fifty Kinot. The best-known author of Kinot was Eleazar Hakallir, who was active in Palestine in the early seventh century C.E. He set the tone and the often complex form (multiple acrostics) that was followed by most poets afterward. The texts make almost constant reference to biblical passages, not only to those related directly to the destruction of the Temple, but also to earlier disasters and warnings. And thus they begin:

> Everything came to a standstill.
> Turn away from me! Those who have besmirched me made me hear.

Kinah no. 6, Eleazar Hakallir.

They made me a filth and refuse amidst the flocks of my
fellow nations. . . .

Kinah no. 6,
Eleazar Hakallir.
The Rose of
Sharon is men-
tioned in the Song
of Songs, 2:1.

O how the Rose of Sharon sits alone
    and joy has been silenced from the mouths
    of those who carried the Ark;
And the priests, the sons of Aaron,
    were removed from their watches,

Kinah no. 15,
Eleazar Hakallir.

Alas! For His quiver is open like a grave waiting for death,
    and He has added a wing to my furious attacker.
I am the man who has seen affliction by the rod
    of His anger.

And a later *kinah*, recalling the First Crusade in 1096,

Kinah no. 25,
anonymous.

Would that my head were water,
    and my eyes a fount of flowing tears . . .
I shall arouse the bitter of heart,
    the confounded ones to weep with me,
        over the beautiful maidens and the tender lads,
        wrapped in their scrolls and dragged to the slaughter…
yet they were trampled and discarded like the
    mud in the streets.
"Turn away from the unclean Jew!"
    they called to each other, lest they come too close. . . .
Please take to your hearts to compose a bitter eulogy,
    because their massacre is deserving of mourning
    and rolling in dust as was the burning of the House
    of our Lord, its Hall and its Palace.

It includes a verse that became a point of rabbinic discussion
when Yom Hashoah was first proposed:

However, we cannot add a new day of mourning over ruin
    and conflagration, nor may we mourn any earlier, only later.
Instead, today on Tishah b'Av I will arouse my sorrowful wailing,
    and I will eulogize and wail and weep with a bitter soul,
    and my groans are heavy from morning until evening.

In some congregations, following Sephardic practice, the book of Lamentations is also read. The study of the book of Job on or before Tishah b'Av is universally recommended; its reading in the synagogue, however, is regarded as a Sephardic custom, though it appears in the 1593 *Minhogim-bukh* and is still observed today by some Ashkenazim.

In the afternoon service, shoes are again removed, but tallit and tefillin are worn and the congregants are seated on chairs. From the Torah, excerpts from the portion *Ki tisa*, Exodus 32:11–14 and 34:1–10, are read, as they are on the seventeenth of Tamuz. It contains two reminders of God's forgiveness and commitment to the Children of Israel: The first segment is the story of how Moses dissuades God from destroying the Israelites after the Golden Calf; the second is the reconfirmation of the Covenant when God gives Moses the second set of tablets to replace the first ones, which were smashed. The haftarah is Isaiah 55:6–56:8, the same as on all public fast days. Its theme: deliverance will be granted to those who keep God's laws. The cantor says the Priestly Blessing, which had been omitted from the morning service.

The evening service is that of a regular weekday. If the moon can be seen, the Blessing of the Moon is recited, deferred from earlier in the month. The Havdalah ceremony is performed over wine, but without the spices, and so we conclude ninth of Av. But the observance doesn't end abruptly; it is the custom to refrain from eating meat or drinking wine until midday on the tenth, because on the ninth the Temple was set ablaze, but it didn't fall until the day after.

*See p. 97 for the Blessing of the Moon (*Kidush levanah*).*

The Month of Av After the Ninth

The Sabbath following the Tishah b'Av is called Shabbat Naḥamu, so named because the haftarah read on that day

begins *Naḥamu naḥamu ami*, "Comfort, comfort my people,"
from the fortieth chapter of Isaiah. This, along with the Torah
portion *Vaetḥanan* (Deuteronomy 3:23–7:11), which precedes
it, does not change with fluctuations in the calendar.

In our model year, this Sabbath falls on Tu b'Av, the
fifteenth of Av, a very joyous—and much ignored—day of
hope for rebuilding in the aftermath of the destruction and
exile. It also commemorates a number of events: the readmit-
tance of the tribe of Benjamin into the community of Israel,
thereby ending a civil war; God's sparing of the lives of the
Israelites in the Wilderness (Numbers 14:32); the rescinding
of the restrictions placed on women's inheritance of property; and the permission to properly bury the dead after the
fall of Betar. If a wedding takes place that day, there is no
need for the prewedding fast (not connected with Tu b'Av).

*The story of the
Benjaminites is
told in Judges
19–21. It is a tale of
rape, revenge, and
the failure of mob
justice.*

*See p. 367 for wed-
ding customs.*

One Torah scroll is taken out from the ark to read the portion *Vaetḥanan* ("And I pleaded"), Deuteronomy 3:23–7:11.
Moses recalls how he pleaded with God to be allowed into
the Promised Land, only to be rebuffed. Moses is told to go
up to Mount Pisgah to look out over the land and to make
Joshua strong, "for he will cause them to inherit the land that
you see." Moses prepares the people to hear his address, to

*Deuteronomy
4:1–2*

> hearken to the laws and regulations that I am teaching you
> to observe. . . . You are not to add to the word that I am
> commanding you, and you are not to subtract from it.

After a few verses of oddly irrelevant material on the towns of
asylum, repeating what had been said in Numbers 35, Moses's
great exhortation begins, occupying the rest of the book
until the final chapter, which tells of Moses's death.

The speech begins magnificently. It evokes awe without
loss of immediacy. All Israel has been assembled to listen and

Moses speaks with insistent rhythm—one can imagine the sound of a great drum, beating on the words "Yes!" "Us!" "Today!" "Alive!"

> Hear, O Israel, . . .
> The Lord our God cut with us a covevant at Mount Sinai.
> It was not with our fathers that the Lord cut this covenant,
> but with us, all of us here today.
> all of us that are alive!

Deuteronomy 5:2–3

Moses has transformed past events into the shared experience of the here and now. Then, all stand as the Ten Commandments are quoted, in a form slightly different from their first appearance in Exodus. Moses reminds the assembly of the first time they heard the words, directly from the mouth of God, "from the midst of fire, cloud, and fog," and how God listened to their words, saying, "It is well, all that they have spoken."

Moses speaks the words of the Shema and instructs when they are to be recalled:

> You are to impress them upon your children and recite them when you stay at home and when you are away, when you lie down and when you get up. Bind them as a sign on your hand and let them serve as a symbol on your forehead; inscribe them on the doorposts of your house and on your gates.

Deuteronomy 6:7–9

Thus begins three fundaments of Judaism: the establishment of the Shema as primary among all prayers; the wearing of tefillin; and the placement of a mezuzah on one's doorpost.

God is not to be tested or questioned, Moses reminds his listeners. Children are to be taught how God brought their forebears out of Egypt—"never forget it." The Israelites are not to mix with any of the Canaanite peoples, whose culture is to be "consigned to destruction." How is this to be

balanced with the themes of justice so clear in the Ten
Commandments?

The haftarah portion *Naḥamu*, Isaiah 40:1–26, gives this
Sabbath its name. It is the first of the seven Haftarot of Consolation, which are read in the weeks following Tishah b'Av.
The events mentioned in the book of Isaiah span about two
hundred years and while traditional Jewish belief holds that
the prophecies were written by one person, it is understood
today that there were at least two authors. The first Isaiah
lived in Jerusalem in the eighth century B.C.E. and prophesied
the fall of the city; Second Isaiah, also called Deutero-Isaiah,
whose words begin with this portion, wrote during the Babylonian captivity and preached a hopeful message of a new
beginning.

After all the foreboding and all the suffering that followed
it, this haftarah gleams with new hope: The punishment is
over and with its end, a life of equanimity and fulfillment of
God's glory is ushered in as Israel enters the Promised Land

This translation is and is delivered—or redelivered—and redeemed. The exultant
especially familiar verse translation below is from the King James Bible.
to English speakers
as the text of sev-
eral segments of   Comfort ye, comfort ye my people, saith your God.
George Frideric   Speak ye comfortably to Jerusalem,
Handel's oratorio   and cry unto her, that her warfare is accomplished,
Messiah. This   that her iniquity is pardoned:
chapter of Isaiah is   for she hath received of the Lord's hand
also an important   double for all her sins.
one in Christian   The voice of him that crieth in the wilderness,
belief, though in a   Prepare ye the way of the Lord,
substantially inter-   make straight in the desert a highway for our God.
preted form. It is   Every valley shall be exalted,
quoted in the third   and every mountain and hill shall be made low:
chapter of Luke,   and the crooked shall be made straight,
where the "voice   and the rough places plain:
who crieth in the
wilderness" is John
the Baptist.

And the glory of the Lord shall be revealed,
  and all flesh shall see it together:
  for the mouth of the Lord hath spoken it.

The reading for the fourth Sabbath of the month is *Ekev* ("As a consequence of"), Deuteronomy 7:12–11:25. For every mention of a great gift that the Israelites will inherit, Moses speaks of a dire consequence if they are disobedient to God's laws. First the carrot, then the stick—a blessing, then a curse—this is his pattern. He tells the Israelites to be unafraid of the numerous Canaanites, for God will dispatch them as he did Pharaoh and all of Egypt, and then warns them against paying heed to their idols; even the gold and silver that adorns them is not to be desired. After Moses describes the bounteous land the people are about to inherit, he hastens to add that only on the condition of their love of God and their remembrance of all that God had done for them will they continue to enjoy these riches. Emphasizing the critical importance of memory, Moses recalls the entire story of the Golden Calf and how it was only through his pleading that the Israelites—a stubborn, "hard-necked people"—were saved from God's wrathful destruction. "So circumcise the foreskin of your heart, your neck you are not to keep hard anymore." Moses tells them of their new lives, urging the people to become more openly loving of God. He tells them, too, that the God who plays no favorites, takes no bribes, and provides justice for widows and orphans also instructs his people to love sojourners and provide them with food and clothing because they, the Children of Israel, were once sojourners in Egypt.

The haftarah *Vatomer Tziyon*, Isaiah 49:14–51:3, the second Haftarah of Consolation, is a mirror image of the Torah portion. As Moses speaks to those who are about to enter the

Promised Land, Isaiah addresses those who are about to *reenter* it. As God had listened to the people at Mount Sinai, he teaches Isaiah to listen and gives him "the tongue of a teacher and skill to console the weary." With God's help the entering Israelites will overthrow the Canaanites; the reentering Israelites, at the end of their captivity in Babylon, will be carried in on the shoulders of the nations, tended along the way by kings and queens. Has God rescinded the divorce decree, described so vehemently by Jeremiah?

Isaiah 50:1 The Lord says,
Is there anywhere a writ of divorce
    by which I have put your mother away?
Was there some creditor of mine to whom I sold you?
No, it was through your own wickedness that you were sold
    and for your own misconduct that your mother was
    put away.

The reconciliation is under way and the second honeymoon is about to begin:

Isaiah 51:3 The Lord has indeed comforted Zion,
    comforted all her ruined homes. . . .
Joy and gladness shall be found in her,
    thanksgiving and melody.

There are five Sabbaths in this month of Av; the Torah portion for the last one is *Reeh* ("See!"), Deuteronomy 11:26–16:17. In it Moses tells the purpose of his blessing-curse pattern: to instruct the Israelites to remember the consequences for not obeying the laws and regulations and, when they cross the Jordan, to give the blessing on Mount Gerizim and the curse on Mount Ebal.

Chapter 12 marks the beginning of the core matter of Deuteronomy: the laws in detail. Unlike the parts of Exodus that deal mainly with social relations, property law, and dam-

ages, the section of Deuteronomy that begins here concerns *For Exodus chapters 19–24, see pp. 339 and 343.*
mostly moral and criminal matters and, to a smaller extent,
dietary laws.

Such laws cannot be abbreviated, but the following list is
offered as a guide to the topics in this portion: demolition of
the Canaanite religious sites; sacrificial offerings and tithes;
animals that may and may not be eaten; that blood may not
be eaten; false gods and prophets are to be destroyed; sabbatical years and release from debts; giving to the needy;
the fair treatment of serfs; observing Passover; observing
Shavuot; and observing Sukkot.

The haftarah is Isaiah 54:11–55:5. It appears that the
Israelites, still captive in Babylonia, required more assuaging
to return home and rebuild the marriage. This third Haftarah
of Consolation is a heavily orchestrated sales pitch, loaded
with buyer incentives. God describes the rebuilt Jerusalem as
a place so magnificent that even its "boundary stones shall be
jewels." The Israelites' children "will be taught by the Lord
and great will be [their] peace."

And in case the promises of security aren't enough, there is
an offer of free lunch:

> Come, all of you who are thirsty, come to the waters;   *Isaiah 55:1–2*
> and you who have no money, come, buy and eat!
> Come, buy wine and milk without money and without
> cost.
> ... Listen, Listen to me, and eat what is good,   *Isaiah 55:3*
> and your soul will delight in the richest of fare.

Yet the most affecting passage, impossible to read today without a sense of tragic irony, is this one:

> Tyranny will be far from you; indeed, nothing will you fear   *Isaiah 54:14*
> and terror will not come near you.

May it be so.

"And the wineskins we filled were new"
(Joshua 9:13)

The Month of Elul

ELUL IS A MONTH OF PREPARATION for the coming New Year and the Days of Awe, the ten-day period from Rosh Hashanah through Yom Kippur, when Jews stand before God to recount and repent their sins of the past year. Elul is considered a time of divine grace and forgiveness, when Moses received the second tablets, thus reassuring the Children of Israel after the Golden Calf episode. Elul is considered an auspicious time to schedule weddings and court cases. But there is more to Elul than preparation alone: it is a time of repentance, prayer, and, above all, of giving. In ancient times Elul had been the "New Year for Tithes" and it remains today the time when annual pledges toward charitable obligations are reviewed and renewed.

Elul is a month without holidays but with many special customs. Rosh Ḥodesh is celebrated for two days and it begins with the blowing of the shofar, a sound heard every day of the month except on Sabbath and on the day before Rosh Hashanah. The *Minhogimbukh* gives three reasons for it:

> When Moses went up to Mount Sinai for the second time to receive the tablets, the shofar was sounded to remind the people that they should not behave the way they did the

Blowing the shofar from the Minhogimbukh, Venice, 1593.

first time, saying Moses was dead and committing the sin of the Golden Calf. It is for this reason that the shofar is blown throughout the month today.

According to another story, the shofar is blown to confuse Satan, so he doesn't know when Rosh Hashanah is. If the shofar were blown only on Rosh Hashanah, Satan would know when it was and would accuse us in front of God, blessed be He.

According to yet another explanation, the shofar is blown throughout the month of Elul in order to remind the people of Israel that they should repent. Once there was a king who told his people they should prepare to face their enemy, and he ordered that the trumpets be blown to remind them. Similarly, the shofar is blown one month before New Year to remind us to repent, since we will soon have to face our own evil inclination (*yetzer hara*). Therefore, we must cry every day in the morning before eating and must remember the sins of the last year and repent. If we do so and give an account of the year that has passed, we will be free of sins when the holy day of the New Year approaches.

The blowing of the shofar in Elul is a custom, not a law, and is not observed everywhere.

Maimonides wrote that the sounding of the shofar is a wake-up call to repentance. The blowing of the shofar usually follows a specific pattern of blasts: *Tekiah* (tuuuuu), *Shevarim* (u-tu, u-tu, u-tu) + *Teruah* (tu, tu, tu, tu, tu, tu, tu, tu, tu), and *Tekiah* again. We shall meet this signalman's vocabulary again in Rosh Hashanah. Exactly when in the Elul morning services the shofar is blown varies among congregations, though most do so before the recitation of Psalm 27, a special addition to the morning service from Rosh Ḥodesh Elul through Hoshana Rabbah. It follows the recitation of the Psalm of the Day at the end of the service

Teshuvah and Selihah: Repentance and Forgiveness

The Hebrew word for repentance, *teshuvah*, has at its root *shuv*, "to return," and it is the idea of returning to God that lies at its center. The fifth benediction of the Amidah begins "Bring us back, our father . . . and influence us to return to your service in complete repentance." According to the sages of the Talmud there are three stages of repentance for sin: *selihah*, "forgiveness," the earnest and active request of one who has sinned against another or against God; *mehilah*, "wiping away," a request to reestablish the relationship as it was before the violation; and *kaparah*, "atonement," through which one demonstrates contrition. The twelfth-century sage Maimonides explains the process in five steps: confess the sin to the injured party; compensate the injured party; resolve never to repeat the transgression; ask for forgiveness from the injured party; and refrain from repeating the act, should the opportunity to do so arise again.

In Jewish tradition, recognition of sins against God is observed not just privately, but as a community, with a sense of collective necessity. This is done through special prayers called Selihot, "forgivenesses," which may be recited anytime but are part of a public prayer ritual in Elul. Ashkenazim gather to say Selihot every day for at least four days prior to Rosh Hashanah as well as on the days between Rosh Hashanah and (including) Yom Kippur. In the Sephardic tradition, the recitation of Selihot begins on Rosh Hodesh Elul. The Selihot constitute a large repertory filling books of their own. At their core is a passage in Exodus (34:6–7) known as the Thirteen Attributes of Mercy, in which God reveals him-

The specific Ashkenazic custom is this: Sunday is always the first day of Selihot; if Rosh Hashanah falls on a Thursday or on Sabbath, the saying of Selihot begins on the preceding Sunday, but if Rosh Hashanah falls on Monday or Tuesday, we start saying penitential prayers on the Sunday of the week before Rosh Hashanah.

self to Moses—not his physical self but his essence. It was with this revealed knowledge that Moses could appeal to God for mercy at times when the Israelites had transgressed. The Thirteen Attributes are reckoned in the Talmud this way:

The verses in Exodus read: "The Lord, the Lord, a God compassionate and gracious, slow to anger, abundant in kindness and faithfulness, extending kindness to the thousandth generation, forgiving iniquity, transgression, and sin, yet He does not remit all punishment, but visits the iniquity of parents upon children and upon children's children to the third and fourth generation." For more on these verses, see p. 34.

1. *Lord.* The name of the Lord denotes mercy; God is merciful before a person sins.
2. *Lord.* God is merciful after a person sins.
3. *God.* God's mercy is even greater than his name.
4. *compassionate.* God is compassionate.
5. *gracious.* God is gracious, even to the undeserving.
6. *patient.* God is slow to anger.
7. *abounding in loving-kindness.* God is abundant in his kindness.
8. *and truth.* God's word is truth.
9. *keeping kindnesses to the thousandth generation.* God preserves acts of kindness through the generations.
10. *bearing with sin.* God forgives even willful sinners if they repent.
11. *and transgression.* God forgives those who anger him if they repent.
12. *and error.* God forgives those who commit sins out of carelessness.
13. *and forgiving.* God cleanses the sins of those who repent.

The Selihot service begins with *Ashrei* (Psalm 145) followed by half Kaddish, prayers of repentance derived from biblical verses interspersed with repetitions of the Thirteen Attributes, the confessional *Viduy ashamnu,* and closing with *Shomer Yisrael* and full Kaddish. The Selihot liturgy comprises petitions that begin *Selah lanu* and *Zekhor lanu,* "Forgive us" and "Remember us," ideas that are combined in prayers *Shema kolenu,* "Hear our cry, Lord our God, and have

mercy upon us and receive with compassion our prayer."
Viduy ashamnu is a series of confessions arranged alphabetically and made on behalf of the community.

For the prayers of supplication and confession, see p. 34.

א. *Ashamnu*: we have been guilty (of disobedience)

ב. *Bagadnu*: we have betrayed

ג. *Gazalnu*: we have stolen

ד. *Dibarnu dofi*: we have spoken falsely

ה. *Heevinu*: we have caused others to sin

ו. *Vehirshanu*: we have caused other to do evil

ז. *Zadnu*: we have had evil hearts

ח. *Hamasnu*: we have become violent

ט. *Tafalnu sheker*: we have become desensitized to lies

י. *Yaatznu ra*: we have advised evil

כ. *Kizavnu*: we have lied

ל. *Latznu*: we have scoffed

מ. *Maradnu*: we have rebelled

נ. *Niatznu*: we have been scornful

ס. *Sararnu*: we have been disobedient

ע. *Avinu*: we have been perverse

פ. *Pashanu*: we have transgressed

צ. *Tzararnu*: we have persecuted

ק. *Kishinu oref*: we have been stiff-necked

ר. *Rashanu*: we have been lawless

ש. *Shihatnu*: we have corrupted

ת. *Tiavnu*: we have committed abominations

Tainu: we have gone astray

Titanu: we have been led astray

Sarnu: we have turned away from Your mizvot

This is followed by the medieval hymn *Shomer Yisrael*, "Protector of Israel," which is part of the daily prayers of supplication. Exactly when the Selihot service takes place is a matter of custom. Some say the best time is at midnight; others say the last third of night. But most agree that the ideal time is the end of night before the dawn, when, according to

For Shomer Yisrael, see p. 37.

the *Zohar*, the divine attribute of mercy is at its strongest. Many congregations gather at this time for the first day but make it part of an earlier-than-usual morning service for the rest of the period, requiring those who attend to awaken before daybreak.

Some people fast during the day throughout the days of Seliḥot. Fasting is considered a particularly great mitzvah, and it is said that it is especially well received in heaven if one gives charity as well. It is taught in the Talmud that "the merit for fasting lies in charity."

Tzedakah: Charity as Justice

The period from Elul through the High Holidays is a time of giving. The Hebrew word most commonly associated with charity is *tzedakah*, though the concepts are not quite the same. Its root is the word *tzedek*, which means "just" or "equitable," and it is in the context of justice that acts of giving are described in the Torah. Giving, caring for the needs of the community and its less fortunate, is described in the Torah as a commandment. Widows, orphans, and the poor are mentioned specifically. The Torah describes a number of tithes as well as a system of taxation through which these needs are to be met. In the Talmud, *tzedakah* becomes part of the broader realm of *gemilut ḥasadim*, "acts of loving-kindness," an idea that inevitably raises questions about the relative merits of certain kinds of giving. In his *Laws of Gifts to the Poor*, Maimonides identifies eight levels of justice in acts of giving, from lowest to highest:

See Leviticus 19:9–10 and Deuteronomy 26:12 and elsewhere.

1. Giving begrudgingly
2. Giving less than you should, but giving it cheerfully
3. Giving after being asked
4. Giving before being asked

5. Giving when you do not know the recipient's identity, but the recipient knows your identity
6. Giving when you know the recipient's identity, but the recipient doesn't know your identity
7. Giving when neither party knows the other's identity
8. Enabling the recipient to become self-reliant

This is part of Maimonides' great code of Jewish law entitled Mishneh torah, *the "Second Torah," not to be confused with the Mishnah, the core of the Talmud.*

Keeping this in mind, in Elul it is appropriate to give to the poor as early as possible so they can fulfill their needs for the holiday. And, the *Minhogimbukh* says, "If one gives with goodwill and with a full heart, the money is worth more."

Torah Portions for Elul

The Torah portions for our model month of Elul continue in Deuteronomy, with the explication of the law that began last month. They are presented here in very brief synopsis. The first week's reading is known as *Shoftim* ("judges") and comprises Deuteronomy 16:18–21:9.

Judges and officials are to be appointed and their justice is to be equitable—no favoritism, no bribes. There is a prohibition against setting up standing-stones, widely used then as fertility symbols. The punishment for idolaters is death by stoning. Animal offerings made to God must be perfect and unblemished. Two or three witnesses are required in capital cases. A higher court shall be established to hear cases too difficult for local courts. The laws of kingship are established, including restrictions on self-enrichment and the requirement to read God's law every day. That which is to be given to the tribe of Levi and the levitical priests is further described. Sorcery is declared an abomination and is prohibited. The official role of the prophet is established and the safeguard against false prophecy is described. Laws concerning accidental killings and cities of refuge are mentioned again. The moving of borders and their landmarks is prohibited. Deliberately false witnesses will be punished for the crime about which they made false accusation.

"Justice, Justice you are to pursue," says Moses, and despite punishments that seem extreme, we witness here the birth of the standards of justice—and of legal organization—that are the hallmarks of our civilization. The independence of judges, the necessity for multiple witnesses, the possibility of appeal to a higher court, and the limiting of power of a nation's chief executive are all laid out. Such is the genius of Judaism and marks its everlasting contributions to the world.

The haftarah is Isaiah 51:12–52:12, the fourth Haftarah of Consolation, which describes further the state of desolation that the Israelites were in at the end of the seventy years of Babylonian captivity. It takes no small amount of consoling and cajoling to get them back to their feet.

Isaiah 52:17   You have drunk from the Lord's hand
the cup of His wrath,
drained to the dregs the bowl of drunkenness;
of all the sons you have borne
there is not one to guide you. . . .

Isaiah 52:20   Your sons are in a stupor . . .
like antelopes caught in the net,
glutted with the wrath of the Lord. . . .

God tells the Israelites to be unafraid, that he is now their comforter and that they may return home from exile at their own will and pace. The time has now come for their oppressors to drink from the "bowl of [His] wrath."

The portion for the second Sabbath, *Ki tetzei* ("When you go out [to war]"), Deuteronomy 21:10–25:19, continues the code of law, mixing the most serious offenses with lesser ones:

Laws are given for the conduct of war, the fair disposition of booty, the fair treatment of women captives, and the extenuating circumstances under which a man may claim exemption from military service (including faintheartedness!). The regulations are established for the disposition of corpses that have been found murdered. Rules are given for the inheritances due to the sons of different wives. A son who is rebellious or stubborn and does not obey his father's discipline, or is a glutton or a drunkard, shall be stoned. Corpses of the executed must be treated properly, so as not to render the soil ritually unclean. Lost property must be returned. Cross-dressing is declared an abomination. A mother bird may not be taken with its young or eggs. A parapet is to be built on your roof so no one is killed falling from it, creating blood-guilt. Two kind of seeds are not to be mixed in a vineyard. An ox and a donkey may not be yoked together. Fabric of mixed wool and linen may not be worn. Fringes are to be made on the four corners of tunics. Laws of marriage that involve accusations of the misrepresentation of virginity, founded and unfounded, are explained. Adultery is defined here as involving a married woman and a man, married or not, and it is to be punished by death for both participants. Laws regarding rape of married and betrothed and unmarried women are explained. A man may not marry the wife of his father. Castrated or sterile males are not permitted to enter God's assembly. The offspring of incest or adultery, Ammonites, and Moabites are not permitted to enter God's assembly for ten generations. Edomites and Egyptians are not to be hated. Care is to be taken that the purity of a military camp is not violated, and directions are given for the disposal of body waste. Fugitive slaves are not to be returned or maltreated. No Israelite is to become a pagan priest. Tainted money may not be brought into the house of God. Interest may not be charged to a fellow Israelite; however, foreigners may be charged interest. Vows must be honored and vows made to God must be accounted to God. One may eat one's fill in a neighbor's vineyard, but not more than is needed to satisfy hunger. A woman who is married and divorced twice may not remarry her first husband. A newlywed husband is exempt from military service for one year so that he may give joy to his wife. Essential items such as milling equipment may not be seized for nonpayment of debts. A man who kidnaps a brother Israelite and sells him into slavery shall be put to death. Special precautions are to be taken regarding those suffering from the skin disease *tzaraat*. Debtors are to be treated with dignity. A worker's wages are not to be delayed. No one may be substituted for another person's capital punishment. Sojourners, widows, and orphans are to receive help, bearing in mind the Israelites' slavery in Egypt. If a man found guilty in a legal quarrel is found to be worthy of corporal punishment, he is not to be struck more than forty times. An ox is not to be muzzled while threshing. The institution and ceremony of "levirate marriage" is described. The hand is to be cut off of the woman who assists her husband in a scuffle by seizing the genitals of his opponent. The falsification of weights and measures is declared an abomination. The cowardly acts of Amalek are to be remembered and avenged.

In the matter of capital punishment and Judaism, there is much conflict between Torah and Talmud. That which is meted out for so many offenses in the Torah is vastly mitigated in the later law and, according to a number of historians, was seldom applied after the destruction of the Temple. The commitment to justice and to simple fairness expressed in so much of the Torah—so evident in this portion—leads inevitably to fundamental uncertainties about the death penalty. While it would be an exaggeration to say that the death penalty was banished from Judaism, its application became extremely rare. In later Jewish history, administration of this ultimate punishment was in the hands of non-Jewish civil authorities, and Jews were their frequent victims. Both the state of Israel and the Reform movement are officially opposed to the death penalty.

In a brief haftarah, Isaiah 54:1-10, God promises the Children of Israel—the forlorn wife—that their children will be more numerous than ever and that they shall spread out into all the land and beyond, to "dispossess nations." He compares the destruction of Jerusalem to the flood of Noah, swearing as before that he will never again let loose such destructive anger. Whereas the God of First Isaiah, the author of chapters one to thirty-nine, chastises the Israelites for every imaginable sin and transgression, the God of Second Isaiah is as apologetic as the strayed, abusive husband in a country song: "In a surge of anger, I hid my face from you for a moment [seventy years], but with everlasting kindness I will bring you back." *Oh darlin', please believe me. . . .*

Isaiah 54:8

Deuteronomy 26:1–29:8, called *Ki tavo* ("When you enter the land"), is the third week's portion. In it Moses instructs the Israelites that in recognition of God's gifts of the land and the deliverance from Egypt, a tithe of the firstfruits is to be gathered and given to the Temple priests for the priests themselves, for sojourners, and for widows and orphans. And with this a blessing is to be made to God as a warrant of one's observance of his commandments and in thanks to him.

There is a double covenant: Israel's obedience to God and God's to Israel. They are to him a "specially treasured people." To seal the covenant, Moses instructs the people to give curses on Mount Ebal and blessings on Mount Gerizim when they cross the Jordan, and he describes the particulars of the ceremony. The fulfillment of this commandment can be found in chapter 4 of Joshua. It's an astonshing scene: men shouting from hilltops at opposite ends of the land.

The haftarah, Isaiah 60:1–22, "Arise, shine, for your light has come," is the penultimate Haftarah of Consolation, in which Israel is told that its grace in the eyes of God is such that all the world will be at its feet. It is promised:

Isaiah 60:20   Your sun will never set again,
                        and your moon will wane no more;
                    The Lord will be your everlasting light,
                        and your days of sorrow will end.

The month's last portion is *Nitzavim* ("All of you stationed here"), Deuteronomy 29:9–30:20. Following the double covenant, Moses returns to his exhortation, recalling the destruction that God brought upon the Egyptians and how, in forty years of wandering, the garments of the Israelites never wore out and they never wanted for food. If they disobey, if they turn their attention to idols, then destruction will be theirs, but if they heed the laws that Moses has spoken to them, then all that was promised will be theirs. Moses speaks also of God's mercy, how he will embrace the one that returns to him. And in summation:

Deuteronomy   I call heaven and earth as witness against you this day: I
30:19   have put before you life and death, blessing and curse. Now
                    choose life—so you and your offspring may live—by loving
                    the Lord your God, heeding His commands, and holding
                    fast to Him, for He is your life and the length of your days,
                    so you shall have life and shall long endure upon the soil
                    that the Lord swore to your ancestors, Abraham, Isaac, and
                    Jacob, to give to them.

In this seventh, and last, Haftarah of Consolation, Isaiah 61:10–63:9, marriage is again the metaphor and just as in a wedding ceremony, the talk is of cherishing, protecting, defending, and a new beginning:

Isaiah 62:4   You will be called Hephzibah ["delight is in her"]
                        and your land Beulah ["maritally consummated"];
                        for the Lord will take delight in you....
Isaiah 62:6   I have posted watchmen on your walls ...
                    They will never be silent day or night....

Never again will foreigners   *Isaiah 62:9*
drink the new wine for which you have toiled.

On Sabbaths preceding Rosh Ḥodesh, it is the custom to
read an alternate haftarah, 1 Samuel 20:18-42. But that is not
the case before Rosh Hashanah, in which neither the special
haftarah nor the announcement of the month is read. There
is no explanation for this other than the folkloric one mentioned by Rabbi Eyzik Tyrnau in his *Sefer Minhagim* ("Book
of Customs"): to confuse Satan about the date so that he
doesn't give a bad account of us before God.

The Day Before Rosh Hashanah

The day before Rosh Hashanah has many customs of its own.
A particularly large number of Seliḥot are said in the morning, and their recitation on this day is considered sufficiently
important that even those sitting shivah, who would ordinarily stay at home, come to the synagogue for this recital.
Viduy, the confession of sins, is said as is Taḥanun, the
prayers of supplication, even though these are ordinarily
omitted on the days before festivals.

The *parokhet*, the cloth that covers the table from which
the Torah is read, is replaced with a white one that will be
used through Yom Kippur.

An interesting custom observed after the morning service
is that of *Hatarat nedarim*, the "cancellation of vows." The
failure to honor a vow is a sin, but it is recognized that in the
course of a year one might make small vows that were forgotten or mistaken. The ritual of *Hatarat nedarim* is a mechanism to cancel any such vows—though expressly not those
that were purposely ignored. The procedure is as follows: the
person who wishes to be released from vows that he or she
may have forgotten declares so in the presence of three

persons who constitute a court (a Beth Din in Hebrew). The court releases the person from these vows by declaring, "You are absolved from all these." Then follows a precautionary declaration against future vows.

After the synagogue, it is customary to visit the graves of loved ones at the cemetery. This is done not only on this last day of Elul, the day before Rosh Hashanah, but thoughout the Days of Awe, the penitential period between Rosh Hashanah and Yom Kippur. Some congregations hold special memorial services on cemetery grounds during this time. Other customs of the day include men bathing at the mikveh (the ritual bath), getting a haircut, preparing one's good clothes. When Rosh Hashanah falls on Thursday and Friday, an *eruv tavshilin* should be made, as in the case of the other festivals, so that one may cook for the Sabbath on the second day.

For eruv tavshilin, *see p. 113.*

The day before New Year is not a public fast day. Nonetheless, it is customary to fast. The *Minhogimbukh* explains the custom with this story.

> A king, followed by a great army, traveled through his land to collect taxes. When he was ten miles from the city, the local dignitaries came to meet him and said, "Most honorable King, we do not have anything. What can we give you?" So the king reduced the debt by one-third. When he was five miles from the city, the middle-class folks came to meet him, also saying that they had nothing to give. So the king reduced their debt by another third. When he got to the outskirts of the city, young and old came to meet him, saying, "Most honorable King, we do not have anything." So the king released the debt entirely. God, blessed be He, the king of the entire universe, does the same when He wants to bring Israel to account for the sins they have committed throughout the year. On the day before New Year, the dig-

nitaries fast, and He forgives one-third. Everyone should consider himself a dignitary and should fast on the day before New Year. Then, during the ten days of penitence, the middle-class fast, and on the Day of Atonement everyone fasts, and God forgives everything.

"You have put gladness in my heart more than
when their grain and wine abound" (Psalms 4:8)

The Month of Tishrei

"**S**PEAK TO THE CHILDREN OF ISRAEL, saying: in the seventh new moon, on the first day of that new moon, shall be a solemn rest unto you, a memorial pro claimed with the blast of horns, a holy convocation. You are not to do any kind of servile work and you are to bring to the Lord a fire-offering." Thus was proclaimed the day that would come to be observed as Rosh Hashanah, the New Year. The prescription continues with Yom Kippur:

Leviticus 23:24

> Note well: the tenth day of this seventh month is the Day of Atonement. It shall be a sacred occasion for you: you shall afflict yourselves and you shall bring a fire-offering to the Lord; you shall do no work throughout that day. . . . Indeed, those persons who do not afflict themselves throughout that day shall be cut off from his kinspeople.

Leviticus 23:27–29

The "affliction" is interpreted both as fasting and as flogging (makot, see p. 250).

And further, on the fifteenth day begins Sukkot, ending eight days later with Shemini Atzeret:

> On the fifteenth day . . . there shall be Lord's pilgrimage fes-tival of Tabernacles, for seven days. The first day is a sacred occasion on which you may not work at your occupation. For seven days you shall bring fire-offerings to the Lord. On the eighth day you shall also observe a sacred occasion on

Leviticus 23:34–36

which you must also bring a fire-offering to the Lord and on which you may not work at your occupation.

The Leviticus verses establish clearly the holy days and festival observances of Tishrei, but they don't explain—at least not directly—how the first day of the seventh month came to be celebrated as the New Year in place of the first of Nisan, which is described in Exodus as "the first of all months." There is no explanation, but the observance on the first of Tishrei was already well established by the time of the Mishnah, which described it as a New Year for calculating calendar years as well as sabbatical and jubilee years. (It wasn't until the fourth century C.E. that a mathematically based Jewish, lunisolar calendar was standardized.) The *Minhogimbukh* gives this concise explanation for Rosh Hashanah as the New Year: "According to the Kabbalah, the Creator, blessed be He, created the first man on Rosh Hashanah. Therefore, we start counting the year from that day." Thus Rosh Hashanah is connected with Creation itself—not with the first day and the heavens and the earth, but with the sixth day: Adam and Eve, the birth of human consciousness.

The Talmud ties a number of other events to Tishrei and Rosh Hashanah: the birthdays of the patriarchs Abraham and Jacob—two who marked new beginnings; the matriarchs Sarah and Rachel, the mothers of Isaac and Joseph; and Hannah, the mother of Samuel—three women who could not conceive a child but for the help of God and whose offspring changed the course of history. On the first of Tishrei, Joseph was released from Pharaoh's prison, and it was on this day, too, that the Israelites stopped working as slaves while the Ten Plagues took their toll. In the Bible readings for the two days of the New Year one may find the fundaments for these stories and others that bear on this time: the birth of Isaac

See p. 16 for more on Jewish time. See the index for "other" New Years.

Sabbatical years occur every seventh year; jubilee years occur every fiftieth. They are described in Leviticus 25:1-10.

Talmud Rosh hashanah 10b-11a

Leviticus rabbah 29:1

and the *Akedah*, his binding for sacrifice; the story of
Samuel's birth to Hannah; and in verses from Jeremiah, the
importance of repentance and the revelation that no matter
how we've sinned, God desires to forgive his people.

*See p. 207 for
Selihot, and p. 205
for the month of
Elul.*

The biblical anthropologist Theodore H. Gaster suggested
that the juxtaposition of Rosh Hashanah, Yom Kippur, and
Sukkot follows a pattern that typifies the ancient world's
understanding of the turning of the year: mortification (the
end of the year), purgation (the atonement of Yom Kippur),
and renewal and jubilation (Sukkot). Passover does not fit
this scenario; it is a foundation story, a journey to freedom,
that contains within it the divine commandment to retell the
story publicly. Rosh Hashanah, by contrast, is not tied to a
great Torah narrative per se, but rather to our own inner story
as we repent the sins we committed through the year, face
God's judgment, and pray for our lives in the next year.

The Book of Life and the Book of Death

The mise-en-scène of Rosh Hashanah is truly awesome: We
stand before God at the Heavenly Court, not knowing
whether judgment will be rendered for us or against us,
whether we will be inscribed in the Book of Life and enjoy a
year of goodness and happiness, or in the Book of Death,
marking us for a year of misfortune. Standing beside us is
Satan, hurling accusations and denunciations, proclaiming
us beyond redemption. We may battle for our lives only
through repentance—only God takes measure of our deeds—
and it is for this reason that Selihot prayers are said days or
even a month in advance; the shofar reminds us of our pend-
ing court date.

Between Rosh Hashanah and Yom Kippur, it is customary
to say the greeting *Leshanah tovah tikatevu vetehatemu*, "May

you be inscribed and sealed for a good year," a reference to the Book of Life and the Book of Death, which are said to be opened on Rosh Hashanah. The origin of this belief is not known, though some scholars conjecture that it may have developed during the Babylonian Exile, as a modification of Babylonian religious writings that speak of similar Tablets of Transgressions and Tablets of Destiny. The *Minhogimbukh*'s account of Rosh Hashanah gives a thorough rendering of how the books are kept:

> On Rosh Hashanah, God, blessed be He, judges all human beings and pays all debts for the coming year. There are some sins that He punishes in this world, others that He punishes in the world to come. He rewards good deeds similarly.
>
> If a person sinned throughout the year, led a frivolous life, and transgressed several commandments, but still abided by some and also performed good deeds, then on the Day of Judgment God will weigh one deed against the other. If God decides to pay in this world for the good deeds performed by the wicked person, then that person becomes like the righteous. He will be written into the Book of Life, which means that he will stay alive the coming year, will become rich, or will receive honor. Similar is the case of a righteous person who performed several good deeds but also sinned some; if God decides that the person has to pay for his sins in this world, he then becomes like the wicked. He will be written into the Book of Death, and he will either die the coming year or will become poor or ill.
>
> There are many righteous people who, in this world, will share the judgment of the wicked; and many who are wicked who will share the judgment of the righteous. What better example than that of Moses, who was prevented from entering the Promised Land because of a minor sin, which God made him pay for in this world.

According to the Talmud, *three* books are opened in heaven on Rosh Hashanah: one for the righteous, one for the wicked, and one for those on the borderline. The wholly righteous are written into the Book of Life right away, just as the wholly wicked are written straightaway into the Book of Death. The fate of those on the borderline hangs in the balance until Yom Kippur. Those who are in the end judged worthy will be written into the Book of Life and they will be compensated in this world. To become worthy one must repent between Rosh Hashanah and Yom Kippur—that mitzvah alone is enough to become worthy. To be inscribed in the Book of Death does not mean that you will surely die, only that you will have a miserable year. Similarly, being written into the Book of Life does not exempt one from tragedy and illness.

The zodiac symbol for Tishrei is Libra, the scales.

Certain mitzvot are so great that they redeem several sins. Similarly, certain sins are so great that they cannot be redeemed even with several *mitsves*. This is all according to God's will. The Creator, blessed be He, judges His people in a month when they can fulfill several commandments and can perform good deeds.

The Yiddish word for "good deed" is mitsve (pl. mitsves), the same as the Hebrew word for "commandment."

ROSH HASHANAH

After the end of the afternoon service on the day before Rosh Hashanah, the last service of the the year, it is a custom to recite the liturgical song *Ahot ketanah*, "Little Sister," a plea for God's mercy on his long-exiled, downtrodden "sister" Israel. Echoing the transition from despondency to hope exemplified by the haftarot from Isaiah that were read in Av and Elul, the heartrending yet hopeful text of this song expresses the mood of repentance mixed with optimism that characterizes the New Year. It was written by the thirteenth-century Spanish poet Avraham Ḥazzan of Geronda:

The sibling reference comes from the Song of Songs.

[cantor] The little sister—hear her prayers
  as she prepares and proclaims her praises.
O God, please heal her ailments
        [congregation] Let the year and its curses end.
  . . .
Lift her up from degradation to lofty majesty,
  for in the pit of exile her soul had melted.
When the lowest are elevated, her heart is poured out;
  among the poorest of the poor are her dwellings.
        Let the year and its curses end.
When will you raise up the daughter from her pit;
  and break the dungeon's yoke? Won't you?
May you act wondrously when you go forth like a hero,
  to bring an end and to her ailments.
        Let the year and its curses end.
  . . .
Be strong, rejoice that her plunder is ended;
  place hope in the Rock and keep His covenant.
You will ascend to Zion and He will say:
  Pave! Pave her paths.
        Let the year and its blessings begin!

The First Day of Rosh Hashanah

FIRST EVENING SERVICE: Rosh Hashanah is observed for two days everywhere, even in Israel. In the Talmud it is described as a *yoma arikhta,* "a double-length day." The evening service is quite similar to that of a Sabbath eve but without the Kabbalat Shabbat. A special *nusah*—the style of chanting—is adopted. When the cantor reaches the end of *Hashkivenu,* the lullaby-like evening blessing, one of the group that follows the Shema, the congregation says, "Blow the trumpet at the new moon, at the full moon, on our festival day, for it is a statute for Israel, an ordinance of the God of Jacob." Then, the cantor says half Kaddish and the congregation recites the Amidah, with the following additions:

See p. 50 for Hashkivenu.

Psalm 81:4–5

First benediction, *Avot*: "Remember us for life, O King who desires life, and inscribe us in the Book of Life."

Second benediction, *Gevurot*: "Who is like You, Merciful Father, who recalls His creatures mercifully for life."

Third benediction, *Kedushat Hashem*: "And so, too, O Lord our God, instill Your awe upon all Your works."

Fourth benediction, *Kedushat hayom*: with the additional line, "And You gave us, Lord our God, with love this Day of Remembrance, a day of the sounding of the shofar, a holy convocation, a memorial of the Exodus from Egypt."

Fifth benediction, *Avodah* (no addition).

Sixth benediction, *Birkat hodaah*: "And inscribe all the children of Your covenant for a good life."

Seventh benediction, *Birkat shalom*: "In the Book of Life, blessing, and peace, and good livelihood, may we be remembered and transcribed before You."

Kedushat hayom: when Rosh Hashanah falls on Sabbath one says, "a day of recalling the sounding of the shofar," since the shofar is not sounded on Sabbath.

The *Minhogimbukh* says that at the end of the Amidah, the verse *Oseh hashalom*, "He who makes the peace," is said aloud because the numerical value of *oseh* is the same as that of Satriel (381), the angel who makes Satan mute and who teaches righteousness to Israel. This custom is not common today.

The cantor says full Kaddish, and kiddush is made, which we will discuss in the home ceremony, then *Alenu*, the mourner's Kaddish, and finally *Adon Olam* or *Yigdal*, depending on congregational custom.

AT HOME: It is customary to light candles on the first night of Rosh Hashanah. The blessing ends with *lehadlik ner shel yom tov*, "who commands us to light the festival candles." Unless it is Sabbath, the blessing precedes the lighting since transferring fire is not prohibited. Kiddush begins with the blessing over wine, *borei peri hagafen*, "Blessed are You, Lord our God, king of the universe, who creates the fruit of the vine." All respond, "Amen." The sanctification is similar to

When Rosh Hashanah falls on Sabbath, the blessing is "who commands us to light the Sabbath and the festival candles."

For kiddush, see p. 66.

that inserted into the *Kedushat hayom*, in the Amidah, but in blessing form:

> Blessed are You, Lord our God, king of the universe, who has chosen us from every people, exalted us above every tongue, and sanctified us with His commandments. And You gave us, Lord our God, with love this Day of Remembrance, a day of shofar blowing, a holy convocation, a memorial for the Exodus from Egypt. For You have chosen us, and You have sanctified us above all the peoples, and Your word is true and established forever. Blessed are You, Lord our God, king over the entire earth, who sanctifies Israel and the Day of Remembrance.

Women recite Sheheheyanu with candlelighting, men with kiddush.

And then the *Sheheheyanu*: "Blessed are You, Lord our God, king of the universe, who has kept us alive, sustained us, and brought us to this season." Since Rosh Hashanah is considered one long day, talmudic commentators debated whether or not one said the *Sheheheyanu* on the second night as well. A halakhic accord was reached, deciding that one would say the blessing on the second night, but out of respect to those on the other side of the debate, one should eat a new fruit or wear a piece of new clothing so that the blessing would have to be said anyway.

If it is Friday night, one starts the kiddush with the paragraph for the Sabbath that begins, "And there was evening, there was morning, the sixth day."

If the second night of Rosh Hashanah is a Saturday night, the order of blessings is: wine, kiddush (sanctification), candles, Havdalah, and *Sheheheyanu*. The rituals follow the Hebrew acronym YaKNeHaZ, a popular mnemonic that in Yiddish sounds like the words for "hunting the hare" and is sometimes portrayed in old haggadot with pictures of hunting scenes.

The Rosh Hashanah meal is a highly symbolic one, not in the ordered, legislated sense of the Passover Seder, but still rich in meaning. Rather than the braided loaves familiar on Sabbath, the challah of Rosh Hashanah is round, sometimes taking the shape of a crown, a reminder of  God's kingship. It is also said that the round shape is a symbol of the circle of life and our hope that our lives will continue without end. Foods that are to be eaten and some to be avoided are known as *Simana milta*, "Significant Omens." To begin the meal, it is customary to take a slice of apple and dip it into honey, reciting the blessing for tree fruits and wishing everyone *Shanah tovah umetukah*, "a good and sweet year." There are other, Kabbalah-inspired symbolic foods, though they are by no means universal custom. Each of them has a specific prayer petition that begins "May it be Your will, Lord." Here are some of them:

"Hunting the hare," from the Minhogimbukh, Venice, 1601

There is a custom to make a ladder on top of the challah as a reminder that God decides who will ascend the ladder of life. A less known custom is baking challah in the shape of a bird, in reference to Isaiah 31:5: "As birds hover, so will the Lord protect Jerusalem."

> *Fenugreek or Carrots*: The Aramaic word for fenugreek is *rubia*, which is like the word for "increase." Similarly, the Yiddish word for carrots is *mehren*, which also means "more." Its prayer is "May it be Your will, Lord our God and God of our ancestors, that our merits increase."
>
> *Ram's or Sheep's Head or Whole Fish*: After the coming of the angel, Abraham substituted a ram for Isaac. It also refers to the verse, "The Lord shall place you as a head and not as a tail" (Deuteronomy 28:13).
>
> *Pomegranates*: It is said that a pomegranate has 613 seeds, the same as the number of Torah mitzvot.
>
> *Fish*: Fish are fertile creatures, but since their reproduc-

tive organs are hidden from view, they are said to have the characteristic of *tzeniut*, "modesty."

Gourds: These are associated with both the enhancement of our ability to fulfill the commandments and the vanquishing of enemies.

Dates, beets, gourds, and leeks are associated with the removal of adversaries, though the first two are also noted for their sweetness. There is an eastern European custom to cook chicken livers at Rosh Hashanah, their connection to the holiday being their Yiddish name, *leberlakh*, which sounds rather like the injunction *leb ehrlikh*, "live honestly." There are some who do not use vinegar on Rosh Hashanah in order to avoid eating anything sour. It is customary to avoid eating nuts on New Year because the gematria, the numerical value of the Hebrew word for nut, *egoz*, seventeen, is said in the Talmud to be the same as that of sin, *het*.

The calculation is incorrect; the value of het *is actually eighteen, but many observe the custom nonetheless.*

In Sephardic households the holiday meal often includes a whole fish, including the head (taking the place of the sheep's head), as a wish for prosperity, fertility, and good luck in the coming year. Another Sephardic custom is that of passing covered baskets of fruit, a symbol of our never knowing exactly what the year will bring. This custom spread to other Jews around the world, and we now wait until Rosh Hashanah to make blessings on new or unfamiliar fruits. It is now an Ashkenazic custom to buy unusual fruits for Rosh Hashanah, types that one doesn't buy ordinarily. The blessings on new fruits are traditionally recited the second night of Rosh Hashanah.

Talmud Rosh hashanah *16b*

Perhaps the most famous of Rosh Hashanah dishes is *tsimmes*, a "mixture" of sweet vegetables (carrots, yams) with cinnamon, prunes, and honey. The carrots are cut in the shape of coins, an obvious symbol of wealth for the New Year.

In the Grace after Meals, the prayer *Yaaleh veyavo*, "May there rise . . . and be noted our remembrance," is inserted, as it is on all festivals. There is also a special *Haraḥaman*.

FIRST DAY'S MORNING SERVICE: This is the *Yom hadin*. According to the Talmud, it is during the day of Rosh Hashanah that God and his Heavenly Court sit in judgment of every person's deeds—a time of awesome seriousness. Three themes pervade the service: acceptance of God's kingship (*malkhuyot*), a plea for divine providence through remembrance of the merits of our ancestors (*ẓikhronot*), and revelation through the blowing of the shofar (*shofarot*). These themes, though common to the day, are expressed explicitly only in the musaf service. Though one dresses in one's best clothes on the New Year, at this service one customarily wears a *kitl*, a white burial shroud, which is a sign of the deepest remorse. The morning service starts early in the synagogue. The morning blessings and the *Pesukei deẓimra*, the Verses of Song, are especially long on this day, with various additions whose order may vary quite a bit. As on Sabbath, they are concluded by *Nishmat*, "the soul of every living thing." There are synagogues that employ as many as three cantors on this day: one to lead the first part centering on the *Pesukei deẓimra*; another who begins with *Hamelekh* and leads the statutory portions of the service; and a third to lead the musaf. This is done on other festival days, too, and also on Sabbath in some synagogues, but during the High Holidays, the need is obvious.

Upon the cantor's incantation of *Hamelekh*, "O King, who sits upon a high and lofty throne," the God who has been portrayed through the year by all his great deeds and

In Yiddish, the word tsimmes *also means a "fuss," a "big deal," no doubt deriving from the number of ingredients and all the chopping.*

For more on Yaaleh veyavo, *see p. 94.*

For Nishmat, see p. 72.

absolute might, for his having brought the Israelites out from bondage, is now through Yom Kippur considered the regent who sits in judgment of us.

> May Your great name be praised forever—our king, the God, the great and holy king—in heaven and on earth. Because for You is fitting—O Lord, our God, and God of our forefathers—greatness and strength, praise and splendor, holiness and sovereignty, blessings and thanksgivings from this time and forever. [*cantor*] Blessed are You, Lord, God, king exalted through praises, God of thanksgivings, master of wonders, who chooses musical songs of praise—King, God, Life-giver to the world.

The ark is opened, and Psalm 130, "A Song of Ascents," is read responsively. Then Kaddish and the Barkhu, the Call to Prayer, and then on to the blessings before the Shema. The *Minhogimbukh* mentions no *yotzerot*—additions to the blessings—though the hymn *Melekh azur gevurah*, "O King Who Is Girded with Strength," is sung in some communities. It was written by the second-century sage Eleazar Hakallir, whose work is prominently represented in the repertory of Selihot and in the repertory of piyutim (hymns).

The statutory parts of the service are described at greater length in the chapters, "The Days of the Week" and "Sabbath."

The Amidah is said, same as the previous night. However, the cantor's repetition of the Amidah is among (with Yom Kippur) the most highly elaborate liturgies in the Jewish year, with the addition of special hymns, specific to the first and second days. In earlier, more leisurely times, such additions were commonplace on special days. The old customs books are filled with references to them. Some are recited by the cantor, some by the entire assembly, and some responsively, showing their origins in choral singing. The ark is opened and closed at various times during the Amidah's repetition, and it is a custom to stand whenever the curtain is drawn.

Some observe the custom of standing throughout the cantor's repetition, and the building of the pleas makes it hard not to. The first hymn begins before the end of the *Avot*, the Amidah's first benediction, sung by the cantor:

> I am frightened as I open my mouth to bring forth
>   words of prayer. . . .
> I am short of worthy deeds and therefore I fear.
> I lack understanding—how can I hope?
> My Creator, make me understand how I may inherit the
>   legacy of Torah.
> Give me strength and courage against faintheartedness
>   and fear.
> May my prayer be as favorable as spices or incense.
> May my expression be as sweet as bees' honey
> May I find favor justly, not like an impostor. . . .

*Attributed to
Eleazar Hakallir*

The congregation and the cantor together plead for mercy in the name of Abraham and Sarah and in memory of their faithfulness:

> The dread of the remembrance day has arrived.
> In awe of it, every living thing puts itself aright. . . .
> In memory of the one [Abraham] who pleaded, "Shall He
>   not do justice?"
> May his supplication [for Sodom] be recalled during
>   the judgment. . . .
> He made Abraham the rock from which all Israel would
>   be hewn,
> On this day the strength of Sarah became rejuvenated,
> to blossom with an heir at ninety years.

*Attributed to
Eleazar Hakallir*

As Sarah's barrenness and relief are recalled, so too are Rebecca's. Both are among the miracles of the day—and symbols of God's favor.

These hymns punctuate the benedictions. There is one

hymn for each of the first three benedictions, parallel in style and related in theme. Then, still within the context of the third benediction, there is another series of hymns leading up to the Kedushah. This is the classic structure of the Kedushah, the composition of seven or more interpolated hymns for the Sabbath or festival Amidah.

The ark is opened again and all stand, for what follows is one of the key prayers of the Days of Awe: *Avinu malkenu,* "Our Father, Our King." The Talmud tells how this supplication was formulated: At a time of a great drought, Rabbi Eliezer led the assembled multitude in an extended version of the Amidah that was said on such occasions. Nothing happened. Rabbi Akiva then improvised a prayer of supplication, *Avinu malkenu,* and the skies burst instantly into rain. The core prayer has become part of the *tahanunim* said most mornings and afternoons by Sephardic and Yemenite Jews. As further trials befell the Jews, more lines were added so that today the Sephardic version contains thirty-two lines and the Ashkenazic version forty-four lines. Here are some excerpts:

Talmud Taanit 25b

> Our Father, our King, we have sinned before You.
> Our Father, our King, we have no king beside You.
> Our Father, our King, reckon with us kindly for Your
>   own Name's sake.
> Our Father, our King, nullify all evil decrees against us.
> Our Father, our King, frustrate the designs of those who
>   hate us. . . .
> Our Father, our King, rid us of pestilence, sword, famine,
>   captivity, destruction, iniquity, and extermination from
>   the members of Your covenant. . . .

For Hallel, see p. 129.

A full Kaddish follows. On all other festivals the psalms of praise known collectively as Hallel (Psalms 113–118) would be recited here, but not on Rosh Hashanah. The Talmud says that the angels had inquired of God about this seeming inconsistency. The reply came, "How can they recite Hallel on so awesome a day when the Books of Life and Death are open before Me?"

Talmud Rosh hashanah 32b

Two Torah scrolls are taken out. A special feature of the Rosh Hashanah and Yom Kippur Torah service is the recitation three times of the Thirteen Attributes of Mercy (Exodus 34:6-7). Five people are called up to the first scroll, from which is read Genesis 21:1-34, which tell of Isaac's (*Yitzhak* means "he laughs") birth to the barren Sarah and the subsequent sending away of Ishmael, Abraham's firstborn son, and his mother, the Egyptian Hagar. Ishmael is looked after by God and is also designated to become a great nation. Half Kaddish is recited then the first scroll is held up and shown, rolled up, bound, and dressed—the *hagbahah* and *gelilah.* Then the second scroll is placed on the table, from which is read Numbers 29:1-6, the Temple sacrifices for this "first day of the seventh month." The haftarah is 1 Samuel 1:1-2:10, another story of a child granted to a long-childless woman, Hannah, who had prayed in the Sanctuary at Shiloh. As Abraham was prepared to show his devotion to God, so, too, Hannah, who pledged to devote her son to God's service, giving him over to the priest Eli as soon as he was weaned. Thus was born the great prophet-judge Samuel, the last such leader before Saul was made the first king and whom the sages considered as important as Moses and Aaron.

For the Thirteen Attributes of Mercy (Exodus 34:6-7), see pp. 34 and 208. These portions are read on Rosh Hashanah regardless of the calendar sequence of portions.

THE BLOWING OF THE SHOFAR: Of the singularly unmusical blast of the ram's horn, the great medieval sage Moses Maimonides wrote, "Although the blowing of the shofar is a scriptural decree, there is an allusion in it, as if the shofar

Maimonides Mishneh Torah (Hilkhot teshuvah 3:4), written in Egypt about 1185.

Blowing the shofar, from the Minhogimbukh, Amsterdam, 1722.

were saying, 'Awake, sleepers, from your sleep! Arise, slumberers, from your slumber! Scrutinize your deeds! Repent with contrition! Remember your creator! Peer into your souls, improve your ways and deeds.'" The shofar, then, is the instrument through which the remembrance of the Jewish people is brought before God. And it is the reminder that there is still time for repentance.

The ritual begins with a recitation—seven times, quietly—of Psalm 47, which contains the verses "God has ascended with a blast, the Lord with the sound of the shofar." The person who blows the shofar, the *baal tekiah*, goes up to the pulpit and recites a silent prayer, a mystical supplication that invokes the names of angels who oversee the shofar blasts and help them to be heard by God. And then the *baal tekiah* recites the blessings—one over the blowing of the shofar, the other the *Sheheḥeyanu*. Conversation is not permitted from this point to the end of the musaf service.

> Blessed are You, Lord our God, king of the universe, who has sanctified us with His commandments and has commanded us to hear the sound of the shofar.

> Blessed are You, Lord our God, king of the universe, who has kept us alive, sustained us, and brought us to this season.

The sounding of the shofar has a vocabulary of four signal patterns: *Tekiah* (tuuuuu), *Shevarim* (u-tu, u-tu, u-tu), *Teruah* (tu, tu, tu, tu, tu, tu, tu, tu, tu), and *Tekiah gedolah* (a very long tuuuuu). A person called the *makri* (the name means "the one who makes it call out") calls out the shofar signals that the *baal tekiah* is to blow:

Tekiah, Shevarim-Teruah, Tekiah
Tekiah, Shevarim-Teruah, Tekiah
Tekiah, Shevarim-Teruah, Tekiah

After a rest, a small modification of the series is blown; then another series of three, another rest, then yet another series of three, ending with the *Tekiah gedolah.* Then the community recites the verse "Happy are the people who know the sound of the shofar, who walk, O God, in the light of Your countenance" (Psalm 89:16). The cantor repeats it after them. The shofar service is followed by *Ashrei* and *Yehalelu,* as the cantor takes the Torah in his or her right arm. With the recitation of Psalm 24, the Torah is brought back to the ark. (If it is a Sabbath, Psalm 29 is recited instead.)

IF THE FIRST DAY IS SABBATH: The three hymns that precede the Shema on Sabbath—*Hakol yodukha* and *El adon al kol hamaasim,* both of which speak of God as the "director" of all things, and *Lael asher shavat,* "To the God who rested," which refers to the origin of the Sabbath—are recited in this service, too. The Amidah is the same as the previous evening, but the reference to Rosh Hashanah becomes *zikhron teruah,* a "recalling" of the shofar's blast, rather than *yom teruah,* the "day" of the shofar's blast, since it is not permitted to blow the shofar on Sabbath. *Avinu malkenu* is omitted. Seven people are called up to the first Torah scroll; in the blessing *Al hatorah,* Sabbath is mentioned together with New Year.

THE MUSAF SERVICE: The musaf service is precded by the Cantor's Prayer:

> Here I am, impoverished of deeds, trembling and frightened from the dread of Him who is enthroned. . . . I have come to stand and supplicate before You for Your people Israel, who have sent me, although I am unworthy and unqualified to do so.

Then follows half Kaddish. The Amidah of the Rosh Hashanah musaf is unlike any other Amidah of the year. Whereas
the usual musaf Amidah has seven benedictions—the first
and last three identical to all other versions of the Amidah,
and the middle benediction particular to the day—this one
has nine benedictions. It is said that the number nine is a reference to the number of times Hannah mentions God's name
in her song of gratitude.

The cantor's repetition of the Amidah is different on the
first and second days, each with its own hymns, though both
are grand liturgies that include the blowing of the shofar
after each of the three middle benedictions. (In some rites,
they also blow the shofar in the silent recitation of the Amidah.) The congregation participates in many of the prayers
and hymns that provide elaboration on the Amidah specific
to the occasion. Two of the most famous precede the Kedushah: the ecstatic hymn *Melekh elyon*, "The Supreme King,"
is recited by the congregation and repeated by the cantor,
stanza by stanza, with the title furnishing the refrain; all
recite together the prayer *Unetaneh tokef*, "Let us now relate
the power of this day's holiness." The legend tells that this
beautiful prayer for Judgment Day was delivered in a dream
by Rabbi Amnon of Mainz, who was tortured to death after
refusing to convert to Christianity.

> You will open the Book of Memory, and it will read itself—
> everyone's signature is in it. The great shofar will be
> sounded, and a still, thin sound will be heard. . . . Behold, it
> is the Day of Judgment. . . . Like a shepherd inspecting his
> flock, making sheep pass under his staff, all mankind will
> pass before You.

Still in the cantor's repetition of the Amidah, we come to
the center of Rosh Hashanah liturgy: the *Malkhuyot*, the

Verses of Kingship; *Zikhronot*, the Remembrance—both of which conclude with the blowing of the shofar—and the *Shofarot*, the elaborated blowing of the shofar. The *Malkhuyot*, in which God's kingship is expounded, is inserted into the Amidah's *Kedushat hayom*, the Holiness of the Day. It begins with an extraordinary recitation by the cantor of the familiar *Alenu*, sung to a special tune, in which everyone bows down with face to the ground. In some congregations only the cantor bows; in others it is the entire congregation. This is followed by the the Verses of Kingship, which describe many aspects of God's sovereignty.

One may not bow down onto a stone floor because stone is a material associated with idolatry. In some synagogues the bowing is done on special mats or carpets.

The *Zikhronot* constitute a separate group of prayers, exploring every aspect of memory and how all is known to God—past, present, and future. Noah, God's covenant with the patriarchs, and the Redemption from Egypt—all are remembered. They speak of our unflagging memory of God's wonders and his memory of our deeds, both physical and spiritual, and how they factor into God's judgment this day.

The shofar blasts were described above. Their liturgical context here in the *Shofarot* prayers begins with awe of the revelation on Mount Sinai, how God appeared to his people in a great, dark, covering cloud.

The three sections conclude with the prayer, "Today is the birthday of the world. Today all creatures of the world stand in judgment. . . . May the utterance of our lips be pleasant before You."

At the end of the repetition of the Amidah, the *Birkat kohanim*, the Priestly Blessing, is made. This ritualized blessing is said every day in Jerusalem and every Sabbath elsewhere in Israel, but in the Diaspora it is the usual custom to say it only during the musaf service of festivals, Rosh Hashanah, Yom Kippur, and in the afternoon service of fast

See p. 133 for further explanation of the Priestly Blessing.

days. Though the blessing itself is only fifteen words long, the ritual is one of the grand gestures of Jewish liturgy.

It has become almost a universal custom to sound one hundred shofar blasts at the morning services. To accomplish this, an additional forty are added in the middle or after the full Kaddish that follows the cantor's repetition of the Amidah. (Those who blow the shofar in the silent Amidah need add only ten.) The service concludes with full Kaddish, *En kelohenu*, and *Alenu*.

TASHLIKH: At a time between the midday festive meal that follows the morning service on the first day of Rosh Hashanah and Hoshana Rabbah, after Yom Kippur, Jews go to a nearby body of water and throw into it breadcrumbs, with a gesture of emptying one's pockets. "You shall cast (*tashlikh*) their sins into the depths of the sea," says the prophet Micah (7:19), thus providing scriptural resonance for this unusual and well-known Rosh Hashanah custom. The origin of *tashlikh* is still debated, but the first description of it appears in the work of the fifteenth-century German rabbi Jacob Moellin, known as the Maharil. Though several midrashic explanations have been given for it, including a story of the *Akedah*, in which Satan tries to block the way of Abraham and Isaac with a body of deep water, some rabbis rejected the custom as non-Jewish in origin. Nevertheless, it remains a popular custom today. Some unusual variants include a Kurdish practice of jumping into the water and the Kabbalists' custom of shaking their clothing to remove even the dust of sin.

Probably the first depiction of tashlikh *in a printed book is in the anti-Semitic tract* The Little Book of Jewish Confessions, *written by* Johannes Pfefferkorn *of Cologne in* 1508. Tashlikh *is associated here with the Jews' poisoning of wells. Pfefferkorn was a converted Jew, an anti-Jewish shill. His* Little Book *is like a* Minhogimbukh *from an evil parallel universe.*

The prayer that accompanies the ritual is taken from
Micah (7:18-20) and Psalm 118:8-9.

Grant truth to Jacob, kindness to Abraham,   *Micah 7:18-20*
As you swore to our forefathers from ancient times.
From the straits did I call upon God,   *Psalm 118:8-9*
God answered me with expansiveness.
The Lord is with me, I have no fear—
    how can man affect me?
The Lord is with me, through my helpers,
    therefore can I face my foes.
It is better to take refuge in the Lord than rely on any man,
It is better to take refuge in the Lord than to rely on nobles.

Moses Cordovero, one of the great Kabbalists of sixteenth-
century Safed, interpreted these verses as the rendering into
action of the Thirteen Attributes of Mercy.

FIRST DAY—AFTERNOON SERVICE: The service is as usual,
with the addition of *Avinu malkenu* following the Amidah.
On Sabbath, *Avinu malkenu* is omitted, as is *Tzidkatkha*.

The Second Day of Rosh Hashanah

SECOND EVENING SERVICE: The service of the second night
is the same as that of the previous night. However, when
reaching *Sheheḥeyanu* in the kiddush, one should think of   *For laws regarding*
new fruit or a new piece of clothing, as explained earlier.   *Sheheḥeyanu, see*
                                                               p. 58.

SECOND MORNING SERVICE: Though the structure of the
first and second days' morning services is the same, the interpolated material in the Shema and Amidah varies greatly.
Some prayer books are arranged so that large sections say
"both days" and others split, joining again later. The hymns
that precede the Shema are martial and majestic. One elaborate one, *Melekh amon*, "O King, Validate," touches on the

three Rosh Hashanah themes: kingship, remembrance, and shofar. This verse ends with a paraphrase of Isaiah 27:13.

> The shofar—may its extended note be heard powerfully, to enwrap and bind them with eternal gladness, thus may those lost in the land of Assyria come. The shofar . . . to proclaim freedom to Judah and Ephraim.

The blowing of the shofar from the Minhogimbukh, Venice, 1603.

Since the second day of Rosh Hashanah is never a Sabbath, the shofar figures even more strongly on this day.

Two Torah scrolls are taken out from the ark and five people are called up. From the first scroll continues the reading begun yesterday, which tells of Isaac's birth. In these verses, Genesis 22:1–24, we are presented the *Akedah*, the "binding," the story of God's test of Abraham's faith. After the grand elaboration on the theme of penitence and forgiveness that we confront in the lengthy liturgies, the compression of this cornerstone story of the faith—devoid of psychological and physical description—transports us to a different dimension. The maftir reads from the second scroll, Numbers 29:1–6, same as yesterday. The haftarah is from the book of Jeremiah, 31:2–20, written in the aftermath of the Babylonian Exile and telling of the efficacy of repentance in keeping God's affection for his people and of his desire for reconciliation, regardless of past sins.

> Is Ephraim [the exiled Northern Kingdom]
>   a darling son to Me?
> Is he a child that is dawdled over?
> For as often as I speak of him,
> I do earnestly remember him still;

Therefore My heart yearneth for him,
I will surely have compassion for him, saith the Lord.

The rest of the service follows the same pattern as yesterday's.

The second day's musaf service follows the same pattern as the first but with different hymns added to the Amidah. The second day's afternoon service is the same, without exception. However, if it is a Friday afternoon, *Avinu malkenu* is not recited.

THE CONCLUSION OF ROSH HASHANAH: *Vehu rahum*, the prayers of supplication that begin the evening service, should be recited only after the sun has set. The service is the same as on a weekday night except that *Atah honantanu* is inserted in the Amidah to mark the end of the holiday, as it does the conclusion of other festivals and Sabbath. Also, phrases particular to the Ten Days of Repentance that will be recited every day until Yom Kippur are inserted into the Amidah: *Zokhrenu*, "Remember us for life," *Mi khamokha*, "Who is like You, merciful Father," and so on. *Besefer hayim*, "In the Book of Life," is recited in the last blessing.

Atah honantanu: *"You have graciously endowed us with the intelligence to study Your Torah."*

Havdalah is recited to mark the end of the holiday. The wine is blessed, but one does not bless or smell the spices, nor does one recite the blessing over light and inspect one's fingernails.

The Fast of Gedaliah

On the third of Tishrei, we observe a minor fast known as *Tzom Gedalyah*, the Fast of Gedaliah. This commemorates the assassination of Gedaliah, the last Jewish governor of Judah following the destruction of the Temple, in 586 B.C.E. After the destruction of Jerusalem, the Babylonian king Nebuchadnezzar kept a small Jewish presence in Judah

under the management of a Jewish governor, to keep and
protect the assets of fields and vineyards. Gedaliah's death
marked the end of the last vestige Jewish rule for more than
a half-century and led to even more misery for the remaining
Jews. The story is related in 2 Kings 25. (If the day after New
Year falls on a Sabbath, the fast is postponed to Sunday.)

One Torah scroll is taken out and the portion for public
fast days is read, Exodus 32:11-14; 34:1-10. Three people are
called up. The portion recalls how Moses assuaged God's
anger after the Golden Calf episode and how the covenant
was renewed. The concentration is on God's Thirteen Attributes of Mercy. In the afternoon service, the Torah portion is
read again. The haftarah is from the book of Isaiah 55:6–56:8
and explores the theme of penitence and forgiveness.

> Let the wicked forsake his way
>   and the evil man his thoughts.
> Let him turn to the Lord,
>   and He will have mercy on him,
>   and to our God, for He will freely pardon. . . .

The morning services between Rosh Hashanah and Yom
Kippur start early because they are longer than usual, retain-
ing some of the liturgies encountered in the Rosh Hashanah
service, such as *Avinu malkenu*, which follows the cantor's
repetition of the Amidah. On Monday and Thursday the
"long" *Vehu raḥum* (prayers for mercy) is said, with the *Nefilat
apayim*, the "falling on one's face," which symbolizes how
Moses, Aaron, and Joshua had cast themselves down before
God in times of trouble.

For the long Vehu
raḥum, *see p. 35.*

During the Ten Days of Repentance

Seliḥot, the penitential prayers, are recited each day during
the Ten Days of Repentance. *Avinu malkenu* is recited every

day after the Amidah, in the morning, afternoon, and evening services, except on Sabbath. Also, *Vekhotvenu besefer ha-hayim*, "May we be inscribed for another year in the Book of Life," is inserted in the *Mi sheberakh* prayer for those who go up to the Torah.

In preparation for the Days of Repentance, the recitation of Selihot begins in the month of Elul. See p. 207 for further explanation.

The *Minhogimbukh* says that one should bake bread at home between Rosh Hashanah and Yom Kippur, or at least, to kasher the oven. It is customary not to promise anything and not to take an oath, not even in a rabbinical court, during this period.

Shabbat Shuvah, the Sabbath of Return

The Sabbath between Rosh Hashanah and Yom Kippur is called variously Shabbat Shuvah, the Sabbath of Return, or Shabbat Teshuvah, the Sabbath of Repentance. The Hebrew word for repentance, *teshuvah*, has as its root *shuv*, "to return," and it is the idea of returning to God that informs it. *Shuvah* is probably a better choice, since it is the first word of the day's haftarah reading.

In the Friday afternoon service prior to Shabbat Shuvah, *Avinu malkenu* is omitted. Both the evening and morning services are as usual for Sabbath. There is no specific Torah reading for this day other than the one that is scheduled according to the calendar. However, there is a special haftarah with three sections.

In our model year, that reading is *Vayelekh*, Deuteronomy 31:1–30, in which Moses tells the assembled Israelites that he will not cross the Jordan with them, but that God and Joshua will lead the way. "Be strong, be resolute," he says. Moses wrote down his Instruction (traditionally interprted as the Torah) and gave it to the priests, that it should be read out loud every seven years at Sukkot. As Moses and Joshua stand before God at the Tabernacle, God tells Moses of his impending death and paints a picture of the idolatry that will follow Moses's departure. As a prevention, Moses writes down a cautionary "Song," which will constitute most of next week's portion.

The haftarah draws from three prophets: Hosea, Micah, and Joel, each on the same theme, that it is not too late to return and repent. The verses of Hosea (14:2–10) begin *Shuvah Yisrael*.

> Return, O Israel, to the Lord your God,
> For you have fallen because of your sin. . . .
> I will heal their affliction,
> Generously will I take them back in love;
> For My anger has turned away from them.
> I will be to Israel like dew;
> He shall blossom like the lily,
> He shall strike root like a Lebanon tree.

The verses from Micah (7:18–20) paraphrase to some degree the Thirteen Attributes of Mercy. It contains the textual basis for the custom of *tashlikh*.

> Who is a God like You,
> Forgiving iniquity
> And remitting transgression?
> Who has not maintained His wrath forever
> Against the remnant of His own people,
> Because He loves graciousness?
> He will take us back in love;
> He will cover up our iniquities,
> He will hurl all our sins
>   into the depths of the sea.

A reference to the blast of the shofar begins two verses from Joel (2:15–17), proclaiming the "solemn assembly" of the High Holidays:

Blow a horn in Zion,
Solemnize a fast,
Proclaim an assembly!
Gather the people,
Bid the congregation purify
    themselves.
Bring together the old,
Gather the babes
And the sucklings at the breast;
Let the bridegroom come out of
    his chamber,
The bride from her canopied
    couch.

It is customary for the rabbi to give a sermon about repentance and it is that custom that is illustrated in the *Minhogimbukh*. The afternoon and evening services are as usual.

The rabbi's sermon on Shabbat Shuvah is portrayed in this woodcut from the Minhogimbukh, *Amsterdam, 1727.*

The Day Before Yom Kippur

MORNING SERVICE: On the morning of the day before the Day of Atonement, Selihot, the penitential prayers, are recited just as they have been throughout the Ten Days of Repentance. But Viduy, the confession of sins, is said only once, not the customary three times, since it will be recited in the afternoon and evening as well. At the end of the morning prayers, Tahanun is omitted but *Avinu malkenu* is recited. If the day before Yom Kippur is a Friday, then *Avinu malkenu* is omitted.

KAPPAROT: Kapparot means "expiation [of sin]." It is an old custom once common among Ashkenazic Jews, observed on the day before Yom Kippur. The ritual is performed like this: after recitation of verses from Psalm 107 and Job 33, a person takes a live fowl by the feet, swings it over his head three

Kapparot from the Minhogimbukh, Venice, 1593.

The scapegoat is a commandment in Leviticus 16:8–10, near the description of the Yom Kippur rituals. See p. 264 for the related Torah passages.

times, saying, "This is my atonement, this is my ransom, this is my substitute." The fowl is then slaughtered and either it or its value in money is given to the poor. By this act, a person's sins are transferred to the fowl, thus bettering the prospect for inscription in the Book of Life.

Kapparot has its origins in the Temple custom of taking a scapegoat to Azazel as a receiver of the people's sins. In this ritual, the high priest placed his hands on the head of the goat and confessed the sins of the nation. The goat was taken a distance then pushed off a cliff, falling to its death. A flag was waved to notify those gathered around the Temple that their sins had been expunged.

Though still practiced in some ultraorthodox circles, kapparot has been mostly replaced by the giving of money or by performing the ritual with money in a handkerchief. The origin of the custom is not at all clear and it is not mentioned in the Talmud. Joseph Caro, the compiler of the great code of law known as the *Shulḥan arukh* (early sixteenth century), rejected it as pagan, and so it is not practiced by Sephardic Jews. But the great Cracow rabbi Moses Isserles, who wrote glosses on the *Shulḥan arukh*, did approve of it because, he said, it provides an opportunity to confront one's sins.

The verses recited at the beginning of the ritual include these:

Psalm 107:17   Some were sick through their sinful ways, and because of their iniquities endured affliction.

Psalm 107:6   Then they cried to the Lord in their trouble, and He delivered them from their distress.

and let them offer thanksgiving sacrifices. *Psalm 107:22*

Then, if there should be for one of them an angel, a media- *Job 33:23–24*
tor, one of a thousand, one who declares a person upright,
and He is gracious to that person, and says, deliver him from
going down into hell; I have found a ransom.

The tradition held further that the father of the family did
this for himself and his household, a cock for each male and
a hen for each female, and both a cock and a hen for a pregnant woman—the first for a boy, the second for a girl.

MIKVEH: It is customary to immerse in a ritual bath, a
mikveh, during the afternoon of the day before Yom Kippur,
as close to the holy day as practicable. Mikveh mean "gathering," a place where water for ritual purification is collected.
The instruction for this may be found in Leviticus 11:36,
"Only a spring, cistern, or collection of waters shall be cleansing." An entire tractate of the Mishnah, *Mikvaot*, is dedicated
to the legal requirements for the building and operation of a
mikveh, though later a body of law developed along with
newer technology. In regard to Yom Kippur, immersion in the
mikveh is a custom, not a requirement, and therefore does
not involve a blessing.

MAKOT: "You are to afflict your very beings," we are commanded in Leviticus, as the Day of Atonement is announced.
From this grew the customs of fasting and *makot*, the act of
flagellation as a personal confession of sin. It is observed the
day before Yom Kippur, though today only in the most
devout circles. Those who do the flogging alternate with
those who are flogged. Thirty-nine lashes are given, as the
words of *Vehu rahum*, the prayer for mercy, are recited three
times very slowly by the person administering the lashes. The
person who is flogged bows and recites the confession saying

one word at each lashing. If specific sins come to mind, these should be mentioned quietly, below the breath.

AFTERNOON SERVICE: In the afternoon, it is customary to go to the synagogue early for the afternoon service. The service begins with *Ashrei* (Psalm 145) and is followed by the Amidah, which includes Viduy, the prayers of confession, to which are added *Ashamnu* and *Al ḥet*, the lists of sins and transgressions, which one says whether or not they apply. After each phrase, one strikes the left side of the chest with the right fist. These recitations are unusual for an afternoon service. The reason they are considered important here is stated bluntly in the *Minhogimbukh*:

Ashamnu, "We have been guilty [of disobedience]," the alphabetically arranged list of transgressions recited collectively, appears on p. 209.

> Viduy is recited because during the meal before the fast one might drink too much, or—God forbid—a bone might get stuck in one's throat, and then one would die without having said Viduy.

Avinu malkenu is not recited at the end of this service, as it is otherwise during the Ten Days of Repentance; neither does one say Taḥanun. It is a custom to wear white at this service.

See p. 113 for the definitions and basic principles of eruvin.

ERUVIN: Since Sabbath-like restrictions apply on Yom Kippur, it is necessary, as it is on Sabbath, to create an *eruv* to "merge" the courtyards and boundaries for those who require unimpaired mobility to get from their homes to the synagogue or from home to home.

Talmud Yoma 81b

SEUDAH MAFSEKET: The Talmud says that just as it is a commandment to fast on the tenth of Tishrei, Yom Kippur, so it is also a commandment to eat on the ninth. This ritual meal is eaten before the fast begins before sunset and before synagogue services. Kiddush, the prayer over wine, is not recited, though the blessing over bread and Grace after Meals are.

CANDLES AND BLESSINGS: It has become a custom to bless one's children on the eve of Yom Kippur, just as on the eve of Sabbath. With parents placing their hands upon the heads of their children, each is blessed thus: to girls, it is recited, "May God make you like Sarah, Rebecca, Rachel, and Leah"; to boys, "May God make you like Ephraim and Manasseh."

In memory of parents who are deceased, it is a custom to light special candles that burn for an entire day. There is a Hasidic custom to light the same sort of candle for every married man in the household. It is called *dos geʒinte likht*, "the light of health." Then the two holiday candles are lit and blessed. *Sheheheyanu*, the second blessing, gives thanks for our lives.

If it is Sabbath, one adds the words, "Sabbath and" before "Yom Kippur."

> Blessed are You, Lord our God, who commands us to welcome Yom Kippur by kindling these lights.

> Blessed are You, Lord our God, king of the universe, who has kept us alive, sustained us, and who has brought us to this day.

When the candles are lit, the prohibitions of Yom Kippur take effect. It is customary to wear a *kitl*, a white shroud, for the services on Yom Kippur, but one should be dressed finely underneath. As on Rosh Hashanah, it is customary to put carpets on the synagogue floor for Yom Kippur because one must bow down.

The prohibitions take effect at sunset regardless of the candles, but if candles are lit earlier, the prohibitions take effect then.

YOM KIPPUR

The Day of Atonement marks the day when Moses came down from Mount Sinai for the second time, his face radiant, when it was understood by all that the sin of the Golden Calf had been forgiven. The instruction for Yom Kippur appears

The event is related in Exodus 34:29–35.

three times: twice in Leviticus, with instructions for its observance (including fasting), and once again in Numbers, with
the specifics of the sacrificial offerings. The following are the
two in Leviticus:

Leviticus 16:29–34

And this shall be to you a law for all time: In the seventh
month, on the tenth day of the month, you are to afflict
yourselves; and you shall do no manner of work, neither the
native nor the sojourner who resides in your midst. For on
this day atonement shall be made for you to cleanse all your
sins; you shall be clean before the Lord. It shall be a Sabbath
of complete rest for you, and you are to afflict yourselves; it
is a law for all time. The priest who has been anointed and
ordained to serve as priest in place of his father shall make
expiation. He shall put on the linen vestments, the sacral
vestments. He shall purge the innermost Shrine; he shall
purge the Tent of Meeting and the Altar; and he shall make
expiation for the priests and for all the people of the congregation. This shall be to you a law for all time: to make
atonement for the Israelites for all their sins once a year.
And Moses did as the Lord had commanded him.

*In the JPS transla-
tion, "afflict your-
selves" is rendered
as "self-denial."*

Leviticus 23:26–32

The Lord spoke to Moses, saying: Mark well that the tenth
day of this seventh month is the Day of Atonement. It shall
be a sacred occasion for you: you are to afflict yourselves,
and you shall bring a fire-offering to the Lord; you shall do
no work throughout that day. For it is a Day of Atonement,
on which expiation is made on your behalf before the Lord
your God. Indeed, any person who does not practice self-
denial throughout that day shall be cut off from his kin; and
whoever does any work throughout that day, I will cause
that person to perish from among his people. Do no work
whatever; it is a law for all time, throughout the ages in all
your settlements. It shall be a Sabbath of complete rest for
you, and you shall practice self-denial; on the ninth day of
the month at evening, from evening to evening, you shall
observe this your Sabbath.

The "Sabbath of complete rest," is, in Hebrew, *Shabbat Shab-baton*, "Sabbath of Sabbaths." What is clear is that there will be no painless forgiveness and none without uncomfortable self-confrontation.

In Everett Fox's translation, The Five Books of Moses, *"sabbath of complete rest" is "a Sabbath of Sab-bath-Ceasing."*

From sunset to dark the next day—twenty-five hours—five kinds of afflictions are in effect:

1. It is forbidden to eat and to drink. A sick person who wishes to be fed should be fed. If a doctor determines that someone must eat, they are to be fed, even against their will. It is forbidden for a nursing mother to fast until three days after childbirth.
2. It is forbidden to wear leather shoes, even for small children.
3. It is forbidden to use emollient creams for pleasure or aromatic oils at all.
4. It is forbidden to bathe; it is forbidden to put even one finger into water for pleasure.
5. It is forbidden to engage in sexual relations.

As said in the Bible passages, it is forbidden to do any work on Yom Kippur. It is a custom that gold not be worn on Yom Kippur, in remembrance of the sin of the Golden Calf. It is forbidden to wear leather shoes. Everyone should ask forgiveness from those one may have wronged or offended. In this regard, it should be remembered that Yom Kippur offers atonement for the sins that are between God and humanity but not for those that are between people.

Kol nidrei: The Eve of Yom Kippur

One of the best-known moments of the Jewish year is the chanting of a dry legal formula, written mostly in Aramaic, which serves as a prelude to the evening Yom Kippur service.

It is called *Kol nidrei*, meaning "all vows." This is its text as it is recited in Ashkenazic synagogues:

> All religious obligations and restrictions we have made forbidden to ourselves, and pledges (declaring something to be done or not done), and items we have (promised to) consecrate to the Temple, that we have vowed and sworn and dedicated, and made forbidden to ourselves; from this Yom Kippur until next Yom Kippur [*some say:* last Yom Kippur to this Yom Kippur], may (all such vows) come to us at a good time. We regret having made them; may they all be permitted, forgiven, eradicated, or nullified, and may they not be valid or exist any longer. Our vows shall no longer be vows, and our prohibitions shall no longer be prohibitions, and our oaths are longer oaths.

These are words that over the centuries have been used against Jews as evidence of their lack of trustworthiness, though what they refer to are vows made between mankind and God, promises made to God in the heat of the moment or as careless speech—expressly not those vows made to fellow persons or those that were ignored purposely. *Kol nidrei* *For* Hatarat nedarim, *see p. 217.* is, in a sense, a last chance of *Hatarat nedarim*, the "cancellation of vows" that was observed on the day before Rosh Hashanah. How this text became infused with the deepest possibility of human emotion is a matter of much speculation. There is a sharp difference of opinion as to whether it refers to vows broken during the past year or vows that *will* be broken in the year about to begin. What is without doubt or controversy, though, is that *Kol nidrei's* widely known tune is among the most heartrending evocations of penitence that was ever created, the musical embodiment of the Days of Awe that culminate with Yom Kippur. It would be as powerful if it had no words at all—such is the power of music to speak with emotional perfect pitch.

For Hatarat nedarim, *see p. 217.*

One of the great ninth-century rabbis, the Amram Gaon, dismissed *Kol nidrei* as a "foolish custom." The Reform Movement removed it from its prayer books from the mid-nineteenth century to 1961, substituting other texts or performing it as instrumental music, but the original text was eventually brought back by popular demand.

The *Kol nidrei* service begins while it is still daylight. Therefore, people may don their tallitot and recited the blessing over them, which may not be done at night. By custom, two or more Torah scrolls are brought out—three in many congregations and as many as seven in some. Three people holding scrolls standing at the pulpit symbolize the Beth Din, the Jewish court. Seven is Kabbalistic in significance, said to represent the seven heavens between man and God.

Before the recitation of *Kol nidrei* itself, the cantor makes a solemn declaration:

> With the approval of the Omnipresent and with the consent of the congregation, in convocation of the court above and the court below, we permit prayers to be said together with transgressors.

The Minhogim-bukh *says that this declaration is made by three dignitaries of the community.*

It is said that this preamble originated at the time of the Spanish Inquisition, when many Jews, under great duress, had allowed themselves to be baptized. Apostate though they were, many joined their fellow Jews at secret houses of worship for Yom Kippur. However, this doesn't explain its use among Ashkenazic Jews.

Kol nidrei must be recited before sundown and is said three times—the same as other declarations of the Beth Din.

EVENING SERVICE: There may be one or two additional cantors sharing the duties of this service. The Barkhu, the Call to Prayer, is recited. The recitation of the Shema is unique in all the year. After the first line, "Hear O Israel, the Lord our God, the Lord is One," one usually recites the second line in a hushed tone, as if parenthetically separating scripture from liturgical response: "Blessed be the name of His glorious kingdom forever." But on Yom Kippur this sentence is said in full voice. A reason for this is given in the Midrash Rabbah, an early collection of stories of Torah interpretation, in which it is said that Moses had heard this line from the mouths of the angels when he was on Mount Sinai. When he came down and related it to the people, it was treated as if it were a stolen jewel, something to be kept hush. But on Yom Kippur, we are all like the angels, so we have no fear showing it off. The closing blessings of the Shema are followed by a verse from Leviticus, "For on this day of atonement is to be effected for you, to purify you from all your sins; before the presence of the Lord, you will become pure."

The special Amidah for Yom Kippur begins the same as Rosh Hashanah and is said throughout the Days of Awe, with interpolated lines asking that we be inscribed in the Book of Life. Following the Amidah, there is a personal recitation of the Viduy, the prayers of confession, which include *Ashamnu* and *Al ḥet*, the lists of sins and transgressions, which one says whether or not they apply. After each phrase, one strikes the left side of the chest with the right fist. *Ashamnu* has been described already, but the formula of *Al ḥet* is as follows:

Leviticus 16:30. If Yom Kippur falls on Sabbath, it is preceded by Exodus 31:16–17, "And the Children of Israel shall keep the Sabbath . . ."

The alphabetical list of sins of Ashamnu *may be found on p. 209.*

If Yom Kippur falls on Sabbath, the Amidah includes those sentences that recognize this.

> For the sin we have sinned before You, whether under duress or willingly; and for the sin we have sinned before You through the hardness of our heart.
> For the sin we have sinned before You without knowledge; and for the sin we have sinned before You through our utterances. . . .
> For the sin we have sinned before You through insincere

confession; and for the sin we have sinned before You
through sexual impropriety.

The alphabetical structure of the confessional prayers expresses a desire for completeness that goes beyond the words
alone.

If it is Sabbath, the Amidah is followed by *Vayekhulu,*
"Thus the heavens and the earth were finished . . . on the sev-
enth day," from Genesis 2:1–3, and *Magen avot,* "Shield of
Our Fathers," also called the "Seven-Faceted Blessing."

This is the only festival evening service that has an extensive liturgy following the Amidah because it is the only festival service after which there is no meal. The series of Seliḥot
that begin *Yaaleh taḥanunenu meerev,* "May our supplications
ascend from evening, and may our cry arrive from morning,
and may our praise find favor by evening," culminates in the
Viduy and *Al ḥet,* and it is followed by a prayer drawn mostly
from Psalms, *Shomea tefilah,* "You who hear prayer, to You all
flesh will come." Central to the Seliḥot is the Thirteen Attributes of Mercy, the passage in Exodus (34:6–7) that tells of
God's nature, the words with which Moses could always seek
God's mercy.

For more on the Thirteen Attri-butes, see pp. 34 and 208.

The Seliḥot are sung responsively in some communities by
the cantor and the congregation. Their structure varies, alternating between straight verses and hymns with strong
repeating phrases and patterns. The order in which these
plaintive prayers are recited makes them all the more fervent.
A verse uttered by Moses in the Wilderness, *Selaḥ na,* "Forgive, please, the iniquity of these people," begging God's forgiveness in the aftermath of the rebellion that followed the
return of the spies from Canaan, becomes here a hymn of
gentle, yet persistent rhythm, with twenty-two verses, one for
each letter of the alphabet.

Numbers 14:19

Forgive, please, the guilt and willful sins of Your nation,
may Your anger not be ignited at the iniquity of Your
children .
Forgive, please, their abomination, and let them live from
the life-source that is You . . .
Forgive, please, all who confess and forsake sin . . .
Forgive, please, wantonness and error . . .
Forgive, please, all who confess and forsake sin . . . .

The *selihah*, *Omnam ken*, "It is indeed true," was written by
Rabbi Yom Tov ben Yitzhak, who died in anti-Semitic riots in
York in 1190. Each verse concludes with the refrain *salahti*, "I
have forgiven!"

It is indeed true that passion rules us;
and so it is for You, O abundantly just, to answer us,
"I have forgiven!"
Abhor the slanderer [Satan] and invalidate his
testimony, O beloved who roars loudly . . .
"I have forgiven!"
Cleanse filth like a fleeting cloud;
Wipe away the willful sin of a delivered people,
and say to us,
"I have forgiven!"

The anonymous *Ki hinei kahomer*, "Like the clay," beseeches
God to think of us as raw material in his artistic hands:

Like the clay in the hand of the potter,
Expanding and contracting at his will,
So we are in Your hand, O preserver of kindness:
Look to the covenant and ignore the accuser.
Like the stone in the hand of the cutter . . .
Look to the covenant and ignore the accuser.
Like the hammer in the hand of the blacksmith . . .
Look to the covenant and ignore the accuser.
Like the anchor in the hand of the sailor . . .
Look to the covenant and ignore the accuser.

> Like the glass in the hand of the blower,
> He shapes and dissolves it at will,
> So we are in Your hand, O forgiver of willful sins and errors:
> Look to the covenant and ignore the accuser.

The evening service after the Amidah may be said to be an expansion of the Viduy, the confessional prayers that include Selihot. Some have insistent rhythmic patterns that take on the quality of drumming:

> Answer us, our Lord, answer us; answer us, our God, answer us; answer us, our Father, answer us; answer us, our Creator, answer us; answer us, our Redeemer, answer us; answer us, You who searched us out, answer us; answer us, faithful God, answer us; answer us. . . .

Then the grand and moving prayer of supplication, *Avinu malkenu*, is recited, as it has been in services since Rosh Hashanah. The the last part of the service includes the customary full Kaddish, *Alenu*, mourner's Kaddish, Psalm 27 (said mornings and evenings from Elul through Shemini Atzeret), *Adon olam* or *Yigdal*, and the Psalm of the Day.

On Sabbath, Avinu malkenu is not recited.

There is a custom among the devout to spend the whole night in the synagogue and recite the entire book of Psalms. If they sleep in the synagogue, they must do so far away from the ark.

The Morning of Yom Kippur

The morning service is a very long one and starts early so that the musaf service may begin no later than 1:00 p.m. The first part of the service is similar to that of Sabbath, concentrating on God's generosity and our praise of Him. The morning blessings are followed by the *Pesukei dezimra* and then *Nishmat*:

> The soul of every living thing shall bless Your name,
> O Lord our God.

The spirit of all flesh shall continually adore and exalt
    the mention of You, O our king.
You are God from everlasting to everlasting.
Other than You we have no king, no redeemer or savior,
    no liberator or deliverer. . . .

*For Hamelekh, see
p. 231.* The cantor starts singing *Hamelekh*, "O King, who sits upon
a high and lofty throne," just as on Rosh Hashanah. He or she
then says Kaddish and Barkhu, the Call to Prayer. The ark is
opened and the cantor begins singing the blessing *Hapoteah
lanu shaarei rahamim*, a poetic insertion to the *Yotzer*, one of
the morning blessings of the Shema, which is, perhaps, a remnant of an old hymn.

> Blessed are You, Lord our God, king of the universe, who
> opens for us the gates of mercy and illuminates the eyes
> of those who await His pardon; who forms light and cre-
> ates darkness, makes peace and creates all. The primeval
> light is in the treasury of eternal life. "Let there be lights
> from the darkness," He declared. And it was so!

The ark is closed and the cantor says, "Forgive the holy
nation on the holy day, O exalted and Holy One," repeated by
the congregation. And in the same order, "We have erred, our
Rock; forgive us, our Maker," which becomes the refrain of a
Yotzer hymn that continues, "Then, on Yom Kippur, You
taught us about forgiveness." (If it is a Sabbath, *Hakol
yodukha* and *El adon* are said, followed by *Lael asher shavat*.)
*For more on these
blessings and
hymns, see p. 74.* Inserted in the *Ofan* is the hymn *Kadosh adir baaliyato*, "The
Holy One, mighty in His lofty heaven." It is recited respon-
sively, with the congregation proclaiming the refrain after
every verse, *Barukh shem kevod malkhuto*, "Blessed is the
name of His glorious kingdom"—the second line of the
Shema, used here in anticipation of its formal recitation, said

loudly only on this day. The Kedushah concludes, "Blessed is the glory of the Lord from His place," followed by the prayer *Ahavah rabah*, "With abundant love You have loved us," which concludes the *Yotzerot*. And then the Shema.

About the loud recitation in the Shema, see p. 260.

The Amidah is the same as in the previous evening, but the cantor's reptition of it is a liturgical tour de force, a veritable catalog of pleading, with hymns inserted in the first four blessings and in the fourth are added extensive Selihot that lead to the Viduy. The ark is then opened, and the cantor says the *Avot*, the benediction of the patriarchs, followed by a brief indulgence (a *reshut*) to justify the insertion of so many extra liturgies into the Amidah.

> Based on the tradition of our wise and discerning teachers and the teaching derived from the knowledge of the discerning, I open my mouth in prayer and supplications to beseech and beg favor before the King who is full of mercy and who pardons and forgives iniquities.

And then the eloquent hymn *Emekha nasati*.

> I bear Your dread as I offer supplication,
>   as I bend my knee on the mission of Your people.
> You who withdrew me from the womb, illuminate my darkness,
>   that I may speak eloquently. . . .
> Protect me like the pupil of an eye from shock and terror,
>   observe my lowliness and come with salvation.

Asher ometz tehilatekha has an unusual gossamer texture and text:

> The force of Your praise is rendered by heavenly angels, by beings that glow like lightening, by lofty hands, with a still, thin sound—and Your holiness is in their mouths.

> The force of Your praise is rendered by pure heavenly nobles, by hastily fleeing angels, by Cherubim of glory, by flaming legions—and this is Your glory!

Al Yisrael emunato is a simple alphabetic list, alternating line by line from cantor to congregation:

> And so, attribute might to God for upon Israel is His pride.
> Upon Israel is His faithfulness.
> Upon Israel is His blessing.
> Upon Israel is His word.
> Upon Israel is His majesty. . . .

En kamokha beadirei malah has the quality of a children's song:

> There is none like You among the mighty ones   above,
> There is nothing like Your works among the elite   below,
> There is nothing like You among the bands   above,
> There is nothing like Your works in the legions   below . . .

Imru lelohim is based on the verses of the Thirteen Attributes of Mercy:

> Give praise to God!
> He is slow to anger and great of strength, readies mountains
>   with strength, giving strength to the exhausted.
> Therefore, let Him be glorified—
>   great is our Master and abundantly strong.

Haaderet vehaemunah is a song of pairings:

> Strength and faithfulness   are His who lives eternally;
> Adornment and purity   are His who lives eternally;
> Beauty and triumph   are His who lives eternally;
> Desire and righteousness   are His who lives eternally . . .

After several more hymns with distinctive, rhythmic refrains and rhyming schemes, the cantor says *Zeh el zeh shoalim,* "They ask one another, 'Where is the God of gods, where is the One who dwells in the heights, and whom they all revere, sanctify, and praise?'" In response to the question, the ark is opened and the cantor and congregation proclaim,

"And so all shall ascribe the crown to You"; then the ark is closed. The Kedushah is in the expanded musaf form—unique to Yom Kippur.

The *Kedushat hayom* (the Holiness of the Day) contains the penitential prayers *Ashamnu* and *Al ḥet*, the lists of sins and transgressions, which one says while striking the left side of the chest with the right fist. One of the inserted hymns is an anonymous medieval one called *Yom asher ashamnu*. In each stanza, the first line begins "A day," the second begins, "Today," and the third a brief verse based on scripture.

For Ashamnu, *see* p. 209; *for* Al ḥet, *see p. 256.*

> A day on which our guilty acts are sunk and locked away.
> Today may You forgive the entire congregation of the Children of Israel and the stranger who lives among them.
>> As it is written in Your Torah: May it be forgiven for the entire congregation of the Children of Israel and for the stranger who lives among them, for the sin befell the entire nation through carelessness.

> A day on which You will pardon and forgive our betrayal.
> Today Your name will be affirmed, O good and forgiving God.
>> As it is written in Your holy words: For You are my Lord, good, forgiving and abundantly kind to all who call upon You.

After the completion of the cantor's repetition of the Amidah, *Avinu malkenu* is recited, except on Sabbath.

After full Kaddish, two Torah scrolls are taken out. Six people are called up to the first scroll—one more than on any other holiday. (If it is Sabbath, seven are called up.) The portion is Leviticus 16:1–34, which begins in the aftermath of the death of Aaron's two sons, Nadab and Abihu, who, in chapter 10, had been consumed by the fire of God, punished for having brought before him a "strange fire." In this portion, God speaks of the matter to Moses for the first time, telling him to warn Aaron that when the cloud appears over the Ark cover, he may not enter the Sanctuary, for he may catch a glimpse of the Lord and perish as a result. God then describes the purgation rituals for the removal of pollution of the Sanctuary and of the community that are to be performed every year on the tenth day of the seventh month. ("To atone" and "to purge" are the same Hebrew verb, *lekhapper.*) The Sanctuary is purged with the blood of a bull that is sacrificed at the altar; the community is purged through expiation, through a tranferrance of sin to an animal. The procedure is described thus: Two hairy goats are brought to the entry of the Sanctuary. By lot, one is chosen for God, the other for Azazel. The one chosen for God is made a sin offering, the other left alive. Aaron places his hands on the head of the live goat, confessing over it all the iniquities and transgressions of the Children of Israel. It is then taken to the wilderness and set free for Azazel. It says in the *Zohar* that those who truly understand this ritual will be forgiven their sins.

The meaning of Azazel has been debated for centuries. Many have said it is ez azel, *"a goat that escapes" (from which we get the word* scapegoat*), though recent scholars believe it is Azazel, a wilderness demon, the vestige of a pagan ritual.*

The maftir reads from the second scroll, the verses Numbers 29:7–11, which repeats the commandment for the observance of "a sacred occasion" and gives the specifics of the sacrificial offerings for this day. The haftarah is from Isaiah (57:14–58:14), a wise balance for the obscurities of reading from the first scroll. Ritual and custom without righteousness are useless hypocrisies.

Isaiah 58:4–6

Behold, ye fast for strife and contention, and to smite with the fist of wickedness; ye fast not this day so as to make your voice to be heard on high.

Is such the fast I have chosen? The day for a man to afflict his soul? Is it to bow down his head as a bulrush, and to spread sackcloth and ashes under him? Wilt thou call this a

fast, and an acceptable day to the Lord?
Is not this the fast I have chosen? To loose the fetter of
wickedness, to undo the bands of the yoke. . . .

On Sabbath the Torah service is followed by the Aramaic
prayer *Yekum purkan*, "May salvation arise from heaven," then
the *Mi sheberakh* prayers for the community.

YIZKOR: A major feature of the Yom Kippur morning service
is Yizkor, the memorial service for the dead. This distinctive
feature of Ashkenazic Judaism is observed on Yom Kippur
and on the three pilgrimage festivals (Passover, Shavuot,
Sukkot). The recalling of the souls of the dead is based in the
belief in the eternity of the soul, which, upon death, rises to
the spirit realm, where it attains a higher level of holiness.
Those who have not lost parents leave the synagogue and
return when the congregations recites the general memorial
prayer *Av harahamim*, "Father of Compassion."

Yizkor is not said on Sukkot, per se, but rather on Shemini Atzeret.

In the Minhogim-bukh, the custom of saying Yizkor is said to be the practice of only Poland, Bohemia, and Moravia.

The Yizkor prayers are accompanied by pledges of charity
made by the mourner to benefit the souls of the deceased.
Though not universal, the pledges are preceded by two recitations, the first a prayer comprising excerpts drawn mostly
from Psalm 144 and Psalm 90, followed by Psalm 91 in its
entirety. There follow the prayers that begin *El malei
rahamim*, "O God, full of mercy," which have in them places
to mention the names of the deceased.

In many congregations, those who have not lost parents remain in the synagogue and recite a prayer for their living parents.

Lord, what is man that You recognize him?
The son of a frail human that You reckon with him?
Man is like a breath, his days are like a passing shadow.

Upon the return of the congregation, *Ashrei* and *Yehalelu*,
the Torah scrolls are taken back to the ark. If there is a circumcision on Yom Kippur, the child should be circumcised
before the musaf service.

Musaf Service

The musaf of Yom Kippur, like that of Rosh Hashanah, is preceded by a doleful, first-person prayer from the cantor, *Hineni heani mimaas*, "Here I am, deficient in worthy deeds, trembling and frightened in dread of Him." It is followed by half Kaddish. The service itself begins, as usual, with the silent recital of the Amidah. In the middle benediction, the *Kedushat hayom*, the Sanctification of the Day, there are variations among different rites, but all of them contain the prayers associated with festival musaf services: *Atah bahartanu*, "You have chosen us from all the peoples," and some verses of *Umipenei hataenu*, "Because of our sins we have been exiled from our land. . . . We cannot perform our obligations in the House of Your choice . . . because of the hand that dispatched against Your Sanctuary," a reference to the destruction of the Temple. They are followed by the reading of the special offerings for the day (Numbers 28:9–10). The silent Amidah is followed by confessional prayers Viduy and *Al het*, as throughout the Ten Days of Repentance.

The cantor's repetition of the Amidah is a grand liturgy, filled with hymns on the themes of atonement, supplication, *For* Unetaneh tokef, *see p. 238.* and awe. Also included is the prayer *Unetaneh tokef*, "Let us now relate the power of this day's holiness." We are reminded that on Rosh Hashanah, God decides our fate and on Yom Kippur it is sealed, though "repentance, prayer, and charity remove the evil of the decree."

The great moment of the service—of the liturgical day, some would say—comes in the cantor's recitation of the *Avodah*, which in this case is the *Avodah* of the high priest, the poeticized reenactment of the Temple rituals and sacrifices performed in Temple times on this day. The recitation is preceded by a series of prayers beginning with *Alenu*, recited to a special tune, during which the congregants bow down face to the floor (an action that will be repeated three times during the *Avodah*). God is beseeched to show us the way to prayer, that it may be a worthy substitute for the Temple ritual. There is an emphasis on getting it right:

> Teach them what to say, make them understand how to speak . . . that their tongues may not blunder nor their abilitie of articulation be stricken.

A matter of great delicacy: in this service, the high priest would speak the Ineffable Name of God ten times and in our word-based counterpart to the Temple ritual, we liturgically allude to the pronunciation of antiquity. At the words "And the kohanim and people used to bow down and kneel and thank and fall down on their faces," everyone bows and falls down face to the floor and stands up again to say the verse "Blessed be the Name."

As is often the case on festivals, the narrative is carried by the piyutim, the hymns. Here are some excerpts from this very lengthy liturgy:

> He [the high priest] strode into the courtyard, where there was a pair of he-goats purchased with community funds.... He cried out in a loud voice, "For YHWH—a sin-offering.". . . When the priests and the people in the courtyard would hear the glorious, awesome Name emanating from the high priest's mouth, they would kneel and prostrate themselves and say, "Blessed is the Name of His glorious kingdom for all eternity."

The various sacrifices are described in considerable detail, the high priest is praised in song, and the loss of the Temple and its rituals are mourned in litanies of the people's sinfulness and the losses suffered because of it.

> And because of our abundant iniquities . . . we cannot relate the extent of our torments, there is calamity and groaning

every day. Trembling has multiplied, pride has descended to the dust.... There is neither prophet nor vision among us.

And then pleas for mercy. As on Tishah b'Av, the tragic story of the Ten Martyrs is also part of this portion of the musaf liturgy, as are Viduy and *Al het*.

The Ten Martyrs were the sages murdered under orders of the emperor Hadrian in the second century C.E.

Orthodox Jews believe that reading the commandments that cannot be be completed, such as those involving Temple sacrifices, is sufficient for their fulfillment. But even the familiar rendition of the sacrifices in this service was apparently a replacement for an earlier set of hymns that were collected from the fifth through the ninth centuries. Reform Jews have no musaf service, but many congregations add extra readings to the Yom Kippur morning service. In place of the *Avodah*, Reform congregations read from Deuteronomy 29 and 30, chapters that describe covenantal responsibilities. After the benediction of thanksgiving, the kohanim gather for the Priestly Blessing. The service ends with full Kaddish, not with the usual *Ashrei* and *En kelohenu*.

Deuteronomy 29 and 30; see p. 215.

For the Priestly Blessing, see p. 133.

Afternoon Service

There is a break between the musaf and afternoon services if time permits.

The afternoon service of Yom Kippur immediately follows the musaf. It begins with the removal of the Torah from the ark. One scroll is taken out to which three people are called up. The portion is Leviticus 18, which describes forbidden sexual unions (and is addressed to men). It's a reading that's not easy to explain in this context, though perhaps we can find part of an explanation in the haftarah that is read when these verses are part of the weekly reading: Ezekiel 22:1–19. It tells how Jerusalem had polluted itself through sexual transgressions and how God would express his revulsion through the Babylonian Exile.

For more on Leviticus 18, see p. 103.

The haftarah is the entire Book of Jonah and three verses from Micah (7:18–20). As the weariness of the hungry congregants grows stronger, hope is held out by Jonah's story—that even in the belly of the whale, it was not too late to ask God's forgiveness. Jonah is the Bible's holy fool, who runs from God's instructions, only to bring misery to himself and those around him. And even when he does what he's told, he becomes angry when things don't turn out exactly as he expects. He's dumb and dumber, unable to understand God's willingness to forgive those who repent.

The juxtaposition of the verses from Leviticus with the book of Jonah provides an important lesson about God's nature, not unlike the Thirteen Attributes of Mercy in Exodus 34:6–7: forgiving of transgression and error (like Jonah's), but not forgiving of willful guilt. Jonah, in his most thick-headed moment, appeals to God to take his life—quoting from the Thirteen Attributes, no less. Indeed, the three verses from Micah are a later version of the same ideas:

> O God, who is like You? Who pardons iniquity and over-looks transgressions for the remnant of His heritage? Who has not held on to His wrath eternally, for He loves kindness. He will again be merciful to us; He will suppress our iniquities and cast into the depths of the seas all their sins. Grant truth to Jacob, kindness to Abraham, as You swore to our forefathers in ancient times.

The *Zohar* writes of these verses from Micah as a "higher" set of Thirteen Attributes, spoken to the Children of Israel under happier circumstances than the first, coming as they did in the aftermath of the Golden Calf episode.

The afternoon service continues with the Amidah, including Viduy and *Al het* in the cantor's repetition. The service concludes with *Avinu malkenu* and full Kaddish.

Neilah, the Last Appeal

Yom Kippur is the only day with five full synagogue services. There is a special service following the afternoon prayers that is called *Neilah*, which mean "closing" or "locking up." Its

purpose is to organize a final rally of appeal by the congregants, to make full use of every last moment before the Book is sealed. The *kotvenu* ("write us") of the earlier services is replaced here by *hotmenu* ("seal us"), underscoring the urgency of the appeal. After half Kaddish, the congregation begins the silent Amidah, which concludes with Viduy, the prayers of confession.

Moses receiving the Law on Shavuot. Minhogimbukh, Amsterdam, 1722. The woodcut was also used for Neilah as a symbol of received judgment.

Al het is not said here. Two paragraphs added to the Viduy are recited only in this service: "What can we say before You who dwells on high. . . . You reach out a hand to willful sinners and Your right hand is extended to accept penitents," a reminder that God is always ready for us to turn to him in repentance. In the *Kedushat hayom* of the cantor's repetition of the Amidah, we come to the final recitation of Selihot. Again the theme is the Thirteen Attributes of Mercy, repeated insistently, again and again, punctuating every prayer. It seems as if every divinely inspired verse of forgiveness is quoted here as well, as if to remind and persuade God of his merciful nature.

In the repetition of the Amidah, two paragraphs dominate the sentiment: the Thirteen Atrributes of Mercy, preceded by *El melekh*: "O God, king who sits on the throne of mercy, who acts with kindness, pardons the sins of His people, removes sins one by one, and grants pardons to careless sinners and forgiveness to rebels." After the last verse of *Avinu malkenu,* which is timed so that it is said at the moment the fast ends, the first line of the Shema is proclaimed, loudly and in unison. The cantor then the congregation recite the second line three times: "Blessed be the name of His glorious kingdom forever and ever." Finally, "The Lord is our God" is shouted, seven times by the cantor and seven times by the congregation. A full Kaddish is followed by the sound of the shofar, and all proclaim, "Next year in Jerusalem."

The Conclusion of Yom Kippur

Yom Kippur ends with an evening service and Havdalah. The service is typical of those that follow festivals and includes in the Amidah the *Atah ḥonantanu* benediction for insight, as well as those for repentance, forgiveness, redemption, health, prosperity, ingathering of exiles, restoration of justice, and so on. When Yom Kippur falls on a Sabbath, many congregations follow the Amidah with the *Pesukei berakhah*, the Verses of Blessing, biblical passages on themes similar to those of the Amidah benedictions.

For Atah ḥonantanu, *see p. 85*

The Havdalah ceremony is performed over wine and, particular to Yom Kippur, over a candle that was lit prior to the beginning of the day; it does not need to be the customary double-wicked candle. If Yom Kippur was on Sabbath, then the blessing over the spices is made as well. After Havdalah, *Kidush levanah*, the blessing of the new moon, is made. Following the instruction to "go from mitzvah to mitzvah," it is customary at the conclusion of Yom Kippur to do something in preparation for Sukkot, usually to start on the building of the sukkah, which must be completed in the four days between Yom Kippur and Sukkot.

For Havdalah, see p. 85. For the blessing of the new moon, see p. 97.

The 1593 *Minhogimbukh* ends its recounting of the Yom Kippur customs with this comforting sentence:

At the conclusion of Yom Kippur, a voice comes from the Heavens and tells us to eat our bread with joy, because God has accepted our prayers.

In our model year, there is a Sabbath between Yom Kippur and Sukkot, and it is a "normal" one. The Torah portion is *Haazinu*, "Give ear, ye heavens, and I will speak," Deuteronomy 32:1–52. The speaker is Moses, and the speech, which covers most of the portion, is known as the the Song of Moses. It is an encapsulation of the story of Israel's relation with God—to date. In it, a steadfast and equitable God gives his inheritance to a people who respond to him unfaithfully. It is a cautionary song, politically canny, a last hedge to assuage God before the people cross into the Promised Land. Moses knows he will not be there to intercede, and in the last verses of the chapter God reminds him—as if he needed reminding—why he will never set foot on the land, *For the offending* because he and Aaron did not wait faithfully and silently *event, see Numbers* before beseeching God when the people needed water in *20, in the portion* *Ḥukat, p. 177.* the Wilderness.

The haftarah, 2 Samuel 22:1–51, is the Song of David (virtually identical with Psalm 18), which provides a study in contrasts with the Song of Moses. Whereas Moses knows that a small infraction might provoke God's rage, David is sure of God's favor, though his words were surely written before his great sin, his adulterous affair with Bathsheba and his complicity in the death of her husband, Uriah.

> The Lord rewarded me as my righteousness deserved;
>   my hands were clean and He requited me.
> For I have followed the ways of the Lord
>   and have not turned away from Him in wickedness;
>   all His laws are before my eyes,
> I have not failed to follow His decrees.

SUKKOT

Sukkot means "huts," a reference to the temporary dwellings in which the Israelites lived in the Wilderness. The festival of Sukkot, the third of the three pilgrimage festivals, commemorates this time and serves also as a festival of the autumn harvest, the ingathering, which during Temple times was marked by a series of sacrifices. The instructions for the observance of Sukkot are given in Leviticus:

On the fifteenth day of this seventh month there shall be the pilgrimage festival of huts. ... The first day shall be a sacred occasion, so you are not to work at your occupations. For seven days you are to bring a fire-offering to the Lord. ... When you have gathered in the yield of your land, you are to celebrate the pilgrimage festival of the Lord. ... On the first day, you are to take for yourselves the fruit of beautiful trees, branches of palms, boughs of thick tree foliage, and willows of the brook. And you are to rejoice before the presence of the Lord your God for seven days ... a law for all time, throughout your generations. ... In huts you are to dwell for seven days, all citizens of Israel are to dwell in huts in order that future generations may know that in huts I had the Children of Israel stay when I brought them out of Egypt.

The complete instructions appear in Leviticus 23:33–43.

A parallel passage in Deuteronomy adds more specific information as to who is to participate:

The pilgrimage festival of huts you are to observe for yourself, for seven days, after the ingathering from your threshing floor and from your vat. You are to rejoice on your festival: you, your son and your daughter, your servant and your maid, the levite, the sojourner, the orphan and the widow that are within your midst.

Deuteronomy 16:13–17

The forty Wilderness years were more than a sojourn; they were a period of growth through moral and legal instruction as well as of living under God's direct protection and through his beneficence. These are the reasons for this "season of our rejoicing."

The Sukkah

"In huts you are to stay for seven days" are the words of the commandment. Since the Torah gives no specific instruc-

tions for these latter-day "tabernacles," it was up to later authorities to codify the law in regard to their construction and use. The Mishnah tractate *Sukkah* is devoted to the subject and is commented upon in both the Babylonian and Jerusalem Talmuds. By strict Jewish law, one is to eat, drink, and sleep in this structure, but many who live in cold climes were sometimes unable to fulfill the obliga-

Sukkah from the Minhogimbukh, Amsterdam, 1727

tions to the letter, so later law was modified to require only the eating of meals or, at least, some bread or other food made from flour. It is considered most important to eat in the sukkah the first night. If the weather does not permit it, one should make kiddush and eat a piece of bread the size of an olive—these are the minimum requirements.

The sukkah must be a temporary structure erected in an open space, with walls strong enough to withstand normal wind. It may be a three-sided structure, though four is more common, with a doorway on one side. Of greater significance is the roof—called the *sekhakh*—which must be made from cut vegetation, such as branches, fronds, slats, or a combination.

It must be sufficiently occlusive to keep out the sun during the day, but open enough so that the stars may be seen. The walls must stand before the roof material is put on. The sukkah may be built against the side of a house or between two houses. It must be big enough to accommodate one person and a table on which to eat, and while there is no limit on its width or depth, its height is restricted to twenty cubits (about thirty feet).

The *Minhogimbukh* offers this unimpeachable decorating advice:

> One should not build a sukkah in a place where it stinks or where it looks miserable.... One should make the sukkah as nice as possible, as if building the nicest room in one's house. And one should adorn and decorate it. One should not put anything in the sukkah that one would not put in a room. Nor should one put anything repulsive in there.

And it also gives a good summary of the traditional regulations regarding the use of the dwelling:

> Throughout the seven days of Sukkot, the sukkah should be considered as one's true dwelling place. Therefore, one should eat, drink, and sleep in the sukkah and should do everything else in there too: work, study, read, and write there. If it rains, one is permitted to leave the sukkah, but only if it rains so hard that one would leave the house as well if it were to rain like that inside. Sick people are exempt from dwelling in the sukkah. It is a greater mitzvah to sleep in the sukkah than to eat there, because between meals on the days of Sukkot one may eat fruits or drink water outside the sukkah as well as in it, but it is forbidden to sleep outside the sukkah, even for a short nap during the day. Nonetheless, some are concerned that they might get ill sleeping in such cold and damp, so not everyone sleeps in the sukkah. But even then, one should build the sukkah in such a way that one might sleep there.

The Four Species

The three pilgrimage festivals comprise the totality of the Jewish people's relationship with God. In Passover, there is

beginning of nationhood expressed in God's deliverance from bondage. In Shavuot, there is the giving of the Law upon which Jewish society would be based. In Sukkot the emphasis is on God's physical gifts to us, as protector of the earth's bounty. If the sukkah is the symbol of protection, then it is in the Four Species that God's gifts of the fruits of the earth are recognized and celebrated. The importance of water, too, is part of our consciousness on Sukkot.

The Four Species, from the Minhogimbukh, *Venice, 1593.*

"On the first day, you are to take for yourselves the fruit of beautiful trees, branches of palms, boughs of thick tree foliage, and willows of the brook," we are instructed in Leviticus. Two of these, the palm and the willow, are specific, but our understanding of the other two comes from the oral law. Three of the species are gathered together into a bouquet called a *lulav* (named for the palm branch), which is used in the key Sukkot rituals. The components are:

The LULAV, determined in the Talmud to be the closed frond of a date palm tree. It should be a nice and whole piece of branch, with leaves converging to a point that is as perfect as possible.

The HADAS, the "boughs of thick trees," was determined to be the myrtle. A kosher *hadas* has three leaves growing out from the same level on the stem, and none is lower than the others. Also, the branch itself must be entirely covered by the leaves.

The ARAVAH is the "willows of the brook." A kosher *aravah* has to have long leaves and red stems.

The ETROG, a citron, is "the fruit of goodly trees." It must be utterly unblemished and grown on an ungrafted tree; the smallest scar or hole makes the fruit ritually unfit.

Care should be taken if the etrog still has its stamen (pitom), which if broken, compromises the etrog's ritual integrity.

The palm frond, two branches of willow, and three sprigs of myrtle are bound together with strips of palm leaves to make the ceremonial *lulav*. The myrtle is on the right and the willow on the left. In the ritual, one holds the *etrog* in the left hand and the *lulav* in the right—together so they touch.

There are various interpretations of the commandment of the Four Species, the most familiar of which comes from *Leviticus rabah*, a collection of early midrash on Leviticus. It is quoted in the *Minhogimbukh*:

> The *etrog*, which is a fruit and has a pleasant fragrance, is compared to a righteous Jew who possesses knowledge of the Torah and performs good deeds. The *lulav* is taken from the tree that grows figs [*sic*] but does not have any smell, so it is like those people who possess the knowledge of the Torah but do not perform any good deeds. The *hadas* smells good but does not bear any fruit, so it is like people who perform good deeds but do not possess the knowledge of the Torah. And the *aravah* has neither fruit nor a good smell, which makes it similar to the wicked, who neither do good deeds nor have knowledge of the Torah.

Another explanation—albeit a botanically spurious one—is that the Four Species all require more water than than other plants, and it is at this time of year that one prays for rain.

The First Night of Sukkot

The first evening service of Sukkot follows the pattern typical of festivals. In some congregations the blessing following

If the first two days
of Sukkot fall on a
Thursday and a
Friday, one is
required to make
an eruv tavshilin
as described in
regard to Passover.
See p. 113.
the Shema is elaborated by a special hymn that enumerates the themes and rituals of Sukkot: the Four Species, the mystical "guests," the sukkah, the recitation of Hallel. Other verses are recited on the second night. The Amidah contains the standard festival *Kedushat hayom*. The service continues with the festival kiddush and concludes with *Alenu*, the mourner's Kaddish, and *Yigdal*.

At home, in the sukkah, candles are lit. As we enter it, we participate in one of the most remarkable of Jewish customs—
Ushpizin, the welcoming of the "guests." These are not guests of the usual kind—though all are welcome at the sukkah table—but the patriarchs, the lights of our forefathers: Abraham, Isaac, Jacob, Moses, Aaron, Joseph, and David. The root of the custom is in this passage in the *Zohar*:

*Ushpizin is the
Aramaic word for
"guests."*

Zohar Emor 103b

> When people sit in a sukkah, the "shade of faithfulness"—the shekhinah [the feminine divine manifestation]—spreads Her wings over them and . . . Abraham, five other righteous ones, and King David make their dwelling with them. And so, people should rejoice with shining countenance every day of the festival, together with these guests who lodge with them. . . . Upon entering the sukkah, Rav Hamuna Sava would rejoice and, while standing in the doorway, say, "Let us invite the guests and prepare the table."

Each day, another one of the patriarchs leads the group. Some Jews determine the order chronologically, but most follow according to their *sefirah*, the ten emanations of God as described by the Kabbalah:

DAY	SEFIRAH	GUEST
1	*hesed* / lovingkindness	Abraham
2	*gevurah* / power	Isaac
3	*tiferet* / splendor	Jacob
4	*netzah* / eternity	Moses

5	*hod* / glory	Aaron
6	*yesod* / foundation	Joseph
7	*malkhut* / kingship	David

The ritual begins with a special *Yehi ratzon*, "May it be Your will, Lord, . . . that You cause Your presence (shekhinah) to dwell among us, that You spread over us the sukkah of Your peace," which is followed by the invitation of the guests: "I invite to my meal the exalted guests: Abraham, Isaac, Jacob, Moses, Aaron, Joseph, and David." Then, with the order of name changing each day as another of the guests moves to the front of the line,

> May it please you, Abraham, my exalted guest, that all the other guests dwell here with me and with you—Isaac, Jacob, Moses, Aaron, Joseph, and David.

It is the custom to donate to charity the value of the meal for the "guests." In egalitarian communities, seven biblical matriarchs are invited in addition to the biblical men. These are, according to the same *sefirot*: Sarah, Miriam, Deborah, Hannah, Abigail, Huldah, and Esther.

There are variations on the list of female Ushpizin.

Kiddush is made over wine, with *Sheheheyanu* at the end; there is a special *Harahaman* in the Grace after Meals. When the first day of Sukkot falls on Sabbath or on Saturday evening, the appropriate blessings for Sabbath or Havdalah are added. There are no statutory foods specific to Sukkot, but those associated with the autumn harvest are most commonly eaten. Meals are generally prepared in the home, as usual, and brought out to the sukkah.

The First Two Days of Sukkot

The morning services are the same as on other festival days, though with particular additions. In the *Yotzer* blessing of the

For typical festival
morning service,
see p. 131.
Shema, verses are said similar to those recited after the Shema in the preceding evening service. Inserted into the cantor's repetition of the Amidah are hymns known as *kerovot*, which recall the celebrations of the day and begin here with a description of our journey from the repentance of Yom Kippur to the joyousness of Sukkot.

> I shuddered in awe on Yom Kippur
>   terrified by the number of sins that were counted.
> I rejoiced when I was judged to be righteous. . . .
> Plantings of supple trees
>   they carry around the altar today. . . .
> They bind the four precious species
>   and observe the mitzvah of the sukkah for seven days.

In some communities, the ritual of the Four Species is conducted in the sukkah prior to the morning service.

The Four Species bouquet is neither blessed nor shaken on the Sabbath.

After the repetition of the Amidah, everyone takes up the *lulav* in the right hand and the *etrog* in the left (reverse for lefties) and recites the blessings: "Blessed are You, Lord our God, king of the universe, who has commanded us concerning the taking of the *lulav*," and then the *Sheheḥeyanu* on the first day the Four Species are taken up. The ritual is explained rather emphatically in the *Minhogimbukh*:

> While facing east, everyone should shake the *lulav* in his hand, then stretch his arms frontward and shake it there, and then draw it back and shake it again—this is repeated three times. Then he should do the same three times to the right, in the southward direction. Then three times behind himself, over his shoulders, toward west. Then three times to the left, northward. And then three times above himself toward the sky, and three times below himself toward the ground. If one waved only to the front and to the back, as some people do, it would not be right. If you do it right, you will yourself understand the reason behind it.

This is followed by full Hallel as on all major festivals. But on Sukkot, the recitation of Psalm 118 is punctuated by the shaking of the *lulav* in a pattern that emphasizes each word in the line (except "the Lord"), "Rejoice in the Lord for He is good; His kindness endures forever":

Hodu ladonai	*ki*	*tov,*	*ki*	*leolam*	*ḥasdo.*
front	right	back	left	up	down

And so through the recitation. The *lulav* is waved again at the verses "Please, Lord, save now!" and, in some communities, at "Please, Lord, bring success now!"

The Torah reading for the first two days of Sukkot is the same: Leviticus 22:26–23:44, in which the instructions for the observance of Sabbath and festivals are given. The maftir reads from a second scroll Numbers 29:12–16, which describes the sacrifices for festival days. The haftarah for the first day is Zechariah 14:1–21. Zechariah prophesied during the Babylonian Exile and offers in these verses an apocalyptic vision of Jerusalem's salvation and God's judgment on its enemies and attackers. After earthquakes and plagues,

For more about this Torah portion in its full context, see p. 159.

> It shall come to pass that everyone who is left of all the nations that came against Jerusalem shall go up from year to year to worship the king, the Lord of hosts, and to keep the festival of Sukkot.

This stresses Sukkot as a universal festival, a thanksgiving to God for all we are given—in contrast to Passover and Shavuot, which are particular to God's relationship with the Jewish people. There are also messianic overtones.

The second day's haftarah is 1 Kings 8:2–21, which tells of the consecration of the Temple that took place over a fourteen-day period, the last seven of which were Sukkot.

MUSAF SERVICE: The musaf is Sukkot is filled with ritual grandeur. It begins after half Kaddish and continues with the Amidah, which is followed by the fully ritualized Priestly

For Ashrei (Psalm 145), see pp. 26 and 48. For the Priestly Blessing, see p. 133.

In the Sephardic rite, the ritual of the Hoshanot is performed in the morning service, following the Hallel.

Blessing, as in the other major festivals. What follows next, though, is unique to Sukkot: the recitation of the Hoshanot, prayers that begin with the words "please save," which are said while the congregants hold the the Four Species—*lulav* in the right hand, *etrog* in the left—and follow the cantor in a circular procession through the synagogue. This is done once on each of the days of Sukkot except on Sabbath; on the seventh day, Hoshana Rabbah, seven circuits are made. (The ritual has its roots in the Sukkot celebration of Temple times.) The cantor recites each stich of the *hoshanah* prayer and the congregations repeats it. Here is a sampling:

Please save	for Your sake, our God,	please save!
Please save	for Your sake, our creator,	please save!
Please save	for Your sake, our redeemer,	please save!
Please save	for the sake of Your truth,	please save!
Please save	for the sake of Your covenant,	please save!
Please save	for the sake of Your mandate,	please save!
Please save	for the sake of Your goodness,	please save!

A different set of poems is said on each day. When the circuit is complete, the following *hoshanah* is said on both days. The words *ani vaho* are of uncertain meaning, but were said by the medieval commentator Rashi to be among the seventy-two three-letter names for God.

> *Ani vaho*, bring salvation now. As You saved the terebinths [a type of tree] in Egypt when You went forth to save the nation—so save us now. . . .
>
> As You saved with the declaration "I shall bring you forth," which is to say, "I shall be brought forth with you"—so save us now. . . .

The service continues with full Kaddish, *Alenu*, the Psalm of the Day, and the mourner's Kaddish.

AFTERNOON SERVICE: The afternoon service begins with *Ashrei* and *Uva letziyon*. If this is a Sabbath, three people are called up to the Torah to read Deuteronomy 33:1–26, in which Moses begins his blessings of the tribes. After the Amidah, full Kaddish is said, then *Alenu* and the mourner's Kaddish.

In the evening following the the second day of Sukkot, one makes Havdalah, though without the double-wicked candle or spices. In Temple times, the Water-Drawing Festival was held at the Temple on the second night of Sukkot. It was related to part of the Sukkot sacrifice and in Isaiah 12:3, "Joyfully shall you draw water from the fountains of triumph." Descriptions of the festival give the impression that the much-celebrated water may have been of the *aquavita* variety: "He who has not seen the rejoicing of the water-drawing ceremony in the Temple has never seen true rejoicing." Another report in the Mishnah tells of Rabbi Simeon ben Gamaliel I juggling eight flaming torches without any hitting the ground. The festival became a bone of contention between the Pharisees, who supported it, and the Sadducees, who held it in contempt. Needless to say, there have been occasional attempts at reviving the ceremony, mainly in student circles. A vestige of it remains in the custom of making a party during Sukkot called *Simhat bet hashoevah*.

For Havdalah, see p. 85.

The Intermediate Days of Sukkot

The pattern of the morning services during the intermediate days (*hol hamoed*) of Sukkot is similar to those of the first two days. Upon reaching Hallel, everyone takes hold of the Four Species as they did the previous day. Then the cantor recites Hallel. At *Hodu*, the *lulav* should be shaken. Full Kaddish is said afterward.

One Torah scroll is taken out on each of the intermediate days and four people are called up to the Torah. The readings *For more on the portion of* Pinḥas, *see p. 179.* are all from the portion of *Pinḥas* and continue the offerings for the days of Sukkot that began in the maftir's portion during the first two days. They are apportioned as follows:

Sukkot intermediate day 1	Numbers 29:17–25
Sukkot intermediate day 2	Numbers 29:20–28
Sukkot intermediate day 3	Numbers 29:23–31
Sukkot intermediate day 4	Numbers 29:26–34

Traditionally, the first three verses are read by a Kohen, the second three by a levite, the third by anyone, then the first three verses are read again.

The musaf service observed each day contains the Hoshanot and the procession around the rostrum with the Four Species. They are similar on all days, though shorter than on the first two. Specific stiches are designated for each day.

Sabbath During the Intermediate Days of Sukkot

The Friday night service is as usual, with additions for the Sabbath and the holiday. At home, the blessing for the sukkah is said immediately after kiddush.

The morning service has a number of special characteristics. As it is throughout Sukkot, Hallel is recited, but without the blessing of the Four Species. Then comes the most distinctive feature of the liturgy, the reading of Ecclesiastes, one of the five scrolls—pure sobriety. For those who may have come away from the Water-Drawing Festival with a major hangover, here is the antidote. The Hebrew name for Ecclesiastes is *Kohelet*, which has been variously translated as "preacher" or "teacher," but is actually the pseudonym of its author. The book begins, "The words of Kohelet, son of

David," which led to the traditional attribution to King Solomon. Though the style and language are quite different from the Song of Songs, the words are those of a wise man, a man of the highest wealth and power.

Ecclesiastes is a patchwork of poetry and prose organized into twelve loosely connected chapters. It is a "wisdom book," in this case the world-weary words of an old man looking back over his experience and observation of the human condition, to which he is both sympathetic and cynical. Yet this is a man who knows God—and knows the value of obeying him. Despite the futility and injustices of life, the author never doubts God's centrality to it all.

> Vanity of vanities, says Kohelet,
> vanity of vanities! All is vanity.
> What do people gain from all the toil
> at which they toil under the sun?
> A generation goes, and a generation comes,
> but the earth remains forever. . . .
> For in much wisdom is much vexation,
> and those who increase knowledge increase sorrow.

Ecclesiastes 1:2–4, 18

For the fate of humans and the fate of animals is the same; as one dies, so dies the other. All go to one place; all are from the dust, and all turn to dust again. Who knows whether the human spirit goes upward and the spirit of animals goes downward to the earth? So I saw that there is nothing better than that all should enjoy their work, for that is their lot; who can bring them to see what will be after them?

Ecclesiastes 3:19–22

> The lover of money will not be satisfied with money; nor
> the lover of wealth, with gain. This also is vanity.
> When goods increase, those who eat them increase; and
> what gain has their owner but to see them with his eyes?

Ecclesiastes 5:10–11

In my vain life I have seen everything; there are righteous people who perish in their righteousness, and there are

Ecclesiastes 7:15–18

wicked people who prolong their life in their evildoing. Do
not be too righteous, and do not act too wise; why should
you destroy yourself? Do not be too wicked, and do not be
a fool; why should you die before your time? It is good that
you should take hold of the one, without letting go of the
other; for the one who fears God shall succeed with both.

Ecclesiastes
9:1–2, 7, 9–10

All this I laid to heart, examining it all, how the righteous
and the wise and their deeds are in the hand of God;
whether it is love or hate one does not know. Everything
that confronts them is vanity, and since the same fate
comes to all, to the righteous and the wicked, to the good
and the evil, to the clean and the unclean, to those who
sacrifice and those who do not. As are the good, so are the
sinners; those who swear are like those who shun an oath.
Go, eat your bread with enjoyment, and drink your wine
with a merry heart; for God has long ago approved what you
do. Enjoy life with the wife whom you love, all the days of
your vain life that are given you under the sun, because that
is your portion in life and in your toil at which you toil
under the sun. Whatever your hand finds to do, do with
your might; for there is no work or thought or knowledge or
wisdom in Sheol, to which you are going.

Ecclesiastes
11:1–2, 7, 9–10

Send out your bread upon the waters,
　　for after many days you will get it back.
Divide your means seven ways, or even eight,
　　for you do not know what disaster may happen on earth.

Light is sweet, and it is pleasant for the eyes to see the sun.
Rejoice, young man, while you are young, and let your heart
cheer you in the days of your youth. Follow the inclination
of your heart and the desire of your eyes, but know that for
all these things God will bring you into judgment. Banish
anxiety from your mind, and put away pain from your body;
for youth and the dawn of life are vanity.

Such a work—proffering as many questions as answers—has
fostered a large body of midrash, much of which transforms

the pessimism of Kohelet into a message of optimism. However, the text on its own has both of those qualities already.

Full Kaddish is said after reading Ecclesiastes and two
Torah scrolls are taken out. Seven people are called up to read
Exodus 33:12–34:26 from the first scroll. The portion concerns a theme that is often repeated in Tishrei—the Thirteen
Attributes of Mercy. The maftir reads from Numbers 29, the
continuation of the sacrifices. The haftarah is Ezekiel 38:18–
39:16, the prophecy of an earthquake brought by God that
will destroy an attack from the North of Gog and Magog,
who constitute an evil alliance intent on destroying Israel. Its
relevance to Sukkot is not clear other than through its relation to the the prophecy of Zechariah read on the first day of
Sukkot.

In the musaf service, Hoshanot are recited, but without the
Four Species and the circuits around the rostrum.

Hoshana Rabbah

The "Great Hoshanah," the last of
the intermediate days of Sukkot, has
been described since the Middle
Ages as the the last possible day on
which one might receive a "good
note" in the Book of Life. To achieve
this end, the Kabbalists of Safed
developed a special *tikun* ("healing")
service that lasted through the night.
In some congregations where this

*Hoshana Rabbah
from the
Minhogimbukh,
Amsterdam, 1722.*

custom is observed, the entire book of Deuteronomy is read;
in others it is all the psalms. Around this belief in a last
chance, there grew a popular superstition: if a man does not
see his shadow on the night of Hoshana Rabbah, it is a sign

that he is to die in the coming year. The *Minhogimbukh* depicts this custom and describes it thus:

> Some have the custom to cover themselves in a sheet and go to a place where the moon can be seen. There they throw off the sheet and stand naked. They stand straight, with all their limbs spread out, and they examine their shadow in the moon. If one's head is missing, he will lose his head. If his fingers are missing, that refers to his relatives. If his right hand is missing, that means his son. If his left hand is missing, that means his daughter. But this shadow that one sees in the moon is not the same as a regular shadow, because this shadow has to move on its own; otherwise it would not be possible that one did not see a part of his own shadow. So the shadow we are talking about is actually the shadow of our shadow. If one examines the shadows very carefully, it is obvious that there are actually two shadows, because the real shadow casts another shadow. Our sages call this a shadow of the shadow (*bevoah bivevoah*). According to the Talmud, if one goes on a long trip over countries and wants to know whether he will return or not, he should examine his shadow. If he sees the shadow of his shadow, he will return home. But at another place in the Talmud the same is repeated, and there it says that one should not take this too seriously, because one might get frightened and ruin his fate because of this; for example, he might not see the shadow out of fear. Therefore, it is all right not to examine one's shadow at all.

This once-popular custom is seldom practiced today. Nonetheless, the holiday is rich in liturgy and symbol, especially in the musaf service. In the morning service, additional psalms are recited in the *Pesukei dezimra*, as on Sabbath. After the Amidah the Four Species are blessed in the Hallel. The Torah reading is Numbers 29:26–34, which concludes the recitation of the Sukkot offerings.

On each day of Sukkot (except Sabbath), the congregation, with *lulav* and *etrog* in hand, makes a circuit around the rostrum while reciting the Hoshanot. On Hoshana Rabbah, all the Torah scrolls are taken out from the ark and seven circuits are made, each with its own set of Hoshanot verses, beseeching God's grace in the realms of the spiritual, the national, and the agricultural, with the last set invoking the merit and strength of the patriarchs. This ritual is said to have been inspired by Joshua's circling of the city of Jericho, *Joshua 6:1–6* which, on the last day he and the Israelite fighters circled seven times. The prayer *Ani vaho* is recited, to which is added *For* Ani vaho, *see p. 283.* the verses *Kol mevaser*, "The voice of the herald heralds and proclaims." The 1593 *Minhogimbukh* mentions the custom of returning one Torah scroll to the ark after each circuit. A fairly common custom is the placing of a lit candle in the empty ark, to stand in for the light of the Torah. The service concludes with the mourner's Kaddish, the Psalm of the Day, full Kaddish, and *Alenu*. Since the holidays continue, no Havdalah is said until after Simhat Torah.

SHEMINI ATZERET

Shemini Atzeret means "Eighth Day of the Solemn Assembly." It is regarded as a festival in its own right and, by custom, as a kind of conclusion to the holiday season in the sense that Shavuot (also called *atzeret* in the Torah) is the conclusion of the season of Passover and the counting of the Omer. Shemini Atzeret is described in Leviticus 23:36: "On the eighth day, a proclamation of holiness [sacred occasion] shall there be for you." In Number 29:35 it is described as a day of rest in which specific offerings were to be made.

In the evening service, some congregations interweave into the blessings of the Shema the hymn *Bayom hashemini*, "On the eighth day," which comprises references to the principles and practices of the day as well as the significance of the number eight:

> The eighth [day] on which I pour heart and soul like water...
> The eighth [day] of the Tabernacle's inauguration...
> The eighth on which the decree for the amount of rain is made...
> The eighth when those assembled in the sukkah are permitted to live in their homes again...
> The eighth day is established in Torah as the time when thirteen covenants were made.

Even circumcision, which takes place on the eighth day of life, is mentioned. The water mentioned in the first line is significant in two ways, with regard to the Water-Drawing Festival of Temple times and in the prayer for rain that is introduced in the musaf service.

Sheheheyanu is added to kiddush on this day. It is a custom to eat the evening meal in the sukkah, though without the blessing or the greeting of the guests.

When Shemini Atzeret falls on Sabbath, additional prayers are said. The morning Torah reading from the first scroll is expanded to accommodate seven readers.

The morning service follows the usual pattern for festivals and includes full Hallel. Two Torah scrolls are taken from the ark and five people are called up to the first. The reading is Deuteronomy 15:19-16:17, which includes a reiteration of the pilgrim festivals—though no mention of Shemini Atzeret. This deficit is addressed in the maftir's portion, Numbers 29:35-30:1, in which the day is announced along with its sacrifices. The haftarah is 1 Kings 8:54-9:1, which concerns the dedication of the Temple, which concluded on Shemini Atzeret. Yizkor, the memorial prayers for the deceased, are said toward the end of this service, before the Torah is returned to the ark.

For Yizkor, see p. 264. For the Priestly Blessing, see p. 133.

The musaf service has two special liturgies, the Priestly Blessing, and unique to this service, *Geshem*, the prayer for rain, which is said in the cantor's repetition of the Amidah. Since Sukkot is the festival closest to the traditional winter rainy season it is after its conclusion that the prayer is said. It is the counterpart of *Tal*, the prayer for dew that is said on Passover. In *Geshem*, God is beseeched to order Af-Bri, the angel of rain, to thicken the clouds, forcing them to give forth rain. It goes on to invoke the patriarchs and the miracles and metaphors of water in their lives, from Abraham's faith to Moses's birth and the parting of the sea. From now until the first day of Passover, this plea for rain will be included in the *Gevurot* of the Amidah.

For Tal, see p. 133.

Before the afternoon service, some follow the kabbalistic custom of saying a brief prayer of farewell to the sukkah:

> May it be Your will, Lord our God, God of our forefathers, that just as I have fulfilled the commandment and lived in this sukkah, so may I merit in the coming year to dwell in the sukkah made from the skin of the Leviathan.

According to the Talmud and midrash, God had made a giant sea creature called the Leviathan on the fifth day of Creation. On the sixth day, he made a giant earth creature called Behemoth. So great were they that God had to destroy their mates so they would not reproduce and kill all other things. When the Messiah comes, these creatures will do battle and both will die. From the brilliant and magnificent skin of the Leviathan, God will make canopies to shelter the righteous from the sun.

This story may be found in Talmud Bava Batra 74b–75a, and Leviticus Rabah 13:3.

SIMHAT TORAH

The "Rejoicing of the Torah" is the occasion on which we celebrate the completion of the year's Torah cycle. Simhat Torah is regarded as an important holiday, though its origins come long after the biblical and talmudic periods—as late as the ninth century c.e. according to some authorities. The early tradition of Torah reading in the land of Israel was on a triennial cycle of 175 portions but was gradually supplanted by the Babylonian system, based on an annual reading cycle.

Simhat Torah is the second day of Shemini Atzeret only in the Diaspora. In Israel, it is part of the observance of Shemini Atzeret and, indeed, their core liturgies are the same. Yet, in the Diaspora, the feeling of the two days are quite different and the liturgical additions to Simhat Torah are invariably joyous, so much so that children take part in the services.

In the evening service, after the Amidah, a series of biblical verses is recited with great animation—a privilege that in many congregations is sold at an auction. They begin with Deuteronomy 4:35, "To you it was shown, that you may know it, that the Lord is God and there is none other like Him." Afterward, all the scrolls are taken from the ark for the *hakafot* ceremony, the circuits, in which the scrolls are carried around the room; children wave flags and hold miniature scrolls. The procession goes seven times around the rostrum. Some congregations add to the circuits joyous songs, some known from the Sabbath repertory, such as *Yedid nefesh*, "Beloved of the soul," and *En adir*, "There is none as powerful as the Lord." The circuits—dancing through the aisles—end with the proclamation "May David the anointed king rejoice with us. Next year in Jerusalem!" This is the only night of the year in which the Torah is read. The customary portion is Deuteronomy 33:1–36, *Vezot haberakha*, "This is the blessing that Moses bestowed upon the Children of Israel." It is followed by a highly elaborate *hagbahah* and *gelilah*, the binding and dressing of the Torah, complete with special hymns.

The morning service is filled with Torah. Some congregations repeat the seven circuits of last night, though others do just one. But the heart of this service is in the Torah readings themselves since it is on this day that the Torah ends and begins again. The *aliyot* are spread out as at no other time—in some communities, everyone is called up to the first scroll, from which Deuteronomy 33:1–26 is read, as it was last night; in others, it is treated like any other holiday reading; in yet others, multiple scrolls are read from simultaneously. For the second-to-last *aliyah*, all the children are called up (with an adult) as the reader recites the verses. Then, as tallitot are spread over the heads of the children, a ḥuppah symbolizing marriage to the Torah, all the adults recite an echo of Moses's blessing—Genesis 48:16, Jacob's blessing of his sons:

Simḥat Torah from the Minhogim- bukh, *Venice, 1593. It is customary for the adults to throw candy to the children on this joyous day so they learn to associate the Torah with sweetness and pleasure.*

> The angel who has redeemed me from all ill-fortune, may he bless the lads. May my name continue to be called through them and the name of my fathers, Abraham and Isaac. May they teem like fish to become many in the land!

For Jacob's blessings see p. 326.

To be called up to the concluding part of Deuteronomy (33:27–34:12)—and of the Torah—is considered a high honor and is reserved for a great scholar or someone who has been of great service to the community. The person is referred to as a *Ḥatan Torah*, "Bridegroom of the Torah" (or *Kalat Torah*,

"Bride of the Torah"), and is brought after an official announcement in a long liturgical poem. The reading is also done under the ḥuppah of the tallit. In these closing verses, God again shows Moses all the land. There he dies, buried by God in a place that no one may know. The Children of Israel, poised at the edge of the Promised Land, wept for him for thirty days. And so it concludes,

> Never again did there arise in Israel a prophet like Moses, whom the Lord knew face-to-face, in all the signs and portents that the Lord sent him to display in the land of Egypt, against Pharaoh and to all his courtiers, and to all his country; and in all the great might and in all the acts of awe that Moses performed before all Israel.

Then all call out: *Ḥazak, ḥazak, venithazek!* "Be strong! Be strong! And let us strengthen one another!"

The next reader is another high honoree, the *Ḥatan* (or *Kalat*) *Bereshit*, the "Bridegroom of Genesis." After his or her announcement, the portion Genesis 1:1–2:3 is recited, which begins at the beginning and continues through God's rest on the seventh day. Then, again, all call out *Ḥazak!*

The maftir reads Numbers 29:35–30:1, which describes the sacrifices of Shemini Atzeret, same as yesterday. The haftarah is Joshua 1:1–18, which tells of Israel's entry into the Promised Land and how, with God's direct help, its armies conquered the land that had been promised them and divided it according to the established plan. Joshua is Moses's successor: part general, part judge, part prophet—and very much God's instrument.

In the evening service, *Atah ḥonantanu* is inserted in the Amidah to mark the end of the holiday. Havdalah is made over wine, the blessing for the spices and the blessing over the candle having been omitted.

"Sow yourselves righteousness"
(Hosea 10:12)

The Month of Ḥeshvan

BUL IS THE NAME given to the eighth month in 1 Kings 6:38, the only time it is referred to in the Bible. Its meaning is uncertain, though; some writers have conjectured a connection to the flood, *mabul* in Hebrew, or to *yevul*, meaning agricultural produce, since it was in Israel a traditional month of plowing and sowing. It was its Babylonian name, *Marḥeshvan* ("eighth month"), that stuck—more or less—and this is the name by which this month is called in the oldest editions of the *Minhogimbukh*. Since *mar* is the Hebrew word for "bitter," as in the *maror* of the Passover Seder, a superstition grew around the name and in most places the offending letters were dropped.

The month is not without its history of bitter occurrences: the Flood, the blinding of Judean king Zedekiah by Babylonian forces, the death of Rachel, Kristallnacht, and the murder of Yitzḥak Rabin. But there are also happy anniversaries, not least of which is that of the Balfour Declaration.

Rosh Ḥodesh Ḥeshvan is observed for two days. As Sukkot has recently concluded, it is a custom to observe the *Behav*, the "Fast of Monday, Thursday, and Monday," to atone for overindulgences in the pilgrimage festivals. Otherwise, there

For more on Behav, see also p. 155, in the month of Iyar.

are no particular customs associated with this month, nor are there any holiday observances.

What it lacks in custom, Ḥeshvan surely makes up in story. The Torah readings for the month are the great foundation narratives of the Jewish people: the book of Genesis from the Flood (6:9) through the death of Abraham (25:13). In years when Rosh Ḥodesh Ḥeshvan falls on a Sabbath, there are five Sabbaths in the month, and the portions go through to the beginning of Jacob's adulthood (28:9).

The first week's Torah portion in our model month of Ḥeshvan is Noaḥ, Genesis 6:9–11:32.

The portion of *Noaḥ* covers not only the story of the Flood, but also a great terrain of moral and political development. It is, in a sense, a second Creation—not a new heaven and earth, but an extreme culling of the bloodlines. God saw that the earth had "gone to ruin" and was "filled with wrongdoing"— and so the deluge and the new beginning. But God had second thoughts and pledged never to do it again, this upon realizing humans are possessed of the *yetzer hara*, "bad tendencies," since "what the human heart forms is evil from its youth." It is often said that the story of Noah is marked by the salvation of the righteous, but that begs the question about what happened to the person who was next in righteousness to Noah. Indeed, a similar question will be taken up by Abraham when Sodom and Gomorrah are destroyed.

The term yetzer hara *is from the rabbinic literature, not from the Bible.*

After the deluge God sets forth a covenant with Noah that never again will he destroy all living things in such a way. Humanity is given dominion over the animals and the permission to eat of them. But killing people is prohibited. The directive is to "bear fruit and be many." There follows an odd incident in which Noah is seen naked by his son Ham, resulting in a decree of inferiority for all Ham's descendants. This is apparently a prohibition of incest. There is then a listing of the seventy nations that will issue from the sons of Noah, establishing all the genealogies that will be encountered in the Torah.

In the midst of these is a brief story, from a time when "all the earth was of one language and one set of words." The people said, "Come now! Let us build ourselves a city and a tower, its top in the heavens, and let us make ourselves a name, lest we be scattered over the face of all the earth!" God came down and saw what they were doing, saying, "Here are one people with one language . . . and this is just the first of their doings. Now there will be no limit to their schemes. Come now! Let us go down and let us baffle their language, so that no man will understand the language of his neighbor." The place was thereafter called Babel (babble), and God scattered the people all over the face of the earth. It is often explained as a cautionary tale, a warning against trespassing God's realm in the heavens. A more plausible explanation is that the story of Babel points to God's further disappointment with humans—another failure. This will soon change with the coming of Abraham, whose name appears in the next verses, among the descendants of Shem, son of Noah. Ten generations will be born between Noah and Abraham.

In the last verses, we meet Abram (as we first know his name), who with his wife, Sarai, and his nephew Lot are taken by Abram's father, Terah, on a journey from Ur of the Chaldeans to the land of Canaan. But they stop and settle in Haran ("crossroads"), where Terah dies, age 205.

The haftarah is Isaiah 54:1–55:5, part of which was encountered in the month of Elul. Isaiah was also the source of the haftarah for last week's portion, *Bereshit*. It's not hard to find a text to complement and compliment God's work in the Creation, since so many verses of praise do just that. However, here in the portion of Noah, the choice of verses is truly

The first week's haftarah in our model month of Ḥeshvan is Isaiah 54:1–55:5.

See p. 214 for a very different context of this haftarah.

inspired. Isaiah is here a "retroprophet"; verses written to herald the rebirth of the nation after the Babylonian Exile are here used as the annunciation of Abraham and the founding of a chosen nation.

> Enlarge the place of thy tent
> And let them stretch forth the curtains of thy habitations,
>   spare not. . . .
> For thou shalt spread abroad on the right hand and on
>   the left;
> And thy seed shall possess the nations.

Isaiah refers to the past, as well:

> For this is as the waters of Noah unto Me;
> For as I have sworn that the waters of Noah
> Should no more go over the earth.

The second week's Torah portion in our model month of Ḥeshvan is Lekh lekha, Genesis 12:1–17:27.

The second week's portion, *Lekh lekha*, "Go forth" (Genesis 12:1–17:27), contains the two central stories of Genesis: the covenant between God and Abraham and the foundation of the tribe. The story begins with an immediate commandment, without the buildup of an introduction:

> Go forth from your native land and from your father's house
>   to the land I will let you see.
> I will make of you a great nation, and I will bless you.
> I will make your name great, and you shall be a blessing.
> I will bless those who bless you, and curse him that curses you,
> And all the families of the earth shall bless themselves by you.

Abram—God makes him Abra*ha*m, "Father of a Throng of Nations," upon giving his covenant—sets out to the land of Canaan with Sarah (she is then "Sarai"), his wife, Lot, his nephew, and their acquired retinue from Haran. Abraham is immediately obedient to God, though some doubts will set in later. When they arrive in Canaan, they are faced with a famine and move on to sojourn in Egypt. Such is Sarah's beauty (she is in her mid-sixties) that Abraham tells her that for safety's sake, she should present herself as his sister. The plan backfires; she is taken into Pharaoh's house as a concubine. For this, God brings plagues upon Pharaoh; Abraham, Sarah, Lot, and their retinue are sent away with great riches that they accumulated there. So vast are their holdings in livestock that when they get back to the the Promised Land, it is necessary for Abraham and Lot to part ways. Abraham settles in Canaan, Lot near Sodom.

A conflict erupts among the area kingdoms. Lot is taken prisoner and is rescued by Abraham and his men, thus establishing Abraham as a big man in the region. In a vision, God again offers his covenant, describing the land that will be given to the seed of Abraham, but tells him that before it becomes so, his heirs must sojourn and be afflicted for four hundred years in another land. Abraham expresses his doubts to God, wondering who shall be his heir, since he has no offspring. Will it be his chief servant? God reassures him that his seed will be as many as the stars in heaven.

A mystery: after Abraham's rescue of Lot, "Melchizedek, king of Shalem, priest of God Most High," comes out with bread and wine. Who is he, a fellow believer in God?

Sarah tells Abraham that since she is barren, he should therefore have children by her Egyptian maid, Hagar. When Hagar becomes pregnant, she becomes insolent to Sarah, who, with Abraham's assent, drives her from the house. God speaks to Hagar, telling her to call the child Ishmael ("God hearkens") and that he, too, will become a numerous nation.

After his brief appearance in Genesis 14:18–20, he never appears again. The character is given broad interpretation in Christian theology.

God speaks to Abraham again about the covenant, how it is to be kept by him and all of his seed through circumcision. At eight days old every male is to be circumcised. God says he will give Abraham a son through Sarah. Abraham collapses in laughter that he, a ninety-nine-year-old man, and his wife, now a ninety-year-old woman, are to have a child! He pleads also for Ishmael, that he should not be ignored by God. God responds that the son is to be called Isaac ("he laughs") and that Ishmael will be blessed, that he will be made many.

That same day, all the males in Abraham's house were circumcised.

The second week's haftarah in our model month of Ḥeshvan is Isaiah 40:27–41:16.

The haftarah, again from Isaiah, is a long echo of the Torah portion, that the God who sought Abraham still seeks us today:

> Why sayest thou, O Jacob,
> And speakest, O Israel:
> "My way is hid from the Lord,
> And my right is passed over from my God?" . . .
> But thou, Israel, My servant,
> Jacob whom I have chosen,
> The seed of Abraham, My friend. . . .
> Fear not, for I am with thee, . . .
> I uphold thee with My victorious right hand.

The third week's Torah portion in our model month of Ḥeshvan is Vayera, Genesis 18:1–22:24.

The intensity and scope of action of Genesis becomes almost overwhelming in the the third week's portion, *Vayera*, "And the Lord appeared." God visits Abraham in the form of three divine visitors to announce the coming of Isaac. Sarah overhears this and laughs silently.

> God asks Abraham, "Why did she laugh?"
> Sarah chimes in, dissembling, "I didn't laugh."
> God responds, "Yes, you laughed."

And then the "visitors" turn their attention to Sodom. God wonders in a rare soliloquy, "Shall I cover up from Abraham what I am about to do to Sodom and Gomorrah?" In the end, he decides to bring Abraham in on it. Abraham is horrified and argues with God.

Will You sweep away the innocent along with the guilty?
What if there are fifty innocent within the city.... Far be it
from You to do a thing like this. ... Will not the judge of all
the earth do what is just?

The Lord said: If I find in the city of Sodom fifty innocent
people, I will forgive the whole place for their sake.

And so it goes: destroy if there are forty-five innocent—no;
forty—no; thirty, twenty, ten—no! But not so many just men
are found. Two of the visitors (angels?) go down to Sodom to
see Lot and his family, and the townsfolk threaten to accost
them. Lot offers the mob his daughters, but they press for
the visitors until they are scared off by a flash of light. Lot
and his family leave Sodom as the towns of the plain are
destroyed by brimstone and fire. They are warned not to
look back. Lot's wife does look back and turns to a pillar of
salt. After taking refuge in a cave, Lot's daughters bemoan
that their father will now have no male heir; they get him
drunk and become pregnant by him. Both bear sons: Moab
("by father"), who becomes the father of the Moabites, and
Ben-Ami ("son of my kinspeople"), who becomes the father
of the Ammonites. Both become troublesome peoples to the
Israelites in the Wilderness. Are Lot's daughters sinners or
practical women protecting their bloodline?

As Isaac's birth approaches, Abraham and Sarah sojourn
among the Philistines, where they come upon King Abimelech. Sarah is again introduced as Abraham's sister, and
Abimelech is nearly killed by God for presuming her avail-
ability. Abimelech is told by God that he should pay heed to
Abraham, who is his prophet. After resolving this initial dis-
comfort, Abraham and Abimelech sign a pact.

Shortly after Isaac's birth, Sarah insists to Abraham that he
remove Hagar and Ishmael from their house. Abraham is

perplexed and wonders about the fate of Ishmael. God tells him to do what Sarah asks—it must be done in order for Isaac to carry on the line—and says that Ishmael will also become a great nation. The presence of Ishmael would have made impossible the next scene: the *Akedah*, the "binding" of Isaac—the passing of the great test of obedience. This is a somber story, told without comment or emotional expression from anyone. The story leads one to assume that Isaac knew all along what was about to take place and that his faith in God was such that he simply obeyed. This is the feat of strength that God sought in his champions—complete and unequivocal obedience. Never again does God speak to Abraham.

At synagogues in which the full, traditional morning service is done, the *Akedah* is repeated daily, followed by the *korbanot*, the recitation of the instructions for the Temple sacrifices. These are a reminder of the ancient standards of obedience to God's commandments, but in the *Akedah* there is also salvation.

The third week's haftarah in our model month of Ḥeshvan is 2 Kings 4:1-37.

Another miracle of a child born to aged parents is the story of the haftarah, 2 Kings 4:1-37. A Shunamite woman and her husband offer lodging to the prophet Elisha, who passes their home from time to time. So gracious are they that they build an upstairs room for the prophet and his servant. In gratitude, Elisha, the heir to Elijah, tells his hostess that on a certain day a son will be born to her. It comes to pass. But after some years an accident occurs and the child dies. As quickly as she can, the woman rides to find Elisha, who gives his staff to his servant and sends him to the boy. Elisha prays and the boy is revived.

The last week's portion, *Ḥayei Sarah*, begins with the death and burial of the matriarch. Abraham weeps and laments her death, but there is no further description and no specifics of the burial other than the acquisition from the Hittites of a cave at Machpelah, near Hebron, in the land of Canaan.

Abraham speaks to his servant, the manager of all his estate, that he is to swear an oath by God that he shall carry out on behalf of Abraham, the choosing of a wife for Isaac. By the terms of the oath, this must be done among Abraham's own people, not from the Canaanites, among whom they are living. Preceded by an angel of God and traveling with ten camels laden with gifts, the servant sets out on his journey, stopping at the spring at Aram-of-Two-Rivers in Mesopotamia, the town of Nachor, Abraham's brother. How to choose a bride for Isaac? He prays to God, hoping that the one who honors his request for a drink from her pitcher and, without asking, offers drink to the camels, will be "the one." And so it unfolds that the beautiful Rebecca appears at the spring. The servant tells the story to her family, gifts are given, and Rebecca agrees to go. And Isaac loves her.

The fourth and last week's Torah portion in our model month of Ḥeshvan is Ḥayei Sarah, Genesis 23:1–25:18.

Abraham had taken another wife, Keturah, who bore him six sons. But all his inheritence goes to Isaac. Abraham dies at the "good ripe age" of one hundred seventy-five and he, too, is buried in the cave at Machpelah.

The offspring of Ishmael are recorded here: twelve sons, twelve leaders of their tribes. Ishmael dies at age one hundred thirty-seven.

Succession is the theme of the haftarah, 1 Kings 1:1–31. As King David is old and withered at age seventy—his interminable cold soothed only by a young Shunamite maiden—there ensues an intrigue over succession to the throne. With Amnon and Absalom dead, Adonijah, David's fourth son, makes claim to the throne, which had been designated for Solomon, David's son with Bathsheba. But Zadok the priest

The fourth and last week's haftarah in our model month of Ḥeshvan is 1 Kings 1:1–31.

and Nathan the prophet and all mighty men that were of David's circle do not support Adonijah. They go to Bathsheba and tell her what is happening, saying that Adonijah will surely slay her and Solomon straightaway if he becomes king. Bathsheba goes to David, rousing him to coherence. Nathan tries to rouse the king's response, but in the end, he says, "Call Bathsheba to me." Bathsheba comes forward and David proclaims:

> As the Lord liveth who had redeemed my soul out of all adversity, verily as I swore unto thee by the Lord, the God of Israel, saying: Assuredly Solomon thy son will reign after me, and he shall sit upon my throne in my stead; verily so will I do this day.

*"A widow, or a divorced woman, or a woman
who has been defiled" (Leviticus 21:14)*

The Month of Kislev

ROSH HODESH KISLEV is celebrated in some years for two days, in other years for one day only. The major observance of the month is Ḥanukkah, which begins on the twenty-fifth. The name Kislev is Babylonian in origin, appearing in the Bible in Zechariah 7:1 and the first verse of Nehemiah. It also appears in the Apocrypha, in which the story of Ḥanukkah and the Maccabees is found. In the Talmud, the fifteenth of Kislev is considered the onset of winter.

*The quotation
accompanying the
woodcut refers to
the marriage
restrictions for
priests.*

Talmud Bava
metzia *106b*

כסלו

ḤANUKKAH

After the death of Alexander the Great, the Greek empire was divided among his generals. Palestine was first administered by the Ptolemies of Egypt, but later the governance fell to the realm of Syria, then ruled by the Seleucid dynasty. The king, Antiochus Epiphanes, ruled over the Israelites with particular harshness, adopting a policy of strict assimilation, which was to be achieved by the destruction of local culture and religion. The observance of Jewish laws and customs was made illegal, and the Temple was turned into a pagan shrine. In the years 165–163 B.C.E., a revolt was incited by the priest

Mattathias and led by his son Judah, called the "Maccabee" (from the Hebrew *makabah*, "hammer"). The revolt was a brilliant success. Antiochus was repulsed and all the lands of Judah and Israel were eventually reclaimed. The Maccabees (known also as Hasmoneans) ruled over a century of considerable success, establishing for greater Israel political power in the region. Israel fell to the Romans in 63 B.C.E., though not without nearly thirty years of continuing resistance.

Ḥanukkah, which means "dedication," is a remembrance of the Maccabees' victory and the cleansing and rededication of the Temple in the aftermath of the revolt. The story is assembled from 1 Maccabees, the Talmud, and the *Megilat Antiokhus*. Maccabees is among the noncanonical texts referred to as Apocrypha. In the Talmud the story was further elaborated to tell of a miracle that took place in which only a single pure jar of lamp oil needed to light the Temple menorah was found, enough for one day and one night. Miraculously, it burned for eight days, seen as a sign of God's acceptance of the Temple's rededication. Thus Ḥanukkah became known as the Festival of Lights and one of its key customs is the lighting of the *ḥanukiyah*, the eight-light lamp or eight-branched menorah.

Talmud Shabbat *21b tells of the miracle of the oil;* Talmud Shabbat *23b described the lighting of candles.*

Why eight days? Some sources say that it took eight days to get new oil from the holy field in which it was produced; others say that it took eight days for those who had been in contact with dead bodies to become ritually pure once again.

This minor holiday is celebrated in a major way among Jews of all persuasions who live in Christian countries. Coming as it does around the time of the winter solstice and Christmas, it is an especially popular observance in Jewish families. In America, as gift giving became pervasively associated with Christmas in the twentieth century, so, too, did it become an increasingly large part of the Ḥanukkah celebration. Perhaps because of its lack of standing in Jewish law, Ḥanukkah became a hotbed of custom. For every reason given for this custom or that, there is always another explanation. The meaning of the word *ḥanukkah* itself is up for grabs. Some sources define it as "dedication," as we have here; other sources, including the 1593 *Minhogimbukh*, say that it comes from *Ḥanu k"h*, meaning "they rested on the twenty-fifth," a reference to the day on which the war was won. Regardless of the word's origin, Ḥanukkah is a holiday about the victory of faith and loyalty to God's commandments.

Ḥanukkah wood-cut from the Minhogimbukh, Amsterdam, 1727. The first depiction of the ḥanukiyah in 1593 showed a candelabrum with a deficient six branches.

The Customs of Ḥanukkah

ḤANUKKAH LIGHTS: There are two fundamental aspects of the Ḥanukkah lights. The first, *pirsumei nisa*, means to "publicize the miracle," which in this case means to light the Ḥanukkah lights in a place where they can be seen, such as in the window or outdoors. The other principle, *leshem mitzvah*, means that whatever is done to fulfill a commandment may not be used for any other purpose. This means that the candles that are lit for the exclusive purpose of the festival are not to be used as a light source. Thus the eight candles are lit with another candle, the *shamash*, which is kept apart from the others.

Is it the placing of the candles (or wicks in oil lamps) or the lighting of the them that fulfills the mitzvah? This was once the source of much debate until it was decided in favor of the lighting. Does one begin with all eight candles and reduce the number by one each day, as said Rabbi Shammai, or does one begin with one and add one each day, as said Rabbi Hillel? Today we follow Hillel.

The rule for the placement of Ḥanukkah candles is that they be no lower than three handbreadths or higher than ten cubits from the ground or floor. The lights may not be closer than a finger's breadth to make sure that they are not mistaken from the distance as a single, great flame.

There are among Iranian Jews two special customs for the candlelighting. One involves two shamash candles: one for lighting the daily candles, the other for ordinary light. The other custom involves the lighting of eight candles on the first day and another eight candles each day after, so that on the final day sixty-four candles are burning in addition to the shamash.

How long must the candles burn? At least one half hour is the legal opinion. If a light goes out before the half hour, do we relight it? It is not required to do so, but it is considered a *hidur mitzvah*, an "enhancement of the mitzvah," if we do.

Do we light from left to right or the opposite? Some legal experts say that the last candle to be set should be the first ignited. The reason for this is that the last light signifies another day of miracle. Other authorities say that we should add the candles from left to right but light them from right to left because this is the way Hebrew is read. The second way is more common today. Do we say the blessings before the candlelighting or say one before and two after? Generally, we say them before. The blessings are as follows:

> Blessed are You, Lord our God, king of the universe, who has sanctified us with His commandments and commanded us to kindle the light of Ḥanukkah.

> Blessed are You, Lord our God, king of the universe, who has performed miracles for our ancestors in olden times and in our times.

And the *Sheheḥeyanu*, recited only on the first night:

> Blessed are You, Lord our God, king of the universe, who has given us life and sustained us and brought us to this happy season.

Even the text of first blessing is the subject of contention: Does it conclude *lehadlik ner shel Ḥanukah*, "the light *of* Ḥanukkah," or *lehadlik ner Ḥanukah*, "the Ḥanukkah light"? Most say that the first is correct. And just where did God command us to light the Ḥanukkah lights, since it is never mentioned in the Torah? The answer usually given is in Deuteronomy 17:11, "According to the instruction that they instruct you, by the regulation that they tell you, you are to do." Such questions make Ḥanukkah an ideal time at which to introduce older children to concepts of Jewish law and custom.

It is the custom that the head of the house kindle the Ḥanukkah lights, though it is now common for it to be done by the oldest child in the house so long as he or she is of sufficient maturity to handle a flame. If one is traveling during Ḥanukkah, some authorities say that you may pay someone to light the candles for you; others say that you may light just one candle each day while you're away.

After the first candle of the day is lit, it is the custom to recite the prayer *Hanerot halalu*, "These lights that we kindle for the miracles, for the wonder, for the salvations, and for the battles which You performed . . ," and sing the hymn *Maoz tzur yeshuati*, "O stronghold, rock of my salvation."

ḤANUKKAH FOOD: Though there are no mandatory ritual meals for Ḥanukkah, special foods are strongly associated with the holiday according to various traditions. Fried foods figure in a big way: *latkes* made of potato, cheese, and vegetable figure in various Ashkenazic communities. Among Jews of Iberian descent, *birmuelos*, fried dough dipped in honey or sugar, are the favorites. An Israeli variation, fried jelly doughnuts called *sufganiyot*, have taken the Jewish world by storm.

In some communities dairy foods are associated with Ḥanukkah. This is through an association with the story of Judith, who fed cheese and wine to Holofernes before she decapitated him. In the midrashic literature, the stories of Judith and the Hasmoneans became somehow intertwined, though there is no actual connection between the two.

THE DREIDEL: Though it has no formal connection to Ḥanukkah, the children's game of dreidel is inextricably linked to its Ashkenazic tradition. Dreidel is the Yiddish word for "spinning top." The Ḥanukkah model has four sides, each with a Hebrew letter: נ *nun,* ג *gimel,* ה *hei,* ש *shin.* The letters represent the words of the Hebrew sentence *Nes gadol hayah sham,* "A great miracle happened there." (In Israel they say "here" [*poh*] and use the letter פ *pei* instead of *shin.*)

Each player begins with ten to fifteen tokens (nuts, raisins, pennies, whatever). At the start, each player antes to the pot one token, then, in turn, each spins once. The results are as follows:

There have been attempts to connect the dreidel to something of greater significance through gematria (Jewish numerology) or more elaborate historical explanations, such as each letter standing for the empires that had conquered ancient Israel.

Nisht, gor, halb, *and* shtel *are Yiddish words.*

- נ   *nun* means *nisht* or "nothing." Player does nothing.
- ג   *gimel* means *gor* or "all." Player takes everything in the pot.
- ה   *hei* means *halb* or "half." Player takes half of what is in the pot.
- ש   *shin* means *shtel* or "put in." Player adds two tokens to the pot.

When there is only one token in the pot, every player adds one. When an odd number of tokens are in the pot, the player rolling *hei* takes half plus one. The game is over when one player wins all.

The Synagogue Customs of Ḥanukkah

Throughout Ḥanukkah, *Al hanisim,* "For the miracles," is inserted in *Birkat hodaah,* the prayer of thanksgiving that is the eighteenth benediction of the Amidah. and also in the Grace after Meals.

In most synagogues the Ḥanukkah lamp is lit by the cantor in the afternoon service, before the prayer *Vehu raḥum.*

Al hanisim is also said at Purim. See p. 355.

The morning services during Hanukkah have a few special features: *Al hanisim*, as mentioned; full Hallel (Psalms 113–118) is recited every day in recognition of how the oil lasted for eight days. Half Kaddish is recited after the Hallel and before the Torah service. Tahanun and *El erekh apayim*, the prayers of supplication and confession, are omitted. One Torah scroll is taken out from the ark, and three people are called up. Over the eight days, the seventh chapter of Numbers is read. These eighty-nine verses list the gifts and sacrifices brought to the newly completed Tabernacle by each of the tribes. This is read in honor of the Second Temple's rededication, which is at the heart of the festival. The services conclude as usual: another half Kaddish is recited after the Torah reading, followed by *Yehalelu*, after which the Torah scroll is returned to the ark. The service ends with *Ashrei, Uva letziyon,* Kaddish, *Alenu*, and the mourner's Kaddish. The sixth day of Hanukkah is always Rosh Hodesh Tevet, so the conclusion of Hanukkah is described in the next month's chapter.

For more about Hallel, see p. 128.

The Torah Portions for Kislev

The first Sabbath of the model month begins with the portion *Toldot*, "And these are the generations of Isaac." Isaac is forty when he marries Rebecca and she remains childless until Isaac makes an entreaty to God. The pregnancy is a very painful one, so much so that Rebecca complains to God, who tells her that in her belly are "two nations . . . two tribes from your belly shall be divided . . . the elder shall be servant to the younger." The first comes out ruddy and hairy, so they named him Esau ("rough one"); the second comes out grasping Esau's heel, so he is named Jacob ("heel holder"). Isaac is sixty when the boys are born, and though he lives a long and

The first week's Torah portion in our model month of Kislev is Toldot, *Genesis 25:19–28:9.*

prosperous life, he remains a reticent and undeveloped character, functioning mainly as a bridge between Abraham and Jacob. But the qualities that make him a less-than-compelling character also allow the story to unfold the way it does. Rebecca is the true protagonist here.

Esau becomes a hunter and is favored by his father; Jacob is a homebody, favored by his mother, who remembers what God had predicted for her sons. Esau is gullible and oblivious to any sense of greater mission, while Jacob is filled with guile. Once when Esau returns home from the field and sees Jacob cooking a stew of red lentils, there ensues a trade:

Genesis 25:30–34
> Esau said to Jacob: "Give me some of that red stuff to gulp down—I am famished."
> Jacob said: "First sell me your birthright."
> Esau said: "I am at the point of death, so of what use is my birthright to me?"
> Jacob said, "Swear to me first."
> So he swore to him, and sold his birthright to Jacob. Jacob then gave Esau bread and lentil stew. . . .

There is a famine in Canaan and Isaac and Rebecca go to the Philistines, where they encounter King Abimelech, with whom Abraham had a treaty. Despite the existing relationship, Isaac does exactly what his father had done and introduces Rebecca as his sister. But Abimelech doesn't fall for it this time, seeing the two fooling around. Isaac prospers among the Philistines, so much so that it gives rise to envy and a falling-out, though it concludes equitably.

As Isaac sits in bed, old and blind, he asks Esau to hunt some game and make him the delicacy he loves so well, promising that when Esau returns he will receive his father's blessing. Esau goes off to the hunt. Rebecca had overheard her husband and tells Jacob that while Esau is gone, she will cook a similar delicacy from goats of the flock and that Jacob will serve it to his blind father and receive the blessing instead. Jacob wonders how the scam will work, especially if Isaac embraces him and feels that he is not the hirsute Esau. And what if he should instead receive his father's curse? Rebecca clothes him in kidskins and says that if there is a curse, she'll take it upon herself.

What unfolds is a vivid scene of deceit, in which Jacob lies repeatedly to assuage his father's doubts. Esau returns after the blessing is given and all that Isaac can offer him is hardly a consolation, telling him that he must live by the sword and only by the sword will he be able to tear Jacob's yoke from his neck. Esau swears blood revenge. Rebecca tells Jacob to flee to her brother Laban's house. Isaac blesses Jacob again—without hesitation—and tells him to take a wife from among Laban's daughters. Both parents warn that under no circumstances is he to take a wife from among the Canaanite women, as Esau had done. When Esau hears this, he takes another wife, from the family of his uncle Ishmael.

It is explained after the lentil-stew-for-birthright episode that Esau became known as Edom, "red one." In the later prophecy and midrash, Esau became associated with every manner of evil, as did his tribe, the Edomites—this despite God's commandment *not* to hate the Edomites in Deuteronomy 23:8. The hatred of Edom is emphasized in the haftarah, from Malachi. Malachi is the last of the biblical prophets and lived in the early Second Temple period. He warned against indifference toward faith in God, that the commandments are a gift not to be treated carelessly, as mere formalities. By example, he compares God's love for Jacob with his disdain for Esau:

The first week's haftarah in our model month of Kislev is Malachi 1:1–2:17.

I have loved you, saith the Lord.
Yet ye say: "Wherein has Thou loved us?"
Was not Esau Jacob's brother? saith the Lord;
Yet I loved Jacob;
But Esau I hated,
And made his mountains a desolation,
And gave his heritage to the jackals of the wilderness.

The Bible's prototypical evildoer, Amalek, is the grandson of Esau, thus creating a bloodline connection from Esau to the later bad guys Agag and Haman. Unlike the caricature of Haman in the story of Esther, Esau is an ambiguous character, as is Jacob. The Torah and the so-called former prophets (Joshua, Judges, Samuel, Kings) show far more complexity of human characterization than do the later books in the biblical canon. In the old books, the bloodlines of good and evil are the same—as they are always.

The second week's Torah portion in our model month of Kislev is Vayetzei, Genesis 28:10–32:3.

In the next portion *Vayetzei*, "And Jacob went out," we follow Jacob's journey into adulthood. It begins with a dream: a ladder from earth to heaven, with angels going up and down it. Standing against him is God, who introduces himself and reiterates his promise first made to Abraham. "I will watch over you wherever you go and will bring you back to this soil; indeed, I will not leave you until I have done what I have spoken to you." Jacob vows to God a tithe in return.

Jacob moves on to Haran, where he meets the beautiful Rachel and embraces and kisses her, as he is embraced and kissed by Laban, Rachel's father, the brother of Jacob's mother. Laban has two daughters, Leah, the elder, and Rachel, the fairer. Jacob offers Laban seven years of work for Rachel, a proffer that Laban accepts. But at the end of the wedding feast, Laban brings to Jacob Leah and her maid, Zilpah, not Rachel. This Jacob realizes only in the light of day—after the wedding night. He goes to Laban and protests, but without satisfaction. Laban says, "Around here we don't give away the younger before the firstborn. But after the bridal week, we'll give you Rachel, too, and her maid, Bilhah—though for her you will serve me yet another seven years." During his time in the house of Laban, Jacob's two wives and two concubines bear him eleven sons and a daughter. To Leah are born Reuben, Simeon, Levi, Judah, Issachar, Zebulun, and a daughter, Dinah. To Bilhah are born Dan and Naphtali. To Zilpah are born Gad and Asher. And to Rachel, who until very late in life was barren, Joseph is born.

After the birth of Joseph, Jacob tries to negotiate with Laban the terms of his release. As God watched over Jacob, his work brought great riches to Laban, who tries clumsily to keep him—not by sharing but by trickery. Jacob offers what Laban thinks to be a fool's bargain: to take only the streaked, spotted, and speckled livestock. Laban gladly agrees. When they show the animals in heat streaked, spotted, and speckled wooden rods, they produce only colored livestock. Jacob leaves with great riches, leaving Laban only with animals past their prime. Jacob sets forth on the journey home and encounters two angels. There ends the portion.

It was a belief of the time—and long after—that the offspring of animals reflected the last colors seen by their parents before conception.

The haftarah is from Hosea (12:13–14:10), a prophet of the Northen Kingdom of Israel, who prophesied the doom that would befall them for their idolatry. The connection with the Torah portion is made in the opening verse: "And Jacob fled into the field of Aram, and Israel served for a wife, and for a wife he kept sheep."

The second week's haftarah in our model month of Kislev is Hosea 12:13–14:10.

The third week's portion is *Vayishlaḥ*, which begins "And Jacob sent messengers before him to Esau his brother." They

The third week's Torah portion in our model month of Kislev is Vayishlaḥ, Genesis 32:4–36:43.

carry and deliver a calculatedly humble message and return to Jacob only to say that Esau is on his way to meet him—with four hundred men. Jacob is terrified of Esau's revenge, for which he is completly unprepared. In panic he prays to God. Jacob splits up his party and separates out an impressive flock as a gift to Esau.

In the middle of the night Jacob awakens and takes his family across the Jabok Gorge. When Jacob is alone, a man appears and wrestles with him until the coming of dawn. The man (an angel) cannot prevail against him, but dislocates Jacob's thigh in an effort to get away. Jacob says to him, "I will not let you go until you bless me."

"What is your name?" asks the angel.

"Jacob," he replies.

"No longer as Jacob, the heel grabber, shall your name be known, but rather as Israel, Fighter of God, for you have fought with God and men and have prevailed."

As the sun rises, Jacob limps along and sees Esau and his men coming toward him. He divides the children among their mothers, sending them out group by group, while he advances ahead of them. He bows seven times before Esau; the brothers embrace, kissing each other and weeping. Jacob addresses his brother beseechingly, in supplication, as one would a king. At last, the crisis of Jacob's youth is over.

Jacob and his family establish a home in Shechem, in Canaan. An unfortunate incident occurs: Dinah, the daughter of Jacob and Leah, goes out to visit with the nearby women. Shechem, the son of the local prince, Hamor, sees Dinah and rapes her. But he falls in love with her and "speaks to her heart" and tells his father that he wishes to marry her. Jacob hears of the incident but chooses to wait until his sons return from the fields before addressing it. In the meantime,

Hamor goes over to see Jacob, and just then the brothers come home. They are very upset; Hamor tries to appease them, putting a good face on the situation, speaking of alliances and a dowry as great as they might ask for. But the brothers demand further concessions. They may not give their sister to anyone who hasn't been circumcised, they say, demanding that all their men must be circumcised. Hamor and Shechem agree to the condition and they persuade the men of their tribe on grounds that if they marry into Jacob's family they will share in their vast wealth and holdings of livestock. On the third day, when all in Shechem are still hurting, Simeon and Levi, Dinah's full brothers, come into the town and kill all the men, including Hamor and Shechem, taking all their property. Jacob is furious, saying they have stirred up trouble with all the neighboring people. Simeon and Levi respond, "Should our sister be treated like a whore?" We never again hear of Dinah, except as a name in a genealogy, but as for Simeon and Levi, their actions will not be forgotten.

God speaks to Jacob, instructing him to build a sacrifice site at Beth El, the place where he had the dream of the ladder. Jacob again sees God, who repeats the words of the angel with whom he wrestled: Jacob will be his name no more; henceforth he shall be Israel. "A host of nations shall come from you, kings shall go out from your loins," says the Lord. On the way back from Beth El, Rachel goes into labor with very great difficulty. She knows she will not survive. As her life slips away, she names the child Ben-Oni, "son of my woe." But his father calls him Benjamin, "son of my right hand." Rachel was buried along the way to Ephrat, later called Bethlehem. Now the sons of Jacob are twelve.

Jacob returns to Isaac, his father, who dies at age one

hundred eighty. Esau and Jacob bury him. There follows a
genealogy of Esau and the Edomites.

*The third week's
haftarah in our
model month of
Kislev is Hosea
11:7–12:12.*

The haftarah from Hosea (11:7–12:12) interweaves the
moments from the life of Jacob with the iniquities of the
prophet's own time: Jacob's altar at Beth El against the
sacrifices to a bullock at Gilgal. Sephardim read an entirely
different haftarah portion, Obadiah 1–21, which is directed
against Edom, the nation descended from Esau.

*The fourth and last
week's Torah por-
tion in our model
month of Kislev is
Vayeshev, Genesis
37:1–40:23.*

The fourth and last week's portion is *Vayeshev*, "And Jacob
dwelt." It is the beginning of the story of Joseph and his
brothers, a story that makes the link between the patriarchs
and Moses. Joseph is the pampered favorite of his old, doting
father, the son of a favorite wife who later dies in childbirth.
That he will be a dreamer or an artist seems inevitable, and
indeed, at age seventeen he is a self-absorbed dreamer who
expects to be listened to, no matter how obnoxious and pre-
sumptuous he might be. This is a kid looking for trouble,
though he doesn't know it. He tells his brothers of his
dreams, which foretell in symbols the day when they all will
bow down to him.

Trouble he finds. Joseph is sent by his father to check on
his brothers out in the fields. When they see him coming, the
brothers suggest to one another that they should kill him and
toss him into a pit. Reuben, the eldest, says no. After Reuben
leaves the group, they throw Joseph alive into a pit, and when
a caravan of Ishmaelites comes by, Judah suggests that they
sell him. While the brothers scheme, a group of Midianites
pulls Joseph from the pit and sells him for twenty pieces of
silver to the Ishmaelites. The brothers take Jospeh's fancy
coat that Jacob had given him and soil it with goat blood,
telling Jacob that a wild beast tore him to pieces. Jacob is dis-

traught. Joseph is taken into Egypt, where he is sold to a courtier called Potiphar.

In an interlude, we hear the story of Judah and Tamar, in which Judah learns what it means to lose a child. Around the same time as the Joseph incident, Judah marries a Canaanite woman who bears him three sons: Er, Onan, and Shelah. Er is struck dead by God for unspecified "wrongdoing" not long after he marries Tamar, whom Judah has chosen for him. By the ancient custom of levirate marriage, the next oldest unmarried brother is obligated to marry her, to continue his brother's line. The next brother is Onan, whose sexual proclivities render him unable to consummate the marriage. He is likewise struck dead. The next son, Shelah, is too young, so Judah tells Tamar to go to her father's house and wait for Shelah to grow up so that he may fulfill his duty and stay alive.

The custom of levirate marriage is still practiced in devout Jewish circles, though mitigated by a release ceremony called ḥalitzah. See p. 168 for more information.

Judah's wife dies and he goes up to see his friends, near the place where Tamar lives. When she hears of his coming, realizing that Shelah must now be grown, she takes off her widow's clothes and veils herself and waits for Judah by the road. Judah mistakes her for a prostitute. Tamar plays along, taking his staff and other effects as a security for payment, but when Judah sends payment, the prostitute and his things are nowhere to be found. Three months later, Judah learns that Tamar has become pregnant. He demands that she be brought to him so that she may be executed. As they bring her out, she sends a message to Judah, along with his things that she had taken. "Recognize these?" Judah is asked. Indeed he does, and he recognizes, too, that he was more in the wrong than she. From their union, twin boys are born. As they are about to be born, one puts out his hand and on it the midwife ties a scarlet thread. But he withdraws it. Then the other one emerges fully; he is named Peretz ("breach"); the

brother with the scarlet thread is called Zerach. From Peretz's
line will be born Jesse and David.

Back in Egypt, Joseph is watched over by God and suc-
ceeds in everything he does. Potiphar puts him in charge of
all his estates. Joseph's most difficult assignment, though, is
fending off the advances of Potiphar's wife—a proto–Mrs.
Robinson. Frustrated by her lack of success, she accuses
Joseph of making advances to her, and for this Potiphar has
him put in prison. God watches over him there, too, and he is
given great leeway by the warden, to whom he becomes a
trusty. In prison he meets Pharaoh's goblet-bearer and his
baker. They have disturbing dreams that Joseph interprets
for them. He tells the royal goblet-bearer that he will be freed
and restored to his position; as for the baker, he will be
hanged from a tree. And so it transpires.

The fourth and last week's haftarah in our model month of Kislev is Amos 2:6–3:8.

Amos is the source of the haftarah. It is not for nothing
that mankind will be punished by God, we are told by Amos,
through whom God speaks of man's inhumanity to man. In a
parallel to the Torah portion, we are presented with the de-
spicable crimes of those who "sell the righteous to the poor"
and "a man and his father who go into the same maid." Amos
is a greatly literary prophet, rich in allusion and high rhetor-
ical style.

> Will a lion roar in the forest
> When he hath no prey?...
> Will a bird fall in a snare upon the earth
> Where there is no lure for it?...
> Shall the horn be blown in a city,
> And the people not tremble?

"Slaughter an animal and make it ready"
(Genesis 43:16)

The Month of Tevet

I N OUR MODEL YEAR, Rosh Ḥodesh Tevet is observed
for two days, the first of which falls on a Sabbath. They
are also the sixth and seventh days of Hanukkah. It was long
debated whether one lights first the Sabbath candles or the
Ḥanukkah lights. Most authorities agree that the Ḥanukkah
lights come first so as not to violate the laws of the Sabbath.
As for cooking and playing Ḥanukkah games, Sabbath laws
take precedence.

In the morning service, all the additions appropriate to
Rosh Ḥodesh are made: the passage *Uverashei ḥodshekhem,*
"At the beginnings of your months" (Numbers 28:11–15), is
inserted into the reading of the sacrifices *(korbanot)* in the
morning service. In the Amidah, *Yaaleh veyavo* is inserted in
the *Avodah,* the seventeenth benediction, as is the custom on
Rosh Ḥodesh. *Al hanisim,* "For the miracles," is inserted in
the *Birkat hodaah,* the eighteenth benediction–specifically
for Ḥanukkah. Full Hallel is recited, as on all the days of
Ḥanukkah. On Rosh Ḥodesh it is followed by full Kaddish.

Three Torah scrolls are taken out of the ark. The weekly
portion, Genesis 41:1–44:17 (discussed later in this chapter),
is read from the first scroll, to which seven people are called

*For more details on
Rosh Ḥodesh and
its readings and
blessings, see the
chapter beginning
on p. 91.*

up. The seventh person is called up to the second scroll, to read the usual verses for Rosh Ḥodesh, Numbers 28:9–15. The maftir is called up to the third scroll to read the continuation of the Ḥanukkah verses—today Numbers 7:42–47—which describe the offerings brought by the tribes for the dedication of the Tabernacle. The haftarah is 1 Kings 3:15–4:1. In years when the last day of Ḥanukkah falls on this Sabbath, the haftarah portion is Zechariah 2:14–4:7.

When there are two Sabbaths that coincide with Ḥanukkah, the haftarah for the first Sabbath is Zechariah 2:14–4:7 and the haftarah for the second Sabbath is 1 Kings 7:40–50.

In the musaf, afternoon, and evening services, the usual additions for Rosh Ḥodesh are made, and also *Al hanisim*, which is added for Ḥanukkah. On Saturday night, Havdalah is made prior to the lighting of the Ḥanukkah lights.

On the seventh day of Ḥanukkah, the portion Numbers 7:48–53 is read; on the eighth and last day, the reading is Numbers 7:54–89, the conclusion of the offerings brought to the dedication of the Tabernacle. There is no Havdalah after the last day of Ḥanukkah.

The Tenth of Tevet

A dawn-to-dark fast is observed on the tenth of Tevet when the armies of the Babylonian king Nebuchadnezzar laid siege to Jerusalem, resulting in the destruction of the Temple in the year 586 B.C.E. The event was one of grave implications, commemorated chiefly on the ninth of Av. Since it was a great tragedy that the people had brought upon themselves, the liturgy includes Seliḥot, penitential prayers. As with all Seliḥot and all fast days, their liturgical emphasis is on the Thirteen Attributes of Mercy. But there are also references specific to the tenor of the day, including quotations from Psalms and the prophets:

See also the months of Av and Elul for more on the destruction of the Temple, Seliḥot, and related readings.

> Record for yourself in the book of prophecy as a remembrance for the nation that is wretched and disgraced—the

essence of this date. . . . . O God! The nations have entered into Your inheritance; they have defiled the sanctuary of Your holiness; they have turned Jerusalem into heaps of rubble.

Psalms 79:1.

One Torah scroll is taken out, and the Torah portion for public fasts is read, Exodus 32:11–14; 34:1–10, which again emphasizes the Thirteen Attributes of Mercy

See p. 34 and p. 208 for the Thirteen Attributes and p. 362 for more about this reading.

Torah Readings of Tevet

"And it came to pass at the end of two full years [after the events of the previous portion] that Pharaoh dreamed he was standing by the Nile, and out from it came seven cows, healthy, well-fed cows, and they grazed in the grass. And then there were seven more cows, skinny and sickly, which ate the well-fed ones." Thus begins the portion *Miketz* (Genesis 41:1–44:17), the continuation of the Joseph story, read on the first Sabbath in our model month of Tevet. Pharaoh has a second dream in which seven ears of grain that grew upon a single, fat stalk were swallowed up by seven measly ears. Pharaoh could not understand the dream, nor could his wise men suggest an explanation. The baker who had been imprisoned tells Pharaoh of the man he met there, a Hebrew named Joseph who had interpreted perfectly his own dream and that of his less fortunate colleague, the cupbearer. Pharaoh summons Joseph, who interprets the dreams as a message from God, a description of what is about to occur: after a seven-year period of great prosperity will come a seven-year period of abject famine. What must be done, says Joseph, is that Pharaoh must appoint ministers to oversee the management of the prosperity so that sufficient stores are laid in to cover the lean times. Pharaoh gives Joseph his signet, appointing him minister over all the land of Egypt. And Joseph becomes

The first week's Torah portion in our model month of Tevet is Miketz, Genesis 41:1–44:17.

a man of great power who manages well the abundance. He is given as a wife, Asenath, the daughter of a priest, who bears two sons, Manasseh ("he who makes me forget my toils") and Ephraim ("double fruit").

After seven years a great famine ensues. Jacob, in Canaan, hears that in Egypt they are giving rations, and he sends his sons there, all but Benjamin, the youngest. The brothers bow before Joseph (now called Zaphenath-paneah) but do not recognize him. He, however, recognizes them and without revealing his identity puts them to a test. He accuses them of spying, so they tell their story, of their families and young brother and old father back home. Joseph places Simeon in custody and tells the others to go home and bring back their young brother (Joseph's only full brother). Only then he will give them the rations they require. On their way back, they are astonished to discover the silver pieces for which Joseph had been sold at the tops of their packs.

Jacob is furious over their bungling, distraught when they return with only a small amount of grain and without Simeon. Now they want to take Benjamin! After considerable persuading and promises, Jacob sends them back—with Benjamin and with twice the silver they come home with, this as a gift of goodwill for Joseph. They return to Egypt and are received by Joseph, who continues to play out his test. Deeply moved to see his young brother, he is careful not to let on, speaking to them only through an interpreter. Joseph prepares for them a great feast, then has their packs filled with food, secretly placing in them the silver they returned and that which they brought as a gift. Joseph's own goblet is placed in Benjamin's pack. After the brothers are sent on their way, Joseph has them pursued. They are questioned and the silver is exposed. They come before Joseph, who says,

"The man in whose hand the goblet is found—he shall become my servant." And there the week's portion ends.

The haftarah, 1 Kings 3:15-4:1, also concerns a king's dream and the fate of a child. The dream is that of the very young King Solomon, who approaches God and asks for only one thing, the wisdom to rule. God is pleased with his selflessness and grants him more than he asked: unparalleled greatness in our time. Solomon's wisdom is demonstrated in the famous story that follows, about the two women who claim to be the mother of an infant.

The first week's haftarah in our model month of Tevet is 1 Kings 2:1–12.

The portion *Vayigash* is read on the second week. Judah, the brother who had wished to sell Joseph out, comes close to Joseph, eloquently telling him how reluctant their father had been to send Benjamin and how returning without the boy would cause their father's death. This they cannot do, so Judah offers to stay in Benjamin's stead. Even though Judah exposes his own dissembling about his brother's disappearance ("he was surely torn to pieces"), the emotion of the reunion overwhelms Joseph, who sends away all his retainers and reveals to his brothers his identity. "I am Joseph. Is my father still alive?" are the first words he pushes out through his tears. Whatever anger he might harbor has been subsumed by a sense of greater purpose:

The second week's Torah portion in our model month of Tevet is Vayigash, Genesis 44:18–47:27.

> I am Joseph, your brother, whom you sold into Egypt. But don't worry about that now or let your guilt get in the way, for it was to save life that God sent me ahead of you. We are two years into this famine and there are still another five to go before there will be another harvest. So God sent me ahead of you to make you a remnant on earth and to preserve life, for you to be a great group of survivors.

"Remnant," "survivors"—words that will ring again and again in Jewish history. Joseph tells them to go back and bring everyone and everything out and settle in Goshen. And then "he flung himself on Benjamin's neck and wept, and Benjamin flung himself upon his neck."

Jacob is revitalized by the news of Joseph's survival and the hope that he will see him again before he dies. Some seventy members of Jacob's household depart from Canaan and settle in Goshen, where Joseph greets them. Jacob meets Pharaoh and gives him his blessing; Pharaoh gives Joseph's family the best part of the land.

The famine worsens and the people sell all they have to Pharaoh for bread, including their land. All Egyptians except the priests become the tenants of Pharaoh, each tithed twenty percent of what they produce. But the house of Israel remains in the region of Goshen, and they become "exceedingly many."

The second week's haftarah in our model month of Tevet is Ezekiel 37:15–28.

See p. 146 for another context of this haftarah.

The haftarah, Ezekiel 37:15–28, tells a parallel story of reunion, nearly a thousand years later, with the very same names. Ezekiel prophesied during the Babylonian Exile, offering a message of the nation's rebirth through God's forgiveness and our acceptance of individual responsibility. Here, the names Joseph and Judah represent the once-divided realms of Judah and Israel. The reading overlaps with one read in the month of Nisan, Ezekiel 36:37–37:14, which also tells the story of the Valley of Dry Bones.

The third week's Torah portion in our model month of Tevet is Vayeḥi, Genesis 47:28–50:26.

In the third week of our model month of Tevet we come to the last portion of Genesis, *Vayeḥi*, the conclusion of the story of the patriarchs. Jacob, who has lived in Egypt for seventeen years, draws near to death. He makes Joseph swear to bury him in Canaan, in the cave with his father and grandfather. Jacob speaks then of how he saw God and how God had blessed him and repeated his promise of great nationhood in the Promised Land. Jacob blesses Joseph and his sons, Manasseh and Ephraim, whom he declares to be as his own sons so that they may share directly in the inheritance. As Jacob places his hands on their heads, it is in reverse order of their birth: his right hand on Ephraim and left hand on Manassah. When Joseph points this out, Jacob makes it clear that it was what he intended, that both will become nations, but Ephraim the greater. Again, the duality of brothers, as it was with Jacob and Esau, Isaac and Ishmael.

The eleven other sons gather at Jacob's deathbed and he blesses them "each according to his blessing." To Reuben, Simeon, and Levi he gives a final rebuke: Reuben for violating his father's bed, Simeon and Levi for their actions after the rape of Dinah. To the others he gives acknowledgment, each according to his qualities. After Jacob's death at age one hundred forty-seven, his wishes for burial are fulfilled.

As Joseph is in his one hundred tenth year, he tells his brothers that he is dying and reminds them that God will take them out of the land and deliver them to the land promised to their fathers. He tells them that when this happens, they should bring out his bones with them.

In the haftarah, 1 Kings 2:1–12, the dying King David imparts his blessing to his son Solomon, with instruction to follow God's laws always and to be mindful of those around them who wish them well and those who wish them ill. The common thread with the Torah portion is not only the obvious deathbed blessings, but also God's participation in all the proceedings. But there the parallels end. The Israelites in Egypt live by faith alone; how the drama of their deliverance will unfold is completely unknown. Under Solomon, they will enter their most secure period of nationhood.

The third week's haftarah in our model month of Tevet is 1 Kings 2:1–12.

The fourth week's Torah portion in our model month of Tevet is Shemot, Exodus 1:1–6:1.

The name of the fourth week's portion, *Shemot,* "names," is the Hebrew name of the book of Exodus. "Now these are the names of the Children of Israel coming into Egypt," it begins and goes on to list Jacob's eleven sons, parenthetically adding Joseph, who was there already. This listing is a kind of balance to the accounting given at the end of Genesis, making for a smooth transition to the Torah's second book. God has delivered on his first promise to Abraham: the Israelites have grown great in number. "They became many, they grew mighty in number—exceedingly, yes, exceedingly." The situation led to fear in Egypt, Pharaoh's fear that the Israelites might overwhelm them. A plan developed: they made the Israelites slave laborers and set them to work building the storage cities of Pithom and Ramses. And as is told in the Passover story, the Egyptians "embittered their lives with all kinds of servitude."

Further steps are taken to keep the Israelite population under control, such as ordering the midwives to kill all male newborns upon delivery. When the plan does not succeed, the boys are thrown into the Nile. A woman from the house of Levi bears a son and hides him for three months, but when she can do so no longer, she builds a little ark and places the child in it. She sends her daughter up ahead, to report what happens. The infant is found by Pharaoh's daughter, who had gone to bathe in the river, and she pities him. The sister asks the princess if she would like her to find a nursemaid from among the Hebrews. Yes, she says, and the sister returns with the boy's mother, whom the princess tells to take the boy and nurse him and that her wages will be paid. The child grows and his mother brings him to Pharaoh's daughter, who calls him Moses—"he who pulls out"—for "it was out of the water I pulled him."

The name Moses was a common one in Egypt. The "pulling out" etymology in Pharaoh's daughter's wordplay is purely Hebrew.

Now an adult, Moses notices the plight of his people. He sees an Egyptian beating a Hebrew man; Moses kills him and buries him in the sand. When Pharaoh learns of this, he sentences Moses to death. Moses flees, settling in Midian, where he comes to the defense of the daughters of the priest Jethro, who were run off while trying to water their sheep. Moses is invited into the priest's home and is later offered in marriage his daughter, Zipporah, who later bears a son, Gershom ("sojourner there"). There he takes up the profession of his forebears: shepherding.

Years pass, the Pharaoh who knew Joseph dies, and the Children of Israel "groan and cry out from their servitude." God hears them and remembers his covenant with Abraham, Isaac, and Jacob. As Moses attends his flock at Mount Sinai, he sees an angel in a burning bush, which burns but is not consumed. God calls him out of the midst of the bush and introduces himself and his purpose. God describes the actions that are to be taken: Moses is to go to Pharaoh and demand that the Israelites be let go. Then he is to go to the Children of Israel and say he was sent by the God of their fathers to bring them out. Moses is a reluctant prophet, by his own admission "heavy of mouth and heavy of tongue," and five times he tries to turn down the job. Moses has doubts: What if Pharaoh won't listen or cooperate? What if the Israelites question the source of the message? God becomes angry and tells Moses that he will be there to guide him and that Aaron, Moses's brother, will speak for him. Moses gathers his wife and son and sets out on the journey back to Egypt.

God also visits Aaron and tells him to meet Moses in the Wilderness. Moses and Aaron speak to the council of elders of the Israelites and show them the signs that God had told Moses. And they believe them. Next they go to Pharaoh and ask that their people be set free to participate in a festival to make offerings to their God so that he doesn't afflict them with pestilence. As God had predicted, Pharaoh says no and adds to their burdens, making them gather their own straw for their brickmaking while demanding that each produce the same daily quota.

The fourth week's haftarah in our model month of Tevet is Isaiah 27:6–28:13 and 29:22–23. Sephardim read instead Jeremiah 1:1–2:3.

In the haftarah, Isaiah speaks of yet another deliverance— from the Assyrians who had overtaken the Northern Kingdom of Israel and, during the prophet's time, nearly taken Jerusalem. But he learns that to be delivered, you must be ready to accept deliverance by adherence to God's precepts. Isaiah reviles the revelers, the ones who will not listen:

> For it is precept by precept, precept by precept,
> Line by line, line by line;
> Here a little, there a little.
> For with stammering lips and with a strange tongue
> Shall it be spoken to this people;
> To whom it was said, "This is the rest,
> Give ye rest to the weary;
> And this is the refreshing";
> Yet they would not hear.
> And so the word of the Lord is unto them
> Precept by precept, precept by precept,
> Line by line, line by line;
> Here a little, there a little;
> That they may go, and fall backward and be broken,
> And snared, and taken.

Sephardic Jews read another haftarah: Jeremiah 1:1–2:3, an apt choice in which the call of Jeremiah is given as a parallel to the call of Moses. Jeremiah also wonders if he is suited to the job:

> And the word of the Lord came unto me, saying:
> Before I formed thee in the the belly I knew thee,

And before thou camest out of the womb I sanctified thee;
I have appointed thee a prophet unto the nations.

The model month's last portion is *Vaera*. "I am the Lord," God says to Moses, "and I appeared to Abraham, to Isaac, and to Jacob as *El Shaddai* (God Almighty), but My name, Yʜwʜ (יהוה), was not known to them." Earlier, in Exodus 3:15, God announced himself to Moses as *Ehyeh Asher Ehyeh*, which means something like "I Will Be There Howsoever I Will Be There," sometimes translated as "I Am What I Am." It is a syntactic enigma, befitting a name that may not be uttered and that represents something beyond comprehension.

The fifth and last week's Torah portion in our model month of Tevet is Vaera, Exodus 6:2–9:35.

God's promise of deliverance is reiterated. Moses tells God that he spoke to the Children of Israel but they did not hearken to him. Again, Moses wonders to God how he with his "foreskinned lips" (a speech impediment? a cleft lip?) will convince Pharaoh to release the Israelites. God tells him that he will make him "as a god for Pharaoh" and that Aaron "will be your prophet."

The confrontation with Pharaoh begins. Moses and Aaron show Pharaoh magical transformations: the staff into a snake, the Nile turned into blood, the land inundated with frogs. These Pharaoh's sorcerers can repeat. But with the third of the Ten Plagues, gnats, the punishments escalate beyond the realm of conjuring. Then come the swarming insects, the pestilence on the livestock, the boils, and the hail. Here the portion ends.

The haftarah from Ezekiel is an uneasy parallel from the period of the Babylonian Exile. At the time of Ezekiel's writing, the reasonably comfortable yet nostalgic exiles followed carefully the precarious situation of those who were still living in the Promised Land, who were about to enter into a pact with a weak Egypt, long in decline. Ezekiel rails on

The fifth week's haftarah in our model month of Tevet is Ezekiel 28:5–29:21.

against the the Egyptians and their lack of trustworthiness, using quotations and paraphrases of passages in Exodus, filled with threats of plagues and other damnations.

Interestingly, Deuteronomy 23:8 enjoins the Israelites "not to abominate an Egyptian, for you were a sojourner in his land." This haftarah has the familiar ring of the overwrought and overemotional machinations of an exile community that schemes from afar to set things straight—without inside support or even up-to-date knowledge.

"He sends the cold and the water stands frozen"
(Psalm 147:17)

The Month of Shevat

"**THESE ARE THE WORDS** that Moses spoke to all Israel . . . in the fortieth year, in the eleventh new moon and day one after the new moon." Thus it was in Shevat that Moses began his great and final instruction that we know as Deuteronomy. The name Shevat is probably Akkadian, and doesn't appear in the Bible until the beginning of Jeremiah.

Deuteronomy 1:1

Shevat is always thirty days and Rosh Ḥodesh Shevat never falls on a Sunday or a Friday.

The connection with Deuteronomy makes Shevat an auspicious month in rabbinic circles, where it has been referred to as a "second Shavuot." But there is only one holiday observance, Tu b'Shevat, which is the "New Year for Trees." This was the date on which the year was determined for the tithing of fruit trees during Temple times. Since a tenth of the fruit was obligated to be given to the levites and Temple priests each year, it was necessary to calculate from a measurable turning point in the growing season. By this time in the Land of Israel, a certain percentage of the fruit had reached the stage at which it can be said to have "begun to ripen"— defined as from the time of blossoming until the fruit reached one-third of its full growth. All fruit so categorized was attributed to the previous year; all the fruit derived from later blossoms was considered to be of the New Year.

"Tu" (טו) is simply the Hebrew expression of "15."

Tu b'Shevat from the Minhogim-bukh, *Amsterdam, 1722.*

There is no widely established liturgy for the Tu b'Shevat Seder, though various examples may be found on the Internet.

There are no special liturgies for Tu b'Shevat, though as on other holidays neither Taḥanun, the prayers of supplication, nor the memorial prayers for the dead are said. Work is not prohibited. There is no requirement for a festive meal, yet it is the custom among Ashkenazic Jews to eat fruits, especially fruits from the Land of Israel. It is a Sephardic tradition to stay up all night to study and recite all the passages in the Bible, Talmud, and Kabbalah related to fruits. The Kabbalists of sixteenth-century Safed instituted a special Seder for Tu b'Shevat, based in the mystical idea that eating a variety of fruits can bring about a *tahyon,* a "correction" of the sin of having eaten from the Tree of Knowledge. During the past century, since the advent of the Zionist movement, Tu b'Shevat has been reinvented as a kind of Arbor Day, a day on which schoolchildren plant trees in the Land of Israel. Jewish children all over the world send money to sponsor the plantings. With the expansion of interest in Kabbalah in recent years, the Tu b'Shevat Seder has undergone a revival. Some groups have added to it a message of ecological *tikun* (restoration). It shows the adaptability of Jewish custom and liturgy.

Torah Readings of Shevat

The first week's Torah portion in our model month of Shevat is Bo, *Exodus 10:1–13:16.*

The first week's portion *Bo,* "Come [to Pharaoh]," continues the plagues: the locusts, which consumed all that remained after the hail, and then the absolute darkness. Still, Pharaoh sets conditions and makes threats. God tells Moses of the final plague, the death of the firstborn males of Egypt—

human and beast alike. After this, God says, Pharaoh will relent. There follows the instructions for the sacrificial lamb, the marking of the doorposts, the Passover itself, the making of matzoh, and the instructions for event's commemoration woven into the narrative.

The haftarah is from Jeremiah, who was an older contemporary of Ezekiel's, and his prophecy here is on the same subject as the previous week's: the folly of seeking help from the Egyptians against Babylon. In 605 B.C.E. Egypt fell to Babylon at the Battle of Charchemish. Again, the words contain innumerable parallels to those of the Torah reading, though each concerns rather different circumstances. Is the practical instruction here that it is unwise to appeal to a former adversary when seeking help with a new one? Nevertheless, Jeremiah, the Poet of Calamity, is in top metaphorical form here, decrying Egypt and its sphere as overfed and useless against powerhouse Babylon in the north:

Many of these passages are quoted at length in the chapter on the month of Nisan, with the Passover observance. See pp. 116 and 117.

The first week's haftarah in our model month of Shevat is Jeremiah 46:13-28.

Egypt is a very fair heifer;
But the gadfly out of the north is come, it is come.
Also her [Egypt's] mercenaries in the midst of her
Are like calves of the stall,
For they are also turned back, they are fled away together,
They did not stand;
For the day of their calamity is come upon them,
The time of their visitation.
The sound thereof shall go like the serpent's;
For they march with an army,
And come against her axes,
As hewers of wood.

Jeremiah 46:20-22

The Sabbath on which the next portion, *Beshalah*, "When it came to pass," Exodus 13:17-17:16, is read is called Shabbat Shirah, "The Sabbath of the Song." Two songs are associated

The second week's Torah portion in our model month of Shevat is Beshalah, Exodus 13:17-17:16.

The Song of the Sea is someimes referred to as "The Song."

Two excerpts of the morning Song of the Sea are part of the Birkat geulah, *the blessing that follows the morning Shema. See p. 31.*

with this Sabbath, and great songs they are. The first, part of the Torah portion, is the Song of the Sea, which Moses and the Children of Israel broke into as they came safely ashore, the Egyptians having been swallowed in their wake. The text is Exodus 15:1–18. It is a moment of the highest exultation, in which God is proclaimed "king for the ages." At its end Miriam, the sister of Moses and Aaron, takes a timbrel in hand and leads the women in dance and in their own version of the song—a frequently depicted scene. The second song comes from the haftarah, the Song of Deborah, the fifth chapter of the book of Judges.

The Song of the Sea is also sung on the seventh day of Passover. A number of special customs are associated with its recitation in different rites, including special forms of cantillation. Many synagogues add a congregational response, "I will sing unto the Lord," between verses. It is the Ashkenazic custom to stand during the song. Moroccan Jews add a special hymn with verses from eight biblical songs. In some Sephardic congregations the song is recited as part of Torah reading, then repeated with a special tune afterward.

The portion begins with the route out of Egypt and a description of how God, appearing as a cloud column by day and a column of fire by night, led the Children of Israel not by the most direct route, but by a circuitous one, purposely avoiding armed confrontations, which might have demoralized the Israelites and made them nostalgic for the simplicity of serfdom. The Egyptians interpreted the path as meandering or lacking in direction, so Pharaoh sent six hundred three-in-hand chariots after them. The scene is planned and played out entirely by God, who wishes to destroy the chariots for his glory, drawing them into the sea that he commanded Moses to split with his staff, leading the Israelites to the safe shore beyond. Upon the destruction of the Egyptians, the song is sung.

The story moves into the Wilderness, in which narrative episodes of survival, complaint, skirmish, and instruction shape a people just emerging from a deprived childhood. The tone established here will be retained through the rest of Exodus and through Numbers. Moses plays the roles of God's agent, leader, judge, conciliator, teacher, policeman, and military commander. Yet through all of this, he never quite develops into a character we know. We are constantly and forever grateful for his presence—there would have been no survival without him. His lack of personality reminds us that the central character is God.

The remainder of the portion includes the people's first grumblings about water and food, the giving of manna and, most important, the declaration of the seventh day as the Sabbath. There also begins here an encounter that will become an occasional but persistent theme, even beyond the Torah: the attack of Amalek, a name first encountered in one of the Genesis genealogies as the grandson of Esau. God declares war against Amalek for "generation after generation" and indeed, Amalek's descendant Haman is the villain of the story of Esther, one of the last books to become part of the biblical canon.

For more on manna and its qualities, see p. 56.

For more on Amalek and the Amalekites, see p. 347.

The haftarah, Judges 4:4–5:31, tells another story of victory over oppression that also ends in song, the victory of the prophetess Deborah over Jabin, king of Canaan, and his nine hundred chariots of iron commanded by his captain, Sisera. After the death of Joshua, the judges served as the national leaders during a time of struggle against the hostile tribes that occupied the area. Deborah, with the help of Barak, develops a divinely inspired plan to gather the Israelite tribes

The second week's haftarah in our model month of Shevat is Judges 4:4–5:31.

of the area on Mount Tabor, drawing the heavily armored Canaanites into an indefensible position. After the Israelites win a total victory, Deborah and Barak burst into song. The Song of Deborah is a moving and sophisticated victory ode, filled with vivid descriptions of the events, giving credit where credit is due yet remaining personal and tender.

> When the men let their hair grow in Israel,
> When the people offer themselves willingly,
> Bless ye the Lord . . .
> Ye that ride on white asses,
> Ye that sit on rich cloths, And ye that walk by the way,
>   tell of it;
> Louder than the voice of archers, by the watering troughs!
> There shall they rehearse the righteous acts of the Lord.

And it includes the story of Jael, the wife of Heber the Kenite, who was an ally of the Israelites. It was Jael who brought down Sisera, the Canaanite king:

> Blessed above women shall Jael be,
> The wife of Heber the Kenite,
> Above women in the tent shall she be blessed.
> Water he [the king] asked, milk she gave him;
> In a lordly bowl she brought him curd.
> Her hand she put to the tent stake,
> And her right hand to the workman's hammer;
> And with the hammer she smote Sisera,
>   she smote through his head.
> Yea, she pierced and struck through his temples.
> At her feet he sunk, he fell;
> Where he sunk, there he fell down dead. . . .
> So perish all Thine enemies, O Lord,
> But they that love Him be as the sun
>   when he goeth forth in his might.
> And the land had rest for forty years.

The third week's portion, *Yitro,* "Jethro," begins with a visit to the encampment by Moses's father-in-law, Jethro, the priest of Midian, bringing with him his daughter, Moses's wife, Zipporah, and Moses's two sons, Gershom and Eliezer. When Jethro sees that Moses is the sole magistrate and peacekeeper in the camp, he warns him against burnout and recommends a structure of government run by "Men of caliber, those who hold God in awe. You should set over the Israelites chiefs of thousands, chiefs of hundreds, chiefs of fifties, and chiefs of tens, so that they may adjudicate at all times." Moses does as Jethro recommends.

The third week's Torah portion in our model month of Shevat is Yitro, Exodus 18:1–20:23.

The Israelites come to the place where Moses first encountered God: Mount Sinai. The story has come now to the covenant, God's revelation, and the giving of the Law. A boundary is set up around the mountain's perimeter, since death will come to those who cross it. The Children of Israel are to be made a holy people: all are to be clean and pure for three days—no sexual contacts. God's presence comes in the form of a thick cloud that blankets the mountain, with thunder and lightning and an exceedingly strong shofar sound. The people tremble. God comes down upon the mountain as fire, causing smoke to rise as in a gigantic furnace. God calls Moses to the mountaintop and tells him to go back down and return with Aaron. Then God speaks the Ten Commandments:

[1] I am Yʜwʜ your God, | who brought you out | from the land of Egypt, from a house of serfs.
[2] You are not to have | any other gods | before my presence. | You are not to make yourself a carved-image | or any figure | that is in the heavens above, that is on the earth beneath, that is in the waters beneath the earth; | you are not to bow down to them, | you are not to serve them, | for I, Yʜwʜ your God, | am a jealous God | calling-to-account the

The translation is by Everett Fox from The Five Books of Moses. *The bracketed numbers are added here to delineate the commandments. The vertical rules denote scansion.*

iniquity of the fathers upon the sons, to the third and fourth (generation) | of those that hate me, | but showing loyalty to the thousandth | of those that love me, | of those that keep my commandments.

[3] You are not to take up | the name of YHWH your God for emptiness, | for YHWH will not clear him | that takes up his name for emptiness.

[4] Remember | the Sabbath day, to hallow it. | For six days, you are to serve, and are to make all your work, | but the seventh day | is Sabbath for YHWH your God: | you are not to make any kind of work, | (not) you, nor your son, nor your daughter, | (not) your servant, nor your maid, nor your beast, | nor your sojourner that is within your gates. | For in six days | YHWH made | the heavens and the earth, | the sea and all that is in it, | and he rested on the seventh day; | therefore YHWH gave the seventh day his blessing, and he hallowed it.

[5] Honor | your father and your mother, | in order that your days may be prolonged | on the soil that YHWH your God is giving you.

[6] You are not to murder.

[7] You are not to adulter.

[8] You are not to steal.

[9] You are not to testify | against your fellow as a false witness.

[10] You are not to desire | the house of your neighbor, | you are not to desire the wife of your neighbor, | or his servant, or his maid, or his ox, or his donkey, | or anything that is your neighbor's.

The people are fearful. Moses says, "Be not afraid! God has come only to test you and the the fear of Him be ever with you, that you do not sin." God then reiterates to Moses that the people are not to make for themselves gods of gold or silver and instructs him to make a sacrifice site, of earth or of unhewn stone.

Isaiah is the source of the week's haftarah. His vision looms large in Jewish liturgy, quoted in the *Kedushat Hashem*, the Sanctification of the Lord in the daily Amidah and in all other forms of the Kedushah. It is Isaiah who quotes the call of the seraphim, "Holy, holy, holy is the Lord of hosts; the whole earth is full with His glory." Isaiah's assignment is to bring back the Israelites from their lives of luxury to the realm of God's teaching. "Lord, how long shall I do this?" Isaiah asks God. God replies:

The third week's haftarah in our model month of Shevat is Isaiah 6:1–7:6, 9:5–6.

> Until the cities be waste without inhabitant . . . and the Lord have removed men far away. And if there be a tenth in it, it shall again be eaten up; and as an oak whose stock remaineth, when they cast their leaves, so the holy seed shall be the stock thereof.

Isaiah 6:11–13

Chapter 7 returns to the political events of Isaiah's time, when Ahaz, king of Judah, fails to join the Northern Kingdom of Israel in alliance against the mounting power of Assyria. This is the backdrop for Isaiah's joyous announcement of the birth of Hezekiah, who it is hoped will bring back piety to the land.

> For a child is born unto us,
> A son is given to us;
> And the government is upon his shoulder;
> And his name is called "Wonderful-in-counsel-is-God-the-
>   mighty-the-everlasting-father-the-ruler-of-peace."

Isaiah 9:5

These are, of course, verses well known to Christians from the Christmas liturgy, though based on translations that alter the original text and intent. As one might deduce, it would not have been likely that an Israelite prophet would have called a mortal person "Mighty God" or "Everlasting Father."

Shabbat Shekalim: The Sabbath of the Shekel Tax

The last Sabbath in our model month of Shevat is Shabbat Shekalim, the first of the four Sabbaths known as the Four Portions. The designation refers to specific Torah verses that Jewish law requires to be read on Sabbaths that occur in specific relation to certain days. In our model year, the second, third, and fourth of the Four Portions occur next month, in Adar. Shabbat Shekalim refers specifically to the verses

Shabbat Shekalim from the Minhogimbukh, Amsterdam, 1727.

Exodus 30:11–16, in which God commanded Moses to take a census and collect a head tax of half a shekel for every healthy man age twenty and over, to support construction of the Tabernacle. No distinction was to be to be made between rich and poor—all were to give the same. This tax continued through the time of the Temple, when the sacrifices were purchased from half shekels donated by the people. The taxes were due by Rosh Ḥodesh Nisan, the month following Adar. It became the custom that the reading of this Torah portion served as the legal notice of the yearly tax, and therefore it is to be read no less than a full month in advance of the beginning of Nisan, which means that the portion must be read no later than Rosh Ḥodesh Adar. There are years in which all the Four Portions fall in Adar.

Today, the tradition is continued as a time when money is raised for charity, especially for building projects in the state of Israel or synagogue construction and repairs.

Two scrolls are taken out and seven people are called up. The regular Torah portion is read before the special one. In our model month it is Exodus 21:1–24:18, called *Mishpatim*, "ordinances." It is the first lengthy explication of the civil and criminal law, following as it does the Ten Commandments. Many of the particulars will be revisited and expanded in Leviticus, Numbers, and Deuteronomy, some more than once. The matters covered are all essentials upon which systematic justice must be based. It begins with the time limitation on the keeping of serfs; during the seventh year of their service they must be offered freedom. Four capital crimes are described: premeditated murder, striking one's father or mother, all forms of kidnapping, and insulting (!) one's parents. This is followed by a variety of remedies for injuries: someone who injures a pregnant woman resulting in the loss of the fetus is to be fined by the husband; serfs injured by their masters are to be set free; an ox that gores and kills someone is to be stoned to death but not eaten; the owner of a deadly animal that does nothing to prevent the killing of a person by that animal is subject to the death penalty. Equal value fines are established—"an eye for an eye." A man who seduces a virgin who has not been spoken for must marry her, though he is entitled to the prevailing dowry amount. A sorceress is to be put to death. Bestiality is punishable by death. You may not mistreat a sojourner, in memory of your sojourn in Egypt. You may not afflict a widow or orphan. A person's only coat taken in pledge for a debt must be returned by nightfall, whether or not the debt is paid.

Don't spread false rumors or side with a guilty person. Do not take the side of a poor or needy person in a dispute just because he or she is poor—or a wealthy person because he or she is wealthy. You may not take a bribe. The land must be given a sabbatical rest after six years of cultivation. All of your household—people and animals—are to be given rest for

The fourth and last week's Torah portion in our model month of Shevat is Mishpatim, Exodus 21:1–24:18.

the Sabbath. The three pilgrimage festivals are described and some rules for the sacrifices are given. The portion concludes with God's specific reassurances that the Israelites should have no fear of the battles to come, that he will go before them in clearing the land.

The fourth week's haftarah in our model month of Shevat is 2 Kings 12:1-17.

For the special Shabbat Shekalim haftarah, Ashkenazic Jews read 2 Kings 12:1-17; Sephardim read more verses, 2 Kings 11:17-12:17. This section of 2 Kings describes a period of disunity after the Northern Kingdom of Israel broke away from the Kingdom of Judah, which was still led by the line of King David. This particular portion concerns the Northern Kingdom and the transition of kingship from Jehu to his son Jehoash. It was a time of regular fighting with the worshipers of the idol Baal. The Northern Kingdom lasted about two hundred years before ending at the hands of the Assyrians. A number intermarried with the local population, and there is some evidence that their descendants are the Samaritans, who survive to this day in very small numbers in the state of Israel.

"And let them grow into a multitude on the earth"
(Genesis 48:16)

The Month(s) of Adar

A DAR, THE MONTH OF PURIM, is considered a joyous time. It is also the leap-year month, meaning that
seven times in the nineteen-year Jewish calendrical cycle—in
years 3, 6, 8, 11, 14, 17, and 19—there are two months of Adar,
the first with thirty days, the second with twenty-nine. All the
major events are celebrated in Adar II, although a minor
observance called *Purim katan*, "Little Purim," takes place on
the fourteenth of Adar I. Bar or bat mitzvah ceremonies are
scheduled for Adar II, but the yearly commemoration of a
death, *yortsait*, is observed in Adar I. Rosh Hodesh Adar is
observed for two days in each month.

In our model year, there is just one Adar. Moses died on the
seventh of the month, and there is a minor fast that day, traditionally observed by officials of Jewish burial societies. The
Fast of Esther is observed on the thirteenth, Purim on the
fourteenth, and Shushan Purim is on the fifteenth. Three of
the special Sabbaths known as the Four Portions are
observed in our model Adar: Shabbat Zakhor, Shabbat Parah,
and Shabbat Haḥodesh. Since Shabbat Shekalim, the first of
the four, must be observed no later than thirty days before
the beginning of Nisan, its observance is recorded here in the

month of Shevat. Shabbat Zakhor must be the Sabbath before Purim, so the first Sabbath of Adar in our model year is a regular Sabbath, not one of the Four Portions.

The reading for this Sabbath is *Terumah* ("Offering"), Exodus 25:1-27:19. On the mountaintop, facing the glory of God, awaiting the presentation of the stone tablets, Moses is commanded by God to build him a sanctuary—a dwelling, a Tabernacle—so that he may "dwell among" his people. This movable structure is to be God's home on earth before the building of the Temple by King Solomon. It is a tent of acacia wood frame and tapestry walls whose two rooms are separated by a screen. The lengthy and highly detailed instructions are, it would seem, an accompanying verbal explanation to a plan or a model that God showed to Moses.

Exodus 25:9   Exactly as I show you—the pattern of the Tabernacle and the pattern of its furnishings—so shall you make it.

Instructions are given for the construction of the Ark, the Holy of Holies, which will hold the stone tablets, and the "mercy seat," a kind of bench or large footstool that sits above it. These, along with a table, a lampstand, and an incense burner, will reside in the northern room of the tent. In the southern room will be located the altar for animal sacrifices and a water basin.

Every material is specified: gold, silver, bronze—in great quantity—fine linen and goat hair dyed blue, purple, and scarlet, acacia wood, incense, oils, and onyx stones. These, say God, are to be collected from the people's freewill offerings. At the heart of the reading are two ideas: that God has *chosen* to live among the Israelites and that the objects enshrined at the heart of the Sanctuary, within the Holy of Holies, are the tablets of the Law—words, not effigies.

The haftarah from 1 Kings (5:26–6:13) tells a parallel story: the building by King Solomon of a permanent Sanctuary, the Temple, four hundred and eighty years after the Children of Israel came out of Egypt. This vast undertaking took seven years and involved some 183,300 workers. God was, again, the supervising architect; Solomon was the contractor, Adoniram the chief engineer, and King Hiram of Tyre, with whom Solomon had friendly relations and had signed a treaty, the subcontractor for the quarry and sawmill work. We are told that the stones were finished at the quarry and that "no hammer or axe or any iron tool whatever was heard in the house while it [the Temple] was being built." This would indicate a kind of construction similar to that of the Pyramids. But regardless of this grandeur, it's still the words that count. God tells Solomon:

> As for this house which you are building, if you are obedi- *1 Kings 6:11*
> ent to My ordinances and conform to My precepts and
> loyally observe My commandments, then I will fulfill My
> promise to you, the promise I gave to your father, David,
> and I will dwell among the Israelites and never forsake My
> people Israel.

Shabbat Zakhor: The Sabbath of Remembrance

Shabbat Zakhor, the Sabbath of Remembrance, is among the most challenging days of the Jewish year. In our model year it is the second Sabbath of the month of Adar. Its Torah portion, Deuteronomy 25:17–19, must be read on the Sabbath before Purim because the villain of the story, Amalek, is said to be the ancestor of Purim's villain, Haman. The portion refers to an earlier event, recorded in Exodus 17:8–16, in which the newly freed Israelites were attacked by the Amalekites. They were the Israelite's first attackers, establishing them as *ur*-enemies. Though they are dispatched handily by the Israelites (Moses brings to the fight a magical power in the lifting of his arms), their evil reputation lives on. The passage in Deuteronomy explains what made the Amalekites' action so heinous: they attacked the sick and weak who were at the rear. Here it is, in its entirety:

Deuteronomy
25:17–19

Remember what Amalek did to you on your way out from Egypt, how he met you on the way when you were weary and faint and attacked you from the rear, where all your downtrodden were. He did not stand in awe of God.

So shall it be: When the Lord your God gives you rest from your enemies that surround you, in the land that the Lord your God is giving to you as an inheritance, you are to blot out the name of Amalek from under the heavens. You are not to forget!

Amalek. Woodcut
from the
Minhogimbukh,
Amsterdam, 1727.

The haftarah for Shabbat Zakhor, 1 Samuel 15:1–34, is the story of the Amalekites' bad end: Following God's instruction, Samuel anoints Saul as Israel's first king and tells him that it is God's commandment that he call up an army to wipe out the Amalekites—men, women, children, babes in arms, livestock, and all. Saul complies, though not entirely: the Amalekites are slain, but their king, Agag, is taken captive, and the livestock is taken by the army as spoils to be sacrificed. Samuel berates Saul:

1 Samuel 15:22–23

Does God desire offerings and sacrifices as much as He desires obedience? Obedience is better than sacrifice; to listen to Him is more important than the fat of rams. Defiance of Him is as sinful as witchcraft, arrogance is as

evil as idolatry. Because you have rejected the word of
God, God has rejected you as king.

Saul admits his sin; Agag is brought before Samuel and is
cut to pieces. In the Purim story, Haman is described as a
descendant of Agag. In Genesis 36:12 Amalek, the founder of
his tribe, is mentioned as the grandson of Esau. In the course
of centuries between the writing of Genesis and the later
prophets Obadiah and Malachi, Esau had gone from being   *See Obadiah 1:10,*
the big, bumbling twin brother of Jacob to the wicked and   *Malachi 1:2–3.*
bloodthirsty root of much evil.

Between the Amalek episode in Exodus and the one in
1 Samuel more than four hundred years passed. Could there
be no redemption for the Amalekites, no peace with them? Is
the fight with Amalek something much older, a proxy blood
feud between Jacob and Esau? We never really learn much
about the Amalekites, though they appear in the Bible several
times, always archetypal evildoers. In Psalm 83 they are mentioned among Israel's ten mortal enemies who surround it.
This makes for harrowing reading, with an all-too-familiar
ring:

> [Say the enemies of Israel] "Let them be a nation no longer,   *Psalm 83:4–8*
> Let Israel's name be remembered no more."
> With one mind they have agreed together,
>   to make a league against thee:
>   the families of Edom, the Ishmaelites,
>   Moabites, and Hagarenes,
>   Gebal, Ammon, and Amalek,
>   Philistia and the citizens of Tyre,
>   Asshur, too, their ally,
>   all of them lending aid to the descendant of Lot . . .
> Like fire raging across the forest,   *Psalm 83:14–16*
>   or flames that blaze across the hills,
>   hunt them down with Thy tempest,

and dismay them with Thy storm wind.
Heap the same upon their heads, O Lord,
until they confess the greatness of Thy name. . . .

Peace is possible. By the time of Solomon's reign, accords of coexistence had been reached with at least some of the enemies, as we learned in the previous week's haftarah about the building of the Temple and the participation of King Hiram of Tyre.

Zakhor is the imperative "remember!"—a word of many implications in Judaism. Six times in the Torah we are commanded by God to remember: the Exodus, the revelation of the Law at Mount Sinai, the evil of Amalek, the Israelites' struggle in the Wilderness, the punishment of Miriam, and the keeping of Sabbath. Three were enshrined in the holidays Passover, Shavuot, and Sukkot. The keeping of Sabbath is a principal regulator—arguably *the* principal regulator—of Jewish life. The memory of God's punishment of Miriam is usually interpreted as a cautionary tale. But what of the Amalekites—how do they rate such imperative remembrance, above, say, the *Akedah*, the binding of Isaac? Is Shabbat Zakhor simply "Enemies Day"?

The story of Miriam's punishment may be found on p. 172.

In the *Minhogimbukh*, the liturgy for Shabbat Zakhor contains one major addition, rarely recited today, a long hymn sung at *Yotzer* in the Shema, *Azkir selah zikhron maasim*, "I will always recall the memory of the events." It is, indeed, a hymn to the biblical enemies, but true to the commandment to obliterate them, their names are never mentioned.

On special Sabbaths, the order of readings begins with the scheduled weekly reading, followed by the special reading, then the haftarah. When there is a special haftarah, that is read in place of the scheduled one, though in a few synagogues they read both.

During these days are remembered and celebrated
A snake descended from venomous serpents,
His vileness we recall so that his memory may rot for
  angering.

The thorn that sprouted from thistles and brambles.
Which from generation to generation continuously
   stabbed Israel . . .
His action that stemmed from hatred over birthright . . .
The first evil nation to merit the commandment
   "Remember!". . .
It should be known that at the time of reckoning,
He will be repaid in the name of the Lord God of hosts.

It goes on to bring upon the memory of Esau every imaginable crime:

Remember the man who caused the death of the patriarch
   before his time; with murder, thievery, and adultery, he
   agitated him. . . .
Remember who raped a girl found in the field
Who spurned his birthright for a cup of bitterness . . . and
   reversed his circumcision.
Remember his perverted acts to sleep with men as if they
   were women.

And on it goes, this ode to infamy, to include the Midianites and Edomites and Babylonians and Haman. And, of course, in our heads it isn't just them. There is something cathartic about confronting one's enemies, rolled into one, in this way, once a year, that allows us to move on and to be thankful for our survival and success despite all the bitter attacks and terrible losses. After all, where are the Amalekites today?

In our model year, the portion *Tetzaveh* ("You command"), Exodus 27:20–30:10, is read on Shabbat Zakhor, before the *Zakhor* verses. It moves from the structure of the Tabernacle to the clothing, adornment, and investiture of its priesthood. It begins with God's instruction to Moses to have the people bring "the clear oil of olives" as fuel for the lamp that was to stand in front of the Holy of Holies. This is the origin of the

Ner tamid, the "eternal light" that burns in front of the ark of every synagogue, traditionally supported by people's contributions.

The description of the priestly garments and their ornaments to be worn by Aaron and his four sons is extraordinary in its detail. As with the Tabernacle design and furnishings in the previous portion, every piece, color, and material is determined in God's description. The ornaments of the breastplate and the turban are described as having the qualities of armor, though not in the usual sense of protection from swords and arrows, but rather as shields from misdeeds, evil, and sin. On the breastplates are the *urim* and *tumim*, objects whose exact nature and meaning has been debated by scholars for centuries. They are oracular tools—divine communication devices. On Aaron's turban was a pure golden plate, engraved with the words "Holiness for the Lord." The portion ends with the investiture ceremony.

The words urim *and* tumim *have been translated as "lights" and "perfections" and have become symbols of the most rarified divine knowledge. They are the Hebrew words on the seal of Yale University.*

PURIM

*The story of Purim is contained in the book of Esther, one of the Bible's five scrolls (*megilot*), along with the Song of Songs, Ruth, Lamentations, and Ecclesiastes. Esther alone is referred to as "the Megillah."*

Purim is the survival story of the assimilated, urban Jews at the Persian court, as told in the book of Esther. *Purim* means "lots"—as in lots drawn in games of chance—and in the story it is by lot that the time of the Jews is to be decided. Despite their contributions to government and society, the Jews of the ancient Persia, whose forebears came there as captives during the Babylonian Exile, occasionally suffered the wrath of their governors. In the Purim story they are threatened with extermination. The mighty arm of God, which often saves the day in Bible stories, is conspicuously absent from this action-adventure burlesque; in fact, God is never mentioned once in the entire scroll. It's guile that gets the job done here.

The story's villain, Haman, is the descendant of old enemies Amalek and Agag and, through biblical genealogy, to Esau, the twin brother of Jacob. As such, Purim completes what might be called the Bible's "villainy cycle" that is worked through in the month of Adar, as if to clear the psychological decks for the upcoming Passover celebration. This story, which begins with Jewish unease as the Persian court celebrates grandly, ends with a revenge fantasy and a great celebration by the Jews.

Purim from the 1722 Amsterdam Minhogimbukh shows Purim revelers in traditional European fools' costumes, complete with belled foolscaps.

The Purim celebration includes uniquely joyous aspects: merriment, drinking, costumes, and plays. It is a Jewish Feast of Fools, a day of escape when all the rules of court and church are turned upside down—the fool is made king, the child is made high priest, men dress as women, all with impunity. The book of Esther contains many elements of satire, a blueprint for the *Purimshpiln* (Purim plays), which are the oldest form of Jewish theater—the only form until the advent of the Yiddish theater in the nineteenth century.

In the nineteenth century, Purim balls organized by Jewish charities became the foremost social event of Jewish life in Europe and in America. To become a sponsor or to serve on an organizing committee of such an event became a statement of one's standing in good society.

THE PURIM NARRATIVE: King Ahasueros, the ruler of one hundred twenty-seven provinces from India to Ethiopia, makes a great feast for all his nobles. When the party is over,

Ahasueros is now identified as King Xerxes I, mid-fifth century B.C.E.

half a year later, he makes a shorter one for all the men of his court in the capital of Susa (Shushan). The king commands Queen Vashti to appear before the gathering. Busy with her own feast, which she's made for all the women of the court, she turns down his request. The king is furious, and, fearing he will be seen as weak, he orders that virgins be brought to him from all the realm so that he may choose a new queen. Mordecai, a Jew at court, puts forward his cousin and ward, Esther, telling her that she should keep her origins secret. Esther wins the king's favor, and she becomes the new queen.

Later, while Mordecai is standing at the palace gate waiting for news of his ward, he overhears a plot against Aḥasueros. He tells Esther, who in turn tells the king. After the plotters are hanged, the much-feared Haman is appointed prime minister. Mordecai refuses to bow to the cruel and imperious Haman—Jews will not bow down, lest their action be interpreted as idolatry. Haman becomes so incensed that he vows that on a day he will determine by the drawing of lots, all the Jews of the empire will be killed. Mordecai tells Esther that since she has the king's ear, only she can save her people. She asks the Jews to fast with her for three days so that she can prepare herself to seek the king's help.

The king, who knows nothing of Haman's plan for the Jews, orders that Mordecai be honored for exposing the plot against him, further roiling Haman. Esther, who knows that charm—and wine—are her most powerful weapons, makes a dinner for the king and Haman. The king is pleased and "merry with wine," he offers to her "whatever you request, up to half my kingdom." She tells the king of Haman's plans and begs that her people be spared. The king rescinds the decree and orders Haman and his ten sons to be hanged on the gallows that had been prepared for Mordecai. The Jews in Susa and the provinces band together and kill seventy-six thousand of their enemies. The king grants to Mordecai all that was Haman's and makes him prime minister. A great celebration ensues.

The Customs of Purim

THE FAST OF ESTHER: Purim begins on a note of apprehension with the Fast of Esther, a minor fast day observed the day before Purim, in commemoration of Esther's fast. The liturgy is the same as on other minor fasts, including the recitation of Seliḥot (penitential prayers) and the reading of the Torah portion for public fasts, Exodus 32:11-14; 34:1-10, which recalls how Moses assuaged God's anger after the Golden Calf episode and how the covenant was renewed. At the afternoon service, everyone is asked to contribute a half shekel—or whatever is deemed an appropriate equivalent—to support the state of Israel and also to give Purim money to the poor.

THE EVENING SERVICE: On the eve of Purim, the service begins as usual, but inserted into the Amidah, in the prayer of thanksgiving, is the prayer *Al hanisim*, also added to the Grace after Meals.

> For the miracles and for the salvation and for the mighty deeds and for the victories and for the battles, which You preformed for our forefathers in those days at this time.

Then the reader spreads out the Megillah, the Scroll of Esther, like a letter, so that it can be encompassed at one glance and recites the following three blessings:

ברוך אתה יהוה אלהינו מלך העולם,

אשר קדשנו במצותיו וצונו על מקרא מגילה.

Blessed are You, Lord our God, king of the universe, who sets us apart with His commandments and commands us to read this scroll.

Since the vanquishing of all the Jewish enemies in Persia took an extra day, the fifteenth of Adar is called Shushan Purim and is the day on which Purim is observed in all ancient walled cities.

Al hanisim is recited also at Ḥanukkah, in recognition of the miracles of the lights. Each version is particular to its holiday.

ברוך אתה יי אלהינו מלך העולם,
שעשה נסים לאבותינו בימים ההם בזמן הזה.

*Blessed are You, Lord our God, king of the universe, who per-
formed wonders for our ancestors at the time of this season.*

The third blessing is the familiar *Sheheheyanu:* "Blessed are
You, Lord our God, king of the universe, for sustaining us
and for enabling us to celebrate this festival."

Then the reader begins the reading of the scroll. Four
verses are read aloud by the congregation then repeated by
the reader:

> "Now there was in Susa, the capital, a Jew named
> Mordecai . . ." (2:5)
> "Mordecai left the presence of the king wearing royal gar-
> ments . . ." (8:15)
> "For the Jews it was a time of happiness and joy . . ."
> (8:16)
> "And all his acts of power and might . . . together with a
> full account of the greatness of Mordecai . . ." (10:2)

This custom was introduced because of the joyousness of
the verses, though there is another explanation: to keep rest-
less children attentive to the whole Megillah while they wait
to participate in reading these verses. The same is done with
the last verse, to make sure that they hear the blessing following the reading. The verses from 9:6 to 9:10, enumerating
the ten sons of Haman, are read in one breath because their
souls left their bodies at the same moment.

One of the most famous Purim customs is the blotting out
with noise (by use of a *purimgreger*) of every mention of
Haman's name (Yiddish: *homenklopfn*). This has its origins in
an ancient custom according to which the name of Haman
was written on a stone that was hit against another stone each
time Haman's name was mentioned in the Megillah, until the

name was wiped off the stone. As the saying goes, "May his name be wiped out," or, as it is in the scripture, "The name of the wicked shall rot." After the Megillah is read, it is rolled up, and into the next blessing is inserted the hymn *Asher heni*, "Who foiled the counsel of nations and overturned the designs of the cunning." Notable is its joyous verse *Shoshanat Yaakov*, "The rose that is Jacob was cheerful and glad."

Proverbs 1:7

MORNING SERVICE: The cantor's repetition of the Amidah has a very special feature on Purim, known by the anagram *krovetz*: *Kol rinah vishuah beoholei tzadikim*, "The sound of rejoicing and salvation is in the tents of the righteous." Though *krovetz* refers to any additional hymns recited during the repetition of the Amidah, on Purim it refers specifically to verses that are inserted before the ends of the benedictions, each one related to both the theme of the benediction and a related aspect of the Purim story. And so the first benedictions is said:

Today these are recited only in some devout communities.

> Blessed are You, Lord our God and God of our ancestors, God of Abraham, God of Isaac, and God of Jacob; God who is great, mighty and awesome; God the most high, who bestows kindnesses that are beneficent and creates everything, who recalls the kindnesses of the patriarchs and brings a redeemer to the children of their children, for His namesake, with love.

To which is added, on a similar, parental theme:

> The adoptive father [Mordecai] loved the orphan girl [Esther] who was worthy. The faith shown by Abraham at seventy-five was for her a protection. Then, long ago, David, who knew how to play music, did foresee that Mordecai, a lion of Judah, a descendant of the wolf Benjamin, would arise as a savior who would be worthy; and Mordecai was strengthened by a thousand shields.

One Torah scroll is taken out and three people are called up to read. The portion read is Exodus 17:8–17:16, the story of the encounter with Amalek, the subject of Shabbat Zakhor. After the recitation of half Kaddish and the return of the Torah to the ark, the Megillah is read, just as on the previous night. This is followed by blessings, hymns, and finally, the prayers *Ashrei, Uva letziyon,* Kaddish, and finally *Alenu.*

MEALS AND FESTIVITIES: The Purim festive meal is supposed to be eaten during the daytime, so some practice the custom of eating dairy foods on the late afternoon of Purim as a kind of half meal. Purim has several customary dishes,

including triangular pastries called "Haman's Ears" (*oznei haman*), which are best known by their Yiddish name, *homentashn* (Haman's pockets).

In addition to the half-shekel gift mentioned in connection with the Fast of Esther, two other types of gifts are to be given on Purim, both with a basis in Esther 9:22, in which Mordecai asks the people to keep the fourteenth and fifteenth of Adar as "days of feasting and joy, days for sending presents of food to one another and giving gifts of money to the poor." Since the words *mishloah manot* (Yiddish *shlakhmones*) are plural, so, too, must be the presents.

It is stated in the Talmud that "One is obligated to drink on Purim until one cannot tell the difference between [the hymns] 'Blessed Be Mordecai' and 'Cursed Be Haman.'" Since this instruction is learned all too readily, it has been the subject of much consternation and spin. The 1593 *Minhogimbukh* explains it thus:

Purim from the Minhogimbukh, Venice, 1601. The Purim revelers here are in the familiar Venetian Carnavale costumes of the commedia dell'arte.

Tractate Megillah 7b

It is taught that on Purim one should drink until one cannot tell the difference between "Cursed Be Haman" and "Blessed Be Mordecai." This actually means until one cannot tell the difference between the *numerical* value of the two, which happens to be the same: 502. Or, that one is allowed to drink modestly, until one cannot count the numerical value of the two. Another explanation is that there was a custom that one person said a rhyme with "cursed be Haman," then another said a rhyme with "blessed be Mordecai," and after drinking a little, they mixed up the order.

Drunkenness leads to several sins. Still, one should drink in order to be joyful. But one should remember that it was the Holy One, Blessed be He, who gave us a great miracle on this day, and we should therefore not neglect the Grace after Meals or the afternoon and evening prayers. While drinking wine, one should remember that wine was part of the miracle: Esther served wine to Haman and it was wine that was the undoing of Queen Vashti—as the verse says in the Megillah, "The king was merry with wine."

Esther 1:10

Shabbat Parah: The Sabbath of the Red Heifer

In the portion *Korah*, Moses's first cousin Korach led a failed revolt against Moses's authority in the Wilderness. The earth opened, and the rebels, who had been duly warned by Moses, were swallowed up, tents and all. Two hundred and fifty more who were not of the priestly caste came forward with incense for God and they were consumed by God's fire; their braziers were then beaten into a cover for the altar. Another fourteen thousand seven hundred were brought down by plague. The portion for this special Sabbath, *Parah* (Numbers 19:1–22), tells of God's instructions to Moses for the ritual cleansing of the Tabernacle in the aftermath of the revolt. God commands

Korah, Numbers 16:1–18:32, read here in Tamuz; see p. 173.

Moses that a red heifer (*parah adumah*) be sacrificed for this purpose, giving detailed instructions for its disposition. In the event a person had become ritually defiled by contact with a corpse, as did many Israelites in the aftermath of the revolt, they could be purified by the ashes from the sacrificed red heifer. Yet, it also says—quite bafflingly—that the persons who prepare the ashes are defiled by the act of doing so.

Shabbat Parah from the Minhogimbukh, Venice, 1593.

The mystery of the red heifer is considered one of the *hukim*, the "unexplainable" commandments. Nonetheless, it remained a topic of interest because it described in great detail a way to become pure in God's eyes. An entire tractate of the Mishnah, *Parah*, is dedicated to the ritual of the red heifer.

Exekiel 36:25–26, 31–32. The sprinkling of water is usually interpretd figuratively.

The haftarah, Ezekiel 36:16–38, was written at the end of the period of the Exile. What it describes is a transformation of faith and notions of purity that will occur even though the Temple will be rebuilt and the sacrifices resumed.

> And I will sprinkle clean water upon you and you shall be clean; from all your uncleannesses and all your idols will I cleanse you. A new heart also will I give, and a new spirit will I put within you; and I will take away the stony heart out of your flesh, and I will give you a heart of flesh.... Then shall you remember your evil ways, and your doings that were not good; and ye shall loathe yourselves in your own sight for your iniquities and your abominations. Not for your own sake do I do this, saith the Lord God, be it known unto you; be ashamed and confounded for your ways, O house of Israel.

And so from this most mysterious of rituals first shown in the Wilderness we come to an emphasis on introspection and conscience as the regulator of purity and obedience. When the sacrifices ended with the destruction of the Second Temple in 70 C.E., the Children of Israel were thus prepared for dedication to prayer.

Among a few small Jewish sects, as well as in the Christian circles that dedicate themselves to the coming of the "end time," the occasional birth of a red heifer in Israel has been seen by some as a sign that a messiah is at hand, the Temple will be rebuilt, and the sacrifices will be resumed—or that the end time is upon us, depending on one's viewpoint. In 1997, the birth of a red heifer in Israel became an international news event, but it soon disintegrated over arguments as to the permissible number of white hairs. (The Mishnah says two white hairs are permissible.)

It is easy to dismiss the ritual of Shabbat Parah as a relic of antiquity and to embrace only the more modern words of Ezekiel. But notions of ritual purity and impurity are easily extended to ethnic and political purity and impurity. The number of people who die each year for and from the abuse of these ideas is hard to ignore. In a crowded world, the dangers of one group's idea of purity abrading another's have greatly increased.

The regular portion of the week, read before *Parah*, is *Ki tisa* ("When you take a census"), Exodus 30:11–34:35. It covers vast ground, much of it echoing throughout the Jewish year. The first six verses are the same as those read last month on Shabbat Shekalim, in which God orders Moses to take a head count of the Children of Israel and collect from each a half shekel for the construction of the Tabernacle. Afterward,

Torah portion Ki tisa, *Exodus 30:11–34:35*

For Shabbat Shekalim, see p. 342.

God continues the description of the Tabernacle implements: the bronze basin in which the priests are to wash their hands and feet, the anointing oil, and the incense and incense burner. The principal craftsmen who are to make all these things are named by God, chief among them Bezalel, whom God has endowed with "practical wisdom, discernment, and knowledge in all kinds of workmanship." However, the final emphasis here is on the Sabbath, the "covenant for the ages; between Me and the Children of Israel a sign it is, for the ages, for in six days the Lord made the heavens and the earth, but on the seventh day He ceased and paused for breath."

The best-known art college in modern Israel is the appropriately named Bezalel School of Art.

And then begins what may well be the key story of the God-Israel relationship: the giving of the tablets and the episode of the Golden Calf. On one hand, there is a very demanding, jealous, but ultimately compassionate God; on the other, the stubborn, untrusting, and sometimes anxious Children of Israel. Between them is Moses—servant, teacher, prophet, mediator—undyingly loyal to both.

The story hardly needs repeating, but for the sake of completeness it is, briefly, this: At the end of his instruction on Mount Sinai, God gives to Moses "two tablets of testimony," written on stone by his own finger. By this time, Moses had been away from the people for nearly forty days and some of the people felt he was shamefully late while others believed he was dead. The people became restive and wanted a god with palpable presence. In an effort to keep them entertained, Aaron told them to bring to him all their gold earrings. From this gold he produced a calf and the people proclaimed, "This is your God, O Israel, who brought you up from the land of Egypt." God tells Moses to go down from the mountain because the people have made ruin. He has decided to destroy them all, leaving only Moses to make "into a great nation." But Moses soothes God's anger, saying, in effect, "Don't You think You'll look silly to the Egyptians and all the others if You destroy the Children of Israel after having brought them so far?"

Moses goes down to the people, sees what they've done, and smashes the tablets before them in anger. He burns the calf into powder, casts it into the water, and makes the people drink it. He then stands at the gate of the camp, saying that all who are with him should come to his side; the others, some three thousand men, he slays. God tells Moses to go on and take the Children of Israel to the Promised Land but that He will not stay in their midst because he would only get angry and destroy them all. Moses moves the Tabernacle outside the camp, to meet there with God. It is there that Moses pleads with God to know him better, to know his nature. Again Moses is up on Mount Sinai, where God reveals to him his nature, the so-called Thirteen Attributes. God repeats certain commandments: against idolatry, to remember the Sabbath and the festivals. The stone tablets are replaced, and Moses returns to the people with the new covenant, his face forevermore glowing from his encounter with God.

For more about the Thirteen Attributes, see p. 34 and p. 208.

The haftarah, 1 Kings 18:1–39, provides interesting counterpoint to the Golden Calf and red heifer stories. It takes place during the secession of Jeroboam, the breakaway Northern Kingdom of Israel and how it suffered continuing problems with the worshipers of the idol Baal who lived to their north. To many in Israel, the Baalist culture proved hard to resist, but the prophet Elijah found a way to discredit it. He told the four hundred fifty prophets of Baal to choose a bull and prepare it for sacrifice; he would do the same. Each would ask their god to set their sacrifice aflame. The prophets of Baal chanted and hollered and danced about, but nothing

The week's haftarah is 1 Kings 18:1–39.

happens. Elijah told them to take their time, lest their god was otherwise engaged or on a journey or busy with a conversation. But still nothing happened. Elijah poured great amounts of water on his sacrifice, making it all the more unlikely to burn, and then prayed to God to accept his sacrifice and burn it. It was set ablaze immediately, and the people bowed down, proclaiming God the one true God.

Shabbat Haḥodesh: The Sabbath of the Month

Shabbat Haḥodesh, which falls on either Rosh Ḥodesh Nisan or the Sabbath before, announces the coming of the month of Nisan and, with it, the observance of Passover. The portion of Shabbat Haḥodesh is Exodus 12:1-20, in which God interweaves his instructions for the commemoration of Passover with his decription of the Passover itself.

The custom of Kidush levanah, the sanctification of the new moon, is depicted in this woodcut from the Minhogimbukh, Amsterdam, 1727. This is the same image used to depict Rosh Ḥodesh.

In the *Minhogimbukh*, a special hymn, little known today, is added at *Yotzer*, before the Shema. It is *Atiat et dodim kegaah*, "When the coming of the season of God's love arrived," and tells how God took the Israelites out from Egypt one hundred ninety years earlier than the four hundred years that God had told Abraham. It tells also of Israelites' awakening and the events of the month to come, both historical and celebratory.

In our model year, the portions *Vayakhel* and *Pekudei*, Exodus 35:1-38:20 and 38:21-40:38, are combined in this weekly portion, which is quite fitting since they concern a single subject: the building of the Tabernacle and the making of its appointments. The story picks up right after the Golden

Calf incident—as if it had never taken place. First is Moses's description of the people's contribution of materials and labor; next the design specifications and the making of the various components by master craftsmen led by Bezalel. God is here the architect and the interior designer, Moses his project supervisor. God takes up residence within and around it. Now the Israelites are ready to continue their journey to the Promised Land.

Combined Torah portions Vayakhel *and* Pekudei, *Exodus 30:11– 34:35 and 38:21–40:38.*

Ezekiel is again the source of the haftarah, this time verses 45:16–46:18. They concern the specific types of offerings and sacrifices involving animals: the burnt offering (*olah*), the peace offering (*shalem*), the sin offering (*hatat*), the guilt offering (*asham*), and various types of grain offerings (called *minhah*, like the afternoon service). In Temple times these were relevant to the Passover pilgrimage.

The haftarah is Ezekiel 45:16–46:18.

In the musaf service, another special hymn is added to the cantor's repetition of the Amidah: *Rishon imatzta*, "The first month you established for salvations." Its theme is also awakening, this time quoting from Isaiah 41, which speaks of the first inklings of redemption after the Babylonian Exile.

Wedding

The Minhogimbukh *ends with brief chapters on the life cycle events: wedding, circumcision, Pidyon haben (the "redemption of the firstborn"), and death. These are especially perfunctory overviews, nearly devoid of the talmudic stories or occasional stern warnings that charm the reader in the earlier chapters. Each of these subjects was once rife with local custom and superstition, and many of the customs mentioned in the 1593* Minhogimbukh *are no longer practiced.*

Woodcut from the Minhogimbukh, Amsterdam, 1722.

ARRIAGE is part of God's plan. In Genesis, husband and wife are to "become one flesh." Marriage is the metaphor for expressing the oneness of God and Israel, Sabbath and the Jewish people, the people and the land—they are described as *beulah*, "maritally consummated." Though the ceremonies that one associates with Jewish weddings are not described in the Torah, marriage's nature as a contractual obligation is unequivocal from the beginning. The Torah offers practical considerations, too, such as this one regarding newlyweds in Deuteronomy 24:5:

Genesis 2:24

Isaiah 62:4

> When a man takes a new wife, he is not to go out to the armed forces. . . . let him maintain his house for one year, and let him give joy to his wife whom he has taken.

According to the *Zohar*, the central work of Kabbalah, there are two parts of a soul—one male, one female. When the soul descends from heaven it splits and enters two different bodies; if they prove worthy, they will be reunited in marriage. Needless to say, by the time the *Zohar* was written, polygamy had virtually disappeared from Jewish life.

Though most of the Bible's first marriages were monogamous, there is, early on, in Genesis 4:19, a reference to the two wives of Lamech, a descendant of Cain. The stories of Abraham and Jacob are much occupied with multiple wives and concubines—and the painful tensions that arise through matters of jealousy and inheritance. When, after the birth of Isaac, Sarah demands that Hagar and her son, Ishmael, be sent away, God tells Abraham to do as she says. It's only through God's promise to make Ishmael a great nation that there is equity in the story. In Deuteronomy 17:17 polygamy is warned against, if not outlawed entirely: "And he is not to multiply wives for himself, that his heart not be turned aside." By the era of the judges (in the books of Joshua, Judges, Samuel), polygamy had become rare and eventually was associated only with kings. Nevertheless, it died out slowly in those places where the majority culture permitted the practice.

The concern in Deuteronomy 17 is less against polygamy than it is against foreign wives and the danger of idolatry.

Concepts and Artifacts of Betrothal and Marriage

SHIDUKHIN: A process is described in Talmud tractate *Kiddushin* 9b called *shidukhin*, an Aramaic word meaning "tranquility," which refers here to the negotiation of dowries between the parents. Since the Jewish legal marrying age was thirteen years for males and twelve and a half years for females, the *shidukhin* was conducted by the parents. It proceeds, "How much are you giving your son?" "How much are

The word Shiddukh is used in Yiddish to mean "a match."

you giving your daughter?" The terms were written in an agreement. The sum pledged was called a *nedunya*, the Aramaic word for dowry.

Among Ashkenazic Jews since the Middle Ages, and still today in traditional circles, a prenuptial agreement is made. First, a verbal agreement—a *vort*, a "word"—is reached by the parents. This is confirmed in a ceremony called a *kinyan* ("acquisition"), which usually takes place around a meal table. The confirming ritual is the taking of a handkerchief, offered by one party to the other. The basis for this is in the story of Ruth (4:7–8), in which Boaz removes his sandal as a pledge to acquire the property of Elimelech and take Ruth as his wife. The second part of the prenuptial agreement is a written document called a *tenayim* ("terms"), which states the financial terms as well as the time and place of the nuptials. The ceremony ends with the two mothers breaking a dish, saying, "Just as the broken shards cannot be repaired, so it is preferable to proceed with the nuptials and dissolve them with divorce than to break this agreement."

See also the description of ḥalitzah, the ceremony of levirate marriage, p. 168.

Though an agreement has been reached between the parents, the couple is not yet betrothed.

EARLY WEDDINGS—KIDDUSHIN/ERUSIN/NISUIN: Betrothal is called *erusin*, and there is a commandment concerning it in Deuteronomy:

> And who is the man that has betrothed a woman and has not yet taken her in marriage? Let him go and return to his house, lest he die in the war and another man take her.

Deuteronomy 20:7

From this it is understood that betrothal is a formal state, though with lower standing than marriage, in which cohabitation is not condoned. The Talmud codified the ceremony, calling it *kiddushin* ("sanctification"), through which the

Talmud Kiddushin 2b

*Forbidden mar-
riages are detailed
in Leviticus 18 and
20 (addressed to
men) and include a
man's mother, step-
mother, sister,
granddaughter,
aunt, daughter-in-
law, sister-in-law,
stepdaughter, and
step-grand-
daughter, and
wife's sister during
the wife's lifetime.
Many more restric-
tions are described
in the Bible, oral
law, and in later
legal codes.*

woman becomes forbidden to all men but her husband-to-be—after the wedding, that is. Before about the fourteenth century this was observed as a sanctification ceremony prior to the wedding, but today it is the first part of a single, two-part ceremony. Kiddush is made over wine and the following blessing is recited:

> Blessed are You, Lord our God, king of the universe, who has hallowed us by His commandments and has commanded us concerning forbidden marriages; who has forbidden unto us those who are betrothed, but has sanctioned unto us such as are wedded unto us by the rite of the nuptial canopy and the sacred covenant of wedlock. . . .

Next a plain gold ring is placed on the bride's finger as a sign of her status, with the declaration, "Behold, you are consecrated unto me with this ring according to the law of Moses and of Israel." By tradition, the bride continued to live in her father's house after the *kiddushin*, awaiting the next step in the marriage processs.

The last stage, after which the bride moves into the groom's home, is called *nisuin*, "marriage," which comes from the verb *nasa*, "to carry." It has three key elements: the reading of the ketubah (marriage contract), the recitation of the Seven Blessings (called *Sheva berakhot* or *Birkat nisuin*), and the presence of two witnesses. The ceremony takes place under a huppah, the wedding canopy. The Seven Blessings, still the center of the marriage liturgy, are:

1. Blessed are You, Lord our God, king of the universe, creator of the fruit of the vine.
2. Blessed are You, Lord our God, king of the universe, who created all things for His glory.
3. Blessed are You, Lord our God, king of the universe, shaper of man.
4. Blessed are You, Lord our God, king of the universe, who

shaped man in His own image, patterned in His likeness,
and enabled them to perpetuate life. Blessed are You,
Lord, shaper of man.

5. May the one who is barren exult in gladness as her children gather to her. Blessed are You, Lord, who bring
   happiness to Zion with her children.

   The "one who is barren" is a reference to Jerusalem.

6. Grant perfect joy to these loving companions, as You did
   your creations in the Garden of Eden. Blessed are You,
   Lord, who bring gladness to the bridegroom and the
   bride.

7. Blessed are You, Lord our God, king of the universe, creator of joy and gladness, groom and bride, mirth, song,
   pleasure, rejoicing, love, harmony, peace, and compan-
   ionship. Lord our God, may there ever be heard in the
   cities of Judah and in the streets of Jerusalem voices of
   joy and gladness, voices of bride and groom, the jubilant
   voices of the wedded from their bridal chambers, the
   voices of young people feasting and singing. Blessed are
   You, Lord, who causes the groom to rejoice with his bride.

KETUBAH: The marriage contract that is read prior to the
nisuin ceremony was first codified in Talmud tractate *Ketubot*
(plural of ketubah) and later by Maimonides in the twelfth
century, and in the works of many other legal authorities. Its
biblical basis is in Exodus 21:9-11, and though those verses
concern serfdom and concubinage, they also refer to a general "just rights for women." The language of the ketubah is
Aramaic—and is still, today. Much of the content is similar to
the *tenayim*, mentioned above in connection with *shidukhin*,
including the value in money and goods of the dowry. Also
described is the husband's financial obligation to his wife.
The ketubah must be signed by two witnesses, neither of
whom may be related to the bride or groom. Though not
legally necessary, it is the custom for both groom and bride
to sign it, too. Beyond the obligatory passages, there were and

In 1953 the Conser-
vative movement's
Rabbinical Assem-
bly decreed that all
officially sanc-
tioned ketubot
would contain a
clause about
divorce, the terms
of which compelled
the parties to abide
by the ruling of a
Beth Din (rabbini-
cal court) in the
event of a dispute.
The measure was
intended to protect
wives from stub-
born husbands.
The legality of the
clause was later
upheld by the New
York State Supe-
rior Court.

are many variations, both in additional language and style of presentation. Ketubot have always been among the most visually rich artifacts of Jewish life. English language ketubot were once popular in the Conservative movement; the Reform movement for a time had preferred simple certificates of marriage. But since the 1960s the original forms have been revived as prized objects of handicraft. Bilingual ketubot are common today.

ḤUPPAH: The ḥuppah, the bridal canopy, is one of the most distinct rituals of a Jewish wedding. It is made from cloth, often highly decorated, usually held up by four posts, which are said to represent four virtues. Traditionally, it was the tallit that served as a ḥuppah and that is often the case still. The word ḥuppah originally meant a domicile, the place where conjugal acts were performed. The first textual reference to the ḥuppah in regard to weddings is in the prophet Joel (2:16): "Let the bridegroom go forth from his chamber and the bride out of her pavillion."

Modern Weddings

Centuries before the 1593 *Minhogimbukh*, the betrothal (*erusin*) and marriage (*nisuin*) ceremonies were combined in both Ashkenazic and Sephardic rites. The customs of *shidukhin* and *tenayim* are still observed in strict traditionalist communities, sometimes done right before the ceremony, though for most in America they have been subsumed into the secular custom of the engagement party, which in Jewish families often includes a blessing said by a family elder or sometimes by a rabbi.

The pattern of Orthodox weddings is fairly uniform, and that is what is presented here. Weddings may be held anywhere, though the preference (if not the majority practice) is to hold them outdoors, in reference to Deuteronomy 1:10-11, "like the stars in the heavens . . . may He add to you a thousand times." According to Jewish law, no clergy are required to perform the ceremony, though since the Middle Ages it has been the norm for a rabbi to officiate.

SABBATH BEFORE THE WEDDING: In the Ashkenazic tradition, the groom is called up to the Torah (Yiddish *oyfrufn*) on the Sabbath before the wedding (Yiddish *brayleft*). Upon completion of the Torah blessings, he is showered with candy by the congregation, to wish him a sweet life, and a special *Mi sheberakh* is said. In Sephardic tradition, the groom (*hatan*) is called to Torah on the Sabbath following the wedding, known as *Shabbat hatan*.

EVE OF THE WEDDING—THE MIKVEH: The bride (*kalah*) immerses herself in the mikveh, the ritual bath, usually on the eve of the wedding. In a few modern egalitarian communities, men also go to the mikveh.

EVE OF THE WEDDING: Local customs prevail. One such example is the Yemenite *hinah*, in which the bride's hands are painted with henna by her friends.

DAY OF THE WEDDING: The *Minhogimbukh* speaks of the couple walking hand in hand in a public place on the morning of the wedding. The onlookers throw grain, saying, "be fruitful and multipy." This is not practiced today, at least not widely. It is the custom for the couple to fast on the day of their wedding and to not see each other. If the wedding takes place before evening, the bridegroom attends the afternoon synagogue service, at which he says the confessional prayers for Yom Kippur, the Viduy with *Ashamnu* and *Al het*.

There are various days and periods of time when marriages may not take place. These are Sabbath and all festival days including ḥol hamoed; the Omer period from Passover to Shavuot, except Rosh Ḥodesh, Lag b'Omer, and 3-5 Sivan; the Three Weeks period preceding Tishah b'Av; and during the Ten Days of Repentance from Rosh Hashanah to Yom Kippur.

The fast is considered a Yom Kippur katan—see p. 93.

See pp. 263 and 209 for the confessional prayers.

BEFORE THE CEREMONY: In some Jewish cultures, especially those in Arab countries, the dressing of the bride is an elaborate ritual fully manifest in the costume. In Ashkenazic weddings, the male guests gather in a room with the groom; the female guests gather with the bride, who sits on a throne. Libations are served in the groom's room, on what in Yiddish is called the *khasnstish*, the "groom's table." The groom or his representative meets the bride and covers her face with a veil.

The meeting of Rebecca and Isaac is recounted in Genesis 24:65. It is described at greater length on p. 303.

This is in memory of Rebecca, who veiled herself when she first saw Isaac, her betrothed. In some communities, especially among Ḥasidim, it is customary to dance a *Mitsvatants* before the wedding, which the men dance with the groom and the women dance with the bride.

The groom dresses in a *kitl*, the shroud of a dead person that one wears also on the High Holidays. This is to signify readiness, that the groom has prayed to be forgiven his sins.

THE CEREMONY: The two ceremonies of betrothal and wedding that have been joined together by custom for nearly a thousand years are still quite distinct; "they show their seam," as the writer Anita Diamant puts it. Though each begins with kiddush over wine, the first ceremony concentrates on the legalities and contractual obligations, whereas the second is elevated into divine realm.

In some groups the leaders of the procession carry candles.

The bride and groom are escorted by their parents to the ḥuppah. It is the custom of some communities for the bride to circle the groom, based on a biblical passage, Jeremiah 31:21, which speaks of the bliss of the Messianic Age: "The woman will go around her husband." It is the usual practice, though only by custom, for the *mesader kiddushin*, the officiator of the ceremony, usually a rabbi, to speak words of greeting to those in attendance and make an invocation. The betrothal ceremony (*erusin*) begins with the sanctification of kiddush over wine. Holding the cup, the rabbi recites the betrothal blessing, which still contains a heavy warning against illict sexual relations:

> Blessed are You, Lord our God, king of the universe, who has made us holy through His commandments and has commanded us concerning sexual propriety, forbidding to us those who are merely betrothed, but permitting to us those to whom we are married through huppah and *kiddushin*. Blessed are You, Lord our God, who makes holy His people Israel through huppah and *kiddushin*.

Many variants have appeared in the more liberal precincts. After the blessing, the glass is given to the groom to drink from, then to the bride. In some congregations, the rabbi drinks first; in others, the wine is passed around among family and friends after the groom and bride drink—a kind of clan consecration. The groom gives the wedding ring to the rabbi, who shows it to witnesses so that they can testify that it has worth. The groom then recites the declaration of the ring, as described above, and places the ring on the bride's right index finger. In liberal congregations, rings are usually exchanged and the bride repeats the declaration. Orthodox legal experts say that to do so negates the idea of *kinyan*—"acquisition"—and makes it more an exchange. Thus ends the betrothal ceremony. As an interlude between the two ceremonies, the ketubah is read aloud, after which the rabbi hands it to the groom, who in turn gives it to the bride.

Ring declaration, see p. 370.

It is forbidden to use a ring with a stone for the purpose of a wedding ring. This is to ensure its genuineness.

In the *nisuin*, the wedding ceremony, there are only two statutory parts: the recital of the *Sheva berakhot*, the Seven Blessings, and *yihud*, a brief period of seclusion for the couple immediately after the ceremony, originally intended as a time to consummate the marriage, today just a symbol.

Woodcut from the Minhogimbukh, Venice, 1601.

The Minhogim-bukh *mentions the custom of the rubbing of ashes on the forehead of the bridgegroom as a remembrance of the destruction of the Temple. This is still practiced in most traditional congregations, observed just before the breaking of the glass.*

See p. 45 for the Grace after Meals.

A second glass of wine is held up by the rabbi as the Seven Blessings are recited. (The texts can be found in their entirety on pages 370–371.)

After the Seven Blessings, the glass is given to the groom and the bride to drink from. At this moment in the ceremony, there may be a sermon from the rabbi, including the civil custom of pronouncing marital status, though these practices vary. The event concludes with the best-known of all Jewish marriage customs, the breaking of the glass by the groom. The custom has no standing in Jewish law, though it is quite old, possibly from talmudic times. German synagogues often had special decorated stones inset into their courtyard walls against which the glasses were thrown. It remains a grand gesture, a powerful symbol of that which cannot be undone. There are many other explanations for the custom, though none that speak more truly to the heart.

As the guests and attendants assemble for the celebration and festive meal, the bride and groom adjourn to a private room for the observance of *yihud.*

The great celebration that follows is filled with traditions and customs of food and dance, most of them tied to local and historical traditions. Since these do not touch upon the realm of religious observance, per se, they are outside the scope of the customs book literature. However, the wedding meal is conisdered a *seudah,* a festive meal, and therefore one's participation is obligatory. The Seven Blessings are inserted into the Grace after Meals.

Circumcision

THE COVENANT God first makes with Abraham in Genesis 15:18-21 is a land grant without mention of reciprocation: "I give this land to your seed." Abraham believes God, but the gift seems moot, since he is over eighty and his wife, Sarah, is over seventy, and they are without an heir. When Abraham is eighty-six, a son is born to him, Ishmael, by Sarah's Egyptian handmaid, Hagar. Thirteen years later he is visited again by God, who reiterates his offer of the land, but now establishes a reciprocal covenant:

Woodcut from the Minhogimbukh, Venice, 1593.

In these verses Abraham is still called Abram.

> This is My covenant which you are to keep, between Me and you and your seed after you: every male among you shall be circumcised. You shall circumcise the flesh of the foreskin, so that it may serve as a sign of the covenant between Me and you. At eight days old, every male among you shall be circumcised, throughout your generations, whether house-born or bought with money from any foreigner who is not your seed. . . . But a foreskinned male . . . shall be cut off from his kinspeople—he has violated My covenant.

Genesis 17:10-14

Following this, God tells Abraham that Isaac will be born to Sarah. Straightaway, Abraham circumcises everyone in his household and has himself circumcised.

*In Yiddish the
ceremony is called,
simply, a bris,
emphasizing its
covenantal aspect.*
The ceremony is a called Brit milah, "the Covenant of Circumcision," and it is a commandment to perform it on the
eighth day after a boy's birth, even if that day is a Sabbath or
holiday. Today it is usually the case that birth times are
recorded precisely, but before time was counted universally,
the calculation was made this way:

*From the 1593
Minhogimbukh.*

If the child is born on Friday after Sabbath has begun, but
before the stars appear in the sky, he should be circumcised
on the following Friday. If he is born on Saturday in the
evening after sunset, but also before the stars appear in the
sky when it is not obvious whether night has fallen, he
should be circumcised on Sunday. The same principle is followed on other weekdays. However, if the child is born on
Thursday evening, also when it is not obvious whether night
has fallen, but Friday, the eighth day after his birth, is a holiday, then the child is circumcised on Sunday. The reason
for this is that circumcision is permitted on the Sabbath and
on a holiday only if it is definitely the eighth day.

In the morning service at the synagogue, when a circumcision will be celebrated by the family of a congregant,
Taḥanun, the prayers of supplication, are omitted. However,
Lamenatzeaḥ, Psalm 20, is recited since it contains the verse
"May God answer you on the day of distress; may you be
made invulnerable by the name of the God of Israel," in
recognition of the baby's distress during the circumcision.
When the child is brought into the synagogue, everyone proclaims *Barukh haba*, "Blessed be he that comes in the name of
the Lord, we bless you out of the house of the Lord" (Psalm
118:26). The Brit milah ceremony traditionally takes places at
the conclusion of the morning services, before *Alenu*, when
the boy's father is still wearing his tefillin and tallit and when
it is easier to raise a minyan.

The ceremony, as it is known today, was influenced greatly

by Kabbalah and is, in many explanations, filled with references to gematria, mystic numerical calculations based on the letters of the relevant Torah verses and blessings. For example, the letters for *haba* equal eight, relating it to the eight days from birth to circumcision. In Sephardic communities, the night before a circumcision is called *Brit Yitzhak* (Covenant of Isaac), on which the family and congregation read from the *Zohar*.

The Brit milah may be performed at a synagogue or at home; the venue is not determined by law. In the Torah, Abraham circumcises Isaac himself, and so anyone who does it other than the father—which is usually the case—is, by law, the father's proxy who must be given formal permission. The person in the community who fills this role is called a mohel, a ritual circumciser who is highly trained in the procedure. The other key players are the parents, the godfather and godmother (called *kvater* and *kvaterin*), and the sandek, the person who holds the baby during the ceremony.

The person is called a moyl in Yiddish.

By Jewish law only the father and the sandek are essential.

It is customary to place two chairs in the room where the circumcision is performed, one of which is proclaimed aloud to be the Chair of Elijah. In 1 Kings 19:10, Elijah stayed in a cave until God asked him what he was doing. Elijah answered, "I have been very zealous for the Lord God of Hosts, because the Israelites have sinned against Your covenant." So God told him, "Because you committed yourself so much for this cause, you are commanded to be present each time the Jews perform a circumcision, to be a witness." The ceremony has three parts: the *milah* (circumcision), the *keriat hashem* (naming), and the *seudah* (ritual meal).

There are some variants of custom in different rites and locales, but the structure remains the same. The following is the order in the Ashkenazic community:

THE CIRCUMCISION: When the mohel is ready, the god-mother (*kvaterin*) takes the child from his mother and hands him to the godfather (*kvater*), who brings the child into the room where the circumcision will be performed and places him on the chair, which the mohel declares to be the Chair of Elijah. Someone (often the father) takes the baby from the chair and puts him in the lap of the sandek, who sits in the adjacent chair. It is on the sandek's lap that the circumcision will be done.

The mohel asks the father if he may serve as the father's proxy for this commandment. As the procedure begins, the mohel uses a probe to lift the *periah*, the underlying mem-brane, into the *orlah*, the foreskin. He then places a shield (*magen*)at the correct place. The *periah* and *orlah* are cut with one sweep along the shield. The knife is called an *izmel*, which is sharpened on both sides. In the last step, blood is drawn (*metzitzah*) from the head of the penis. An anesthetic and dressing are applied. The procedure takes less than a minute. The removed foreskin is buried in earth, often a waiting pot.

The parents recite the blessing "Blessed are You . . . who has sanctified us by His commandments and commanded us to enter our sons into the covenant of Abraham, our father." The mohel and the community respond, ". . . even as this child has entered into the covenant, so may he enter into a life of Torah, the ḥuppah, and good deeds."

The child is then held by the mohel, sandek, or other hon-ored guest. With cup in hand, the mohel makes the blessing over wine, giving a drop to the child. A second blessing prais-ing God, "who established a covenant with His people, Israel," is also said.

THE NAMING: The mohel recites a prayer for the welfare of

the child, "just as he has entered the covenant, so may he enter into the Torah, the ḥuppah, and good deeds," which includes a formal announcement of the child's Hebrew name. This is the essence of the naming ceremony, which concludes with another drop of wine given to the child. Naming holds great significance, especially in this context, since it was upon Abraham's fulfillment of the covenant that God changed his name, from Abram to Abraham and his wife's name from Sarai to Sarah. Then follows the festive meal.

A naming ceremony for girls is not dictated by Jewish law, but has been practiced with great joy and in various forms for centuries. A girl is named in the synagogue on a day when the Torah is read—Monday, Thursday, or Sabbath—so that a parent may go up to the Torah. There is no set time but it is generally done as soon as possible. A new custom called Simḥat bat, "joy of a daughter," or Brit habat, "covenant of the daughter," is widely practiced today in all denominations. It is a celebration akin to the ritual meal that follows a circumcision.

The *Minhogimbukh* refers to circumcision by an old Yiddish word, *yidishn*, "to make [him] a Jew," which is rooted in Jewish folk belief that one could not be a Jew without circumcision. Though the word is long gone from the vocabulary, the belief in *yidishn* persists in an interesting way, especially among those whose Jewish identity is marginal and who wonder why they should subject their child to pain and risk if they themselves are not observant. And yet most do, even if they do so in the hospital, without ceremony.

It should be mentioned, too, that a baby's health is the highest priority in Jewish law, taking precedence over the timing of the Brit milah. There are also exemptions to circumcision in some rare circumstances.

Pidyon haben: The Redemption of the Firstborn Son

A father sits across the table from a kohen, a member of the

priestly class, and places five silver coins on the table. He tells the kohen that neither he nor his wife is of the priestly caste and that his wife gave birth thirty-one days ago to her firstborn, a son, and he is there to hand over the boy to the kohen and his cohort. Without a trace of surprise, the kohen asks the man if he would wish to redeem his son. The man says yes, and they agree that the price of redemption will be the coins on the table. Blessings are said by both men, who go their respective ways. This is a ritual called Pidyon haben, "redemption of the firstborn son," a modern playing out of a biblical commandment, making good on the terms that God set when he freed our ancestors in Egypt:

> Sanctify unto Me every firstborn, breacher of every womb among the Children of Israel, of man or of beast—it is Mine. . . . And every firstborn of men, among your sons, you are to redeem. It shall be when your child asks someday, "What does this mean?" You are to say to him: "By strengh of hand the Lord brought us out of Egypt, out of a house of serfs."

And so, in return for the Tenth Plague in which all the male firstborn of Egypt were slain and Pharaoh relented, the male firstborn were to be given over to the priests or redeemed, the price for which was set at five shekels in Numbers 18:16.

It remains as a ritual and as a mitzvah. In earlier times, when a firstborn son had no father, an amulet was hung on his neck saying that he had not not been redeemed. He was to redeem himself when he became an adult.

Bar and Bat Mitzvah

THE WELL-KNOWN CUSTOM of bar mitzvah, the Jewish coming-of-age ceremony, with its synagogue ritual and great feast, is not mentioned in the 1593 *Minhogim-bukh*. Though Jews of nearly every rite and denomination celebrate bar mitzvah today, its history is, in fact, quite sketchy.

This is not to say that bar mitzvah is without precedent before the modern era, but as a custom without biblical basis or legal manadate, it had lower standing. In the published record, it becomes something recognizable to us as recently as the second half of the sixteenth century, and only in the mid-nineteenth century does bar mitzvah become the ritual we know today. Certain religious influences contributed to bar mitzvah's development in nineteenth-century western Europe, but perhaps its greatest encouragement came from the advent of a middle-class culture that had adopted as one of its cornerstone values a new sociological concept of children and childhood. It's little wonder that the modern bar mitzvah first took shape in western Europe after Emancipa-

The old Minho-gimbikher *did not contain chapters on bar or bat mitzvah. The illustration above is a detail from a copperplate engraving from a 1748 German book by J. C. G. Boden-schatz about synagogue practices.*

The author acknowledges the contribution of Szonja Ráhel Komoróczy, who assisted in many aspects of this book, but especially with the compilation of background information for this new chapter.

tion at the beginning of the nineteenth century, when Jewish families could express their accomplishment and social standing outside the circle of the immediate family. The railroad, the steamship, and the telegraph all contributed, too, making plausible celebrations that gathered together friends and family from afar.

The Background of Bar and Bat Mitzvah

Bar mitzvah ("son of the commandment") was originally the term for every adult male Jew who is obligated to fulfill the commandments; it appears five times in the Talmud. In Jewish law, boys reach religious and legal maturity at thirteen years and one day, girls at twelve years and one day. Though these ages are not mentioned in the Bible, they are regarded as part of the oral law and a number of sources from the first centuries of the common era, such as the *Pirkei deRabbi Eliezer* and *Genesis Rabah*, attach the age of thirteen to certain actions in the Bible. Until then, parents bear responsibility for their children. Regardless of age, the idea of bar mitzvah is linked with education, a fundamental principle of Jewish belief expressed in the Shema:

Ages of maturity: Talmud Kiddushin 16b. Rabbinic law derived from Maimonides and the Shuḥan arukh require the presence of pubic hair to achieve the status of religious adulthood.

Deuteronomy 6:7

> You are to repeat them [the words of the Shema] with your children and are to speak of them when you are sitting in your house and as you walk on your way, when you lie down and when you rise up.

Education should start very early, the Talmud says. In the story of Joshua ben Ḥananya, one of the Talmud's sages, it is said that his mother took his cradle into the study house so he would become accustomed to the "voice of the Torah." The Mishnah speaks of five stages of maturity: "at five years of age to the Torah, at ten to the Mishnah, at thirteen to the com-

Mishnah Avot 5:21

mandments, at fifteen to the Talmud, at eighteen to the wedding canopy." In a fourth-century C.E. commentary on *Avot*, Rabbi Natan speaks of the maturing of moral sensibilities at age thirteen:

> Until the age of thirteen the evil inclination (*yetzer hara*) is greater than the good inclination (*yetzer hatov*), and at the age of thirteen the good inclination is born.

Avot deRabbi Natan 16

The earliest reference to a bar mitzvah ceremony similar to the one known today is from the sixteenth century. In his legal treatise *Yam shel Shelomo* ("Sea of Solomon"), the great Lithuanian rabbi and teacher Solomon Luria writes, "There is a feast for the bar mitzvah that the Germans do, in which they celebrate and praise God that a boy has reached this age and that his father has lived to see his son fulfill the commandments of the Torah." He also mentions that the child delivers a sermon at this feast. A century later, in another treatise on Jewish law, *Magen Avraham*, the Polish rabbi Abraham Abele ben Hayim Halevi Gombiner (c. 1637-1683) says that it is compulsory for the parents to arrange a feast when a boy reaches the age of bar mitzvah since in the Torah Abraham "made a great drinking feast on the day that Isaac was weaned" (Genesis 21:8).

In the beginning of the nineteenth century, the early Reform movement in Westphalia instituted a public group ceremony for Jewish boys and girls in their late teens called confirmation, influenced by the Christian ceremony of the same name. It was intended not to replace bar mitzvah but to supplement it by creating an additional milestone of further Jewish education. But in some Reform circles it did replace bar mitzvah, as some rabbis equated confirmation with a modern faith based on free will, in contrast to bar mitzvah, which some called a "primitive" act of rote learning. Significantly, it also included girls. As confirmation gained in popularity through the course of the nineteenth century, traditional congregations in western Europe (Reform Judaism barely existed in eastern Europe) upped the ante on bar mitzvah as more families invested it with a kind of feast that appealed to "sophisticated" social sensibilities. Since bar mitzvah was an individual ritual and confirmation a group ritual, the attraction of the bar mitzvah with a big party became more popular than ever. By the early twentieth century, when the center of Jewry had moved westward from Europe to America, three (and eventually four) branches of Judaism competed to put their stamp on these rituals that filled the synagogues and ensured a role for them in Jewish education. Conservative synagogues added confirmation ceremonies, using the terms *ben* or *bat torah* to describe the participants. Only the most "classical" of Reform synagogues denied their children bar mitzvah. And only the most pious of Orthodox congregations discouraged big parties.

The greatest change to bar mitzvah came with the advent of an equivalent ceremony for girls, which eventually became known by the obvious name bat mitzvah, "daughter of the commandment." The earliest of these were in the 1880s and 1890s in Germany, France, and Italy. In America, the first known bat mitzvah ceremony was that of Judith Kaplan, in 1922. She was the daughter of Rabbi Mordecai Kaplan, the founder of Reconstructionist Judaism—and she read only the haftarah. But more than anyone could realize at the time, women's participation at this level, as readers of scripture on the rostrum, would forever change the course of Judaism.

The Customs of Bar and Bat Mitzvah

In Jewish law, children who have reached the age of maturity (*benei mitzvah*—plural of both bar and bat mitzvah) are held responsible for their acts and for the control of their desires. They are considered adults for religious purposes whose vows are valid, who may become members of a religious court, who may be counted in a minyan, who may lead prayer services, and who may be called up to the Torah. However, there are some exceptions for certain kinds of testimony and the work of ritual slaughtering, for which one must be eighteen years old—partly an issue of physical strength.

TEFILLIN AND TALLIT: The first obligation of the benei mitzvah is to do something they may have done for years: recite the evening Shema on the day of their birthday. The first ritual obligation comes in the morning service, where for the first time the young person dons tefillin in public. For pedagogical reasons it is customary to start wearing tefillin earlier, to educate the young man or woman in the commandment. In the case of an orphan, it is done an entire year earlier. In many communities children start wearing the tallit on the day of their benei mitzvah.

Some Sephardim and Hasidim say that tefillin may not be worn even one day before benei mitzvah.

TORAH READING: To be called up to the Torah to recite from the weekly portion and the week's haftarah is a key honor of the benei mitzvah. Exactly how this is executed varies. Traditionally, the benei mitzvah would come up to the Torah on the next possible opportunity immediately following their thirteenth birthday, which may be Sabbath, Monday, or Thursday. The Torah blessings are said by the youngster and, depending on the custom of the congregation and his or her ability, the recitation may be the entire portion or, as is usually the case on Sabbath, the maftir's portion and the haftarah. It is a common custom that the parents, adult siblings, and other distinguished family members also be called up to the Torah. In traditional congregations, after the benei mitzvah complete their Torah readings, their parents recite a benediction, *Barukh shepetarani,* "Blessed be He who has relieved me of the punishment due on this child's account." This is a legal formula to say that what sins the young adult now commits are now his or her own responsibility. It is usually followed by a special *Mi sheberakh* prayer said for the benei mitzvah and their families. In some Reform congregations the *Sheheḥeyanu* blessing is said instead.

In the context of daily speech, Barukh shepetarani is a way of saying "good riddance."

After the benei mitzvah complete their reading, it is customary to throw candy at them—for a sweet life—just as at weddings.

The benei mitzvah ritual also includes a *derashah,* a discourse on the Torah portion given by the benei mitzvah to show understanding of rabbinical commentaries and interpretation and to honor and thank their parents. This was frequently written by a teacher, but that is less often the case today. After the *derashah,* it is customary for the congregation to give presents to the benei mitzvah (*droshegeshenken* in Yiddish). It is also customary for the rabbi to give a sermon when a bar or bat mitzvah is celebrated and often it concerns the commandments.

The service concludes as usual on Sabbath morning.

Benei mitzvah ceremonies are usually not held on festivals or on Rosh Ḥodesh, Shabbat Shekalim, Shabbat Zakhor, Shabbat Parah, or Shabbat Haḥodesh.

The festive celebration is considered a *seudat mitzvah* and may be celebrated on another day.

Death and Mourning

THE BABYLONIAN SAGE RAV, a formulator of Talmud, asserted that the mitzvot, the commandments, "were given only in order to refine humanity." We are further refined by the other kind of mitzvah, the honorable deeds that we do out of goodness and a sense of obligation to our fellows. Nowhere is this more evident than in the Jewish rituals of dying, death, and mourning. It is a mitzvah to comfort the dying and encourage their deathbed confession. And it is a mitzvah to perform the funeral rituals. It is a mitzvah to comfort those who mourn. To do these things for those in need or those who have no family or friends and are considered *met mitzvah*, is a very great goodness that is of lasting credit to those who do them.

Woodcut from the Mınhogımbukh, *Amsterdam, 1727.*

The Jewish rituals of death are simple and expeditious. The scholar Ruth Langer has written an excellent summation:

> Among all life-cycle events in traditional forms of Judaism, the rituals surrounding death are at the same time the most tightly choreographed and the least liturgical. While, in general, Jewish rituals tend to be accompanied by a relative torrent of encoded verbal prayers, the performance of funerary rituals are striking in their combinations of silence and

free speech. The result is the creation of a time that is markedly different, that responds powerfully to the emotions of the moment, and that effects the dual transition of accompanying the deceased to the grave and only then of comforting the mourners.

The *Minhogimbukh* covers five aspects of the subject: comforting the dying and their family, the moment of death, preparing the corpse, the performance of funeral rituals, and mourning. Here is its description of how the dying are to be comforted:

> It is a mitzvah to visit the sick, especially for a minor to go visit an adult. It is taught that the person who goes to visit the sick will be protected against the judgment of *gehinom* [purgatory] and will enjoy the fruits of his good deed in this world—its glory will be remembered also in the world to come. However, one should not visit a sick person when he is asleep, nor should one visit a sick person against his will. By visiting the sick, one causes one sixtieth of their illness to go away.
>
> If there are friends or relatives crying near the patient, they should be made quiet, in order not to distress him. The commandment of visiting the sick cannot be fulfilled without praying that God should bring remedy.
>
> A patient who is close to dying should be encouraged to say confession. He should be told that confessing his sins brings remedy and that many who had not confessed their sins died, whereas many who had confessed their sins lived.

A person hovering between life and death is called in Hebrew a *goses*. The Talmud states that a person's deathbed wishes *Talmud* Gittin *13a* must be honored just as a signed contract. Though Jewish law emphasizes that life is to be cherished and preserved, there is a body of law that states that a terminally ill person who suffers greatly should not be prevented from dying. New medical technologies continue to bring about changes in rabbinical legal rulings and opinions.

The deathbed confession, called Viduy, same as the daily and special holiday confessions, is a brief expression of hope for life and acceptance of death. It ends with the Shema.

> I acknowledge before You, Lord, my God and God of my ancestors, that my cure and my death are in Your hands. May it be Your will that You heal me completely. But if I die, may my death be an atonement for the sins, transgressions, and violations that I have sinned, transgressed, and violated before You. May You grant my share in the Garden of Eden, and let me merit the world to come reserved for the righteous. Hear, O Israel, the Lord our God, the Lord is One.

There are many versions of this prayer.

When someone feels the need for further confession, they are to recite the Viduy for Yom Kippur. Death itself is considered the greatest atonement.

At the Time of Death

Those present at the moment of death recite the abbreviated benediction, *Barukh dayan haemet*, "Blessed be the true Judge," which will be heard again in the funeral service. In some communities the relatives of the deceased also recite the series of prayers *Tziduk hadin*, "Acceptance of Judgment," which will be said at the cemetery as well. It is an expression of our acceptance of God's will. The act of rending garments (*keriah*) is considered the deepest expression of grief, and it is mandated that seven relatives of the deceased must perform this ritually within the thirty-day mourning period: spouse, mother, father, son, daughter, sister, and brother. Those relatives present at the time of death should do this spontaneously, though in some traditions one pins a piece of torn cloth to one's outer clothing.

There is a considerable body of Jewish law on the ritual of keriah, *touching on such areas as the time that a soul remains present to issues of modesty.*

As soon as death is determined, the eyes are shut. This is traditionally done by a son, if present. In Genesis 46:4 God assures Jacob, "And Joseph shall put his hand upon your eyes." In some communities it is customary to spread dust or soil over the eyes. The mouth is to be closed (tied closed if necessary) and other orifices filled. The pillow is removed, and the body covered and placed on the floor. This is done because a corpse is considered *tamei met*, the source of the greatest ritual impurity. Everything and everyone it touches becomes impure except the soil to which it must be returned. The laws for this are expounded in Leviticus and elsewhere in the Torah, as well in the Talmud and later law. However, it is law that a corpse must be shown the greatest respect since it is a belief that though the body has died, the soul remains present, at least for a time. Candles are lit near the head of the corpse, and from the moment of death through interment, the corpse is never left unattended.

Preparation of the Corpse

Preparing the body for burial is considered a great mitzvah and since it is a good deed that can never be returned, it is regarded as one of the most meritorious acts. Burial is to take place as soon as possible; only the travel of distant family members can delay it. In Orthodox communities it is rare that burial is delayed more than twenty-four hours. Even a *Deuteronomy 21:23* criminal who is hanged is to be buried the same day. However, funerals must be postponed until after Sabbath. They are also postponed until after festivals, though not by law.

In order to fulfill the rituals and obligations, "Holy Societies"—volunteer burial societies—were formed to assure the proper ritual treatment of bodies. In places where few Jews live, it is considered an imperative to form such a group, even before forming a prayer congregation. This is still the custom today, though the work of the *Ḥevra kadisha* (its name in Aramaic) is mostly carried out at funeral homes rather than at private residences, as in the past. To protect modesty, men perform the duties for men, women for women. Members of the family share the duties as *shomerim*, reading the Psalms while keeping watch over the body.

The corpse must be purified (*tohorah*) by washing. Those performing the task recite a brief prayer before beginning, asking for strength to do the work. A verse from Ezekiel 36:25 follows: "And I will pour upon you pure water, and you shall be cleansed; from all your uncleanliness and abominations will I purify you." Otherwise, the work is done in silence. Embalming of any kind is not permitted by Jewish law, though in the Torah Jacob and Joseph were embalmed in the Egyptian manner. In some groups, the hair is washed with eggs, the roundness of which is a symbol of mourning. The corpse is kept covered as much as possible throughout these procedures.

For roundness and tragedy, see also p. 190.

Jews are buried in white linen shrouds, without shoes, so that there be no difference between rich and poor. A man is to be buried with his tallit, but its tassels (tzitzit), which are reminders of God's 613 commandments, are cut since the deceased cannot fulfill them anymore. In traditional communities, the thumbs of deceased men are bent behind the fist, so that the fingers form the letter *shin* for the word *Shaddai*, "Almighty." Then the fists are tied with the fringes of the tallit. It is customary to be buried in a plain wood coffin. (By tradition, cremation is not permitted.) In some communities the bottom of the coffin is opened by the pulling of a rope so that the shrouded corpse is buried directly in the earth, in fulfillment of the biblical verse, "Dust you are, and to dust

Coffins are not permitted in Jerusalem.

Genesis 3:19

you shall return." A person may also be buried under stones. Throughout the Bible, an unburied corpse is considered the greatest curse and indignity—"food for the dogs," "food for the birds."

The Funeral and Burial

In Hebrew, a graveyard is called *bet kevarot,* a "house of graves." As in English, it is more widely known by euphemistic names—*bet haḥayim* ("house of life") or *bet olam* ("eternal home").

The service is always simple, though it varies slightly in different communities. It is customarily led by a rabbi. Those who have not been to a cemetery in over thirty days are obliged to begin with the blessing "Blessed are You . . . who fashioned you with justice . . . and will revivify and preserve you with judgment." First in the formal liturgy is the *Gevurot,* "Your might is boundless," the second benediction of the weekday Amidah. Then the series of prayers *Tziduk hadin,* "Acceptance of Judgment," which in some communities is said outside the gates of the cemetery while in others people assemble at the gravesite before saying it. The last of its biblical verses refer to the Thirteen Attributes of Mercy (Exodus 34:6–7), God's telling of his own characteristics that Moses would paraphrase when seeking God's mercy.

For Thirteen Attributes, see pp. 34 and 208.

The first verse of Tziduk hadin is a quotation from Deuteronomy 32:4.

> The Rock, perfect in His work, for all His ways are just; a God of faith without iniquity, righteous and fair is He.
> The Rock, perfect in every act. Who can say to Him, "What are You doing?" He rules below and above, causes death and restores life, lowers to the grave and raises up. . . .
> Great in counsel and mighty in deed, that Your eyes are attentive to all the ways of mankind, to give each man according to his ways and according to the consequences of his deeds.

> Declare that the Lord is just. My Rock, there is no wrong in
> Him. The Lord gave and the Lord took away; let the
> name of the Lord be blessed.
> He, the merciful One, is forgiving of iniquity and does not
> destroy; frequently He withdraws His anger, not arous-
> ing His entire wrath.

Tziduk hadin is not recited on days when Taḥanun, the prayers of supplication, are not said in the synagogue.

In those communities where *Tziduk hadin* is recited in a place other than the graveside, a procession now begins, during which the rabbi recites Psalm 91, stopping three times to allow the mourners to grieve.

> O thou that dwellest in the covert of the Most High, and
> abidest in the shadow of the Almighty;
> I will say of the Lord, who is my refuge and my fortress,
> my God, in whom I trust . . .
> He will cover thee with His pinions and under His wings
> shalt thou take refuge; His truth is a shield and a
> buckler.
> Thou shalt not be afraid of the terror by night, nor of the
> arrow that flieth by day. . . .
> For thou hast made the Lord who is my refuge, even the
> Most High, thy habitation.
> There shall no evil befall thee, neither shall any plague
> come nigh thy tent.
> For He will give His angels charge over thee, to keep thee
> in all thy ways.

As the coffin or shrouded body is lowered into the grave, the rabbi says, "May he (she) rest in peace." The male mourners cast three shovefuls of earth into the grave, placing the shovel in the ground for the next person to take. Then the special burial Kaddish is said, for "Blessed is He beyond any blessing and song, praise, and consolation that are uttered in *For Kaddish, see p. 26.*

For El malei
raḥamim,
see p. 77.
the world." Many communities add the memorial prayer *El malei raḥamim,* "O God, full of compassion."

Those present form two rows through which the mourners walk, and as they pass, the people recite the prayer of consolation: "May God console you among the other mourners of Zion and Jerusalem." As the participants leave, they pull some blades of grass and toss them over their right shoulders, *Psalm 103:14* saying, "May people blossom from the city like the grass of the earth. He is mindful that we are dust." Upon leaving the cemetery, one ritually washes one's hands, saying,

Isaiah 25:8
> May He swallow up death forever, may the Lord wipe away tears from every face, and the shame of His people He will remove from all the land, for the Lord has spoken.

After the funeral, the mourners are served a ritual meal, a *seudat havraah,* which contains foods of symbolic significance: eggs and lentils, round like the cycles of life. Wine and meat are not to be eaten since these are associated with pleasure. Mourners may not eat their own food; providing the meal is a community obligation.

The source for this custom is Ezekiel 24:17, "And eat not the bread of other men."

Mourning

There are seven relations one has to mourn: father, mother, son, daughter, brother, sister, spouse. From the time of the death to the burial, the bereaved are called *onen* and *onenim* (pl.), and their state, *aninut,* is one in which their only obligation is to the funeral, exempting them from all positive commandments such as praying, wearing tefillin, and saying Grace after Meals—even the Shema. They are in a suspended state, beyond comfort. After the funeral, their state is called *avelut,* in mourning still, but with the intent to establish a new normalcy. It is a community obligation to help the bereaved through mourning by providing food and comfort.

The first seven days of *avelut* are called shivah, which means simply, "seven." It is a period in which the prohibition of pleasure is similar to Tishah b'Av and Yom Kippur—though fasting is not permitted. Prohibited are leather shoes, washing and shaving, sexual relations, working, having a haircut, greeting people, sitting on chairs, participating in joyous events, studying Torah. In addition, all the mirrors in the house must be covered. After seven days mourners formally end the shivah by leaving their homes and walking around the block.

The common verb for the shivah observance is "sitting shivah."

One may sit on stools or benches— no backs—or on the floor.

The next twenty-three-day period of mourning is called *sheloshim*—"thirty," since it technically includes the shivah. Now the intensity is lessened after a week of intensive mourning. The mourner returns to work and may bathe for cleanliness, though not for pleasure, though the other prohibitions remain. Mourners recite the Kaddish at every service for the entire thirty-day period. A husband who has lost his wife may remarry after the thirty-day period; the wife, by tradition, may not remarry until after three months—to be certain she is not pregnant by her late husband. Those who have lost a parent maintain their mourner's status for twelve months, avoiding public pleasures and reciting Kaddish.

The occurrence of holidays may truncate the mourning period, the rules for which are complicated but important. This is the way it is presented in the 1593 *Minhogimbukh*:

> If one started counting the seven days of mourning just one hour before the Sabbath, that one hour is counted as the first day, and the Sabbath as the second day. The same is the case if it was one hour before a holiday, but then the holiday substitutes all the seven days. Similarly, if one already observed shivah for seven days, the last day of which was the eve of a holiday, the holiday substitutes for the whole thirty-

day period of mourning. If it was just one hour before Passover, that one hour is considered the seven days, and then together with the eight days of Passover it is already fifteen days of mourning. If it was one hour before Shavuot, that one hour counts as the seven days, and Shavuot itself counts as another seven days, as it is explained in the holy books, so altogether it is already fourteen days of mourning, and with the second day of Shavuot it is fifteen. If it was one hour before Rosh Hashanah, that counts as seven days. And Yom Kippur counts as the thirty days of mourning. If it was one hour before Sukkot, that counts as seven days, then with the seven days of the holiday it is fourteen. The first day of Shemini Atzeret counts as another seven, so it is then twenty-one days, and with Simḥat Torah altogether twenty-two days of mourning.

If someone dies in the intermediate days (*hol hamoed*) of a holiday, the mourners should do as on the Sabbath that falls within the first seven days of mourning: they should not mourn in public, but friends should go to visit and comfort them. They should begin observance of the seven days of mourning after the end of the holiday and should sit for the whole period of seven days, though they are allowed to do work at home after the seventh day after the burial. Also, the concluding day of the holiday may be counted as one day of mourning, so shivah is observed for only six days more.

Notes and Bibliography

Transliterations and Translations

ABOUT THE TRANSLITERATIONS: This book uses a simplified phonetic system for transliterating Hebrew, based mainly on sound rather than on orthography. The vowels are pronounced as follows: a = father; e = pay; i = feed; o = dome; u = dune. Consecutive vowels denote multiple syllables: *geulah* = geh-oo-lah; *hodaah* = ho-da-ah. The ḥ and kh are pronounced similarly, both as in the Scottish lo*ch*. Words that are found in *Webster's Third New International Dictionary* are spelled as they are there. Yiddish words follow the similar system established by YIVO Institute for Jewish Research.

TRANSLATIONS. Over time we develop our own repertory company of biblical players and in this book I present various styles of Bible translation to suggest the sounds I associate with the different eras of the texts. I was among the generations that grew up with *The Pentateuch and Haftorahs* edited by J.H. Hertz (London: Soncino Press, 1937). Hertz was the American-trained chief rabbi of the British Empire and his work, which was used across the denominational spectrum, incorporated the English translation published in 1917 by the Jewish Publication Society. It is a fine work and I have relied on it here, as I have the JPS *Tanakh* of 1985 and the *Etz Ḥayim chumash* of 2003. Everett Fox's *The Five Books of Moses* (New York: Schocken Books, 1995) has been a great inspiration. More than any other English translator, Fox attempts to capture the rhythm and spareness of the ancient Hebrew of the Torah. Others that have informed my choices are Robert Alter's translation of 1 and 2 Samuel (*The David Story: A Translation with Commentary of 1 and 2 Samuel* [New York: W. W. Norton, 1999]) and the books by James Kugel, cited below.

The major prophets, especially the later Isaiah, speak to me in Shakespearean language and I have used the King James version in several passages and the Revised Standard Version in some others—almost always with modifications. In the Psalms and other writings, I have relied on a mixture of sources, including the many fine biblical studies from Jewish Publication Society.

Page Notes

xiv. BIBLIOGRAPHIES OF CUSTOMS BOOKS. Though there are no thorough bibliographies of the customs book literature, some preliminary lists have been made. The oldest is Moritz Steinschneider's catalog of Jewish books at the Bodleian Library, Oxford, published 1852–1860. More up-to-date information has appeared mainly in the work of three leading scholars of Old Yiddish literature, the late Chone Shmeruk of Hebrew University, Jerusalem, Jean Baumgarten of the Centre National de la Recherche Scientifique, Paris, and Chava Turniansky, also of Hebrew University.

xv. EYZIK TYRNAU. Born in Vienna, Tyrnau had been a disciple of Rabbi Abraham Klausner, who had written his own *Sefer haminhagim*, later published (in Hebrew) in Riva di Trento in 1558. Klausner had also been the master of the Worms authority on law and custom, Jacob Moellin, known as the Maharil, whose *Sefer hamaharil* was published in Sabbioneta in 1556. Their work was in the tradition of customs collections from France and Germany that date back to the eleventh century, some of which predate the *Mahzor Vitry*, one of the main sources for daily and holiday liturgies and life cycle customs. I am grateful to Jean Baumgarten for sharing with me his unpublished paper, "Prayer, ritual and practice in Ashkenazic Jewish society: The tradition of Yiddish customs books, 15th c.–18th c."

A legend about Eyzik Tyrnau and his beautiful daughter, who was pursued by a Christian prince, was the subject of a story published in Yiddish in Frankfurt-am-Main, ca. 1715. It was later translated into Hebrew as *Etzba Elohim*, "The Finger of God," and published in Königsberg in 1857.

xvi. EDITIONS. The following is a far-from-complete list of editions up to the year 1800 compiled from the aforementioned works and my own research. *YIDDISH EDITIONS (illustrated through 1768, unless noted otherwise)*: Venice 1590 (listed mistakenly by Steinschneider as Mantua, this first Yiddish edition has no illustrations); Venice 1593, *first illustrated edition*; Venice 1601; Basel 1610; Basel 1611; Prague 1611; Prague 1620; Amsterdam 1645; Amsterdam 1662; Prague 1665; Frankfurt a.M. 1690; Frankfurt a.M. 1690; Dyhernfurt;

1692; Amsterdam 1707; Frankfurt a.O. 1707; Frankfurt a.M. 1707; Frankfurt a.M. 1708; Frankfurt a.M. 1714; Frankfurt a.M. 1715; Frankfurt a.M. 1717; Amsterdam 1723; Frankfurt a.M. 1723; Amsterdam 1727; Hamburg 1729; Hamburg 1729; Frankfurt a.M. 1729; Frankfurt a.M. 1733; Furth 1752; Furth 1756; Frankfurt a.M. 1762; Amsterdam 1768; Amsterdam 1768, *Ladino*; Offenbach 1779; Furth 1779; Sulzbach 1787; Sulzbach 1800. HEBREW EDI-TIONS (*not illustrated unless noted otherwise*): Venice 1566; Lublin 1570; Cracow 1578; Venice 1591; Cracow 1593; Cracow 1597; Cracow 1598; Venice 1598; Basel 1598; Frankfurt a.M. ca. 1674, *illustrated*; Prague 1682, *illustrated*; Amsterdam 1685, *illustrated*; Amsterdam 1708, *illustrated*; Frankfurt a.M. 1708, *illustrated*; Amsterdam 1768, *illustrated*; Amsterdam 1774, *last illustrated edition?*; Nowy Dwor 1784. I thank Prof. Jerold Frakes for first pointing me in the direction of some of these sources.

xvi–xvii. ITALIAN YIDDISH PRINTING and the *Minhogimbukh*. See Chone Shmeruk, "Defusei yidish beitalia," in *Italia* 3 (1982); Jean Baumgarten: "Giovani di Gara, printer of Yiddish books in Venice (16th c.)," *Revue des Études Juives* (2001); M. Epstein: "Simon Levi Ginzburg's illustrated customal of Venice, 1593 and its travels," *Proceedings of the Fifth World Congress of Jewish Studies* 4 (1973); Chone Shmeruk: "Haiyurim min haminhagim beyidish Venitzia 1593," *Studies in Bibliography and Booklore* 15 (1984); Chone Shmeruk: *Haiyurim lesifrei yidish bameot ha16-17* (Jerusalem: Akademon, 1986); Chone Shmeruk: "Reshimah kronologit shel hamahadurot beyidish shel haminhagim shel Shimon Halevi Ginzburg ad 1800: Haiyurim min haminhagim beyidish (Venitzia 1593)," *Studies in Bibliography and Booklore* 15 (1984).

For a concise panorama of Jewish life in Italy the period of the *Minhogimbukh*, see Elliott Horowitz, "Families and Their Fortunes: The Jews of Early Modern Italy" in *Cultures of the Jews*, ed. David Biale (New York: Schocken, 2003). Also *The Jews of Early Modern Venice*, ed. Robert C. Davis and Benjamin Ravid (Baltimore: Johns Hopkins University Press, 2001); and Robert Bonfil's *Jewish Life in Renaissance Italy* (Berkeley: University of California Press, 1994). The most voluminous works on the subject are Shlomo Simonsohn's dozen documentary histories of Jewish life in Italy and its relations with the Holy See. These include his *History of the Jews in the Duchy of Mantua* (Jerusalem: Kiryat Sepher, 1977), and his four-volume *A Documentary History of the Jews in Italy* (Jerusalem: Kiryat Sepher, 1982–1986). In the aforementioned works as well as in his *The Apostolic See and the Jews* (Toronto: Pontifical Institute for Medieval Studies, 1991), Simonsohn describes an occurrence in 1595, in which all Jewish libraries were searched, under orders from Rome, for anti-Christian material. The legacy is four hundred thirty inventories, which give us an extraordinary record of what books Jews read— or, at least, bought.

For early Yiddish literature in general, see Jean Baumgarten, *Introduction à la littérature yiddish ancienne* (Paris: Le Cerf, 1993); Joachim Neugroschel, *No Star Too Beautiful: Yiddish Stories from 1382 to the Present* (New York: W. W. Norton, 2002; and Jerold Frakes's forthcoming *An Anthology of Old and Middle Yiddish, 1100–1700* (Oxford University Press).

About *Tsenerene*. This most enduring of Yiddish religious works was written in the late sixteenth or early seventeenth centuries by the itinerant Polish rabbi Yaakov ben Yitzhak Ashkenazi and first published about 1608. The title is a quotation from the Song of Songs, *Tzeenah ureenah*, "Come out and see [you daughters of Zion]." The book's biblical paraphrases are excerpts of classic midrash translated into Yiddish. It would be hard to underestimate the importance and ubiquity of this work in the lives of European Jewish women. (See also note to p. xxiv.)

xviii. TYPOGRAPHY. Herbert C. Zafren, "Variety in the Typography of Yiddish, 1535–1635," in *Hebrew Union College Annual* 53 (1982); and by the same writer, "Early Yiddish Typography," in *Jewish Book Annual* 44 (1986).

There are passages in the *Minhogimbukh* that address women directly, explaining their obligation to observe certain commandments and lack of obligation toward others. Recognizing the desire of some women to involve themselves with mitzvot that were the domain of men, Gunzburg writes in the *Minhogimbukh*, "I shall provide women with some consolation: if they nevertheless do keep the commandments that they are not obligated to, they shall receive reward for that, albeit a small reward. According to the Talmud, a person obligated to observe a commandment receives a great reward for doing so, and the person not obligated to do so receives a smaller one. If you wonder what the reason behind this is and say that it should be the other way around, I shall give you several explanations—if you do not like one, you should choose the other. . . ."

xx–xxi. BIBLIOTHÈQUE NATIONALE MS HEBR. 586. I am grateful to Prof. Jerold Frakes for first bringing this document to my attention and especially to Prof. Diane Wolfthal for sharing with me her research on it that is now collected in her book, *Picturing Yiddish: Gender, Identity, and Memory in the Illustrated Yiddish Books of Renaissance Italy* (Leiden: Brill, 2004).

xxii. WOODCUTS. Who made the *Minhogimbukh* woodcuts has been a matter of some speculation and has been written about by Shmeruk and by Naomi Feuchtwanger-Sarig in her article "How Italian are the Venice Minhagim of 1593? A Chapter in the History of Yiddish Printing in Italy" published in *Schöpferische Momente des europäischen Judentums 16. bis 18. Jahrhundert*, ed. Michael Graetz (Heidelberg: Heidelberg University, 2002). There has also been discussion as to whether the blocks were cut by Jews or gentiles. The only compelling evidence that would suggest one way or the other is the Ḥanukkah woodcut in the 1593 edition, reproduced here on page 1, which shows a six-branched menorah (plus *shamash*) rather than the appropriate eight-branched model. It's difficult to imagine a Jewish artist making that mistake. The error was corrected in all subsequent editions.

xxiv. TKHINES. See Chava Weissler's book about this important literature, *Voices of the Matriarchs: Listening to the Voices of Early Modern Jewish Women* (Boston: Beacon Press, 1998). A new edition of a Yiddish *Seyder Tkhines*, the early women's prayer book, has just been published (2004) in English by Jewish Publication Society. First published in Amsterdam in 1648 it is here translated and introduced by Devra Kay. The books of *tkhines* were rather small and appeared in many editions, perhaps more than the *Minhogimbukh*.

xxv. MEMORIZATION and the transmission of knowledge. I thank Jean Baumgarten for reminding me of this aspect of Jewish learning. On the subject of language and learning, see his article "La littérature juive en langue yiddish: crise religieuse, culture vernaculaire et propagation de la foi" in *Annales* 51/2 (1996). Also see Jacob Neusner's *The Memorized Torah: The Mnemonic System of the Mishnah* (Chico, Calif.: Scholars Press, 1985).

1–2. THE OBJECTIVES OF MINHAG. The list of objectives is based on that of Rabbi Yitzḥak Lipietz of Shedlitz, from his *Sefer hamateamim* ("Worthy sources of hallowed Jewish customs"), published in Warsaw in 1889. It was quoted in Abraham Chill's *The Minhagim: The Customs and Ceremonies of Judaism, Their Origins and Rationale* (Brooklyn: Sepher Hermon Press, 1979). Chill's book is a compendium of twenty-seven sources from the twelfth to twentieth centuries. The fifth item was suggested to me by Prof. Ruth Langer.

3. CUSTOM AND LAW. For further explications of the differences and nuances of these subjects, see Ruth Langer's *To Worship God Properly: Tensions between Liturgical Custom and Halakhah in Judaism* (Cincinnati: HUC Press, 1998). Some of the fundamental issues of biblical law are taken up with clarity in Edward L. Greenstein's essay "Biblical Law" in *Back to the Sources: Reading the*

Classic Jewish Texts, ed. Barry W. Holtz (New York: Summit Books, 1984). See also *An Introduction to the History and Sources of Jewish Law*, ed. Neil S. Hecht (Oxford: Oxford University Press, 1996).

8. HISTORY AND DEVELOPMENT OF JEWISH PRAYER. See *Texts and Traditions: A Source Reader of Second Temple and Rabbinic Judaism*, ed. Lawrence H. Schiffman (Jersey City: KTAV Publishing, 1998); and *The Canonization of the Synagogue Service* by Lawrence A. Hoffman (Notre Dame, Ind.: Notre Dame University Press, 1979).

13. HEADCOVERING. See *A History of Jewish Costume* by James Laver and Alfred Rubens (New York: Crown, 1973).

13–15. MUSIC. Joshua R. Jacobson's *Chanting the Hebrew Bible: The Art of Cantillation* (Philadelphia: Jewish Publication Society, 2002) is an authoritative guide to the subject. Salamone Rossi and his world have been covered well by Don Harrán, who has edited the composer's complete works (pub. American Institute of Musicology), and has written a fine biography: *Salamone Rossi, Jewish Musician in Late Renaissance Mantua* (Oxford: Oxford University Press, 1999). Of particular interest is the connection between Rossi and the polymath rabbi Leon Modena, a vigorous proponent of art music in Jewish liturgy. The diversity of Jewish music is covered in Amnon Shiloah's *Jewish Musical Traditions* (Detroit: Wayne State University Press, 1992) and Marsha Bryan Edelman's *Discovering Jewish Music* (Philadelphia: Jewish Publication Society, 2003). Sephardic music is also documented in the work of musicologists Israel J. Katz, Shoshana Weich-Shahak, and Edwin Seroussi. An Internet search on their names will lead to many book, recording, and journal sources.

18. REUVEN HAMMER's *Entering Jewish Prayer* (New York: Schocken Books, 1994), has been supplemented by *Entering the High Holidays* (Philadelphia: Jewish Publication Society, 2003).

49. *Birkat maariv*. Translation from Hayim Halevy Donin's *To Pray As a Jew* (New York: Basic Books, 1980).

57. BETZAH. I thank Maggie Glezer for informing me about the *betzah* (egg) as a unit of measure in talmudic and halakhic sources. Some of this information will be referenced in her forthcoming book, *A Blessing of Bread* (New York: Artisan, 2004).

59. KABBALAT SHABBAT. For more about this service and its development, see *Kabbalat Shabbat: The Sabbath Evening Service* by Chaim Raphael (Springfield, N.J.: Behrman House, 1996).

62. GOLEM. Moshe Idel's *Golem: Jewish Magical and Mystical Traditions on the*

Artificial Anthropoid (Albany: State University of New York Press, 1990) places the Golem story in the contexts of Kabbalah and Jewish superstition.

69–70. ZEMIROT. There are a number of good collections of Sabbath songs with musical notation. My favorite is the *Harvard Hillel Sabbath Songbook* (Boston: Godine, 1992), which was my first Judaica project. It contains the core repertory of the Zemirot literature as well as many other songs, old and new.

71. SHABBES GOY. The history of the shabbes goy as a widespread practice is not especially old, according to Jacob Katz in his book *The Shabbes Goy: A Study in Halakhic Flexibility* (Philadelphia: Jewish Publication Society, 1995).

118. HAGGADOT. There are more editions of the haggadah than of any other Jewish book, a testament to the power and adaptability of its text and imagery. Many facsimiles have been published of the great illuminated haggadot from the Middle Ages to recent times, but the more humble printed haggadot earned the place of honor in Yosef Hayim Yerushalmi's magisterial *Haggadah and History: A Panorama in Facsimile of Five Centuries of the Printed Haggadah* (Philadelphia: Jewish Publication Society, 1975).

120. ROMAN DIPPING. See *Art, Culture, and Cuisine: Ancient and Medieval Gastronomy* by Phyllis Pray Bober (Chicago: University of Chicago Press, 1999).

136. NOAHIDE LAWS. The Toronto ethicist David Novak has written a provocative book on this subject, *The Image of the Non-Jew in Judaism: An Historical and Constructive Study of the Noahide Laws* (Lewiston, N.Y.: Mellen Press, 1984).

145. SONG OF SONGS. Two studies with new translations may be found in Ariel and Chana Bloch's *The Song of Songs: A New Translation with an Introduction and Commentary* (Berkeley, Calif.: University of California Press, 1998 [reprint]), and Michael V. Fox's *Song of Songs and Ancient Egyptian Love Songs* (Madison: University of Wisconsin Press, 1985).

149–151. HOLOCAUST REMEMBRANCE DAY. At this time the history of Yom Hashoah and its acceptance is to be found mainly in the journalistic record. Among the various efforts at creating a narrative and liturgy for the day are Abba Kovner's *Megilot haedut*, published in Hebrew in 1993, and translated into English as *Scrolls of Testimony* (Philadelphia: Jewish Publication Society, 2001); and *The Six Days of Destruction: Meditations Toward Hope* by Elie Wiesel and Albert H. Friedlander (New York: Paulist Press, 1988). Kovner's unusual work, part fiction and part documentary, alludes to the physical form of the Talmud—text surrounded by commentary; Wiesel and Friedlander take their inspiration from the Creation. Synagogue services for Yom Hashoah have been compiled by a number of liturgists, including Rabbi Avi Weiss and

Yiddish scholar David Roskies; the latter's work *Nightwords: A Liturgy on the Holocaust* is available online in PDF format.

The quotation from Primo Levi's "Shemà" is from *Collected Poems*, translated by Ruth Feldman and Brian Swann (London: Faber and Faber, 1988).

153. BAR KOKHBA REBELLION. A concise and richly contextual study of this complicated and important subject was written by Moshe and David Aberbach, *The Roman-Jewish Wars and Hebrew Cultural Nationalism* (New York: Macmillan, 2000).

156–159. YOM HAZIKARON, YOM HAATZMAUT, YOM YERUSHALAYIM. As with Yom Hashoah, the history of these holidays has not yet been written and may be found, primarily, in the journalistic record.

181. PHINEAS. James Kugel's fine and enjoyable work on the Bible and its sources, *The Bible As It Was* (Cambridge, Mass.: Harvard University Press, 1997), cites the "alternate" source Targum Pseudo-Jonathan and two early Torah commentaries that mention Phineas's transformation from zealous priest to Elijah the prophet, perhaps the only grant of immortality in the Torah.

195. KINOT. The two well-known collections of Kinot are those of Abraham Rosenfeld, *Kinot for Tisha B'Av* (Brooklyn: Judaica Press, 1965), and the ArtScroll Kinnos / Tishah B'Av Siddur published in both Ashkenazic and Sephardic editions (Brooklyn: ArtScroll, 1992 [both editions]). Recently published is the *Sim Shalom Siddur for Tishah B'Av* (New York: Rabbinical Assembly, 2003).

225–294. ROSH HASHANAH AND THE HIGH HOLIDAYS. See Reuven Hammer's *Entering the High Holidays* (Philadelphia: Jewish Publication Society, 2003). Philip Goodman's seven holiday anthologies, first published by Jewish Publication Society in the 1960s and 1970s, are still in print. The *Rosh Hashanah Anthology* as well as the volumes for Yom Kippur and Sukkot / Shemni Atzeret cover a broad range from scripture to recipes.

306. HASMONEAN. The Hasmonean period has been the subject of much study, but the best place to start is with the the books of Maccabees and the writings of a descendant of Judah Maccabee, the historian Flavius Josephus, author of *The Jewish War* and *Jewish Antiquities*, a history of the Jewish people.

The Apocrypha (Greek for "hidden things") refers to a series of writings from the end of the biblical period. They were excluded from the Jewish canon, but were accepted by the early Christians. The books include Maccabees (1 and 2), Esdras, Judith, Tobit, the Wisdom of Solomon, and Baruch.

350. ZAKHOR. The tensions between the traditions of memory and modern writ-

ing of history are addressed in Yosef Hayim Yerushalmi's renowned essay *Zakhor*, published first in 1982 and in a revised edition in 1996 (Seattle: University of Washington Press).

368. *SHIDUKHIN*. Since the *Minhogimbukh* discusses only the customs of weddings, not of courtship or married life, it does not mention the traditional role of the *shadkhn*, the "matchmaker" responsible for making the *shidukh*.

374. TWO CEREMONIES. See Anita Diamant's *The New Jewish Wedding* (New York: Simon and Schuster, 1986).

380. MOHEL. Part of the mohel's equipment is a book, called in Yiddish a *moylbukh*, which contains the intructions for the procedure and the blessings. In back is recorded the boy's names. Old *moylbikher* are an important source of genealogical information.

381. BNEI MITZVAH. I thank Prof. Daniel Sperber for pointing out to me two sources for more information about these rituals: *Bar Mitzvah: A Study in Jewish Custom* by Isaac Rifkind (New York, 1942 [in Hebrew]), and Ora Wiskind Elper's recent *Traditions and Celebrations for the Bat Mitzvah* (Jerusalem and New York: Urim Publications, 2003).

In *Life Cycles in Jewish and Christian Worship* (Notre Dame, Ind.: Notre Dame University Press, 1996), author Debra R. Blank states that confirmation was introduced to America by Isaac Mayer Wise in 1846, in Albany, New York. Wise was later the founder of Hebrew Union College, the first rabbinical college in the United States.

389. FUNERARY. Rabbi Langer's paper is available online at www2.bc.edu/~langerr/jewish_funerals.htm. There are good books on this subject from many points of view. The best known in English is Maurice Lamm's *The Jewish Way in Death and Mourning* (Middle Village, N.Y.: Jonathan David, 2000). Leon Wieseltier's *Kaddish* (New York: Knopf, 1998) is a moving, personal reflection that begins with the loss of his father. Related to the *Minhogimbukh* is Sylvie-Anne Goldberg's *Crossing the Jabbok: Illness and Death in Ashkenazi Judaism in Sixteenth- through Nineteenth-Century Prague* (Berkeley: University of California Press, 1996 [first published in French in 1989]).

Other Works Consulted (not listed above or in the sidenotes)

Adler, Morris. *The World of the Talmud.* New York: Schocken, 1976.

Agassi, Judith Buber. *Martin Buber on Psychology and Psychotherapy: Essays, Letters, and Dialogue.* Syracuse, N.Y.: Syracuse University Press, 1999.

Alter, Robert. *Genesis: Translation and Commentary.* New York: W.W. Norton, 1996.

Bell, Catherine M. *Ritual: Perspectives and Dimensions.* New York: Oxford University Press, 1997.

Biale, Rachel. *Women and Jewish Law: An Exploration of Women's Issues in Halakhic Sources.* New York: Schocken, 1984.

Bloch, Abraham P. *The Biblical and Historical Background of the Jewish Holy Days.* New York: Ktav, 1978.

Buber, Martin and Franz Rosenzweig. *Scripture and Translation.* Bloomington, Ind.: Indiana University Press, 1994.

Chill, Abraham P. *The Minhagim: The Customs and Ceremonies of Judaism, Their Origin and Rationale.* Brooklyn: Sepher-Hermon Press, 1979.

Cohen, Richard I., *Jewish Icons: Art and Society in Modern Europe.* Berkeley, Calif.: University of California Press, 1998.

Cox, Harvey. *Common Prayers: Faith, Family, and a Christian's Journey Through the Jewish Year.* Boston: Houghton Mifflin, 2001.

Eliach, Yaffa. *There Once Was a World: A Nine-Hundred-Year Chronicle of the Shtetl of Eishyshok.* Boston: Little Brown, 1998.

Elon, Menachem. *Jewish Law; History, Sources, Principles* (four volumes). Philadelphia: Jewish Publication Society, 1994.

Encyclopaedia Judaica. 16 vols. New York: Macmillan, 1971.

Encyclopaedia Judaica, CD-ROM edition. Jerusalem: Judaica Multimedia, 1996.

Epstein, Marc Michael. *Dreams of Subversion in Medieval Jewish Art and Literature.* University Park, Pa.: Pennsylvania State University Press.

Forst, Binyamin. *The Laws of Kashrus: A Comprehensive Exposition of Their Underlying Concepts and Application.* Brooklyn: ArtScroll, 1999.

Freehof, Solomon B. *Reform Jewish Practice and Its Rabbinic Background, Volumes I and II.* New York: Union of American Hebrew Congregtions, 1964.

Gaster, Theodor Herzl. *Festivals of the Jewish Year: A Modern Interpretation and Guide.* New York: Morrow, 1953.

Gelbard, Shemuel P. *Rite and Reason: 1050 Jewish Customs and Their Sources.* Nanuet, N.Y.: Feldheim, 1998.

Goldberg, Harvey E. *Judaism Viewed from Within and from Without: Anthropological Studies.* Albany: State University of New York Press, 1987.

Grimes, Ronald L. *Deeply into the Bone: Re-Inventing Rites of Passage.* Berkeley, Calif.: University of California Press, 2000.

Heilman, Samuel C. *Synagogue Life: A Study in Symbolic Interaction.* New Brunswick, N.J.: Transaction Publishers, 1998.

———. *When a Jew Dies: The Ethnography of a Bereaved Son.* Berkeley, Calif.: University of California Press, 2001.

Hoffman, Lawrence A. *Covenant of Blood: Circumcision and Gender in Rabbinic Judaism.* Chicago: University of Chicago Press, 1996.

Jacobs, Louis. *Tree of Life: Diversity, Creativity, and Flexibility in Jewish Law.* Oxford: Oxford University Press, 1984.

Katz, Jacob. *Tradition and Crisis: Jewish Society at the End of the Middle Ages.* New York: Free Press, 1961.

Klein, Isaac. *A Guide to Jewish Religious Practice.* New York: Jewish Theological Seminary of America, 1979.

Klein, Michele. *A Time to Be Born: Customs and Folklore of Jewish Birth.* Philadelphia: Jewish Publication Society, 1998.

Knobel, Peter S., Bennett M. Hermann, and Ismar David. *Gates of the Seasons: A Guide to the Jewish Year—Shaare Moed.* New York: Central Conference of American Rabbis, 1983.

Kugel, James. *The God of Old: Inside the Lost World of the Bible.* New York: Free Press, 2003.

Kushner, Lawrence. *The River of Light: Jewish Mystical Awareness.* Woodstock, Vt.: Jewish Lights, 2000.

Levenson, Jon D. *The Hebrew Bible, the Old Testament, and Historical Criticism: Jews and Christians in Biblical Studies.* Louisville, Ky.: Westminster/John Knox Press, 1993.

Langer, Ruth. *To Worship God Properly: Tensions between Liturgical Custom and Halakhah in Judaism.* Cincinnati: Hebrew Union College Press, 1998.

Linafelt, Tod. *Surviving Lamentations: Catastrophe, Lament, and Protest in the Afterlife of a Biblical Book.* Chicago: University of Chicago Press, 2000.

Maimonides, Moses, ed. Isaac Klein. *The Code of Maimonides*, Yale Judaica Series; v. 8–9. New Haven: Yale University Press, 1949.

Matt, Daniel C., trans. and ed. *The Zohar: Pritzker Edition*, vols. 1 and 2. Palo Alto, Calif.: Stanford University Press, 2003 and 2004.

Millgram, Abraham Ezra. *Jewish Worship.* Philadelphia, Jewish Publication Society, 1971.

Moore, Deborah Dash, and S. Ilan Troen. *Divergent Jewish Cultures: Israel and America.* New Haven: Yale University Press, 2001.

Petuchowski, Jakob. *Prayerbook Reform in Europe: The Liturgy of European Lib-

eral and Reform Judaism. New York: World Union for Progressive Judaism, 1968.

Pollack, Herman. *Jewish Folkways in Germanic Lands (1648–1806).* Cambridge, Mass.: MIT Press, 1971.

Rappaport, Roy A. *Ritual and Religion in the Making of Humanity.* Cambridge and New York: Cambridge University Press, 1999.

Roskies, Diane K., and David G. Roskies. *The Shtetl Book: An Introduction to East European Jewish Life and Lore.* New York: Ktav, 1979.

Sarna, Jonathan D. *American Judaism.* New Haven: Yale University Press, 2004.

Sarna, Nahum M. *Exploring Exodus: The Origins of Biblical Israel.* New York: Schocken Books, 1996.

Sarshar, Houman, ed. *Esther's Children: A Portrait of Iranian Jews.* Philadelphia: Jewish Publication Society, 2002.

Schauss, Hayyim. *The Jewish Festivals: History and Observance.* New York: Schocken, 1973.

Segal, Eliezer. *Holidays, History, and Halakhah.* Northvale, N.J.: Jason Aronson, 2000.

Shachar, Isaiah. *The Jewish Year Iconography of Religions.* Leiden: Brill, 1975.

Sperber, Daniel. *Why Jews Do What They Do: The History of Jewish Customs Throughout the Cycle of the Jewish Year.* Hoboken, N.J.: Ktav, 1999.

Sperling, Abraham Isaac. *Reasons for Jewish Customs and Traditions (Taamei Haminhagim).* New York: Bloch Publishing, 1968.

Steiman, Sidney. *Custom and Survival: A Study of the Life and Work of Jacob Molin Known As the Maharil.* New York: Bloch, 1963.

Stemberger, Günter, Markus N. A. Bockmühl, and Hermann Leberecht Strack. *Introduction to the Talmud and Midrash.* Edinburgh: T. & T. Clark, 1996.

Strassfeld, Michael. *The Jewish Holidays: A Guide and Commentary.* New York: Harper & Row, 1985.

Trachtenberg, Joshua. *Jewish Magic and Superstition: A Study in Folk Religion.* New York: Atheneum 1977.

Trepp, Leo. *The Complete Book of Jewish Observance.* New York: Behrman House and Summit Books, 1980.

Zfatman, Sara. *Yiddish Narrative Prose, 1504–1814: A Bibliography* [in Hebrew]. Jerusalem: Hebrew University, 1985.

Acknowledgments

M Y GRATITUDE is great to those who were so generous with
their advice, counsel, and work on this book. Saul Touster, professor emeritus at Brandeis—poet, teacher, scholar, friend—helped me
keep focused on the words and ideas, reading every page as if it were his
own. Irene Tayler, emerita of MIT, a dear friend who is also Saul's wife,
was no less committed to a close and helpful reading. My excellent
research assistant, Szonja Ráhel Komoróczy, of Oxford University, who
made for me the preliminary translation of the 1593 Venice *Minhogimbukh*, also helped me translate and understand other old sources that
would have eluded me otherwise. She brought to this material both vast
knowledge and an intuitive grasp. I am grateful to Brad Sabin Hill, dean
of the library at YIVO Institute for Jewish Research, for recommending
her. Rabbi Ruth Langer, professor of theology at Boston College, was my
principal and invaluable advisor on matters of Jewish law and custom,
the intersection of which is her particular expertise. Her care and erudi-
tion are reflected in the best parts of the book.

My first conversations about this project were with Menahem
Schmelzer and David Roskies, and they pointed me in all the right directions. I thank them. I have been the beneficiary of the kindness of some
of the leading practitioners in the field of Old Yiddish: Jerold Frakes and
Jean Baumgarten were very helpful in the early stages of the work, and

shared with me key information about manuscript sources, early imprints, and the persistence of the Eyzik Tyrnau text. Diane Wolfthal kindly shared with me her research on the visual representations of Jewish-Christian dynamics and women's roles in sixteenth-century Europe. She added important things to my understanding. Professor Daniel Sperber, one of the world's leading experts in Jewish custom, was very generous and enthusiastic.

I am deeply grateful for the encouragement and suggestions I received from friends and colleagues who read parts of the book along the way, especially Arthur Boyars, a vital poet and veteran of more than fifty years at the creative center of publishing, who provided the delightful translation of the 1593 prefatory poem. To be no more than one degree of separation from the right connection is a blessed thing and my special blessings who always know the right person, e-mail address, and phone number are my friends at the Jewish Publication Society and my collaborator and friend Jonathan Sarna.

I am a book and typeface designer who also writes about Jewish texts and life; Rabbi Lawrence Kushner is an expert in Jewish life and texts who also designs and typesets his own notable books. Who else in all the world could have written such an appropriate and graceful foreword? I am honored by Larry's participation and friendship and I thank Marjie and Bob Kargman for introducing us.

Gideon Weil, my editor at Harper San Francisco, is a great calmer of nerves and giver of courage. I enjoyed working with him. I thank Harper staffers Terri Leonard, Laina Adler, Claudia Boutote, and Jim Warner for their hard work and for their good faith in— and tolerance of— an author who is also a designer and typesetter. I am especially grateful to Brettne Bloom, my excellent agent at Kneerim & Williams, whose faith, energy, and vision never flag, and whose literary sensibilities never miss.

While this book took shape over the past two years my son, Milo, was born and my daughter, Sophie, began college. As I write this, Milo runs in and out of my office, laughing, showing me his latest drawings. And all the while other work carried on. Without the loving help of family and friends, this good idea for a book would have remained little more than just that. My wife's parents, Bill and Val Sarles, were constant in their encouragement and did everything possible to help ease the burdens. Steve Sarles and Ann Walters, and Chris Lipscomb and Monique Segarra were always there to provide good company and delicious food while I was in the thick of work. They are great friends.

Above, beyond, and most of all I thank Betsy Sarles, my wife and partner in life and work, whose good counsel and unfailing sense of the essential is reflected throughout these pages. She suffered gracefully not only my heavy work schedule, but, worse still, my breakfast-table disquisitions on biblical texts. She is the definition of loving-kindness and I dedicate this effort to her.

The author gratefully acknowledges permission to quote from the following works. Segments from *The Five Books of Moses* translated by Everett Fox. Reprinted by permission of the author. Copyright © 1997 by Everett Fox. Translation of *Nishmat kol ḥai* from *Entering Jewish Prayer* by Reuven Hammer. Reprinted by permission of the author. Copyright © 1994 by Reuven Hammer. Translation of *Birkat maariv* from *To Pray As a Jew* by Hayim Halevy Donin. Reprinted by permission. Copyright © 1980 by Hayim Halevy Donin.

The translation of the prefatory poem on pages xxxii–xxxiv is copyright © 1997 by Arthur Boyars.

Index